FINANCIAL REGULATION AND MONETARY ARRANGEMENTS AFTER 1992

CONTRIBUTIONS
TO
ECONOMIC ANALYSIS

204

Honorary Editor:
J. TINBERGEN

Editors:
D. W. JORGENSON
J. WAELBROECK

NORTH-HOLLAND
AMSTERDAM • LONDON • NEW YORK • TOKYO

FINANCIAL REGULATION AND MONETARY ARRANGEMENTS AFTER 1992

Edited by

Clas WIHLBORG
Department of Economics
University of Gothenburg
Gothenburg, Sweden

Michele FRATIANNI
School of Business
Indiana University
Bloomington, IN, U.S.A.

Thomas D. WILLETT
Department of Economics
Claremont Graduate School
Claremont, CA, U.S.A.

1991

NORTH-HOLLAND
AMSTERDAM • LONDON • NEW YORK • TOKYO

ELSEVIER SCIENCE PUBLISHERS B.V.
Sara Burgerhartstraat 25
P.O. Box 211, 1000 AE Amsterdam, The Netherlands

Distributors for the United States and Canada:

ELSEVIER SCIENCE PUBLISHING COMPANY INC.
655 Avenue of the Americas
New York, N.Y. 10010, U.S.A.

Library of Congress Cataloging-in-Publication Data

Financial regulation and monetary arrangements after 1992 / edited by
  Clas Wihlborg, Michele Fratianni, Thomas D. Willett.
       p.   cm. -- (Contributions to economic analysis ; 204)
    Includes bibliographical references and indexes.
    ISBN 0-444-89083-1
    1. Financial services industry--Government policy--Congresses.
  2. Monetary policy--Congresses. 3. Financial services industry-
  -Government policy--Europe--Congresses. 4. Monetary policy--Europe-
  -Congresses.   I. Wihlborg, Clas. II. Fratianni, Michele.
  III. Willett, Thomas D. IV. Series.
  HG63.F56 1991
  332.4'94--dc20   91-33789
                                                              CIP

ISBN: 0 444 89083 1

PRINTED IN THE NETHERLANDS

INTRODUCTION TO THE SERIES

This series consists of a number of hitherto unpublished studies, which are introduced by the editors in the belief that they represent fresh contributions to economic science.

The term "economic analysis" as used in the title of the series has been adopted because it covers both the activities of the theoretical economist and the research worker.

Although the analytical methods used by the various contributors are not the same, they are nevertheless conditioned by the common origin of their studies, namely theoretical problems encountered in practical research. Since for this reason, business cycle research and national accounting, research work on behalf of economic policy, and problems of planning are the main sources of the subjects dealt with, they necessarily determine the manner of approach adopted by the authors. Their methods tend to be "practical" in the sense of not being too far remote from application to actual economic conditions. In additon they are quantitative.

It is the hope of the editors that the publication of these studies will help to stimulate the exchange of scientific information and to reinforce international cooperation in the field of economics.

The Editors

Preface

This volume contains the proceedings of a conference held in the city of Gothenburg on May 21-23, 1990, preceded by a planning conference held on the island of Marstrand just north of the city on September 6-7, 1989. The conferences were organized to launch financial and monetary economics as a major focus for study and research at the School of Economics and Commercial Law within the University of Göteborg. With the city's traditional role as the major port and center for international trade activity in Sweden it was natural to focus the conferences, as well as the school's education and research program, on international aspects of monetary and financial economics.

The major objective of the conference was to stimulate research on the linkage between structural and regulatory development in the financial services industry, on the one hand, and monetary arrangements and exchange rate regimes, on the other. A second objective, with the background of rapid development of a framework for economic integration in Western Europe, was to analyze and discuss potential future regulatory policy conflicts among insiders in the European Community (EC), as well as between the EC and major "outsiders". These objectives are discussed in more detail in the Objectives and Overview chapter.

It is risky to produce a volume such as this one, containing the proceedings of a conference on a topic in rapid development. The academic papers are sufficiently general, however, not to depend for their relevance on specific reforms within the EC. Contributions within this volume discussing reforms from the perspectives of individual countries run a greater risk of being overtaken by real world events. The risk is small, however, since the formal reforms that take effect before the end of 1992 provide only a framework for further development of EC-institutions and regulation during the foreseeable future.

Major unanticipated events did occur during the planning period for the conference. The Berlin Wall fell, Soviet domination of Eastern Europe was broken, and market oriented reforms were initiated even within the Soviet Union. For a while, it looked as if the 1992 process was going to stall in the face of the overwhelming transition problem facing the former communist bloc. Reforms within the EC continued, however, and they may even have obtained greater urgency.

One session was added to the conference in order to incorporate the East European perspective on financial market reform in the EC, and on problems of transition to convertibility of currencies. The participants also obtained a vivid account of the negotiations between East and West Germany on conditions for creating a German monetary union. Hans-Joachim Huss came directly from the conclusion of these negotiations to the conference. His insightful after-dinner presentation of the historic agreement was highly appreciated.

My deepest gratitude for contributions to the success of the conference, as well as to the completion of this volume, goes to Ms Karin Hane, my assistant in the Department of

Economics. Without her administrative and organizational talents and capacity, the conference would not have reached even the planning stage. She understood and handled with great skill the complexity (unforeseen by myself) of the organizational task. Similarly, without her efforts this volume, with all the extra work related to the preparation of a camera-ready manuscript, would not have been completed.

I am also grateful to Jan Nilsson, President of the University of Göteborg, and Lars Nordström, Dean of the School of Economics and Commercial Law, for their support. Valuable input during the conference or to the preparation of this volume has been provided by Göran Andersson, Mats-Ola Forsman, Anders Johansson, Joao Loureiro, Asal Maher, Cunwu Pan, Lulseged Yohannes, and Max Zamanian, Ph.D. students in the department of economics, and Boo Sjöö, research fellow in the department.

Finally, I would like to thank the sponsors of the conference, whose contributions were essential complements to Karin Hane's skills. Skandinaviska Enskilda Banken, Volvo, and PK-banken (now Nordbanken) were sponsors at an early stage. I am grateful to Otto Wrangel, Lennart Jeansson, and Mikael Wallgren in these firms for their personal support that made the planning conference possible. Additional support was obtained from Första Sparbanken, Handelshögskolefonderna at the Gothenburg School of Economics and Commercial Law and the Center for Economic Policy Studies at the Claremont Graduate School. Last but not least, I would like to thank the Tore Browaldh, Jan Wallander Research Foundations at Svenska Handelsbanken for sponsoring the main conference.

Gothenburg, June 7, 1991

Clas Wihlborg
Felix Neubergh Professor
of Financial Economics

List of Conference Participants
Marstrand, September 6-7, 1989, and Gothenburg, May 21-23, 1990

Sven Arndt	Professor, Claremont McKenna College, Claremont
Göran Bergendahl	Professor, Gothenburg School of Economics and Commercial Law
Stanislav M. Borisov	Professor, Institute of World Economy and Foreign Relations, Moscow
William H. Branson	Professor, Princeton University
Franco Bruni	Professor, Bocconi University, Milan
Richard Burdekin	Professor, Claremont McKenna College, Claremont
Wlodek Bursztyn	Dr, Gothenburg School of Economics and Commercial Law,
Nigel Carter	Dr, Bank of England, London
Emil-Maria Claassen	Professor, University of Paris-Dauphine, Paris
J. Kimball Dietrich	Professor, University of Southern California, Los Angeles
Patricia Dillon	Professor, Scripps College, Claremont
Igor G. Doronin	Dr, Institute of World Economy and International Relations, Moscow
John Driffill	Professor, Queen Mary and Westfield College, University of London
B. Espen Eckbo	Professor, University of British Columbia, Vancouver
Gunnar Eliasson	Professor, Director, The Industrial Institute for Economic and Social Research (IUI), Stockholm
Emil Ems	Senior Officer, Economic Affairs Department, EFTA, Geneva
Peter Englund	Professor, University of Uppsala
David Folkerts-Landau	Deputy Chief of Financial Studies, International Monetary Fund, Washington, DC
Elena Folkerts-Landau	Dr, World Bank, Washington, DC
Thomas Franzén	Dr, Deputy Governor, Central Bank of Sweden, Stockholm
Michele Fratianni	Professor, Grad. School of Business, Indiana University, Bloomington
Alberto Giovannini	Professor, Grad. School of Business, Columbia University, New York
Reuven Glick	Dr, Federal Reserve Bank of San Francisco, San Francisco
Linda S. Goldberg	Professor, New York University
Morris Goldstein	Dr, International Monetary Fund, Washington
Charles Goodhart	Professor, London School of Economics
Daniel Gros	Dr, Centre for European Policy Studies, Brussels
Thorvaldur Gylfason	Professor, University of Iceland, and IIES, Stockholm
Jürgen von Hagen	Professor, Grad. School of Business, Indiana University, Bloomington

Mats Hallgren	Senior Advisor, Skandinaviska Enskilda Banken, Stockholm
Bengt Hane	Director Financial Relations, AB Volvo, Gothenburg
Robert Hodrick	Professor, Kellogg School of Management, Northwestern University, Chicago
Bengt Holmström	Professor, Yale School of Organization and Management, New Haven
Hans-Joachim Huss	Dr, Ministry of Finance, Bonn
Michael Hutchison	Professor, Bank for International Settlements, Basle, and Crown College, University of California, Santa Cruz
Jan Häggström	Dr, Svenska Handelsbanken, Stockholm
Lars Jonung	Professor, Stockholm School of Economics
Björn Kårfalk	Vice President and Treasurer, AB Volvo, Gothenburg
Karen K. Lewis	Professor, University of Pennsylvania, Philadelphia, and New York University
Nils Lundgren	Dr, Nordbanken, Stockholm
Johan A. Lybeck	Professor, Gothenburg School of Economics and Commercial Law
Michael Melvin	Professor, College of Business, Arizona State University, Tempe
John O. Montgomery	Dr, Board of Governors of the Federal Reserve System, Washington DC
Niels Chr. Nielsen	Professor, Copenhagen School of Economics and Business Administration
Eva Nisser	Financial Consulting, Stockholm
Yoshiharu Oritani	Manager, Research Division, The Bank of Japan, Tokyo
Lars Oxelheim	Professor, Gothenburg School of Economics and Commercial Law, and IUI, Stockholm
Richard Portes	Dr, Centre for Economic Policy Research, London
Aris Protopapadakis	Professor, Claremont Graduate School, Claremont
Tad Rybczynski	Professor, City University, London
Anthony M. Santomero	Professor, The Wharton School of the University of Pennsylvania, Philadelphia
Stefan Schönberg	Dr, Deutsche Bundesbank, Frankfurt
Boo Sjöö	Dr, Gothenburg School of Economics and Commercial Law
Göran Skogh	Professor, School of Economics and Management, Lund University
Roy C. Smith	Professor, Stern School of Business, New York University, and Goldman Sachs, New York
Ulf Sternhufvud	Dr, Skandinaviska Enskilda Banken, Gothenburg
Richard M. Sweeney	Professor, School of Business Administration, Georgetown University, Washington, DC
Hans T:son Söderström	Dr, Centre for Business and Policy Studies (SNS), Stockholm
Hiroo Taguchi	Dr, The Bank of Japan, Tokyo
Niels Thygesen	Professor, University of Copenhagen
Ingo Walter	Professor, Stern School of Business, New York University, and INSEAD
Sir Alan A. Walters	Director, Putnam, Hayes & Bartlett, Washington, DC
Roland Vaubel	Professor, University of Mannheim

Steven R. Weisbrod	President, Weisbrod Group Ltd, New York
Clas Wihlborg	Professor, Gothenburg School of Economics and Commercial Law
Per Wijkman	Dr, EFTA Secretariat, Geneva
Thomas D. Willett	Professor, Claremont Graduate School, Claremont
José Vinals	Dr, Bank of Spain, Madrid
Pehr Wissén	Dr, Svenska Handelsbanken, Stockholm

Table of Contents

List of Tables

List of Figures

Financial Regulation and Monetary Arrangements after 1992
C. Wihlborg, M. Fratianni and T.D. Willett (Editors)
© 1991 Elsevier Science Publishers B.V. All rights reserved

Objectives and Overview

Clas Wihlborg, Michele Fratianni, and Thomas D. Willett

1. 1992: INITIAL FINANCIAL AND MONETARY REFORMS

The Single Market Programme, or more familiarly Europe 1992, is more a process of economic and political integration than a specific event. The process is no longer limited to the 12 EC members but encompasses an increasingly wide array of "outsiders" as well. With the exception of some new regulations due to take place before the end of 1992, the timing of regulatory change, private sector adjustment, and secondary regulatory responses among inside and outside countries remains unknown. The one certainty is that most of the process will work itself out after 1992.

Reform of the financial services industry and monetary reform is at the center of the 1992 process. The formation of a currency union is the most dramatic and potentially the most tangible aspect of the Western European integration process. Whether its creation is a necessary condition for the realization of major benefits from the formation of an economic union is a fundamental issue for this volume. The realism of the plans for a currency union with one central bank for all EC-countries is subject to much debate as well. Analysis and discussion of the transition process, as envisaged by the Delors Committee on Economic and Monetary Union, are also important.

At the time this book is completed, there is an agreement in principle among central bankers to proceed with the three stages in the transition process towards a currency union with an independent central bank being responsible for monetary policy. An inter-governmental conference, charged with the task of drafting the necessary "monetary articles" to amend the Treaty of Rome, was formed at the Rome Summit in 1990. The conference is expected to convene towards the end of 1992. In the planning process for this conference there is substantial disagreement on how to organize the European central bank, as well as on the implementation of different stages in the transition. The outcome is by no means certain.

The monetary integration process has a very direct bearing on the financial services industry, since one central bank implies centralization of control over the payment system and the supply of credit through the banking system. Notwithstanding the uncertainties about the monetary union, reform of the regulation, and supervision of the financial services industry have proceeded at a rapid pace with important and direct implicaitions for the industry itself, other sectors of the economy, and economic policy making.

The financial services industry has been greatly protected in most countries, either through explicit government regulations and/or through cartel-like agreements sanctioned by governments. Thus, the scope for structural change is particularly wide in this sector. There is an increasingly widespread view among economists and politicians alike that structural adjustment and increasing competition in the financial sector influence not only the prices of financial services, but, more importantly, conditions for industrial restructuring and competition, as well as conditions for monetary and fiscal policies.

Among the regulatory changes in the financial sector that have been implemented, or seem certain to be introduced, the following are of particular interest as a background for the papers in this volume. First, exchange controls within the EC were for the most part abolished as of July 1, 1990. Second, the Second Banking Directive has introduced the concept of a "single banking license", "mutually recognized" within the EC. This implies that a bank, chartered by its home country's authorities to conduct a set of activities, is allowed to conduct the same set of activities in all member states. Third, some elements of regulation, such as minimum capital requirements, will be common throughout the Community.

Fourth, relative to the rest of the world, the principle of reciprocity in banking becomes interpreted as "national treatment" subject to "effective access" requirements. In other words, an outsider's bank may be able to select a European home country and be treated within Europe as any other bank with the same home country. This interpretation of reciprocity is conditional on "effective access" in the outsider-bank's original home country. This conditionality is a "loop hole" that may enable regulatory authorities to discriminate based on nationality of ownership and control.

Fifth, in the investment banking field it seems inevitable that similar rules will apply. One reason is that in Germany traditional banking and investment banking fall under the single banner of "universal banks", whereas in other EC countries restrictions on banking activities are more severe. Furthermore, investment banking is already highly competitive internationally since trade in services across borders within this sector is possible without physical presence in the customer's country.

Sixth, with respect to the insurance industry, the difficulties of implementing a single license with mutual recognition are larger than in banking and investment-banking. The links between the public sector and parts of the insurance industry are strong. It seems, however, as if for non-life insurance the principle of a single license and mutual recognition may apply for "large" risks, meaning for companies with more than 250 employees. For life insurance (including life, pensions, and general annuities) on the other hand, host country authorization is incorporated in a second directive. Cross-broder sales would be allowed at the initiative of an applicant.

In this description the current status of monetary and financial reforms, developments in Eastern Europe and the Soviet Union must be mentioned as well. During the planning period for our conference (which proceedings are published in this volume), the Iron Curtain was raised for several countries while the Berlin Wall came down. Conditons for monetary union between East and West Germany, agreed upon only days before the conference, have added new economic and political dimensions to reforms in Western Europe.

2. AFTER 1992: OBJECTIVES AND PERSPECTIVES OF THIS VOLUME

The reforms described above will mostly not take effect before 1992. They constitute the starting point for regulatory and structural change in the monetary and the financial sectors. Developments in these sectors will in turn influence industrial and ownership structure through "markets for corporate control" as well as conditions for monetary, fiscal, and industrial policies. The proposed reforms leave many regulatory issues unresolved.

As a result, it is highly uncertain how far and how fast regulatory and structural change will proceed. There is also uncertainty about repercussions between changes within the EC and adjustment of financial and monetary arrangements outside the EC.

The objective of this volume is, in general terms, to analyze economic and potential regulatory consequences of initial financial and monetary reforms in the EC for both "insiders" in the EC itself and important outsiders, such as the USA, Japan, EFTA countries, and Eastern Europe. These consequences are obviously too far-reaching and too diverse to be captured in one volume. Furthermore, the body of economic knowledge and tools is insufficient to develop a complete analysis. Therefore, we have chosen to include two types of papers. One set consists of academic papers designed to improve our understanding of benefits and costs of regulation of financial activities and of alternative monetary arrangements. A second set of papers discusses more specifically from either an insider's or an outsider's point of view the conomic and political repercussions of initial reforms on prospects for further regulatory reform and structural change. These papers are more speculative.

We have chosen to include analyses of both financial regulation and monetary arrangements in the same volume because of the naturally strong links between these sectors. The prospect for a monetary union, for example, depends strongly on the degree of capital mobility and the integration of financial institutions across borders. Macro-economic analyses proceed usually from rather general assumptions about capital mobility. With the restructuring of the financial sector, it is important to consider the relation between the institutional setting in financial markets and macro-economic adjustment. Similarly, analysis of the financial sector is generally carried out under the implicit assumption that the jurisdiction for financial regulation coincides with the jurisdiction of a central bank and a monetary area within which certain means of payments are used. The initial reforms in the 1992 process undermine such assumptions with consequences that have not been analyzed sufficiently.

In the second set of papers, we have chosen to include the policy-perspectives of different kinds of insiders and outsiders relative to the EC. The reason for this broadening of the perspective is that the process of reform in the EC after 1992 will depend on how conflicting interests are resolved. It is necessary to take into account conflicts among EC-members as well as between the EC and the outside. For example, EC rules for internal and external trade in financial services will be heavily influenced by the responses in European countries outside EC, in the USA, and in Japan to such rules. Optimal monetary arrangements within the EC and exchange rate arrangements with the world will similarly depend on the simultaneous choice of monetary arrangements of major trading partners.

Future developments of financial and monetary arrangements can be expected to be heavily influenced by the impact on the real economy of the 1992 reforms. It is therefore our objective to incorporate analysis of important economic consequences in the real economy of foreseeable reforms in the financial and monetary sectors. The financial services industry, like monetary arrangements, influence costs of performing transactions within the non-financial sector, and information transmisison from agents with potential investment projects to those supplying funds. Thus, regulatory change in the financial services industry influences conditions for reorganization of ownership, industrial structure, and competition. Awareness of this central role of financial institutions is reflected in EC proposals for rules related to mergers and acquisition activity, such as disclosure, bidding, and insider trading rules, as well as in proposals for limiting the size of mergers and acquisitions that can occur without approval by the Commission.

The consequences of initial financial and monetary reforms in the EC on competitive and ownership conditions in industries and on macroeconomic adjustment is bound to touch on politically sensitive nerves. Economic forces, unleashed by the initial reforms, could well generate pressure for re-regulation to prevent politically unpopular consequences in individual countries.

3. THE CONTENTS OF THIS VOLUME

As noted, the volume consists of analytical papers as well as more speculative policy oriented "perspective"-papers. The analytical papers in Parts One through Four deals with under-researched topics, contributing to improved understanding of consequences of initial 1992-reforms. Most of these papers have comments, as well. Parts Five through Seven contain the shorter "perspective"-papers.

Before describing the individual papers in some detail we provide a brief overview of the seven parts.

Part One, "Implications of 1992 for Regulation, Competition, and Structure of the Financial Services Industry", contains four papers on determinants of market structure in banking, and the economics of optimal regulation of banking (in a broad sense) and insurance. The papers are written by J. Kimball Dietrich; David Folkerts-Landau, Peter M. Garber, and Steven R. Weisbrod; Anthony Santomero; and Göran Skogh.

In *Part Two*, "Investment Banking and the Industrial Sector", economic consequences of a deregulated and harmonized financial environment for the non-financial sector are analyzed. The three papers by Roy C. Smith and Ingo Walter; Espen Eckbo; and Gunnar Eliasson, focus on changes in ownership structure through merger and acquisition activity, on potential effects on competition in industry and the financial sector, and on important sources of productivity gains through markets for corporate control.

In *Part Three*, "Barriers to Capital Mobility and Financial Intermediation", John O. Montgomery and Alberto Giovannini bridge the gap between analysis of financial markets and macroeconomic issues in two papers focusing on "natural" or non-regulatory barriers to perfect integration. In the first paper, Montgomery applies recent developments in the theory of banking to the question of regional and national monetary policy independence. Giovannini analyzes determinents of currency substitution and its effect on monetary policy and financial market volatility.

The subject of *Part Four* is "Economics and Politics of the EMS". The papers by Reuven Glick and Michael Hutchison; Jürgen von Hagen and Michele Fratianni; and Clas Wihlborg and Thomas D. Willett deal with issues raised by plans to form a currency union or at least to coordinate monetary policy more closely. One such issue is whether fiscal policy need to be coordinated or whether there exists incentives to do so in a coordinated monetary policy area. The nature of shocks to the EMS members and adjustment to them in a coordinated monetary policy area is the second issue addressed in this part. The final academic paper reviews and updates the theory of the optimum currency area including questions of how to accomplish the transition to such an area.

We turn next to the perspective-papers in Parts Five through Seven. The papers in these parts are intended to bring out potential policy-conflicts among nations, as well as conflicts between developments caused by market forces in the new regulatory environment, and policy objectives in different countries.

Part Five, "Economic Policy Perspectives on Financial Market Regulation and Supervision" contains papers by Tad Rybczynski; Nigel Carter; Emil Ems; and Igor G. Doronin representing general EC-, U.K.-, EFTA, and Soviet perspectives respectively. Thereafter, in *Part Six*, "Economic Policy Perspectives on Monetary Arrangements", perspectives are presented by Yoshiharu Oritani, Sven Arndt, Karen Lewis, Thomas Franzén, Sir Alan A. Walters, and Aris Protopapadakis. These authors present large and small outsiders' perspectives and raise questions about the proposed transition path within a strengthened exchange rate mechanism (ERM) within the EC.

Part Seven, finally, "The Transition to a Convertible Currency for a Centrally Planned Economy" with papers by Stefan Schönberg, Emil Claassen, and Stanislav M. Borisov brings up issues raised by the rapid monetary unification in Germany, as well as by the slower pace towards convertibility in other Eastern European economies.

Part One: Implications of 1992 for Regulation, Supervision, and the Structure of Banking

The initial focus is on banking. *J. Kimball Dietrich's* "Consequences of 1992 for Competition in Financial Services: Banking" sets two competing hypotheses to explain what Europe 1992 entails for banks. The first is that banks, through mergers and acquisitions, will become bigger and reap the benfits of economies of scale. Incidentally, this is the view of many European bankers. The alternative hypothesis is that deregulation will force banks to become more competitive. The first hypothesis implies a higher degree of concentration; the second is somewhat silent on market concentration. The latter issue appears again in the paper by Eckbo in Part Two. The evidence presented in the Dietrich paper favors the competition hypothesis. He examines factor shares to determine whether input prices are priced efficiently and finds that they are not.

Anthony Santomero notes that the contribution of Dietrich's paper lies in having "introduced a new technology to the issue of economies of scale and scope...[and] that recourse to primary financial statement data is possible in a market where standardized Call Reports and Functional Cost Analysis studies are not available." The issue of production and factor market efficiency will undoubtedly generate a great deal of attention by other researchers. For example, are the inefficiencies in the deposit and loan markets related to bank size? Dietrich does not provide a direct test of this proposition. Yet, it is quite plausible that smaller banks may price both inputs and outputs in a more distortive way (larger deviations from marginal value product) through some "public-choice" mechanism that insulates smaller banks in small communities relative to large banks with a national branch network. On the other hand, we see in the following papers that large money center banks may receive a relatively strong deposit insurance.

The next two papers analyze the case for supervision and regulation of bank activity. They take very different views on what economic role banks perform in society and therefore on the role of supervision and regulation.

In a theoretical paper, "The Supervision and Regulation of Financial Markets in the New Financial Environment", *David Folkerts-Landau, Peter M. Garber* and *Steven R. Weisbrod* make the controversial argument that banks' uniqueness stems from their ability to be the cheapest source of liquidity and not from a comparative advantage in processing information about borrowers. One implication of the hypothesis is that, since bank loans are not a unique form of credit, bank borrowers do not bear the cost of reserve requirements to a higher degree than other borrowers with the same need for liquidity. With this view of banking activity central banks and supervisory authorities face a trade off between an efficient allocation of capital resources and the need to limit risk-taking in banks obtaining liquidity assistance in times of crises.

Peter Englund in his comments remarks that the uniqueness of bank liabilities "does not imply the rejection of the uniqueness of bank loans", and that banks cannot extract the "tax" implied by reserve requirements from borrowers. Potential tax bearers include holders of bank liabilities, bank owners and the ordinary "Joe the taxpayer" as well. Careful empirical work will eventually shed light as to which of the four actors bears the largest burden of reserve requirements.

According to the view of banking presented here the reserve requirement "tax" is partial payment for credit risk absorbed by central banks when guaranteeing liquidity. This proposition gives the central bank the opportunity of trading off more efficiency in capital allocation with less regulation against more credit risk absorbed to reduce systemic risk. The authors conclude their paper on a controversial note by suggesting that at present there is an "insufficiently stringent and regulatory structure", if systemic risk is to be avoided. The implication is that securitization would have to be reduced if central banks are unwilling to absorb credit risk by guaranteeing the liquidity of bank liabilities. The optimal constraint on banks' asset position is left for future research.

Anthony Santomero in "The Bank Capital Issue" analyzes in more detail proposals for and alternatives to imposing constraints on banks' asset position in the form of capital requirements related to the nature of assets. Such constraints are agreed upon and are being implemented in Europe, the USA, and Japan.

Santomero emphasizes that any policy recommendation with respect to capital requirements as well as to deposit insurance is based on an explicit or implicit view of whether banks provide any positive externalities, and, if so, on the source of uniqueness of banking activity. The paper by Folkerts-Landau, Garber, and Weisbrod is clearly arguing that externalities exist in the provision of liquidity with central bank backing to avoid systemic crises. Santomero does not rule out such an externality but views the uniqueness of banks as resulting from client-information advantages, while their uniqueness in the previous paper is based solely on the central bank's guarantee of liquidity. A third view of banking discussed by Santomero is that banks neither provide externalities nor are unique. Under these conditions there is obviously no case for regulation or supervision.

It is in the information-advantage view of banks' uniqueness that capital adequacy ratios become controversial. Essentially, the risk on a specific asset can only be evaluated by the bank. *Ad hoc* rules for capital ratios against different assets imposing differentiated "taxes" on lending will be distortive. Santomero argues that current proposals will distort banking acitivites seriously.

Differentiated deposit insurance is a substitute for differentiated capital ratios but suffers from the same problem. Without the bank's information an optimal insurance rate structure cannot be identified. The paper discusses other alternatives for controlling banks' risk-taking and the social costs and benefits associated with each.

Santomero concludes with a discussion of whether regulatory competition within the EC with the suggested mixture of home and host country regulation of banks could induce countries to implement optimal constraints on banking activity. His view is not optimistic. The same issues appear again in the perspective papers in Part Five, where Rybczynski points out the *ad hoc* nature of bank-regulation.

The information advantage view of financial institutions continues in *Göran Skogh's* paper, "The Structure and Future of the Insurance Market". Skogh emphasizes that understanding of the specific information required to provide different kinds of insurance services is required to predict how the industry will develop in a deregulated environment based on competitive advantages of firms and synergies among activities. He questions the widespread contention that bank and insurance activities have natural synergies. Banks invest in customer-specific and transaction-specific information that is difficult to trade; this investment in turn implies small economies of scale and an emphasis on decentralization. Property and liability insurers, on the other hand, invest in information about low-probability events; this investment in turn implies large economies of scale and an emphasis on centralization. Skogh concludes that Europe 1992 will not affect significantly the structure of the insurance industry. Changes are more likely to occur in the distribution systems, which cater to specifc customer needs, than in the risk-assessment and claims-settlement areas of the industry, where the sources of information advantage for firms can be found. This part of the study questions conventional wisdoms about economies of scale in banking, economies of scope between banking and insurance, and proposed principles for regulation and supervision. Many issues are unresolved, however, and need further research before new regulatory structures are imposed and "frozen".

Part Two: Investment Banking and the Industrial Sector

The three studies in Part Two of the volume demonstrate the far-reaching effects that deregulation and harmonization of rules for investment banking can exert on industrial activity.

Roy C. Smith and Ingo Walter's "The European Market for Mergers and Acquisitions" offers an overview of merger and acquisition (M&A) activities in Europe and examines the implications of harmonized tax and regulatory structures for industrial restructuring. The evidence presented in the paper undescores the extent to which M&As in continental Europe have "taken off". The implementation of Europe 1992 is bound to produce a great deal more of it. One obvious alternative to M&A is firm expansion through investment. Is the activity in M&A a sign that asset prices are low relative to prices of reproducible goods, or is the M&A activity a sign that target firms are taken over by lower-cost producers, or does it reflect a strategy of large firms to gain market power? These issues are only partly resolved by Smith and Walter who point to the productivity gains derived from M&As.

B. Espen Eckbo's "Mergers, Concentration, and Antitrust" focuses on the impact that M&As have on competitive conditions and thus provides answers to some of the above questions. Two alternative hypotheses of merger activity are contrasted in the paper. The first hypothesis stresses efficiency gains (or lower agency costs); the second larger market power. The first hypothesis implies that rates of return of the acquired and rival firms rise after the merger; the second hypothesis implies that the rate of return of the acquired firm rises, whereas those of the rival firms can either rise or fall. The tests are implemented on US and Canadian data for non-financial and financial firms. The weight of the evidence comes out clearly in favor of the efficiency hypothesis. The implications of the findings for anti-trust policy are rather obvious: anti-trust activities are more likely to lower efficiency than to prevent monopolies from occurring. *Steven R. Weisbrod* agrees with Eckbo's criticism of market structure regulation but objects that a common European anti-trust policy regulating monopolistic pricing behavior would not be better. As an example, Weisbrod refers to the U.S. practice of determining dumping which "has become a lightening rod for trade policy rather than an attempt to reduce the threat of monopoly in the U.S. marketplace."

Gunnar Eliasson in "Financial Institutions in a European Market for Executive Competence" presents a view of how capital markets and internal labor markets interact as mechanisms for allocation of managerial and firm-specific competence contributing to productivity growth in a way that is neglected in most discussions of a new European industrial policy. Most industrial policy discussion is based on the concepts of economies of scale in production functions and industry-learning over time and by becoming larger. Eliasson objects to the "production-function" view of the firm commonly held by economists. He emphasizes instead that the crucial factor enabling a firm and a country to hold a sustainable competitive advantage is "organizational learning" meaning the firm's ability to continuously upgrade its competence base, especially in individuals and teams at executive and managerial levels.

The market for corporate control, relying very much on capital markets, is crucial in Eliasson's view of organizational learning. Competent teams and individuals on the managerial level can be "traded" through mergers and acquisitions, substituting for trade in internal and external labor markets. In addition, the competition among executive teams through performance requirements in capital markets and take-over threats provide incentives for organizational learning in internal labor markets. Eliasson compares the efficiency of "organizational learning" in two different financial environments, taking into account the nature of asymmetric information about competence, and its often intangible nature. Within so-called industrial banking groups, common in Germany, Japan, and Sweden, a quasi-internal market for executive competence is created. Monitoring of individual's and team's skills are performed internally. If the group is sufficiently large, diverse, and international a highly efficient market can be created. The drawback of this financial market structure is that a stagnating group is not easily dissolved and reorganized.

The decentralized financial market structure characterizing the USA and U.K. is more easily reorganized and take-over threats require firms to work on their organizational learning capabilities. Asymmetric information problems are harder to resolve, however, and the mobility of competent teams and individuals reduces incentives for investment in internal competence upgrading.

Niels Chr. Nielsen is sceptical about these conclusions partly because they are not grounded on empirical evidence. He refutes the arguments and evidence demonstrating that M&A activity generally benefits shareholders and points to several reasons why such activity often occurs in the interest of management groups.

Part Three: Barriers to Capital Mobility and Financial Intermediation
This part analyzes barriers to the provision of financial and monetary services across borders, that may remain even after regulatory impediments are removed. We used the phrase "natural" barriers above to denote those remaining barriers, although they are no more natural than the "natural rate of unemployment". Furthermore, "natural" barriers need not be constant and could well peter out over time through learning. Nevertheless,

information problems, habits, and cultural barriers could be important for the evolution of banking and payment systems for quite some time after regulatory barriers are removed.

The papers in this part provide a link between analysis of financial institutions and markets and the macroeconomic topics that follow. *John O. Montgomery* in "Market Segmentation and 1992: Toward a Theory of Trade in Financial Services" analyzes theoretically and empirically how local information monopoly of banks could limit efficiency gains within the financial sectors, as well as more general welfare gains in the form of an equalization of capital costs internationally. On the other hand, segmentation could allow a degree of monetary policy independence.

The testable implication of Montgomery's thesis is that regional loan rates are positively correlated with external regional borrowings, evidence that banks have market power or that interregional capital mobility is imperfect. The empirical work, using Italian data, cannot refute the hypothesis that regional fund supply curves are upward sloping and loan demand curvesare downward sloping. These findings in turn, are consistent with several hypotheses that the test cannot distinguish among: (1) informational advantage by banks, (2) search costs borne by banks' clients, (3) differences in regulation, and (4) non-profit maximizing behavior on the part of banks.

Daniel Gros comments that it is hard to reconcile the results of the paper with the fact that "in Italy, as in most other industrialised countries, there is an active inter-bank market through which, at least apparently, all banks can obtain funds at the posted market interest rates." Another difficulty in interpreting the correlation between interest rates and net regional capital flows stems from the fact that these contain a good deal of government transfers. Again quoting Gros "...the aid programme for the 'Mezzogiorno' includes a substantial proportional subsidy on capital costs, which implies that firms will be less concerned about the interest rate they pay." *Richard Sweeney,* in a comment in Chapter 10 below, points out that Montgomery's theoretical structure is inconsistent with the Modigliani-Miller theorem of capital structure irrelevance, since the marginal costs of funds are determined in loan markets. Further empirical work along the lines initiated by Montgomery is certainly desirable. If the market power of local banks is non-negligible then local monetary conditions can be differentiated, for example, by means of reserve requirements.

Alberto Giovannini in "Currency Substitution and Monetary Policy" analyzes the potential for currency substitution under financial and monetary arrangements implied by 1992, and discusses welfare consequences, as well as consequences for monetary policy, of currency substitution. He also asks whether it is likely that a monetary union would occur through a market driven evolution, as some have argued, when there are not restrictions on choice of currency in transactions. Imperfect substitutability of foreign for domestic currencies is grounded in legal restrictions (e.g., tax payments), explicit constraints (e.g., reserve requirements) and in the "network" value (i.e., the bulk of the transactions are local using local currencies). Trade and financial openness raises the residents' demand for other countries' currencies. Giovannini does not believe that any one currency would dominate in the absence of currency-restricting regulations. This argument is interesting for the controversy about proposals for currency competition as a transition towards a Monetary Union.

Michael Melvin in his comments points out that the transactions demand for foreign currencies cannot be directly linked to bilateral trade flows because the currency of invoice need not coincide with the currency of either trading country. On the other hand, this demand is driven by parallel-currency considerations. On dominance, Melvin reports findings indicating the pre-eminence of the Deutsche mark over other European currencies including the ECU.

The second part of Giovannini's paper deals with the effects of higher currency substitution. Here the author contrasts the Hayek-U.K. Treasury view of a stable evolution with the instability view of currency substitution. According to the former, currency substitution, under flexible exchange rates, has the desirable properties of pressuring government to maintain a low rate of inflation and of stabilizing exchange rates. The very nature of currency competition would prevent any currency from dominating. This contrasts sharply with the view that currency substitution would be a major source of exchange rate instability. Under fixed rates an important question is whether "Cresham's Law" (bad money drives out good money) would take effect, as Hayek and Wihlborg and Willett in Ch. 12 in this volume argue. Giovannini points out that "Cresham's Law" can actually work in reverse making "good money" dominate, if the user-values of currencies are different and the expected rates of inflation are identical. This result is, as noted, controversial. It focuses attention on the issue whether currencies are useful to different degrees when exchange rates are truly fixed and legal restrictions on their uses are abolished.

Part Four: Economics and Politics of the EMS
This part of the book looks at political economy aspects of the EMS with the purpose of evaluating the viability of a proposed currency union, as well as the viability of the proposed transition-process.

In "Fiscal Constraints and Incentives with Monetary Coordination: Implications for Europe 1992" *Reuven Glick* and *Michael Hutchison* investigate theoretically the fiscal policy implications of an economic and monetary union in the European Community. One of the most intensly debated issues surrounding monetary union has been the possible need for multilateral constraints on member countries' fiscal deficits. Using an intertemporal model with maximizing private and public agents, the authors asks whether institutional change affect incentives facing fiscal policy-makers and whether the feasible mix of government expenditure and financing arrangement may change in a monetary union. The answer is affirmative to both questions and the critical conclusions of the paper are: Monetary integration induces fiscal integration, provided governments see "beyond their noses"; monetary dominance in a fixed-exchange-rate area forces fiscal convergence. In other words, concerns that mechanisms for fiscal coordination must be agreed upon before a European Central Bank is created are exaggerated.

Linda S. Goldberg, in her comments, cautions the reader that the Glick-Hutchison conclusions stem from strong assumptions. For example, while there is economic integration in the two-country setting of the authors, currency substitution does not take place. Yet, currency substitution alters the determination of optimal monetary and fiscal policies. She argues, for example, that "...when consumers in each country hold some of their own currency as well as the currency of their trading partner, there is an incentive for the domestic government to print excess money since it can ...export some of the inflation tax." On this pointss, Giovannini disagrees. Richard J. Sweeney in his comments accepts the results of the paper but would like to see how robust are the paper's results across models that relax the flex-price, market-clearing approach. He notes that the model is essentially Ricardian in the sense that government debt is not considered net wealth. This assumption is clearly important in discussion of monetary authorities' incentive to monetize debt.

There are two commonly held views about the role of EMS. Some economists and central bankers in general view it as an anti-inflationary device for countries pegging to Germany. Others argue that the shock absorbing properties of EMS are more important. *Jürgen von Hagen and Michele Fratianni* belong to the latter group. In "Policy Coordination in the EMS with Stochastic Asymmetries", they investigate the shock-absorbing properties of the EMS. The analysis is based on numerical simulations of a relatively small, three-country model consisting of two EMS countries and the US. The paper evaluates policy coordination among the European countries in the form of full cooperation with flexible exchange rates and two EMS-like fixed exchange rate arrangements. The focus is on the robustness of the welfare benefits from coordination. Stochastic asymmetries limit severely the scope for European coordination, but the benefits of European coordination to these asymmetries rises with economic integration. In essence, 'Europe 1992' is good news for the EMS. *Thorvaldur Gylfason*, while agreeing with the main results of von Hagen and Fratianni, raises the issue of a comparison of their model with another where "employment does not depend solely on unanticipated monetary policy changes" but also on the anticipated component and where non-market clearing mechanisms substitute for the rational expectations market clearing approach.

"Optimum Currency Area Revisited on the Transition Path to a Currency Union" by *Clas Wihlborg* and *Thomas D. Willett* reviews and extends the determinants of optimum currency areas. They conclude that in traditional criteria the EC is not an optimum currency area but question these criteria. First, if real shocks are sectoral, they require relative price adjustment and internal labor market adjustment in each country. Exchange rate adjustment and macroeconomic policies are far from first best responses to such shocks. Second, political economy considerations are often neglected. Third, within rational expectations models the criteria for evaluating exchange rate regimes switch from the variability of output to the variability caused by confusion of agents about sources of disturbances. In conventional rational expectations models, flexible exchange rates are superior to fixed rates under this criteria, but the relative superiority based on this criteria denoted "informativeness" depends on the relative variability of different shocks.

Wihlborg and Willett extend the analysis of informativeness allowing for imperfect information about structural parameters and monetary policy rules. They argue that a case for a currency union as opposed to fixed rates with several central banks can be made on grounds of informativeness.

In the analysis of a currency union in Europe the transition path is an important factor to consider when evaluating the feasibility of the plan. Wihlborg and Willett argue that the three stage transition process may spell the doom for plans to create a union and recommend a "big-bang" approach with flexible exchange rates until the date a union is created and responsibility for monetary policy shifts to one central bank.

In the comments by *John Driffill* the emphasis is on issues that are treated too lightly by the previous authors. For example Driffills sees "the need for greater interregional transfers in a monetary union". This concern is central in in the fiscal federalism literature and potentially of great importance in Europe after 1992. Wihlborg and Willett, on the other hand, suggest that regional transfers within countries may suffice. This disagreement can only be settled with more research into the nature of shocks, their relative impact on different countries, and these countries ability to adjust. This is the central theme of von Hagen and Fratianni's paper.

Part Five: Perspectives on Financial Market Regulation and Supervision

Tad Rybczynski addresses the problem of regulatory framework in an integrated area like the European Community. Rybczynski notes that "there is at present no established, accepted and comprehensive body of theory giving guidance of what is the optimal structure of regulation during different stages of economic and financial evolution." He sees proposed regulation in the 1992 process as one of many examples of *ad hoc* responses to economic and political pressures of the moment rather than regulation by a careful design. Rybczynski points out that several aspects of the EC 1992 Single Financial Market Programme are responses to the revolution in information technology. The view of regulation presented here explains well the disparity between optimal and actual regulation discussed by papers in Part One.

Nigel Carter provides an insider perspective and reviews the U.K. government's basic economic policy stance and its relationship to the principles underlying the U.K. approach to financial market regulation domestically and internationally. Carter hopes for greater regulatory convergence across countries to enhance the containment of systemic risk emphasized in the Folkerts-Landau, Garber and Weisbrod paper.

Emil Ems takes a small outsider perspective and discusses how EFTA countries have reacted to and will benefit from Europe 1992. Since cartel-like arrangements have prevailed in EFTA, the financial liberalization in Western Europe will lead to a reduction of producers' surplus and gains in consumers' surplus in EFTA. Also EFTA countries' public sectors will lose to the extent that tax rates on capital and financial transactions will have to be reduced to Western European standards. In other words, Europe 1992 is good news for the EFTA consumers. Yet, as Ems points out "There is a risk that public decision makers will try to renege on their pledges to liberalize capital movements and financial services." By joining the EC financial area this risk would be greatly reduced if not eliminated.

Igor Doronin relates economic reforms currently under way in the USSR with the Europe 1992 programme. He sees the need for an integration of the Soviet financial system with Western Europe in the longer term but warns that current institutional structures would put Soviet institutions at a disadvantage if all barriers between financial markets were removed. It is perhaps significant that Doronin, after discussing the overwhelming problems facing the Soviet Union in the financial sphere, concludes that economic statistics must be improved. It seems as if economists in Soviet Union simply lack the most basic input in economic analysis.

Part Six: Economic Policy Perspectives on Monetary Arrangements

Yoshiharu Oritani looks at European monetary union from the perspective of a Japanese central banker. To begin with, he argues that the decisions taken by the Commission in the financial area are more consistent with the spirit of deregulation than with the notion of Fortress Europe. He then moves to compare two strategies to achieve monetary union: the "top down appraoch" and the "bottom up approach". The "top down approach" starts with the formation of a central bank that begins first with monetary policy responsabilities and then acquires resposabilities for payment services. The "bottom up approach" would reverse the sequence. Oritani seems to prefer the latter emphasizing like Folkerts-Landau, Garber and Weisbrod in Ch. 2 the role of central banks in the payment system.

Sven W. Arndt discusses the consequences of economic integration and monetary arrangements in Europe for the USA and outsiders. He emphasizes sector and firm specific effects on outsiders resulting from increased competitiveness of some European industries. The effects of monetary arrangements would depend largely on their impact on European inflation, monetary stability, and economic growth. Arndt also makes the point that during the transition to full economic and monetary union Europe may be the source of real and financial shocks, further complicating coordination and cooperative schemes among the three large players in the world.

Karen Lewis does not take a country perspective but asks how adjustment to internal trade and fiscal deficits and surpluses will occur within a monetary union. There are economic, as well as political aspects to this issue. For example, will the market assess a sufficient risk-premium on government debt to induce fiscal discipline? Another question is whether internal trade deficits will have repercussions on intra EC politics.

The papers by Thomas Franzén, Sir Alan A. Walters and Aris Protopapadakis take contrasting viewpoints on the current exchange rate mechanism (ERM) within the EMS as a transition arrangement to a monetary union or, from the Swedish and the U.K perspectives, as a mechanism for reducing inflation. At the time this is written the U.K. has joined the ERM and the Swedish currency became pegged to ECU in May 1991 after having been pegged to a basket since 1977.

Thomas Franzén, Deputy Governor of the Swedish Central Bank, offers a very favorable assessment of the EMS and states that "a Swedish EMS-association is not excluded from further consideration in the future...a Swedish association would be in line with our ambition to achieve closer cooperation and integration with the EC." Is this a political statement or a purely economic evaluation of the EMS? As a political statement, Franzén's position appears to reflect the mood of Swedish public opinion, which favors more EC participation. (Since the paper was written Sweden has declared the intention to apply to the EC, and at publication time it is likely that the application has been submitted.) As an economic assessment, Franzén's position contrasts with that presented in von Hagen and Fratianni in Ch. 11. These authors argue that there is a "real" EMS grounded on a mechanism that lowers the variability of exchange rates and inflation rates and a "mythical" EMS grounded on the popular notion that high-inflation countries gain credibility in their anti-inflation program upon joining the EMS. This notion is theoretically weak and empirically unproven.

Sir Alan Walters's view of the EMS stands in sharp contrast with that of Franzén and many of the conference participants. Sir Alan starts by repeating his well-known critique that capital flows in the EMS move towards the relatively high-inflation EMS countries. These flows are perverse and exacerbate inflation divergences rather than bring about convergence. Walters' critique presupposes that an investor who buys Italian government securities at a higher interest rate than German government securities is assured the stability of the exchange rate. But this is not true so long as there is a probability of a realignment. Indeed the significant differences between Italian and German interest rates reflect the probability of realignments. The Walters' critique seems to be more relevant in the "new EMS", that is since the last realignment of January 1987, than in the old EMS. As to monetary union, Sir Alan thinks it can be as good as flexible exchange rates, depending on how the European central bank will behave. He suggests that both regimes can be improved by creating a commodity standard.

Aris Protopapadakis questions the proposition that a regime like the ERM can ever be credible. Thereby he associates himself with those considering the ERM and the EMS as an anti-inflationary device. What Sir Alan calls a "half-baked" system Protopapadakis calls a fixed rate with a realignment-option for central banks. The fact that policy makers retain this option implies that it is valuable to them. The pegged exchange rate cannot therefore be perfectly credible.

The traditional criteria for optimum currency areas often referred to as arguments why the EC is not such area, are also questioned by Protopapadakis on grounds similar to those in Wihlborg and Willett. He also develops an interpretation of a currency union in terms of integration of markets for credit. Thereby, he links the issues of monetary union with the integration of financial markets more broadly, and raises again the issue of jurisdiction of and division of labor among different national and supranational monetary and financial authorities. The future will tell what the scope for jurisdictional conflict is.

Part Seven: The Transition to a Convertible Currency for a Centrally Planned Economy

Stefan Schönberg views German monetary unification and European monetary union as different types of monetary reforms. "In Western Europe we are engaged in a process of harmonizing national monetary and economic policies...by transferring national sovereign powers towards a European institution...In contrast, the abolition of the East German mark [resulted from] East Germany's complete loss of sovereignty in monetary policy matters." He proceeds to discuss elements and objects of the German monetary unification process. In hindsight and in light of recent statements from the Bundesbank about the choice of an inappropriate conversion rate, Schönberg's assessment seems optimistic.

Emil-Maria Claassen's analysis does not support the view that the conversion rate was inappropriate and the cause of unemployment in Eastern Germany. He distinguishes between monetary stabilization aspects of the rules of conversion and price reform and liberalization to restore a market determined relative price structure. Relative real wages between Eastern and Western Germany are not obviously determined by the conversion rate.

Stanislav M. Borisov gives an appraisal of the importance and the timing of introducing rouble convertibility in the USSR. In contrast to East Germany, other eastern European countries have the choice of delaying convertibility. Borisov reminds the Western audience that a currency can either be externally or internally convertible, the former implying the existence of an exchange market for roubles outside the Soviet Union in addition to the ability of Soviet residents to convert freely between domestic and foreign currency. While external convertibility is more demanding than internal convertibility, the latter is far more important at this stage. Yet, Borisov reminds us that internal convertibility should not be considered a panacea; that the improvement in the quality of the means of exchange should be separated from the need to proceed with economic reforms; and that a policy of low money growth rates is more important than the introduction of parallel currencies. Concerning the timing of rouble convertibility, Borisov makes it conditional on (i) significant progress towards a market economy, (ii) achievement of lower inflation rates and smaller budget deficits and (iii) the creation of a foreign exchange market. As he puts it "...it is perfectly clear that rouble convertibility is not the case in the nearest future..."

Part One

Implications of 1992 for Regulation, Competition and Structure of the Financial Services Industries

Financial Regulation and Monetary Arrangements after 1992
C. Wihlborg, M. Fratianni and T.D. Willett (Editors)
© 1991 Elsevier Science Publishers B.V. All rights reserved

1 Consequences of 1992 for Competition in Financial Services: Banking

J. Kimball Dietrich

School of Business, University of Southern California, Los Angeles, CA 90089-1421, USA

1. INTRODUCTION: 1992 AND ALL THAT

The European Economic Community (EEC) has undertaken a bold initiative to fully integrate its goods and capital markets. While still not in place, the Community has drafted banking directives focused on allowing the unrestricted operation of banks throughout the EEC. The economic benefits of the movements towards goods and capital market integration are presumed to be large. For example, in The "Costs of Non-Europe" in Financial Services (Price Waterhouse, 1988), part of the so-called Cecchini Report, the increase in consumer surplus from financial services market integration is estimated to be in the range of 11 to 33 billion European Currency Units (ECUs), or roughly $8.8 to $26.5 billion[1]. Gains in the banking sector alone were estimated to be in the range of $6.6 to $17.5 billion, or around two thirds of the gain in surplus from integration in financial services.

The Cecchini Report estimates of increased efficiencies in financial markets are based on reductions in prices for a standard list of banking services. These services were priced in seven EEC markets using survey techniques by Price Waterhouse. The average of the lowest quotes were assumed to be the level to which market integration could bring the costs of services. The source of estimated economic gains are entirely in the form of estimated increases in consumer surplus, ignoring the impact of integrated banking markets on financial service providers[2]. While the Cecchini report analysis provided banking market comparisons not before available, the study did not focus on the relative impact of changes in banking market competition or the potential sources of increased efficiency of service providers.

Efficiencies from banking market integration could come from two basic sources: more efficiency in the provision of services and increased competition. Increases in operating efficiency could come from economies of scale to be realized from larger market size or reductions of distortions in local factor markets. Efficiencies from competition could come from an increased number of low cost suppliers or from price-cutting induced by the threat of new competitors with the removal of barriers to entry by foreign competitors.

The questions of the relative importance of the possible sources of the cost reductions assumed in the Cecchini report analysis are of policy and strategic interest. If the efficiencies are likely due from economies of scale, substantial restructuring and increased size of financial institutions should be tolerated if not encouraged by regulators. If the cost savings come from increased competitive conditions in the individual country product and factor markets, realization of the savings do not necessitate dramatic shifts in banking relationships but only the credible threat of competition from potential entrants in now contestable markets and increased flexibility and competitive behavior by existing firms, regulators, and suppliers.

This study assesses the impact of these two sources of savings on banking markets in the EEC by examining the efficiency of microeconomic banking units in the EEC and three other European countries. The intention is to sort out the potential for increased efficiency among the European banking markets. The identification of major sources of banking market efficiencies to be expected from either increased competition or cost reductions from larger scale organizations, or both, should have an important impact on the focus of policy towards banks and banking related institutions in the future.

2. APPROACH, METHODS AND DATA USED IN THIS STUDY

2.1 Approach

Studies of bank efficiency have often foundered on the definition and/or measurement of bank output. Most studies such as those reviewed and summarized in Kolari and Zardkoohi (1987) have used loans and deposits as measures of output in estimating cost functions. The cost function estimation typically uses detailed cost data from a survey of participating banks.[3] Efficiency in this framework consists of relatively low cost provision of bank services in the form of loan and deposit dollar amounts and/or numbers of accounts.

The current literature on the efficiency of banks has not explicity incorporated current developments in banking practice or modern developments in financial theory concerning the sources of value added in banking. In practice, developments in off-balance sheet activities, such as interest rate and currency swaps, credit guarantees in the forms of letters and lines of credit and note issuance facilities, mean that bank output is not completely represented by activity measures such as loans and deposits, although they may be complementary to these traditional banking functions. Other commercial bank activities, such as currency and securities trading and investment banking activities like private placements, mergers and acquisitions, and financial advising, have grown tremendously in importance in modern banks. Neither the new or expanded traditional banking services output levels can be captured solely by output measures based on loans and deposits.

Modern developments in financial theory as applied to banking have concentrated on banks' role in resolving principal-agent problems arising from information asymmetry and moral hazard in lending arrangements. In short, these theories note that borrowers have an incentive to distort their earning prospects and risks from investments when borrowing money, and that there is always the temptation to take the money and run. In reviewing models of bank firms, Santomero (1984) stresses the contribution of information economics analysis in both the asset transformation problem (converting nonmarketable loans to liquid financial claims, namely deposits) and the role of information asymmetries in loan pricing.[4] Fama (1985) attributes the difference in banks' cost of funds (after the reserve requirement tax) and yields on loans to information giving banks "a comparative cost advantage in making and monitoring repeated short-term inside loans (p.38)."

The approach used in this study concentrates on analyzing value added by banks in all their activities. Much of this value cannot be captured by traditional bank activity measures such as loan and deposit volume. Value added represents partly net interest margins, namely the difference between the yield on loans and costs of funds including deposits. In concentrating on value added, however, these margins can be the result of carefully negotiated and structured deals in line with the information economics view of bank production. Value added also includes fees and concessionary terms on deposits which may have been part of loan deals or other banking activities. Of course, value added also includes trading profits, capital gains, and other traditional sources of value production in banks. Value added is net of all non-labor costs, including not just the financial costs implicit in net interest margins, but unallocated costs associated with the provision of services as part of non-price competition.

Value added is a composite production measure which includes value from both traditional and new banking services, and includes that portion of the value produced which is received by an often experienced and highly trained labor force. Banking services to customers may produce value which is returned to employees in the form of commissions, bonuses or profit-sharing plans to traders and lending officers. In focusing on value added and related return measures, this study avoids the direct measurement of bank production and concerns on whether the economic value of banking services is captured by workers or investors in banks.

To summarize, value added has several advantages as a measure of bank productivity. First, banking is a labor intensive business and value added includes both profits and remuneration to labor. Second, value added captures all sources of the value of services provided by banks: this value may be provided in exchange for explicit fees for service, or may represent services provided in the form of customer conveniences like branches which are paid for in terms of higher lending rates or below market rate deposits or compensating balances. Third, value produced by off-balance sheet activities and traditional banking activities like deal-making and trading not directly related to loans and deposits are included in value added.

2.2 Method

Using data described in the next section, two basic methods are employed to examine the sources of potential change in the production of value added in banking services following market integration after 1992. The first is to examine basic relationships measuring bank performance and market structure in the form of graphs and tables, presented as Tables 1 to 4 and Figures 1 to 3 in Appendix. These representations of data are intended to set the stage for more rigorous examinations of differences in bank performance in different European countries.

More formally, a model of value added using a Cobb-Douglas production function is developed. This model assumes that in addition to the exogenous input equity capital, labor and financial inputs in the form of loan and deposit amounts are employed to produce value. This model is similar to the work by Hancock (1985a) in assuming both real and financial inputs in production. Accordingly, the value added estimation equation is:

$$\text{Log(VA)} = \alpha_o + \alpha_N * \text{Log(N)} + \alpha_K * \text{Log(K)} + \alpha_L * \text{Log(L)} + \alpha_D * \text{Log(D)} + e_{VA}, \quad (1)$$

where VA is value added, N is total employees, K is equity capital and L and D are loans and deposits, respectively, and e is an error term.[5]

Since factor shares will be simultaneously determined by competitive conditions in the markets for loans, deposits, and workers in each European market, three factor share equations are specified as follows[6]:

$$wN/VA = \alpha_N + \Sigma_i \beta_{Ni} DUMMY_i + e_N \qquad (2)$$

$$r_L L/VA = \alpha_L + \Sigma_i \beta_{Li} DUMMY_i + e_L \qquad (3)$$

$$r_{MM} D/VA = \alpha_D + \Sigma_i \beta_{Di} DUMMY_i + e_D \qquad (4)$$

where w is average wages bank and r_L is the average loan rate for each bank. The factor share for deposits is computed using the average local country money market rate, r_{MM}, times deposits. Money rates are assumed to be the marginal costs of funds in competitive funds markets and departures from these rates reflect competitive conditions in deposit markets. All variables are described in detail in the data description, below. The dummy variables are for each European banking market included in the sample, exluding one to avoid singularity.[7]

The system of equations in value added and factor shares is estimated using three stage least squares (3SLSQ). In estimation, the coefficients of the production function are constrained to equal the constants in the factor share equations, as demanded by the model. In estimation, observations are weighted to reflect lower measurement errors when more years are used to compute bank data averages.[8] The 3SLQ estimation technique is efficient, and takes account of cross-equation correlation of error terms.[9] The results of the estimation are included in Table 5.

This econometric formulation enables ready interpretation of differences in European banking markets. Given Cobb-Douglas production in the specified inputs and outputs, country dummies represent departures of factor average compensation or cost from the marginal product. To see this, cross multiply value added per employee in equation [2], obtaining:

$$w = \alpha_N*(VA/N) + \Sigma_i \beta_{Ni} DUMMY_i*(VA/N). \qquad (2')$$

The first term on the right-hand side of equation (2') is marginal product. Significant coefficients on dummy variables signal a departure of average wages from the marginal product of labor. Positive coefficients on dummy variables mean that wages are higher than marginal product, conversely for negative coefficients, and similarly for other factor shares.

The above specification allows financial factors like deposits and loans to be classified as inputs or outputs depending on their contribution to value added. Inputs reduce value added while outputs increase value added. This classification scheme follows Hancock (1985b) and is very general in the sense that deposits may be a net input acquired in the market at a cost or a net output with services provided in the form of transactions services in exchange for fees or below market funds adding value.

2.3 Data

Data on individual banks in each of the EEC countries and the three non-EEC countries, Austria, Finland, and Sweden, were gathered from individual annual reports. In total, 89 banks were analyzed for possible inclusion in the sample. In each case, the objective was to gather comparable data on bank operations for as many years in the period 1984 to 1988 as were practical. Table 1 lists the banks used in the analysis.

All bank data were transformed either into operating ratios or comparable currency units for analysis. Local currency data for the period 1984 to 1988 as given in the annual reports were translated into real terms using the Consumer Price Index (CPI) for the country in question as reported by the International Monetary Fund (IMF) in the International Financial Statistics (IFS) with 1985 as a base. These local real currency units were translated into U.S. dollars using the average 1985 dollar exchange rate for the local currency as reported by the Federal Reserve Board in the Federal Reserve Bulletin. Averages for each bank's data were computed for all years available and the observations weighted to reflect the improved accuracy from more observations per bank, as discussed above.

The final sample represents banks which responded to the request for information and represents the largest three banks for all countries except France, Italy, and Portugal, where two of the three top banks are represented. In all but two cases, Algemene Bank in the Netherlands and Barclays Bank in Great Britain, data from the banking units, rather than the corporate group, were used in an effort to make data as comparable between individual units as possible.

Microeconomic data have not been used in a study comparing European banks.[10] Enormous effort is necessary to translate detailed operating data into comparable numbers. There are also potential problems associated with reports of financial institutions operating under different regulatory and tax regimes. For example, regulators until the Basle Agreement had different capital requirements and tax authorities allow different deductability of items like tax losses to reduce taxable income. These problems have been resolved or confronted in this study in two ways: use of aggregated items such as value added and before tax income attempt to minimize the effects of differing tax treatments. In estimation as discussed above, the country dummy variables reflect differing country regulatory effects. Nonetheless, noncomparability of data render the interpretation of data and estimation results herein hazardous.

Data describing macroeconomic and country total banking conditions in each country over the period 1984 to 1988 were collected from IFS. While every effort was made to make data comparable across countries, variations in regulatory and reporting requirements in different jurisdictions mandate caution in interpreting these data. Loan and deposit shares were computed as individual bank total loans and deposits expressed as a percent of the totals for each country. For each country the largest bank share was identified as another measure of market concentration.

Table 2 provides descriptive statistics for the 15 countries and definitions for values calculated to represent financial market conditions. Table 3 presents some descriptive information on bank operations in the countries analyzed: the table provides the average equity capital as a percent of assets, the return on equity, the average bank loan market share and for each country the largest single bank loan market share, for banks included in the analysis and for which data were available. While caution again is urged in using these numbers because of omission of some large banks and differences in comparability across jurisdictions, the data suggest a wide variation in competitive conditions in different loan markets.

Table 4 and Figures 1 to 3 are summary representations of the data. Table 4 gives the pairwise correlation coefficients between countries' average bank operating statistics and banking market variables. Figure 1 shows individual bank total assets by country. Figure 2 presents value added per employee and Figure 3 presents return on equity, both plotted against average total assets.

3. ANALYSIS OF BANKS IN EUROPEAN MARKETS

To gain an overview of the European banking scene, look at Table 1, showing average real total assets, loans, and deposits, arranged by country in descending order of assets, and Figure 1, depicting average total assets for the banks in the sample for each country. An initial observation is that the largest banks are in the largest economies, namely France, Great Britain, Italy, and West Germany. Nonetheless, among the large banks over $10 billion in assets, there is no apparent tendency for these larger banks to cluster in the largest economies; for example, Belgium, Finland, Denmark, Spain and Sweden all have several banks over $10 billion, despite their widely differing levels of income and population.   As a comparison, in the United States, banks from $4.7 to $50 billion account for 92 of the top 100 banks.[11]

Table 1 shows that the largest banks in the analysis are the Barclays Group and the Banque Nationale de Paris, with average real assets of $95 billion and $94 billion, respectively. The smallest bank is the Isle of Man Bank with $ .8 billion. All countries except Portugal have one or more banks over $5 billion in assets, and Portugal has at least three $3 billion banks.

Table 2 indicates that real per capita income ranges from $2,071 in Portugal to $12,135 in Sweden. Five of the countries in the analysis represent per capita real incomes over $10,0000, namely Denmark, Finland, Luxembourg, Sweden and West Germany. More interesting perhaps is the range of average per capita bank loans, ranging from $1,616 in Greece to $22,368 in Luxembourg, and average per capita deposits, ranging from $903 in Greece to $16,032 in Denmark.

Table 3 demonstrates substantial variation in bank operating characteristics for the countries analyzed. For example, banks in France average 2 percent capital relative to assets while in Ireland the average is 7.3 percent. As another example of differences, in West Germany the largest bank loan share is given as 4.9 percent of the private loan market, whereas the largest Irish bank has 83 percent share. The average bank return on equity ranges from 18 percent in Spain to 2.3 percent in Austria.

Table 4 and Figures 1 to 3 confirm that few generalities can be made in the relations between bank size, average bank operating characteristics and countries, and levels of economic activity. For example, of the bank operating characteristics, the only significant positive correlation reported in Table 4 is between growth in gross domestic product and average return on equity. On the other hand, the correlations between per capita loans and deposits and economic growth are not significant. Loans per capita is negatively correlated with the largest bank loan share of total country loans, but the ratio of loans to gross domestic product is not significantly correlated to any of the bank operating statistics like leverage, return on equity, or economic growth.

The relation between two measures of banking performance and size are shown in Figures 2 and 3. As can be seen in Figures 2 and 3 and of particular interest here is that there is no discernable pattern in the relation between average bank size and value added per employee or the return on total assets. If patterns governing future banking market conditions in Europe are related to productivity of labor and return on capital, size of banking firms as measured by average total assets based on the evidence appearing in these graphs looks to be an unimportant factor.

A tentative conclusion to be drawn from these observations is that differing growth rates of countries in Europe will not necessarily be associated with major changes in banking structure as represented by the average size of banks or in changes in the share of banks in total loans. Furthermore, loans and deposits per capita, representing the extent of bank intermediation in various countries, do not seem to be importantly related to economic conditions in various European countries.

To explore the relation between different country labor and financial markets and bank operating efficiency more rigorously, we turn to the estimates for the model of value added in equations [1] to [4]. These results provide some guidance into the prospects for major adjustments in the banking sector following banking market integration after 1992. The model results reported in Table 5 are quite strong, with an overall model R^2 of .835. The negative coefficient on deposits indicates that deposits are an input into value production of banks.

The first important inference from these results is that there is no evidence of economies of scale. The production function coefficients sum to nearly unity, and the statistical test reported at the bottom of Table 5 does not allow rejection of the hypothesis of no economies of scale at the 15 percent level. However, the model estimates indicate many departures in individual country markets from efficient allocation of both real and financial inputs as measured by equality of marginal productivity and factor compensation, but these departures differ across markets in different countries.

According to the estimates, Denmark, Luxembourg, Sweden and West Germany compensate labor less than its marginal product. The results for Belgium and France both indicate that wages are above the marginal product of labor, although not significantly. Since in the use of labor banks are likely to be price takers, several explanations can be offered for these departures from marginality. Among possible explanations are that efficient banks, such as those whose wages are less than marginal product, develop organizational capital and effective systems increasing the productivity of workers.

Where labor is paid its marginal product or more, labor shortages or labor organizations may allow determined bargaining on the part of workers, putting wages above competitively sustainable levels. An alternative explanation for high labor compensation relative to productivity is that government interference produces excessive employment of labor. A third reason could be lack of trained labor in an interim adjustment period, such that productivity is below long-run expected levels.

While this evidence is preliminary, differences in labor compensation and productivity in different country markets does suggest that integration of banking markets may unleash pressures in labor markets as banks adjust to potential competition from abroad. Some countries may experience labor market adjustments which could be politically difficult to reconcile with deregulation of banking markets.

Deposit market regressions suggest that in many countries money market rates are substantially above the marginal cost of deposits in the production of bank value added, as for example in Greece. The evidence in these markets, where banks can be assumed to be price setters, is that money market rates are above the marginal cost of the deposit funds in terms of services provided and interest paid. These departures from efficiency occur in all countries in the sample, although not significantly for Great Britain and the Netherlands. The departures are largest in Greece, Sweden and Luxembourg.

The Cecchini report did not analyze deposit markets at all. These results suggest that the major inefficiencies in European banking markets are probably in deposit markets. Since the general results of these inefficiencies is to reduce the return to savers below the value of money market rates prevailing in the different countries, the potential elimination of these inefficiencies could be pervasive. One conclusion is that the impact of banking market integration would seem to be largest in deposit markets. The increased returns to savers and the overall increase in savings are beyond the scope of this study, but would seem to be of a large magnitude.

On the other hand, using United States experience as a reference again, deregulation and competition in deposit markets does not necessarily lead to overwhelming effects on banking structure. Abstracting from the major crisis in deposit-taking institutions in the United States caused by increases in deposit insurance ceilings and expansion of investment authorities, the average size and scale of operations of banks in the United States have not dramatically changed. While bank mergers have accompanied interstate banking, a development analogous in many ways to European bank market integration, small banks continue to thrive and new banks are chartered. In summary, competitive deposit markets in Europe do not necessarily imply the demise of locally prominent banking institutions, even those of relatively small scale.

European loan markets demonstrate a number of departures from efficiency in the sense used above. In a number of countries, average loan returns are estimated to be above marginal productivity in terms of value of services. Luxembourg appears to be a country were marginal loan returns are substantially above average loan rates. Sweden and West Germany are also out of line from relations in Great Britain and the Netherlands, where loan share reflects marginal value productivity.

It cannot be said whether the loan market results are due to less than perfectly competitive conditions or to superior banking services provided by some country's banks. For example, there is no obvious relation between these estimated departures from efficiency and loan market concentration measures displayed on Table 3, where Danish banks have half the average loan market share compared to Finland and Sweden. The results do indicate potential realignments from loan market intergration challenging current bank managements.

4. CONCLUSION: IMPLICATIONS FOR POLICY AND STRATEGY

Two conclusions are warranted by this analysis of individual European bank and country banking market data. First, there are few significant patterns in banking markets which would suggest that particular growth patterns in the period following banking market integration will induce particular changes in bank markets. For example, measures of loan shares in given country markets will not necessarily change with economic growth or higher levels of financial intermediation in terms of per capita loans and deposits. Second, there is no evidence that only the largest pan-European banks will survive banking market integration. There is no evidence of economies of scale in this bank sample. If smaller banks can produce value in local business markets through local knowledge and expertise, it seems clear that smaller banks can coexist with larger banks in individual country markets, much as they do in the United States. These smaller banks can provide value in markets which differ from other country bank markets by language and unique business conditions.

These observations do not rule out substantial changes in banking in Europe after 1992. The econometric analysis reported on Table 5 and the related discussion suggest that labor markets and loan and deposit markets display varying patterns of inefficiency. Integrated banking markets and reduced barriers to entry will bring potential competitors which will likely force adjustments in the banking practices in many countries. However, given freely adjusting labor and financial markets, it is to be expected that local banks, even in the smallest markets, may continue to play a key role in the future development of the European economy.

The implications for policy are that the temporary adjustments accompanying banking market integration may produce strong political pressures to interfere in the process with ad hoc regulatory responses, but in the long run the health of even smaller institutions is benefited by market discipline focusing bank management on their particular sources of comparative advantage. The implication is to resist the pressure to interfere in the adjustment process. The strategic implications for banks are the counterpart to this: bank managers should not fear market integration, but should identify where they can produce value in the market they can best serve, whether it be a smaller local retail or business market or a broader multinational wholesale market.

FOOTNOTES

I acknowledge with gratitude the major contribution of Kersti Schantz of the Gothenburg School of Economics to this work in obtaining, creating, and checking the data used in this study. I appreciate the many useful comments and criticisms provided by the participants of the Conference on Financial Regulation and Monetary Arrangements after 1992 and owe special thanks to Aris Protopapadakis and Anthony Santomero for their careful critiques.

1. Dollar figures use a value of the ECU of $1.246 as reported in the Wall Street Journal for May 11, 1990, "Currency Trading" table

2. See pp. 139-170 for details on method and assumptions. The gains are calculated using a constant elasticity demand curve with an elasticity of -.75 and assuming competitive conditons in markets at the assumed reduced cost and price levels

3. See Kolari and Zardkoohi (1987) for a complete review and discussion of this literature. Many studies have used the Functional Cost Analysis surveys conducted by vairous Federal Reserve Banks in the United States

4. See Section 1, "Why Do Banks Exist", 577-579, and Section 7, "Credit Rationing Models", 599-602

5. Most current work in estimating bank efficiency employ transcendental logarithmic (translog) approximations of the production frontier. This specification is desirable in allowing for U-shaped costs

functions and for estimation of economies of scope in multiproduct firms. Data limitations and the focus on economies of scale of a single output measure made use of a Cobb-Douglas specificaiton, a special case of translog functions, appropriate here.

6. Additional factors in principle should be included to exhaust the set of inputs and outputs. Hancock (1985b) specifies loans, time and demand deposits, cash, labor and materials (p. 867). Experiments with other factors inputs available with the current data (other operating expenses) did not change the reported results and data limitations prevented more precise enumeration of inputs and outputs. Specification on factors will be the focus of further study.

7. More precise modeling than dummy variables of competitive and regulatory effects in different countries would allow explicit analysis of the sources of distortions of efficiency in banking markets. Analysis along this line will be explored in future research.

8. Weights are the square root of the number of years of data available to compute each bank's averaged data.

9. See Pindyck and Rubinfeld (1976), 282-283

10. See Revell (1980) for a detailed comparison of banks and bank accounting and regulatory treatment in OECD countries. While this study used data from individual banks financial statements, the data have been aggregated. It is one of the most complete analyses of differences in banking performance known to the author

11. Fortune, "The Top 100 Largest Commercial Banks", June 1, 1989

REFERENCES

Fama, E.F. (1985), "What's Different about Banks," Journal of Monetary Economics 15, 29-39.

Hancock, D. (1985a), "The Financial Firm: Production with Monetary and Nonmonetary Goods," Journal of Political Economy 93, 859-880.

_____ (1985b), "Bank Profitability, Interest Rates, and Monetary Policy," Journal of Money, Credit and Banking, 17, No. 2, 189-202.

Kolari, J. and A. Zardkoohi (1987), Bank Costs, Structure and Performance, Lexington Books, Lexington, Massachusetts.

Pindyck, R. S. and D. L. Rubinfeld (1976), Econometric Models and Economic Forecasts. McGraw-Hill Book Company. New York.

Price Waterhouse (1988), Research on the "Cost of Non-Europe": Basic Findings, Volume 9, "The 'Costs of Non-Europe' in Financial Services", Commission of the European Communities, Brussels-Luxembourg.

Revell, J. R. S. (1980), Costs and Margins in Banking: An International Suvey, Organization for Economic Co-Operation and Development, Paris.

Santomero, A. M. (1984), "Modeling the Banking Firm," Journal of Money Credit and Banking, Volume XVI (4), Part 2, 576-644.

U.S. Department of the Treasury (1986), National Treatment Study: Report to Congress on Foreign Government Treatment of U.S. Commercial Banking and Securities Organizations

Table 1
Banks and Average Balance Sheet Items
(Millions of 1985 dollars)

	Average 1984-1988[*]		
	Assets	Loans	Deposits
Austria			
Creditanstalt-Bankverein	17,539	7,424	1,976
Girozentrale & Bank der Österreichischen spa	12,508	5,178	1,340
Osterreichische Landerbank	9,333	3,677	1,517
Bank fur Arbeit & Wirtschaft	8,046	3,894	1,730
Österreichische Volksbanken	2,563	858	16
Bank fur Oberösterreich & Salzburg (Oberbank)	1,846	875	650
Belgium			
Générale de Banque	31,100	10,738	14,695
Banque Bruxelles Lambert (BBL)	22,802	5,194	7,620
Crédit Communal de Belgique	22,348	12,547	5,806
Kredietbank	17,217	4,473	7,238
Ippa Savings Bank	1,848	720	1,723
Denmark			
Den Danske Bank af 1871	12,081	5,427	5,896
Copenhagen Handelsbank	10,019	4,545	4,395
Privatbanken	7,252	3,548	3,158
Provinsbanken	4,398	2,294	2,047
Andelsbanken Danebank	4,216	2,384	2,137
Jyske Bank	4,066	1,785	1,927
Finland			
Kansallis Osake Pankki	13,387	6,880	4,697
Union Bank of Finland	12,565	6,508	4,693
Postipankki Ltd	7,345	3,445	2,963
Skopbank	4,228	1,244	211
Osuuspankkien Keskuspankki Oy (Okobank)	3,324	864	206
France			
Banque Nationale de Paris	94,059	37,462	35,168
Crédit Lyonnais	89,288	36,172	31,111
Banque Indosuez	20,346	8,524	5,557
CIC-Union Europeenne, Internat. et Cie	4,053	874	465
Great Britain			
Barclays Bank (Group)	95,353	56,025	80,388
National Westminster Bank	55,682	29,082	47,145
Midland Bank	45,044	28,023	38,025
Lloyds Bank (BLSA)	44,730	27,365	.
TSB England & Wales PLC	13,404	3,619	11,252
Ulster Bank	1,977	771	1,371
Isle of Man Bank	882	126	772
Greece			
National Bank of Greece	15,231	5,044	13,091
Commercial Bank of Greece	3,986	1,520	3,355
National Mortgage Bank of Greece	3,132	1,761	1,608
Ionian and Popular Bank of Greece	1,957	679	1,587
Credit Bank	1,734	663	1,458
Ireland			
Allied Irish Banks PLC	7,740	4,257	5,067
Bank of Ireland	6,235	3,357	5,286

Table 1 (cont.)

	Average 1984-1988*		
	Assets	Loans	Deposits
Italy			
Istituto Bancario San Paolo di Torino	35,429	15,865	12,484
Banca Commerciale Italiana	34,326	11,738	15,523
Banco di Roma	29,707	9,456	8,802
Credito Italiano	29,442	7,380	11,260
Monte dei Paschi di Siena	24,935	6,950	12,539
Istituto Mobiliare Italiano	12,753	11,092	395
Luxembourg			
Banque Internationale a Luxembourg	5,486	1,255	4,149
Banque Generale du Luxembourg	5,210	1,059	3,415
Kredietbank Luxembourgeoise	4,438	531	2,717
Société (Financiere) Européenne de Banque	826	194	170
Netherlands			
Algemene Bank Nederland (ABN-Bank Group)	45,869	19,343	15,585
Amsterdam-Rotterdam Bank	41,311	13,720	4,405
Nmb Bank	21,061	9,016	2,415
Postbank	16,916	8,235	8,745
F. Van Lanschot Bankiers	1,748	823	628
Portugal			
Banco Portugues do Atlantico	3,775	1,637	3,196
Banco Espirito Santo & Comercial de Lisboa	3,489	1,230	2,813
Banco Pinto & Sotto Mayor	2,935	1,342	2,232
Banco Borges & Irmao	2,171	916	1,790
Spain			
Banco Central	15,417	6,784	10,580
Banco Bilbao Vizcaya	15,052	7,178	9,567
Banco Espanol de Credito	13,825	6,370	10,543
Banco Hispano Amaricano	12,164	5,681	8,201
Sweden			
S-E-Banken	17,376	9,290	8,025
Svenska Handelsbanken	15,986	7,616	6,378
PK Banken	15,936	8,063	10,820
Gotabanken	4,353	2,595	2,115
Nordbanken	3,311	2,043	1,641
Skanska Banken	1,657	812	686
West Germany			
Deutsche Bank	54,235	27,581	27,892
Westdeutsche Landesbank Girozentrale	47,815	21,919	8,228
Bayerische Landesbank Girozentrale	40,168	17,577	4,838
Dresdner Bank	36,369	18,135	21,901
Commerzbank	30,784	15,991	19,168
Bayerische Vereinsbank	28,376	21,097	9,139
Bayerische Hypotheken & Wechsel Bank	27,530	20,496	9,055
DG Bank (Deutsche Genossenschaftsbank)	24,835	6,838	2,474

Source: Bank asset, loan and deposit data from individual bank annual reports, 1984-1988. Consumer Price Index from <u>International Financial Statistics</u> (IFS), International Monetary Fund, January, 1990. Average 1985 dollar exchange rate from Federal Reserve Board <u>Bulletin</u>.

* In cases where all data not available, average of years available.

Table 2
Country and Bank Market Data (1985 dollars)

| | Average Per Capita 1984-1988: | | | Total Income |
	Income ($)	Loans ($)	Deposits ($)	Growth (%)
Austria	8,702	7,024	5,696	1.923
Belgium	8,408	3,041	2,363	2.299
Denmark	11,407	19,750	16,032	1.524
Finland	11,214	5,509	7,766	3.134
France	9,684	3,872	4,386	2.356
Great Britain	8,448	3,849	3,383	3.835
Greece	3,371	1,616	903	1.912
Ireland	5,427	1,858	1,447	2.588
Italy	7,664	4,822	2,599	3.036
Luxembourg	11,136	22,368	9,129	3.606
Netherlands	8,786	6,289	6,230	2.023
Portugal	2,071	2,298	979	4.017
Spain	4,448	2,700	2,732	3.935
Sweden	12,135	5,869	5,531	1.900
West Germany	10,509	5,704	9,238	2.369

Source: Income is real gross domestic product from line 99b.p, except for France, Great Britain, Italy and Germany, which are line 99b.r, and Netherlands, line 99a.r (gross national product). Deposits are current local currency sum of total bank amounts of demand and time deposits (lines 24 and 25), and loans are current local currency bank claims on private sector (line 22d), and midyear estimated population data, all from IFS, January, 1990. All financial data are transformed to 1985 inflation adjusted amounts using CPI from IFS, January, 1990 and all local currency items converted to dollars using average 1985 dollar exchange rate from Federal Reserve Board _Federal Reserve Bulletin_. Income growth computed from income figures.

Table 3
Bank Average Operating Statistics by Country (Averages 1984-1988[*])

	Capital Ratio (%)	Return on Equity (%)	Average Loan Share (%)	Largest Loan Share (%)	Deposit Velocity
Austria	2.864	2.339	8.424	17.228	1.239
Belgium	2.216	6.913	28.478	54.263	2.765
Denmark	6.333	6.576	4.056	6.607	0.578
Finland	5.793	4.446	9.918	18.051	2.036
France	2.099	9.345	8.276	14.716	2.501
Great Britain	6.518	10.882	11.313	32.489	2.195
Greece	2.538	11.859	21.651	57.570	2.086
Ireland	7.296	.	74.199	83.047	2.921
Italy	5.458	6.083	6.888	9.935	1.589
Luxembourg	4.747	15.494	23.380	38.039	0.498
Netherlands	3.362	10.092	11.011	21.338	1.397
Portugal	2.620	27.278	12.810	16.380	0.901
Spain	5.493	18.389	6.059	6.684	1.647
Sweden	6.941	4.747	11.227	20.069	2.068
West Germany	3.662	7.970	3.305	4.858	1.842

Source: Bank operating data from annual reports as in Table 1, loan market data uses loans from IFS as in Table 2.
* Average of years available.

Table 4
Correlation Coefficients between Banking Market Variables

	Capital Ratio	Return on Equity	Value Added/ Employee	Average Assets	Growth in Income	Largest Loan Share	Average Loans
Capital Ratio	1.00000 0.0000 15	-0.21142 0.4681 14	0.00571 0.9845 14	-0.21610 0.4392 15	0.15409 0.5835 15	0.06251 0.8248 15	0.23829 0.3924 15
Return on Equity	-0.21142 0.4681 14	1.00000 0.0000 14	0.28911 0.3161 14	-0.20832 0.4748 14	0.67744 0.0078 14	0.03101 0.9162 14	0.16211 0.5798 14
Value Added/ Employee	0.00571 0.9845 14	0.28911 0.3161 14	1.00000 0.0000 14	-0.05473 0.8526 14	0.33212 0.2460 14	0.11516 0.6950 14	0.36919 0.1939 14
Average Assets	-0.21610 0.4392 15	-0.20832 0.4748 14	-0.05473 0.8526 14	1.00000 0.0000 15	-0.01102 0.9689 15	-0.29197 0.2910 15	-0.30705 0.2656 15
Growth in Income	0.15409 0.5835 15	0.67744 0.0078 14	0.33212 0.2460 14	-0.01102 0.9689 15	1.00000 0.0000 15	-0.08056 0.7753 15	-0.01340 0.9622 15
Large Loan Share	0.06251 0.8248 15	0.03101 0.9162 14	0.11516 0.6950 14	-0.29197 0.2910 15	-0.08056 0.7753 15	1.00000 0.0000 15	0.90553 0.0001 15
Average	0.23829 0.3924 15	0.16211 0.5798 14	0.36919 0.1939 14	-0.30705 0.2656 15	-0.01340 0.9622 15	0.90553 0.0001 15	1.00000 0.0000 15
PC GDP	0.27578 0.3198 15	-0.70237 0.0051 14	0.20334 0.4857 14	0.23588 0.3974 15	-0.37441 0.1692 15	-0.31736 0.2491 15	-0.29639 0.2834 15
PC Loans	0.23871 0.3915 15	-0.36516 0.1992 14	0.13702 0.6404 14	-0.05391 0.8487 15	-0.35953 0.1881 15	-0.45333 0.0897 15	-0.37721 0.1657 15
PC Deposits	0.20880 0.4552 15	-0.09193 0.7546 14	0.54222 0.0452 14	-0.26662 0.3368 15	-0.11438 0.6848 15	-0.20710 0.4589 15	-0.17465 0.5336 15
Velocity	0.03047 0.9142 15	-0.33772 0.2376 14	-0.34893 0.2214 14	0.38094 0.1612 15	-0.13197 0.6392 15	0.52216 0.0459 15	0.47450 0.0739 15
Loans/GDP	0.15971 0.5697 15	-0.11717 0.6900 14	0.08126 0.7824 14	-0.12982 0.6447 15	-0.22409 0.4220 15	-0.55010 0.0336 15	-0.44004 0.1007 15

Table 4 (cont.)

	PC GDP	PC Loans	PC Deps	Velocity	Loans/GDP
Capital	0.27578	0.23871	0.20880	0.03047	0.15971
Ratio	0.3198	0.3915	0.4552	0.9142	0.5697
	15	15	15	15	15
Return on	-0.70237	-0.36516	-0.09193	-0.33772	-0.11717
Equity	0.0051	0.1992	0.7546	0.2376	0.6900
	14	14	14	14	14
Value Added per	0.20334	0.13702	0.54222	-0.34893	0.08126
Employee	0.4857	0.6404	0.0452	0.2214	0.7824
	14	14	14	14	14
Average	0.23588	-0.05391	-0.26662	0.38094	-0.12928
Assets	0.3974	0.8487	0.3368	0.1612	0.6447
	15	15	15	15	15
Large Loan	-0.31736	-0.45333	-0.20710	0.52216	-0.55010
Share	0.2491	0.0897	0.4589	0.0459	0.0336
	15	15	15	15	15
Average Loans	-0.29639	-0.37721	-0.17465	0.47450	-0.44004
	0.2834	0.1657	0.5336	0.0739	0.1007
	15	15	15	15	15
PC GDP	1.00000	0.73934	0.57344	-0.10456	0.51157
	0.0000	0.0016	0.0254	0.7108	0.0513
PC Loans	0.73934	1.00000	0.81355	-0.54816	0.94400
	0.0016	0.0000	0.0002	0.0344	0.0001
	15	15	15	15	15
PC Deposits	0.57344	0.81355	1.00000	-0.71786	0.76499
	0.0254	0.0002	0.0000	0.0026	0.0009
	15	15	15	15	15
Velocity	-0.10456	-0.54816	-0.71786	1.00000	-0.69389
	0.7108	0.0344	0.0026	0.0000	0.0041
	15	15	15	15	15
Loans/GDP	0.51157	0.94400	0.76499	-0.69389	1.00000
	0.0513	0.0001	0.0009	0.0041	0.0000
	15	15	15	15	15

Note: PC = per capita, GDP = gross domestic product.

Table 5
Estimation of Value Added and Factor Share Equations

Weighted Mean Square Error for System =   1.809610 with 187 DFS
Weighted R-Square for System = 0.8351

Dependent Variable: Log(Value Added)

VARIABLE	DF	PARAMETER ESTIMATE	STANDARD ERROR	T RATIO	APPROX PROB>|T|
Intercept	1	-3.732683	0.272276	-13.7092	0.0001
Log(Employees)	1	0.790741	0.037689	20.9809	0.0001
Log(Deposits)	1	-0.144004	0.044108	-3.2648	0.0019
Log(Loans)	1	0.365395	0.084772	4.3103	0.0001
Log(Equity)	1	0.045762	0.083219	0.5499	0.5847

Dependent Variable: Wage Share

VARIABLE	DF	PARAMETER ESTIMATE	STANDARD ERROR	T RATIO	APPROX PROB>|T|
Intercept	1	0.790741	0.040972	19.2996	0.0001
Belgium	1	0.049523	0.087440	0.5664	0.5740
Denmark	1	-0.234394	0.070657	-3.3173	0.0018
Finland	1	-0.063920	0.070036	-0.9127	0.3664
France	1	0.015450	0.076503	0.2019	0.8409
Great Britain	1	-0.123134	0.149064	-0.8261	0.4132
Greece	1	-0.095562	0.070930	-1.3473	0.1848
Italy	1	-0.132037	0.073982	-1.7847	0.0812
Luxembourg	1	-0.262401	0.083023	-3.1606	0.0028
Netherlands	1	-0.109251	0.103158	-1.0591	0.2954
Spain	1	-0.082235	0.092265	-0.8913	0.3776
Sweden	1	-0.210129	0.066922	-3.1399	0.0030
West Germany	1	-0.172341	0.062908	-2.7396	0.0089

Table 5 (cont.)

Dependent Variable: Deposit Share

VARIABLE	DF	PARAMETER ESTIMATE	STANDARD ERROR	T RATIO	APPROX PROB>|T|
Intercept	1	-0.144004	0.047951	-3.0032	0.0044
Belgium	1	-1.746375	0.636254	-2.7448	0.0087
Denmark	1	-2.084419	0.479384	-4.3481	0.0001
Finland	1	-1.233532	0.481849	-2.5600	0.0140
France	1	-2.031491	0.540855	-3.7561	0.0005
Great Britain	1	-2.201551	1.182675	-1.8615	0.0694
Greece	1	-7.983663	0.490991	-16.2603	0.0001
Italy	1	-2.506290	0.517801	-4.8403	0.0001
Luxembourg	1	-4.571840	0.612761	-7.4610	0.0001
Netherlands	1	-0.799924	0.780740	-1.0246	0.3112
Spain	1	-2.699776	0.681285	-3.9628	0.0003
Sweden	1	-3.598107	0.446827	-8.0526	0.0001
West Germany	1	-0.684860	0.409782	-1.6713	0.1018

Dependent Variable: Loan Share

VARIABLE	DF	PARAMETER ESTIMATE	STANDARD ERROR	T RATIO	APPROX PROB>|T|
Intercept	1	0.365395	0.092156	3.9649	0.0003
Belgium	1	3.168397	1.298341	2.4403	0.0188
Denmark	1	1.504905	0.969333	1.5525	0.1277
Finland	1	1.557123	0.949828	1.6394	0.1083
France	1	4.008617	1.095640	3.6587	0.0007
Great Britain	1	2.294743	2.406057	0.9537	0.3454
Greece	1	2.546558	0.978021	2.6038	0.0125
Italy	1	2.783839	1.039094	2.6791	0.0103
Luxembourg	1	7.926019	1.224111	6.4749	0.0001
Netherlands	1	0.944645	1.591565	0.5935	0.5559
Spain	1	1.459101	1.383658	1.0545	0.2974
Sweden	1	3.678332	0.900716	4.0838	0.0002
West Germany	1	3.924494	0.816267	4.8079	0.0001

Test of Hypothesis that $\alpha_N + \alpha_L + \alpha_D + \alpha_K = 1$

Numerator:	3.75776605	DF:	1	F VALUE:	2.0766
Denominator:	1.80961000	DF:	187	PROB > F:	0.1512

Figure 1
Average Total Assets for Banks
By Country (in 1985 Dollars)

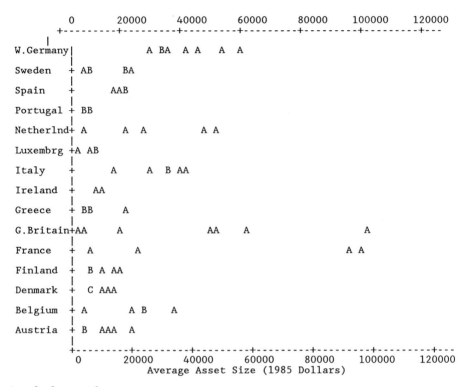

```
               0       20000     40000     60000     80000    100000    120000
              +---------+---------+---------+---------+---------+---------+---
              |
 W.Germany|                    A BA  A A    A  A
              |
 Sweden    + AB       BA
              |
 Spain     +      AAB
              |
 Portugal + BB
              |
 Netherlnd+ A       A  A          A A
              |
 Luxembrg +A AB
              |
 Italy     +      A      A  B AA
              |
 Ireland   +    AA
              |
 Greece    + BB      A
              |
 G.Britain+AA      A           AA    A                    A
              |
 France    +  A        A                          A A
              |
 Finland   +  B A AA
              |
 Denmark   +  C AAA
              |
 Belgium   + A        A B      A
              |
 Austria   + B   AAA   A
              |
              +---------+---------+---------+---------+---------+---------+---
               0       20000     40000     60000     80000    100000    120000
                        Average Asset Size (1985 Dollars)
```

A = 1 observation
B = 2 observations
C = 3 observations

Figure 2
Average Value Added per Employee (in 1985 Dollars)
Versus Average Total Assets (in 1985 Dollars)

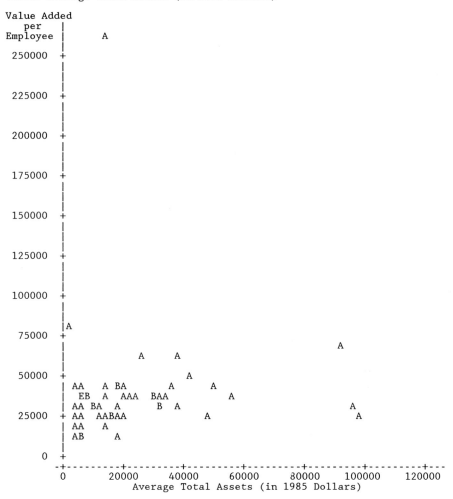

A = 1 observation
B = 2 observations

Figure 3
Return on Equity versus Average Assets (in 1985 Dollars)

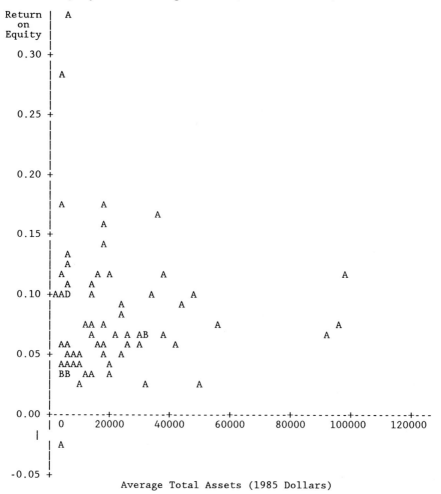

Average Total Assets (1985 Dollars)

A = 1 observation
B = 2 observations
C = 3 observations
D = 4 observations

Financial Regulation and Monetary Arrangements after 1992
C. Wihlborg, M. Fratianni and T.D. Willett (Editors)
© 1991 Elsevier Science Publishers B.V. All rights reserved

Comment

Anthony M. Santomero

Finance Department, The Wharton School of the University of Pennsylvania,
Philadelphia PA 19104-6367, USA

Discussant's comments are usually in one of two forms. In one version, he or she responds to the title of the paper to be discussed by offering his or her own version of the subject matter. In the other, he or she briefly makes specific comments on the main paper presented with observations that can only be understood in the context of the original work. At the outset of my comments on the Dietrich paper, I had to choose which version of a discussant's role I would accept. Upon reflection, I decided to try to combine the two by outlining the landscape covered by the title of this paper, and then critiquing the paper's contribution to some of the details of this landscape.

1992 AND THE FUTURE OF EUROPEAN BANKING INSTITUTIONS

The impact of the Second Banking Directorate, passed in the fourth quarter of 1989, will prove to be substantial. In one step, the banking environment of the EEC will become harmonized with the adoption of the single banking license, the principle of mutual recognition, and home-country control of banking entities in the post 1992 era. To quote Sir Leon Brittan, Vice President of the Commission of the European community, "in one bound...(Europe) has moved from 12 fragmented and confusing structures of national (banking) regulation, to a single market of a size and simplicity unmatched anywhere else in the world" ("Opening World Banking Markets", speech delivered at the American Enterprise Institute, March 23, 1990). Trying to grasp the consequences of such a major step is exceptionally difficult. Many questions and issues come to mind as potentially important effects of the new environment on the banking industry and the EEC. However, to my mind, five issues appear paramount and warrant careful consideration.

First, the single banking charter provision of the Second Banking Directorate is likely to substantially change the currently fragmented structure of in-country banking entities within the member countries of the EEC. The Act clearly favors the establishment of universal banks, with German-like charters, over their counterparts, which may be characterized as segmented and functionally distinct, as in the U.K. for example. One key issue facing a student of the European banking environment is what will be the effects of this unilateral expansion of the role of universal banks on both financial structure and competition. Another is the viability of banking regulation both within individual countries and across national borders.

Second, the creation of a single market for a wide range of financial products raises substantial production economy issues for the industry. In essence, one would like to know whether there are exploitable economies of scale and/or scope within the EEC market which will result in lower unit costs for financial products and a commensurate increase in real sector capital intensity and an investment boom. To be sure, the Commission presumes that there are such economies and that they are substantial. However, evidence from the United States has not been as felicitous to this view. (Dietrich notes this point in his paper and offers several references to support it.) In addition, estimates recorded thus far within the EEC in the so called Cecchini Report have been exceptionally crude. To make matters worse, little production data for European banks is available to be brought to bear on this important issue.

Third, there is a presumed benefit of such an expansion of the banking franchise both across product lines and national borders to the consumers of financial products. The exact nature of the benefits associated with an integrated market, functioning under a universal banking charter, has not been carefully articulated, however. One would like to have a better notion of the nature of the consumer-side gains associated with this alleged bonanza. Are they merely declines in market prices associated with increased potential and/or actual competition? Or, are customers indeed served better, i.e., do they find more value in a financial market that is broader and deeper?

Fourth, an integrated market is likely to result in a stronger EEC banking industry. Least cost production associated with out-sourcing and optimal-sized firms is alleged to result in a stronger European banking industry relative to the trading blocks of the United States and Japan. With the expansion of the Japanese banking industry's world market share, participants have welcomed the increased strength of European banks. However, they have not carefully articulated the alleged reasons that an integrated market will increase the European banking industry's ability to function and compete on the world stage.

Fifth and finally, as banks with leading franchises in individual countries look to the 1992 deadline they see a clear decline in their relatively exclusive position domestically. Many have questioned whether the demise of national boundaries and the establishment of national treatment will substantially reduce or even eliminate the so-called home country advantage. In short, many participants wonder whether, and by how much, domestic market shares will change in the new transnational banking environment of the EEC.

To my mind these five questions are at the heart of the concerns centering around the 1992 deadline facing the European financial service industry. While we know quite a lot about what will be allowable activity, substantial questions remain as to the effect these changes will have on each of the outlined areas above.

COMMENTS ON PAPER

Kim Dietrich's contribution, "Consequences of 1992 for Competition in Financial Services: Banking" is substantially less encompassing than the broad menu above. Nonetheless he addresses a critical part of this controversy. Mapping his contribution to my landscape above, he addresses a limited part of question number two. The paper concentrates on characteristics of the production function, looking for economies of scale to see if there is evidence to support the notion that banking has production characteristics that are consistent with a natural monopoly. In addition, he examines factor shares to see if particular inputs are efficiently priced across countries. As indicated above, these are not uninteresting questions, but they represent only a subset of the larger agenda outlined here.

A substantial contribution of the current paper is the fact that it centers around the use of individual bank data in its cross-country investigation. Eighty-nine banks are analyzed over the period 1984-1988. However, given the limited nature of some information, his paper at times investigates only one year of data.

His methodological contribution is equally important. Rather than using standard translog technology, which has received considerable attention both pro and con in the United States (see Herring and Santomero, 1990, Gilbert, 1984, and Shaffer, 1990). Dietrich presents a new methodology titled, "A Value-Added Approach." Centering on labor, deposits and loans, he estimates a Cobb Douglas production function and three factor share equations using three-stage least squares. In addition, he uses dummies that are country specific to represent deviations in factor average compensation from marginal products

The first set of results of the study suggests that there are few significant patterns in European banking markets which would suggest substantial changes in market share in post 1992. Most specifically, there is no tendency for large countries to have banks with a competitive advantage over their smaller country counterparts. Further, there appears to be no correlation between bank size and bank performance.

A second set of findings centers around the production technology and the three product markets. Here, no clear economies of scale appear to exist. However, factor market inefficiencies are important. Most notable of these is both the absence of an efficient, i.e., competitive, labor market across countries, and strong evidence that the deposit markets exhibit substantial non-competitive tendencies. Indeed, Dietrich's results state "the impact of banking market integration would seem to be largest in deposit markets."

The results obtained by this study appear both sensible and in accordance with expectations. Further, the use of this value-added approach is an exciting addition to the literature.

CONCERNS AND RESERVATIONS

Yet, discussants are supposed to be critical. Accordingly, I would like to indicate where I have concerns and at times substantial reservations about these results. First, on a theoretical level, the value-added model presented, while novel, is not sufficiently rigorous for my tastes. I would hope that in subsequent papers using this approach, a more rigorous development of the theory that leads to the estimated equations could be included. I do not suggest that this is impossible. Nonetheless, I would like to see it presented.

On the empirical side, I so have severe reservations about the comparability of the data. Accounting standards across countries are notoriously uneven (see Revel, 1980). Even conventions such as book vs. market valuation vary substantially from country to country. In addition, allowable banking activity, i.e., differential product offerings, will change the meaning of any reported data. It remains unclear to me how one can compare the efficiency of universal and specialized banks across countries using virtually any methodology or standard accounting reports.

Finally, countries differ by more than bank charters differ. There is substantial evidence suggesting that the financial infrastructure across Europe differs dramatically (see Dermine, 1990). The result is that the value added in standard bank products will also differ as some European banks must compensate for the lower quality of such infrastructure as telecommunication and postal services which are readily available to their geographic counterparts. The point here is that country differentials may not be associated with relative efficiency in factor markets, but differential cost structures that are geographically relevant and not institutionally defined.

SUMMARY

The above notwithstanding, however, the Dietrich paper is an important contribution. He has introduced a new technology to the issues of economies of scale and scope which can be replicated with the aid of better data and a larger data set. He has shown us that recourse to primary financial statement data is possible in a market where standardized Call Reports and Functional Cost Analysis studies are not available. Since he is a pioneer, we will no doubt sharpen his aim but follow his direction.

His concentration on production efficiency and factor markets will prove to be most important, as several things appear clear. Post 1992 is likely to have fewer but larger banking entities in the EEC. This will come about by a combination of increased intra-country mergers and cross-border acquisitions. This trend is already evident in our host country, Sweden. This will result in more competition, but hopefully, neither more banking firms nor banking outlets. As is the case in their counterparts, Japan and the United States, Europe is over-banked. Therefore, the future is more comparable to competing for market shares in a declining market than in an expanding one. In this regard, Dietrich's concentration on market inefficiencies and production economy may prove most important. In the European banking market of the 1990s, only the efficient institutions will survive.

REFERENCES

Dermine, J. (1990), <u>European Banking after 1992</u>, Basil Blackwell Publ.

Gilbert, G. (1984), "The Bank Market Structure and Performance: A Review", <u>Journal of Monetary Banking</u>, Nov.

Herring, R. and A. Santomero (1990), "The Corporate Structure of Financial Conglomerates", in A Meltzer (ed.) <u>International Competitiveness in the Financial Services Industry</u> and <u>Journal of Financial Services Research</u>, Dec.

Revel, J.R.S. (1980), <u>Costs and Margins in Banking: An International Survey</u>, Organization for Economic Cooperation and Development, Paris

Shaffer, S. (1990), " A Revenue-Restricted Cost Study of 100 Large Banks", Federal Reserve Bank of New York, Feb.

Financial Regulation and Monetary Arrangements after 1992
C. Wihlborg, M. Fratianni and T.D. Willett (Editors)

2 Supervision and Regulation of Financial Markets in the New Financial Environment

David Folkerts-Landau
International Monetary Fund, Washington, DC 20431, USA

Peter M. Garber
Department of Economics, Brown University, Providence, RI 02912, USA

Steven R. Weisbrod
Weisbrod Group Inc., 114 East 32nd Street, Suite 1306, New York, NY 10016, USA

1. INTRODUCTION

Recent developments in world financial markets, in particular the liberalization of cross-border financial transactions and the restructuring of domestic financial institutions in some major industrial countries, have profoundly altered the environment in which central bank supervisory and regulatory policy is made. Two developments have been particularly important in this regard. First, the ability to locate financial institutions and transactions outside the purview of the "home country"-financial authorities has been significantly enhanced by the liberalization of cross-border transactions and by technological advances in communications and data management. This development has meant that the ability of any national financial authority to impose unilaterally a desired supervisory and regulatory structure is limited. Second, the growth in the gross volume of domestic and cross-border financial transactions supporting any given volume of underlying real transactions has meant that the potential cost of liquidity crisis, borne by the central bank as lender-of-last-resort, has risen accordingly. Thus, while the first development limits the ability of the central bank to reduce the probability of liquidity crises through the imposition of a more stringent supervisory and regulatory structure, the second development increases the expected cost to the central bank of liquidity crises. In this paper we attempt to formulate the financial policy problem facing central banks in the new financial environment and discuss its solution.

In broad terms, the central bank's financial policy seeks to achieve an efficient allocation of capital resources and to limit the real effects of financial disturbances, i.e., of liquidity crises. The first aim is achieved by implementing policies supporting the establishment of a competitive market structure to ensure the efficient pricing and allocation of financial resources. The second objective is achieved by providing liquidity assistance in times of systemic crises. In pursuing the second objective, the central bank assumes the credit risk associated with the claims it acquires when expanding its liabilities to supply liquidity. As a partial remuneration for such credit risk, the central bank receives the income from holding the reserve balances of the banking system. This credit risk can be reduced by financial policies that reduce the number and severity of systemic liquidity crises that lead to central bank intervention. Such policies, however, tend to restrict the activities of banking firms, limit the range of available financial instruments, and increase the cost of operating the payments system. Hence, such policies generally increase the total cost of financial transactions supporting a given volume of real activity. Thus, the basic structure of the central bank policy problem emerges as having to choose a desired point on this trade-off between the credit risk assumed by the central bank and the total cost of financial transactions.

In the next section we identify the main sources of systemic disturbances. In Section III we formulate the central bank's policy paradigm, and in Section IV we explore the implications of recent developments in financial markets for central bank financial policy. Section V concludes the paper.

2. THE SOURCES OF SYSTEMIC RISK IN FINANCIAL SYSTEMS

Systemic risk is the risk of economy-wide disturbances of the financial system during which the making of payments is disrupted by a generalized illiquidity in the banking system.[1] The insolvency of individual financial institutions is generally not a source of concern unless such a disturbance threatens to become systemic through its effect on other institutions. There are two effects of insolvency of a single institutions that can produce a systemic liquidity crisis. First, other financial institutions may not be able to settle on payments made during the day to third institutions if the insolvent institution fails to settle on the payments it made during the day. Second, short-term liquid claims on the insolvent institutions become illiquid pending a resolution of bankruptcy proceedings and thus claimants may not be able to settle their own obligations to third institutions. In the first case, the initial disturbance is magnified and transmitted through certain features of the payments system relating, inter alia, to the finality of payments, the netting of payments, and the settlement period. In the second case, the disturbance will be magnified when there exists markets in securitized short-term, liquid short-term claims, which include those issued by the insolvent institutions.

In order to provide an analytical structure to the financial policy problem of central bank, we identify in this section the main sources of systemic risk in the typical financial system so as to be able to identify appropriate central banks policy instruments. First, we note that in the financial systems of the major industrial countries the prevailing institutional arrangements, in particular the access to central bank liquidity facilities, has endowed large money center banks with a comparative advantage in providing liquidity to the rest of the financial and nonfinancial system. Because of their specialization in supplying liquidity the failure of such banks has become a source of systemic risk in that the disruption in their supply of liquidity could precipitate a generalized shortage of liquidity. Second, we identify certain features of the payments system, in particular, those that tend to magnify the failure of individual institutions.

This section thus points to a particular set of financial institutions, namely wholesale or money center banks, and to the payment systems as the source of systemic risk, and it identifies these ingredients of the financial system as the main objects of central bank financial policy.

3. THE BANKING SYSTEM AS SUPPLIER OF LIQUIDITY

Recent literature on the role of banks in financial markets has focused on banks' special information about borrowers relative to that of other financial institutions.[2] For example, Fama (1985) presented evidence that securitized short-term unsecured corporate obligations, such as commercial paper, trade at the same yields as bankers' acceptances, and bank certificates of deposit. Banks must hold reserves against deposits, which most researchers interpret as a tax paid by bank customers.[3] Because commercial paper does not have a reserve requirement, Fama inferred that depositors do not pay for reserves. He concluded that the tax incidence falls on customers who borrow from banks and that, therefore, bank loans are a unique form of credit. Otherwise, borrowers would switch to an untaxed source of credit.[4]

We propose an explanation of why banks are unique among financial intermediaries which does not rely on an informational advantage.[5] Instead, we argue that banks are unique because they are the cheapest source of liquidity in the economy. This advantage is not derived from the special nature of individual banks but from the special nature of the banking system which can mobilize good funds more easily than competing financial institutions.[6]

In particular, we note that recent literature ignores an important element in the market for short-term corporate obligations, such as commercial paper markets. Corporations which issue commercial paper maintain credit lines, representing the right to borrow good funds from a bank during a certain period. Credit lines give commercial paper issuers access to the liquidity of the banking system. Commercial paper issuers sometimes require bank loans to pay off their commercial paper; as occasional bank borrowers themselves, they must also pay for reserves according to the conventional view that bank borrowers pay for reserves.

Commercial paper issuers attach a line because they must assure lenders that they can deliver good funds at maturity. Normally, issuers can obtain funds by reissuing or rolling over commercial paper; during times of liquidity stress in the money markets, however, it is difficult for even high quality borrowers to issue short-term paper. Even in normal times, a CP issuer may face technical problems in rolling over its paper. A cash delivery can be assured only by buying a line from a bank which, in turn, has access to the banking system and to the liquidity services of the central bank.

The bank will find it necessary to hold reserves against the lines of credit it extended as backing for CP, and the reserves held against the CP line and the CD can be shown to be equivalent. The opportunity cost of holding additional reserves to cover its liquidity commitment on its customer's line will be covered in the price of the line on the commercial paper. The CP issuer will offer a commensurably lower yield to cover this cost of providing liquidity, so the CP holder bears the cost of reserves needed in the payments mechanism to provide liquidity. Both short-term and liquid, CP and CD are perfect substitutes; and they should, therefore, pay the same yields, as confirmed by Fama. Both depend on the holding of good funds as reserves against *demand deposits* to assure liquidity, however, so both pay for the cost of such reserves. It follows, therefore, that the cost of reserve requirement do not fall on the banks' borrowers and that bank loans are not a unique form of credit. If banks have a comparative advantage in some activity, it has to be in something else besides making loans.

Instead, access to central bank liquidity facilities gives banks a comparative advantage in supplying liquidity. Issuers of securities obtain assurances of access to good funds by establishing a line of credit with a bank and then draw on these lines to deliver good funds when their paper matures or obligations become due. Banks may, of course, extend regular term-credit but they have no particular advantage in doing so over other forms of credit.

Access to good funds makes banks suppliers of cash to commercial paper issuers. Since any financial institution can hold good funds in the form of a currency inventory, it is useful to explore the organization of the banking system to understand why banks are the lowest cost market maker in good funds.

Banks hold only a small percentage of their assets in good funds. Individual banks can make a credible statement about delivering good funds to their deposit customers and borrowers on demand because banks are part of a banking system, tied together by the clearing and settlement mechanism of a clearing house. Members agree to lend good funds to members who experience a drain on good funds on any particular day, i.e., to banks whose market-making activities in good funds cause them to have end-of-day net debit positions from large volumes of payment orders.[7] Final settlement of payments among banks occurs with the delivery of good funds.[8]

In a system of *continuous settlement*, each payment message from one bank to another is accompanied by the good funds specified in the message. As long as the sending bank has sufficient reserves on hand, payments messages will be processed without delay. In continuous settlements, receiving banks bear no credit risk from participating in the payment mechanism.

In a continuous settlement system, when the amount of payment exceeds the good funds on hand, the payment must be blocked until more funds are received. If numerous banks face a similar situation, the payments system can become gridlocked. Banks wish to make large payments to each other but cannot send payments because they have not received payments.

The gridlock problem can be solved by breaking up payment orders into smaller parts. This increases the payment traffic on the communication system and may result in incomplete delivery of agreed values, thereby creating credit risk. Alternatively, the banks can generally increase their reserve holdings. This would involve selling loans to other investors in return for good funds. Bank customers would have to pass through a higher cost of reserves. Thus, a system of continuous settlement eliminates credit risk among banks from the day's payments, thereby reducing systemic risk. But it does so by reducing the potential speed of transmitting payments. That is, it reduces systemic risk by reducing liquidity, i.e., by increasing the cost of financial activity.

To avoid breaking up transactions or increasing reserves, banks can engage in *net settlement* at the end of the day. They would pay the difference between total payments and total receipts at the end of the day, forming a clearing house for the purpose of executing the net settlement. All good funds held by banks would be transferred to the clearing house to collateralize bank payment orders. Banks can execute delivery of good funds without increasing their reserves because the individual members of the clearing house and their customers believe that net due to positions cumulating during the day will be covered by delivery of good funds at settlement. Members are justified in their belief if the clearing house guarantees due to's and holds reserves exceeding the sum of the net due to exposures to the clearing house that crop up between settlement periods.[9]

The Federal Reserve is an example of a clearing house with the power to create good funds by purchasing government or private securities. The Fed's power freely to create reserves does not obviate reserves as a source of liquidity. Nor does this power make reserves a tax, as in the conventional interpretation. The Fed bears the same risk of settlement failure as the private clearing house: reserves serve as a guarantee to the Fed of the delivery of good funds against end-of-day net due to positions.

In Fedwire payments, banks with net positions due their reserve account at settlement borrow Fed funds from other members. The Federal Reserve guarantees unconditionally that a bank payment message sent over Fedwire will be honored as good funds at settlement. If a bank fails to deliver good funds, the Fed supplies them without assessing other banks for the deficit in reserves resulting from the failure. During the day, the Fed then insures the market in wholesale payments. The revenue on reserves deposited with the Fed serves as a compensation for the risk it bears.[10] Hence, the Fed significantly increases liquidity in the money markets and the efficiency of the payments mechanism; but as a result, it assumes the risk of making payments for a bank in default.

The interconnection among banks and their connection to the central bank permits the quick movement of good funds from banks with a surplus of good funds to deficit banks. Of course, nonbank institutions could establish similar networks and supply similar assets and liabilities, but this would effectively make them banks, though lacking in payment insurance. That banks can turn to the central bank for funds, however, makes it certain that their net due to's issued between settlement periods will be settled in good funds, while the net due to's of other financial institutions lack such guarantees.

Aside from operational expense, the cost to the banks of the liquidity provided to borrowers and depositors through access to the banking system is the forgone interest on the reserves banks hold with the central bank to guarantee liquidity. Other financial institutions are not required by regulators to bear this cost, and they typically do not form independent organizations that impose reserve requirements on members.[11] If banks alone are forced to hold reserves and membership in a central banking system has no offsetting value, banks would go out of business because no investor or borrower would be willing to pay for the reserves. The banking system gives banks the advantage of providing to potential borrowers a credible guarantee of delivery of good funds without holding reserves on their balance sheets to cover all lines.

While money center or clearing banks, as suppliers of liquidity or lenders of last resort to nonbanks, are the main pillars supporting the domestic and international financial systems, it is the clearing and settling of payments among banks that transmits disturbances from one bank to another thus turning local financial disturbances into a systemic financial problem. *Credit risk* in payment systems arise due to the possibility that any of the parties in the chain of transactions may default on its obligations. For example, the sender could initiate a transfer with his sending bank without having sufficient funds in his account to cover the transfer. The sending bank incurs credit risk if it transmits the payments message before the sender supplies the covering funds. Secondly, the sending bank may fail to provide funds to the receiving bank at settlement. Finally, the payee runs the risk that the receiving bank will not make the funds available. These three risks-*sender risk, receiver risk, settlement risk* - are to be found in most payments systems. If the clearing house operates under settlement finality, then the credit risk of the sending bank is distributed over the receiving banks according to the loss-sharing formula adopted by the clearing house.

Systemic risk occurs as an outgrowth of settlement risk. The failure of one participant to settle deprives other institutions of expected funds and prevents these institutions from settling in their turn. Thus, although a participant does no business directly with a failed institution, chains of obligation may make it suffer because of the impact that the failed institution has on a participant's ability to settle, i.e., the cost of settlement failure reaches beyond the exposure of credit bank to the failing bank. While it is generally not difficult to identify credit risk in a payments system, there are difficulties in properly identifying systemic risk.

A private or public payments system with settlement finality, such as the Fedwire system in the United States, is not subject to systemic risk. Liquidity crises are avoided through a sharing of the debit balance of the failed institutions among the solvent members of the system or through a funding of the debit balance by the central bank. Concerns about the intra-day credit exposure in net-settlement payments systems with payment finality led the Federal Reserve to introduce caps on debit positions with Fedwire and CHIPS, and to propose interest charges on such debit positions.[12] The presence of a cap on the debit position that an individual bank is allowed to run with Fedwire effectively limits the loss that could be incurred by the United States Federal Reserve as a result of payments instructions sent out over the Fedwire by a failing bank. However, in a situation where investors have lost confidence in a large money center bank and fail to renew short-term funds, such as maturing certificates of deposit and repurchase agreements, the bank would quickly reach its net debit limit and may then be unable to repay its short-term creditors. As a result, the central bank could be faced with the need to provide funds to the bank through the discount window and hence be once again subject to the credit risk inherent in the bank asset used as collateral.[13] Thus, if some banks are regarded as too-large-to-fail, then it may be difficult for the central bank to avoid credit risk completely in a liberalized financial system.

The main *international payments system* - CHIPS - has only recently adopted payment finality and hence its members were significantly exposed to the credit risk of lending banks. The 150 member bank of CHIPS are international banks of varying credit ratings. Credit risk arises when banks send out payments for a customer during the day before receiving good funds in the customer's account. For example, a bank might receive a message from the clearing house that an account will be credited with a given amount of dollars at the end of the day. The bank might then be asked by the holder of the account to make payments to other banks from the account through CHIPS even though the bank has not received good funds. Competition has generally forced banks to be prepared to make such payments. All such payments messages are netted at the end of the day by CHIPS and net balances are cleared through Fedwire transfers among the settlement banks.[14] Thus a central element of the international payment system is the extension of credit among the banks that are members of CHIPS.

In the event of a disturbance in the financial markets, such as the bankruptcy of a major nonfinancial company, it is possible that some CHIPS members might be unable to settle, debit balances by borrowing in the interbank market for federal funds. In this case, payments to and from that participant would be unwound, and new net positions will be calculated for the remaining participants. If one of these remaining participants were unable to settle, this process of calculating new net positions would continue until settlement is achieved. Participants in CHIPS permit most of their customers to use credits for CHIPS payments during the day prior to settlement while reserving the right to charge back such credits if the transferring bank does not settle its CHIPS position. Simulations of the unwinding of transactions under the assumption that one large CHIPS participant would be unable to meet its payment obligations suggest that such failures could change drastically the net positions of other participants, thus inducing a series of failures to settle by the remaining participants.[15] This suggested that earlier CHIPS rules and the practice of unwinding thus could potentially have contributed to systemic risks in the banking system and put pressure on the Federal Reserve to provide liquidity assistance while losses and solvency problems are determined.

Since the Federal Reserve does not regulate and supervise the foreign members of CHIPS, it could only guarantee the domestic transactors on CHIPS (as is done on Fedwire). Moreover, attempts by CHIPS itself to impose regulations on its foreign member banks would require the approval of bank regulators in other countries. Under current arrangements, the failure of a major international banking institution could nonetheless cause a systemic crisis if it were to spread illiquidity across the CHIPS system.

4. THE FINANCIAL POLICY PROBLEM

The previous section identified money-center banks and their interaction through the payments system as the source of liquidity for other financial and nonfinancial firms. Thus the possibility of a disturbance in this structure represents the main source of systemic risk. In recent years there has been a particular concern that developments in the major financial markets - increased international integration, higher volatility of asset prices, growth of derivative markets and, above all, substantially larger trading volumes in all markets - are severely testing the adequacy of the existing infrastructure for clearing and settling large-value payments among major international financial institutions, thus worsening the central bank policy trade-off. The settling of payments by the delivery of good funds at periodic, usually daily, intervals is a key test of the solvency of financial institutions in the international financial system. An international financial crisis, if one were to occur, would most likely first manifest itself through an inability of a financial institution, or a group of institutions, to settle their obligations in one of the major payments systems. The fear is that such an event would cause inadequately prepared payments system to "freeze"--become unable to effect payments among institutions. Such an inability to settle payments could then be expected to lead to a severe liquidity shortage as healthy institutions, not having received payments expected at settlement time, might be unable to settle on their own payments obligations.

In the absence of central bank intervention, such a liquidity crisis could easily lead to a loss of confidence in depository institutions, which, in turn, could precipitate multiple failures of otherwise healthy financial institutions.[16] As a result, major central banks have reassured financial markets of their liquidity support during times of stress. However, the sheer size of average *daily* payments flows - $1.4 trillion in 1988 - through the domestic and international U.S. dollar wholesale payments system and the difficulties experienced in settling trades and payments following a computer breakdown at a single clearing bank in New York in 1985[17] and during the October 1987 equity price downturn have contributed to a sense of unease. In fact, some observers believe "that the greatest threat to the stability of the financial system as a whole during the October stock market crash was the danger of a major default in one of the clearing and settlement systems."[18]

Why is it desirable that one of a central bank's goals is the maintenance of "orderly" markets? What are the gains and costs of such a policy? In many markets trading strategies such as stop loss sales or portfolio insurance are used to create liquidity, though traders using such rules may not prepare formal lines to banks to assure the liquidity of their positions. For any one small player, the assumption of price continuity is probably reasonable. If all of the selling strategies are triggered simultaneously, however, they will prove to be infeasible. The rest of the market participants may have no knowledge of the existence of such traders because their sell orders lie buried in the future. They will explode on the market only if stepped on by the proper contingency. When the time comes for these massive sales to occur, the sellers may find no buyers prepared to take the other side of the market at the last reported price, and the price may suddenly collapse.

A lack of liquidity in the market may cause a snowballing of sell orders. If the price falls below its fundamental value due to liquidity problems, further sales may be triggered. Banks may make margin calls on their loans to security holders and cancel lines. This may either bankrupt them or force a sale of their stock. In either case, it precludes their entry as market makers in the stock. This expanding volume of trades of the security generates an expanding demand for liquidity to undertake the transactions along with a possible diminishing supply.

The occurrence of such a problem might bankrupt a large segment of market makers, making many securities less liquid and forcing securities issuers to rely directly on the banking system for finance. This shift to increased intermediation would raise the cost of liquidity and channel capital away from smaller firms which issue less liquid liabilities.

If such problems were obviously temporary liquidity difficulties, it would be desirable for the banking system to expand its delivery of liquidity to avoid bankruptcies and to channel funds to less liquid firms.

Alternatively, the price fall in the securities market may itself be fundamental. Suppose that the central bank erroneously adds liquidity to a market when the price of the security is higher than its ultimate level. It expands reserves and pressures banks to lend against the securities. If the security price eventually falls as central bank liquidity is withdrawn, market makers will be bankrupted, leaving bad loans on the books of the banks and reducing bank capital. Depositors will have less confidence in banks, and banks will be less able to provide liquidity services in the future. To reduce the damage to the banks of this mistake, the central bank may not contract reserves to their normal level. This leads to a permanent expansion in the money stock and to a rise in the price level.

The ability to create currency through the open market purchase of securities or direct lending against eligible collateral has allowed central banks to supply liquidity in times of crises and thereby guarantee the exchange rate between bank deposits and currency. In fact, during the period from 1793 to 1933 the United States experienced at least 17 banking crises, while none have occurred since 1933,[19] the beginning of active Federal Reserve intervention. Thus the systemic financial instability in banking and payment systems was eliminated through the introduction of the central bank clearing house where banks would hold their clearing balances and that stood ready to convert bank deposit liabilities into currency taking bank assets as collateral.

In the absence of regulatory and supervisory restraints on the activities of banks, however, under a broad class of assumptions about the stochastic properties of the occurrence of liquidity crises, the central bank should expect to experience losses on the bank assets acquired in the course of providing liquidity. This is the case when the market value of the collateral is less than amount of central bank assistance deemed necessary to prevent the failure of a bank from creating a systemic liquidity problem. While the monetary effects of the liquidity operation can be sterilized, the central banks' losses on acquired bank assets fall to the taxpayers. The public sector, therefore, assumes some of the credit risk of bank assets in return for an efficient banking system. Thus, as has occurred at various stages in the evolution of the payments and banking system, a certain amount of credit risk has been accepted, in this case by the central bank, as the cost of providing an efficient payment system. In effect, the taxpayer has assumed the credit risk inherent in bank assets that serve as collateral for central bank lending in return for an efficient payment system.

In order to reduce the credit risk incurred during liquidity operations to a desired level, monetary authorities can impose a regulatory and supervisory regime on financial systems (not only on banking systems) designed to reduce the expected losses on acquired bank assets to a desired level. In particular, regulations can be designed so that disturbances from the non-payments activities of banks do not spill over into the payments system and become systemic. Such regulations include risk-related capital requirements, separation of investment banking activity from payments activity, position limits, and assessment of the solvency of the bank through supervision and inspection of the bank's assets. Furthermore, regulatory policy can limit the credit risk of the central bank through its choice of payments system. The more restrictive the regulatory and supervisory regimes, however, the greater the total cost of financial transactions, in particular the cost of making payments.

In limiting the risks that central banks are prepared to assume in providing liquidity to the financial system, they must decide the allowable range of available securitized money market instruments. In practice, such decisions fall along a spectrum, ranging from the highly liquid securitized money markets of the United States to the traditionally restricted money markets in the Federal Republic of Germany. Securitization in money markets shifts credit to larger, liquid institutions from bank balance sheets directly to the money market. With restricted money markets, even large and relatively low risk firms seeking access to liquid funds must be carried on bank balance sheets.

If a central bank permits large-scale, liquid, and securitized money markets, potential issuers of liquid, short-term securities remove themselves from bank balance sheets, thereby reducing the demands for bank reserves. The price of accessing bank liquidity falls for less liquid issuers of securities. A policy of permitting a liquid money market favors issuers of illiquid securities and allows them to access capital more cheaply. If such issuers are concentrated among the smaller, riskier and perhaps more innovative firms, the structure of investment by type of firm and type of activity is altered. Alternatively a highly restricted money market will raise the cost of capital to less liquid firms, channeling capital to the larger, lower risk, and perhaps less innovative firms.

A central bank might restrict markets if it can reduce its own credit risk. Why would liquid money markets increase the credit risks assumed by a central bank? An unrestricted system is prone to a greater probability of periodic liquidity crisis because of the network of dealers that must materialize to make the money markets. A sudden piece of negative information may cause the usual dealer lines of bank credit to disappear as potential lenders become momentarily uncertain of the solvency of the market makers. The potential systemic nature of such a situation invites a central bank liquidity intervention and assumption of risk. If the borrowers and lenders on the money market were forced to intermediate through banks, there would be fewer credit lines that might unravel and a smaller chance of a systemic problem emerging from the same disturbance. Eliminating the money market reduces the range of securities that lean on banking system liquidity, thereby reducing the chances of central bank liquidity interventions.

Hence there exists a trade-off between the amount of credit risk assumed by the public sector and the efficiency of the financial system. Casual observation suggests that there exist significant differences in the willingness of the public sector in various countries to assume credit risk of bank assets. For example, recent history suggests that the United States is willing to tolerate a significant amount of credit risk in the interest of a liberal financial system, whereas financial authorities in Germany appear willing to accept a less liberal financial system (e.g., the absence of well-developed short-term money markets) in the interest of lower credit risk for the public sector.

5. IMPLICATIONS OF RECENT DEVELOPMENTS FOR CENTRAL BANK FINANCIAL POLICY

Recent developments in financial markets have generally worsened the trade-off between the total cost of financial transactions supporting a given level of real activity and credit risk facing central banks. First, increases in the magnitude of financial flows have greatly increased the expected size of central bank liquidity support in the event of a systemic liquidity crisis. Second, the improved ability of financial firms to transform the type and to shift the location of financial transactions and balance sheets towards the less regulated activities and jurisdictions has led firms to arbitrage regulatory differences. Such arbitrage has generally reduced the effectiveness of a given financial policy.

Cooperation vs. Competition in Financial Policy

The redesign of financial transactions into less regulated transactions and the geographic shifting of financial activity into less regulated jurisdictions has generally induced financial authorities in the more stringently regulated jurisdictions to liberalize regulatory constraints in order to ensure that financial activity will remain within their jurisdiction.[20] Regulatory authorities have prevented a redistribution or loss of regulatory or fiscal control by liberalizing regulatory or fiscal constraints in the high-cost jurisdictions, that is, by leveling the playing field around a lower common denominator. This approach is thus one of competition for "regulatory market share" by the regulators. In particular, the disintermediation from banking markets to securities markets or the shifting of financial transactions from onshore to offshore locations provided incentives for the deregulation of the adversely affected banking sector and some other domestic transactions.[21] The desire to avoid a sharp decline in the market share of the banking sector, for example, led to the gradual removal of interest rate restrictions on bank liabilities in the United States and Japan. It is likely that the growth of competition from the securities industry for traditional banking business will lead to the dismantling of some of the more onerous provisions of the Glass-Steagall Statute in the United States or Article 65 in Japan. The decline of U.S. banks in importance at the international league table is also likely to bring further pressure on banking regulators to amend financial policy toward banking.

Loss of trading activity from the securities markets of some countries has led to a significant restructuring of the intermediary industry by removing fixed commissions schedules in securities markets and by allowing foreign ownership. In order to bring Euromarket activities back into the domestic regulatory purview, some countries are liberalizing their domestic regulatory and fiscal restrictions. For example, the United States has recently permitted bonds to be converted from bearer (Eurobonds) to registered form and back after a ninety-day seasoning period, thus linking the Eurobond and domestic bond markets more closely. Similarly, German and Swiss financial authorities have abolished to have turnover taxes in order to induce trading activity to return the domestic market and to prevent further shifts of activity in primary and derivative instrument to London. The introduction of a German public sector debt futures contract on the London International Financial Futures Exchange also provided the decisive incentive to permit the trading of such contracts on the Deutsche Termin Boerse in Frankfurt.

The effort of the EC to establish, inter alia, a single financial market relies on some harmonization of national financial policies combined with home country control over financial policy. Efforts are underway to implement a sufficient degree of harmonization to obtain an EC-wide agreement that will allow a financial institution to establish itself anywhere within the EC and remain under the jurisdiction of its home country. Once the necessary harmonization of financial policy has been put in place, a bank or securities firm from, say, Spain would be allowed to conduct financial business in London while remaining entirely subject to Spanish financial policy. A rigorous implementation of this approval is essentially noncooperative in nature as banks will be able to choose the jurisdiction under which they want to obtain a banking license. Thus countries will tend to adapt their regulatory structure to the least regulated jurisdiction if they wish to prevent a loss of financial activity.

Fostering competition may well be an efficient method of achieving financial sector liberalization when faced with a highly regulated financial system. Noncooperation among regulators has until recently provided world financial markets with substantial benefits. For example, when foreign exchange controls were removed in Japan in the early 1980s, Japanese corporations were free to buy and sell securities in international financial markets, freeing them from dependence on their main bank. The heightened competition forced liberalization of domestic money markets, which, in turn, increased the investment alternatives for consumers. It is quite plausible that without a relatively free international market, financial reform in Japan would note have occurred so quickly.

However, there exists no mechanism whereby continued competition for market share by regulators will result in a stable distribution of financial activity across jurisdictions governed by financial policies that are optimal, in the sense that the expected cost of liquidity support operations by the central bank is balanced by the reduction in the cost of financial activity. However, cooperation has developed not only because of the inefficiency of the competitive approach, but also because in an important instance there exists some degree of regulatory monopoly in world financial markets. This limited monopoly is created by the U.S. dollar's preeminent role in the international economy. The international dollar payments system, CHIPS, is operated by the major New York City banks that are regulated by the U.S. Federal Reserve. The burden of a liquidity crisis on this system will likely fall on the Federal Reserve and the U.S. taxpayer. This places the U.S. central bank in the position to seek a cooperative solution to payments risk reduction. Because the New York banks are regulated by the Federal Reserve, it has the tools at its disposal to generate an outcome that reduces risk. The Federal Reserve can, for example, insist that these banks write rules that reduce the possibility of nonsettlement.

These rules have the potential to raise the cost of clearing dollar payments that might invite regulatory competition. Suppose the central bank of a major industrial country prefers a more liberal set of rules for clearing international payments. It might encourage its major banks to establish an international clearing system in its own currency. Due to the more liberal rules of the alternative clearing house, the cost of making payments in that currency would be lower than the cost of making dollar payments, if financial markets in that currency had the depth of dollar markets.

Given the dominance of the dollar in world markets, it is unlikely that another central bank could compete with the Federal Reserve. Nor could that central bank set up a competitive dollar clearing system because no one would believe the liquidity guarantees of a central bank that cannot print dollars. Thus, the U.S. has a powerful tool to establish cooperative supervision of payments risk.

The U.S. securities regulatory authority, the Security and Exchange Commission (SEC), on the other hand, has no such power over international securities markets. The SEC does not regulate an institution like CHIPS that, for all practical purposes, market participants must use if there is to be settlement of transactions. As a result, securities market regulation has tended to be unilateral in nature.

6. CONCLUSION

In this paper we have formulated the financial policy problem of central banks and investigated the implication of recent developments in financial markets for central bank financial policy. Other than assuring the competitive structure of the financial sector, central bank financial policy should be limited to reducing the real cost of liquidity crises. We have shown that banking systems have a comparative advantage in supplying liquidity and that systemic liquidity crises occur when the banking system fails to distribute liquidity through the payments system. In this case the central bank should generate liquidity, i.e., good funds, in exchange for bank assets. The credit risk assumed by the central bank during such interventions should be contained by a regulatory and supervisory policy designed to reduce the expected number of systemic liquidity crises. Such policy should be designed to reduce the risk of insolvency of and illiquidity of an individual bank and it should determine the features of the payments system. It should likewise affect the potential demand for liquidity by deciding on the allowable type of securitized money market instruments. However, such regulatory policies increase the total cost of financial transactions supporting a given volume of real transactions. The financial policy problem of central banks then consists of choosing a point on the trade-off between credit risk and the total cost of financial transactions. We conclude that recent developments in financial markets imply that the noncooperative, unilateral design, and implementation of national financial policy will produce an insufficiently stringent supervisory and regulatory structure.

FOOTNOTES

The views expressed in this paper are those of the authors and do not necessarily reflect the position of the International Monetary Fund. The authors are indebted to W. Branson, C. Goodhart, and R. Herring for comments on an earlier draft of this paper.

1. For a history of banking panics and liquidity crises, see Schwartz (1988).

2. For a recent review of this literature and of other perspectives on the role of banks, see Gertler (1987).

3. For example, see Black (1975) for such an interpretation. James (1987) confirms Fama's evidence on insignificant spreads between certificates of deposit and commercial paper, showing that the average spread remained unchanged across changes in reserve requirements. Black (1975) and Goodfriend (1988) have also suggested that banks obtain their special information because of their role in the payments system. They argue that a bank benefits from having a demand deposit relationship with a customer which provides it with current information about the state of the borrower's financial condition. Another nonbank lender, however, could easily erode this competitive advantage by requesting that the borrower provide real time access to his on-line bank financial statements.

4. James (1987) developed additional evidence that capital markets regard banks as possessors of private information about borrowers not available to other lenders. He found that the announcement of a bank line of credit causes the stock of the recipient company to exhibit excess returns immediately after the announcement. In constrast, he found that the announcement of a commitment to lend by an insurance <company causes no such reaction in the stock market.

5. See also P.M. Garber and S.R. Weisbrod (1990), "Banks in the Market for Liquidity".

6. "Good funds" can mean either cash or, more typically in the wholesale markets we examine, deposits at the Federal Reserve or at banks, items whose delivery always constitutes settlement of a claim for dollars.

7. Whenever a deposit is cashed or a loan made, a bank becomes a buyer of goods funds at a posted bid price because it must make delivery of funds to a customer or another bank. Whenver a loan is repaid or a deposit made, a bank becomes a seller of good funds at a posted offer price.

8. Of course, settlement may be in any mutually acceptable medium. In actual banking systems, settlement is not final unless payment is made in good funds, currency or central bank deposits. Whether this arises through legal constraints or through choice is not at issue here. For a detailed discussion of payments systems, see D. Folkerts-Landau (1991).

9. In settling net positions, the clearing house makes a claim that in the event that one member is in bankruptcy, it has the right to offset payments due from that member with pyamnets due to that member. The clearing house makes prior claim over all other creditors to the bankrupt member's liabilities to the clearing house to the extent that they are offset by that member's loans to the clearing house. Much of the security the clearing house adds to the payments mechanism is derived from liability rules. Reserve requirements protect the payments mechanism in a similar fashion. They are assets of the several member banks, but the clearing house has prior claim to them in the event of bankruptcy.

10. The Fed may or may not earn a profit from the user charge represented by reserves, depending on its magnitude. Moreover, there may be more efficient means of charging for this risk bearing. Since the Treasury taxes the Fed's revenues, it ultimately bears the risk of operating the payment system.

11. In the United States, any depository institution which offers transaction accounts, that is, deposits that permit third party payments services, must hold reserves with the Federal Reserve. The role of non-banks in wholesale payments is very small, however. Clearing houses in organized financial markets provide liquidity

services for members and regulate member liquidity, but ultimately they rely on the banking system for the delivery of good funds to cover net positions.

12. See Folkerts-Landau (1991) for discussion of recent reform measures.

13. A large proportion of the assets of money center or clearing bank are financed by short-term funds - certificates of deposit, repurchase agreements, interbank loans - and it is possible that a loss of such funding could make it necessary for the bank to discount assets other than the eligible government securities. In this case the central bank would be exposed to the private credit risk inherent in such assets.

14. Foreign banks clear through a CHIPS settlement bank.

15. See Humphrey (1986).

16. Some of these concerns have been discussed in recent conferences and symposia. For example, the Group of Thirty Symposium on Clearance and Settlement Issues in the Global Securities Markets in London in March, 1988, the International Symposium on Banking and Payment Services, sponsored by the Board of Governors of the Federal Reserve System, June 7-9, 1989, and the Williamsburg Payments System Symposium of the Federal Reserve Bank of Richmond, May 20, 1988.

17. The Bank of New York, a major clearing bank in the U.S. payments system, experienced a computer breakdown on November 21, 1985, which led the U.S. Federal Reserve to make an overnight loan of $22.6 billion from the discount window, collateralized by $36 billion in securities.

18. See Greenspan (1989).

19. See Schwartz (1988).

20. See Folkerts-Landau (1990).

21. A further motive for deregulating interest rate ceilings and restrictions on the investment choice of some financial intermediaries has been the need to finance fiscal deficits. A greater volume of government bonds outstanding acted as a stimulus to the development of secondary markets for debt securities with market-determined yields and presented an investment asset alternative to bank liabilities.

REFERENCES

Bank for International Settlements (1989a), Report on Netting Schemes, Basle, February.

_____ (1989b) Payments Systems in Eleven Developed Countries, May.

Black, F. (1975), "Bank Fund Management in an Efficient Market", Journal of Financial Economics, 2, 323-339.

Cannon, J.G. (1911), Clearing-houses: Their History, Models and Administration (London: Smith, Elder, and Company, 1901), reprinted in National Monetary Commission, Vol 6, Washington.

Corrigan, E.G. (1986), "Financial Market Structure: A Longer View", Federal Reserve Bank of New York, Annual Report

_____ (1987), "Financial Market Structure: A Longer View", Federal Reserve Bank of New York, Annual Report.

Eichengreen. B., and R. Portes (1987), "The anatomy of financial crises", in R. Portes and A. Swoboda, Threats to International Financial Stability, Cambridge: Cambridge University Press.

Fama, E. (1980), "Banking in a Theory of Finance", Journal of Monetary Economics, Vol 6, 39-57.

_____ (1985), "What's Different About Banks?", Journal of Monetary Economics, 15, January, 29-40.

Federal Reserve Bank of New York (1987-88), "Large-Dollar Payment Flows from New York," Federal Reserve Bank of New York, Quarterly Review, Vol. 12, 6-13.

Folkerts-Landau, D. (1985), "The changing role of international bank lending in development finance", IMF Staff Papers.

_____ (1991), "Systemic Financial Risk in Payment Systems", Occasional Paper, No. 77, Washington, IMF)

Folkerts-Landau, D. and D.J. Mathiesen (1988), "Innovation, Institutional Change, and Regulatory Response in International Financial Markets", in W.S. Haraf, R.M. Kushmeier (eds), Restructuring Banking and Financial Services in America, Washington, 392-423

Garber, P.M. and Weisbrod, S.R. (1990), "Banks in the Market for Liquidity", NBER Working Paper.

Gertler, M. (1988), "Financial Structure and Aggregate Economic Activity: An Overview", Journal of Money, Credit and Banking, Vol. 20, No. 3, Part 2, August.

Goodfriend, M. (1988), "Money, Credit, Banking, and Payments System Policy," in D.B. Humphrey (ed) The U.S. Payments System Efficiency, Risk, and the Role of the Federal Reserve, Kluwer Academic Publishers.

Goodhart, C.A.E. (1987), "Why Do Banks Need a Central Bank?" Oxford Economic Papers, Vol. 39, 75-89.

Greenspan, A. (1989), "International Payment System Developments", speech before the International Symposium on Banking and Payment Services, Washington.

Humphrey, D.B. (1986), "Payments Finality and Risk of Settlement Failure", in A. Saunders and L.J. White (eds), Technology and the Regulation of Financial Markets, Lexington Books.

James, C. (1987), "Some Evidence on the Uniqueness of Bank Loans", Journal of Financial Economics, 19, 217-36.

Johnson, M.H. (1988), "Challenge to the Federal Reserve in the Payments Mechanism", Issues in Bank Regulation Summer, 13-16.

Kane, E. (1983), "Policy Implications of Structural Changes in Financial Markets, American Economic Review 73 (no.2).

Schwartz, A. J. (1988). "Financial Stability and the Federal Safety Net", in W.S. Haraf and R.M. Kuschmeider, (eds) Restructuring Banking and Financial Services in America, Washington, DC, American Enterprise Institute.

Financial Regulation and Monetary Arrangements after 1992
C. Wihlborg, M. Fratianni and T.D. Willett (Editors)

58

Comment

Peter Englund

Department of Economics, Uppsala University, P.O. Box 513, S-751 20 Uppsala, Sweden

The recent liberalization of financial markets - both domestically and internationally - has raised a set of new policy issues. In particular there is today a widespread concern with the potential fragility of the financial system. On one hand a number of events and indicators suggest that markets have become more volatile in the last few years and that the real economy may be more sensitive to financial disturbances than previously. On the other hand the proliferation and sophistication of these markets and, in particular, the rapid international integration apparently have made the financial system more difficult to control. The concern with the policy problems raised by these two phenomena is particularly deep in a country like Sweden - previously heavily regulated and strongly dependent on international financial markets.

In this innovative paper Folkerts-Landau, Garber, and Weisbrod (FGW) identify the central policy problem of central banks as a trade off between two basic regimes: on one hand an unregulated, and thereby efficient, financial system with sizeable credit risk assumed by the central bank which may have to act as lender of last resort, and on the other hand a regulated and less efficient financial sector but a lower probability that the central bank (and the taxpayers) have to step in.

Much of the analysis in the paper derives from a somewhat novel view on the functions performed in the economy by financial institutions in general and banks in particular. The traditional view, well-known from generations of textbooks, is that banks are unique in being the only providers of means-of-payment, apart from central banks. Real effects of monetary policy comes via a stable money demand function, derived e.g. by a cash-in-advance constraint. A further tenet of the traditional view is that the banking system is susceptible to bank runs, and that a lender of last resort is needed to guarantee the stability of the system. In the traditional analysis the asset side of bank balances plays a subordinated role.

In the last decade or so the traditional view has been challenged by a competing paradigm which stresses the special features of bank loans as opposed to other types of credit. This "new" view - with an ancestry at least back to Gurley and Shaw (1960) - recognizes that bank loans are typically characterized by asymmetric information between lender and borrower. Economies of scale in monitoring of borrowers explain why such loans are handled by a financial intermediary, and economies of scope between monitoring and production of transaction services (handling transaction accounts gives useful information about the creditworthiness of a borrower) explains why this typically is a bank. This view has emerged largely from theoretical work on the economics of asymmetric information; see e.g. Gale and Hellwig (1985) and Diamond (1984).

The "new" view gained added credibility from an empirical observation made by Fama (1985). He noted that bank certificates of deposit trade at the same interest rate as commercial paper of the same risk class. Since the former but not the latter are subject to reserve requirements, he argued that CD's - the marginal financing of banks - cannot bear the tax burden of the reserve requirement. Hence these must be borne by bank borrowers, that is, bank loans are "special".

FGW challenge Fama's conclusion based on an analysis previously presented in Garber and Weisbrod (1990). Their basic observation is that companies issuing commercial paper typically have access to bank credit lines, and that banks charge for this service since they have to hold reserves against these lines of credit. Consequently Fama's conclusion is not valid. Instead FGW suggest that the unique role of the banking system is that of supplying liquidity, in the sense of mobilizing "good funds", i.e. ultimately central bank money, in times of liquidity crises.

There is much to be said in favour of this view, and it is here said clearer and more forcefully than elsewhere. I think, however, that one can raise objections against the evidence put forward by FGW. First, the argument seems to presume that the size of bank reserve holdings are freely chosen at the margin, in which case a commercial paper program with an associated credit line would lead to increased reserves. On the contrary if reserve requirements are binding and force banks to hold larger reserves than they would like to, then a new credit line would not imply additional reserve holdings, since credit lines are not part of the base against which reserve requirements arecalculated (at least not in Sweden). Hence, the argument seems to build on the counterfactual assumption of non-binding reserve requirements.

Second, let us anyway presume that banks hold extra reserves against credit lines. Under such circumstances it is certainly possible that bank liabilities are unique in the sense suggested, but this does not imply the rejection of the uniqueness of bank loans. Indeed the most reasonable position is probably that there are unique items on both sides of bank balance sheets.

Such a more eclectic view of the functions of banks and the financial system in general obviously affects the conclusions about the policy trade-off. Perhaps one should worry more about the effects of sudden contractions of bank credit than the analysis of Folkerts-Landau, Garber and Weisbrod leads us to do.

REFERENCES

Diamond, D. (1984), "Financial Intermediation and Delegated Monitoring", Review of Economic Studies, 1984, 51, 393-414.

Fama, E. (1985), "What's Different About Banks?", Journal of Monetary Economics, 15, 29-40.

Gale, D. and M. Hellwig (1985), "Incentive-Compatible Debt Contracts I: The One-Period Problem", Review of Economic Studies, 52, 647-64.

Garber, P.M. and S.R. Weisbrod (1990), "Banks in the Market for Liquidity", NBER Working Paper, 3381, Cambridge: Massachusetts.

Gurley, J. and E. Shaw (1960), Money in Theory of Finance, Brookings Institution, Washington D.C.

Financial Regulation and Monetary Arrangements after 1992
C. Wihlborg, M. Fratianni and T.D. Willett (Editors)
© 1991 Elsevier Science Publishers B.V. All rights reserved

3 The Bank Capital Issue

Anthony M. Santomero

Finance Department, The Wharton School of the University of Pennsylvania, Philadelphia PA 19104-6367, USA

1. INTRODUCTION

Finance has long worried about optimal debt-to-equity ratios. This has occupied the literature at an institutional level for years and on a theoretical level since at least the time of the seminal contribution of Modigliani and Miller (1958). Over the years there have been substantial advances in our understanding of the issue, associated with (i) efficient market theory, such as the work of Fama (1970), (ii) information theory, such as Leland and Pyle (1977) and (iii) incentive compatibility with the work of Jensen and Meckling (1976). Nonetheless, it remains an area of continual evolution in standard corporate finance.

The applicability of this work in standard financial theory to firms in the banking industry has been rather contentious. This can be explained by the fact that intermediation theorists often have different views of the leverage issue, as a result of their own perspective on the role performed by banks in the real economy. This has resulted in several different views of the banking firm's decision process applicable to the determination of optimal bank capital ratios, and increased interest in the public policy consequences of whatever decision it reaches. Academic researchers centering their interest on the firm level optimization issues have attempted to meld the standard corporate finance literature with the unique characteristics of the bank franchise to obtain optimal leverage level. Here, such works as Orgler and Taggart (1983) and Sealey (1983) are representative. On the other hand, work by Fama (1980) and Galai and Crouchy (1986) argue against any special consideration for the position of banks and in favor of the standard finance theory results on optimal capital. By definition, these authors either reject or ignore the role of banks within the economy and the externalities they provide. However, there is a large body of literature, recently reviewed by Gertler (1988) and Santomero (1991) suggesting that the banking industry has important externalities in the real economy. This has led some to argue that this privileged place requires government policy intervention on their operations, financial decisionmaking and risktaking.

The dichotomy of perspective, which roughly corresponds to a firm level focus and a financial market focus, respectively, has led to discussions of bank capital and its regulation that are often at cross purposes. Regulators and policymakers presume a unique place is occupied by the banking sector and concern themselves with externalities associated with bank failures. They argue that such macro issues require consideration in the choice calculus of optimal leverage ratios, (see, e.g., Corrigan, 1987). They, therefore, tend to foster greater capitalization than members of the industry would like to see. Proponents of a firm level perspective argue correctly that their products have close substitutes and are offered in highly contestable markets. They argue that, in an efficient financial market, regulation can destroy an otherwise healthy industry, (see, e.g., Galai and Crouchy, 1986). Armed with this view, industry representatives and several students of the industry call for less capital intervention, and more free market solutions to the leverage issue.

The above notwithstanding, the recognition of a regulatory umbrella associated with such phrases as, "too big to fail," "federal insurance," and "implicit guarantees," has renewed interest in the establishment of a credible bank capital standard at a time when the cost of such regulatory support is ballooning. Yet, the nature of such a policy is no less controversial than a need for it. Some have argued that the government should merely eliminate the inefficiencies of bank regulation and liability insurance to allow the marketplace to efficiently regulate bank capital ratios, e.g., Kareken and Wallace (1978). Others have argued in favor of the establishment of a narrow bank along the lines of Friedman-Simons, e.g., Litan (1987) or the Brookings Panel (Benston et al, 1987). Still others argue for better capital regulation of the industry in its present form, e.g., Furlong and Keeley (1987).

It is the last issue that will be the focus of the present discussion. In short, the current paper will attempt to answer the question of what do we know about optimal bank capital regulation and what needs to be done for efficient implementation of such a policy? The sections that follow will attempt to address these two issues, trying to keep as narrowly focussed as possible on this narrow agenda. This is not always possible, however, as it is extremely difficult, indeed nearly impossible, to discuss bank capital without touching on market efficiency, regulation and managerial incentive issues. Bank capital must, at times, be put into the broader perspective of the financial structure. In short, the analysis must carry some baggage.

The paper itself is divided into seven sections, including this introduction. Section 2 contains a review of the role performed by banks. Thereafter, I turn to the trade-off between profit and risk in banking with and without deposit insurance in Section 3. Section 4 asks what the limits are to banks' willingness to take risks. Sections 5 and 6 discuss capital regulation and alternative proposals to limit risk-taking. Section 7, finally, contains conclusions and implications of potential competition in regulation as envisioned in the EC for efficiency of regulation.

2. THE ROLE OF BANKS IN SOCIETY

The analysis of optimal bank capital regulation begins by evaluating the role performed by banks within the developed financial markets of the late twentieth century. This perspective is presented here for context and will be shown to have evolved and changed substantially over the past decade. This evolution is a result of the fact that the financial market and the services provided by various participants has been altered by a number of well-defined economic forces. These include globalization, technology and competition, to name the most obvious ones, following Santomero (1989). All of these have changed the financial markets and institutions, leaving them with a different set of products and services provided to the real sector. In summarizing the roles performed by financial institutions, I will refer to a large body of academic literature that has developed on this growing area of interest and direct interested readers by explicit citation.

The emerging view of the role of banks in financial markets argues that they serve two primary functions. First, they are generators or creators of assets. Through their role as evaluator of business proposals and spending opportunities, they screen the set of borrowing opportunities presented to them using an expertise and specific-capital that is unique to this sector. Once evaluated and found worthy, the bank begins its second activity, i.e., ongoing surveillance and monitoring. In essence, borrowers are monitored and loans serviced by the same institutions that initiated the funding and reviewed the offering proposal. The works of Leland and Pyle (1977), Diamond (1984), and Campbell and Kracaw (1980) are the initial contributions in this view of bank activity and serve as fundamental references for such additions to the literature as the works of Williamson (1986), Diamond (1988), or Smith (1984).

Notice that while the funding of such loans had previously been combined with evaluation and monitoring, this last role is increasingly segmented from the banking industry per se. With the advent and increasing importance of loan sales and asset securitization, a buy and hold decision is merely one of the funding mechanisms available to institutions that create financial assets; see Pennachi (1988), Greenbaum and Thakor (1987) and Santomero (1988).

The bank's central feature is sorting through the endless stream of sometime subjective information provided by a prospective borrower in the marketplace. They are efficient providers of this service due to their ability to economize on evaluation time on behalf of their depository clients and by offering specific information skills to the less than perfectly informed real world that funds such investments.

In addition to the above functions, banks are viewed as also providing a series of services to depositors that are essentially secondary in importance. These services include those associated with the lack of divisibility of assets, as in Klein (1973), and the minimization of transaction costs in transfer activity, as in Benston and Smith (1976) and Sealey (1983). Together these ancillary services provide banks with ample opportunity to offer liabilities and attendant clearing services to the marketplace. Through various types of deposits, the services provided to liability holders include both transaction cost minimization for various types of demand deposit and savings deposit accounts, as well as risk pooling to obtain higher returns for various types of time deposits. However, except for some payment services, the franchise to provide such services is increasingly not exclusive, as these products are offered also by other financial firms.

In essence, banks create assets and service liabilities. Their franchise is limited in both dimensions. Assets that have no specific certification requirement, for example, triple A credits, have already left the banking industry in favor of direct market borrowing through commercial paper, and the bond market in the U.S. and the U.K. particularly. At the same time, liabilities that are strictly seeking the highest risk adjusted return must be fully competitive with other market alternatives or they will leave the banking sector. Both these points have been made by Fama (1985).

The franchise is delicate and shrinking. As information becomes more available, the proportion of assets that need bank certification continues to decline. As alternative financial instruments become more efficient at facilitating transactions or pooling risks, the bank's share of household assets has likewise declined. It is for these reasons that the percentage of capital market activity going through depository institutions has been declining through time, as evidenced by the Federal Reserve Flow of Funds (1990).

Attempts to reverse this trend of declining market share have involved banks in increasing the risk profile of their assets and/or offering more investment type liability alternatives. The first of these implies a decline in the quality, or at least the liquidity of bank created assets. Therefore, one should not be surprised to find bank balance sheets increasingly filled with highly leveraged assets and complicated loans rather than traditional blue chip corporate lending. On the liability side, meanwhile, in an effort to expand the investment vehicles available to bank customers, money market instruments of various kind has replaced standard demand and savings accounts, and upscale banking have attracted increasing attention. Indeed, in the U.S. the combined value of both areas now account for the overwhelming majority of the funding base of banking institutions. Both of these areas of emphasis will retain their importance as the banking industry attempts to remain profitable in an ever more efficient financial market.

3. PROFIT AND RISK FOR THE BANKING FIRM

Within the above view of the banking industry, the individual institution must find an appropriate niche and adequate profitability to retain invested and needed capital. If its competitive advantage is in loan evaluation, it must be sufficiently accurate and its volume sufficiently large to obtain adequate returns. However, no evaluation is perfect and within an imperfect information setting, both ex ante and ex post mistakes are made. Accordingly, with the ability to evaluate loans comes the potentiality of loss as well as return. A challenge to the firm is optimal portfolio structure to reduce this vulnerability as discussed by Santomero (1984), by Hart and Jaffee (1974), or by Flannery (1985, 1989) focussing on optimal portfolio structure. On the liability side, product profits are also not assured. While some institutions make substantial returns from this activity, others make little. It has recently become clear that in order to exploit market imperfections, scale becomes a critical issue, as noted by Schafer (1990). With reasonably high fixed operating costs and transactions-driven cost functions, profits require sufficient scale in both dollar and transaction terms. With the erosion of demand deposits and savings account monopolies brought about by the advent of money market substitutes, standard retail banking products continue to decline in profitability. These are increasingly being replaced by fee-income activity and transaction service fees as noted by Furash (1987).

In addition to the two market niches listed above, banks have also found a third way of turning their charter into profit. Unlike their competitors in the securities business, banks have the ability of transmutation - a word out of old Money and Banking texts such as Chandler and Goldfeld (1977). In earlier years we thought of this as term structure intermediation. However, we have come to recognize it as something quite different. Through the benefits of deposit insurance, both implicit and explicit, banks transform risky assets into riskless liabilities. Unfortunately, both the regulator and deposit insurer bears the risk and the associated cost.

This governmental intervention is justified by an appeal to the importance of the role performed by banks in providing investable capital, as argued by Bernanke and Gertler (1988), or to the importance of their deposit liabilities argued by Corrigan (1987). Others such as Diamond and Dybvig (1983) see the need to assure the stabilization of the financial system. Intervention is based on these views which trumpet the role of banks in our society and mandate public policy to assure the integrity of the services they provide. Thus, banks have been allowed to issue liabilities with risk characteristics that are independent of, or at least not perfectly correlated with, their assets.

Banks buy risky assets by issuing liabilities that are explicitly or implicitly guaranteed by the government. Such a guarantee is provided through the FDIC or the Federal Reserve discount window in the U.S. and by central banks in many European countries. Deposits of large banks are repaid by the issuing bank or a federal agency. In good times the banks pay all of their liabilities. In bad times, the insurance agency pays the contracted returns to liability holders. The net result of this governmental guarantee is to reduce both the average and marginal cost of funding the banks' risky portfolio of assets. Recent empirical data by Avery, Belton and Hanweck (1988) and Gorton and Santomero (1990) demonstrate this bias exists even in the most sensitive market, i.e., the market to subordinate debt. They demonstrate that funds are raised at below true expected cost because the bank is not fully liable for and the depositor is not sufficiently fearful of bad returns.

This profit opportunity associated with exploiting the insurance guarantee is optimized by a high risk-asset portfolio, as Kane (1985) and Benston et al (1986) clearly demonstrate. It, therefore, establishes a set of incentives that encourage risk-taking by the bank. Risk generates expected economic returns as the bank receives returns in good times and leaves the bank to the regulators in bad ones. Depositors recognize this but ignore the behavior of the bank due to governmental assurances of full payment of nearly all liabilities in nearly all cases. To use the words of the literature, i.e., Merton (1977) and Sharpe (1978), the bank holds a put option, whereby it always has the option of turning the institution over to the deposit insurer in the event of a bad outcome. We have seen all too much of this in the U.S. thrift debacle of the last two decades.

4. LIMITS ON BANK WILLINGNESS TO TAKE RISK

Healthy firms, however, will not necessarily run headlong into an extremely risky portfolio strategy. There are factors that mitigate the profitability or desirability of unrestrained risktaking. While this fact is often neglected in much of the discussions of the effects of deposit insurance, it is worth recognizing here. In practice, three factors work to reduce the bank's appetite for risk. The first is that managers themselves may not find it in their professional interest to do so. This point was made first by Kahane (1977) and Koehn and Santomero (1980) based upon the agency work of Ross (1973). Human capital rarely is fully diversified or diversifiable, and is severely damaged by bad outcomes. This has led the above authors to argue that managers will be somewhat risk-averse in their portfolio selection and, at some level of risk, arrive at a point where additional expected return is not worth the added underlying risk of failure.

Some would disagree with this perspective and have indeed done so in the academic press, e.g., Keeley and Furlong (1990). They argue that stockholder valuation is optimized by maximizing expected return and ignoring risk. They, therefore, contend that it is not appropriate to think of professional managers as risk-averse, but rather as risk neutral agents, or worse yet, risk-lovers exploiting the imperfection of deposit insurance. Clearly, limited liability and deposit insurance exacerbates the manager's gain from risktaking in the portfolio, as it truncates the loss to managers and reduces the market's pricing of default outcomes. However, such arguments do not vitiate the concern of managers about a high-risk portfolio. The result that risk aversion of bank managers may be a sufficient risk limiting force remains, if somewhat mitigated by the combination of limited liability and depositor insurance.

Notwithstanding the above, a second rationale exists for limited risk-taking by member firms in the industry. Simply put, owner-managers and owners with substantial capital in the banking firm will not find it in their best interest to take unlimited risks. To the extent that bank equity capital is a large percentage of total assets, owners will be reluctant to accept a high-risk portfolio because the expected gain associated with the mispricing of liabilities is small while the capital risk is large. This is the view taken by Benston and Kaufman (1988), and proved rigorously by Keeley and Furlong (1990). Therefore, independent of any other factors, increasing capital encourages prudence.

Thirdly and finally, Marcus (1984) and Herring and Vankudre (1987) demonstrate that the charter itself has the ability to constrain risk-taking. These authors show that, to the extent that the firm has specific capital or, equivalently, a valuable franchise, the threat of its loss deters the risk-taking tendency of the banking firm. This argument assumes, however, that regulation can be established to assure that the franchise is surrendered quickly and predictably when losses are observed, as the Shadow Financial Regulatory Committee has noted. If this can be achieved, the penalty to a bad outcome from a risky portfolio looms large in the mind of bank management. To the extent that this charter has value as a going concern, it will not be put at risk lightly by large portfolio risks.

Taken together the above arguments suggest that it is probably unreasonable to assume that banks have an unmitigated taste for risk. While one could contest any one of these constraints on risk-taking, it appears unlikely that all are irrelevant. Nonetheless, this does not necessarily suggest that the tendency towards risk, associated with deposit insurance mispricing and/or government guarantees, is completely offset. This has led many to suggest that there is an appropriate role for bank regulation beyond just the chartering decision. Historically, such regulation has taken the form of constraints on pricing and product mix. However, we have increasingly seen the ineffectiveness and inefficiencies of such schemes. Accordingly, there is a recent trend toward increased emphasis on capital regulation as a mechanism to offset the willingness of the insured bank to absorb risk.

5. CAPITAL REGULATION AS A LIMIT TO RISK

Capital regulation has a long history in bank supervision worldwide. It has, however, changed radically over the years. Initially, regulators hoped that one could constrain bank risk by both imposing a simple capital ratio, i.e., capital to total assets, and using moral suasion on the banking industry. However, it soon became apparent that all assets were not the same, and moral suasion was ineffective as a long-term risk-limiting technique. Accordingly, the simple ratio fell into disfavor and initial interest centered on a ratio which took at least some recognition of the assets held. This led to a move toward the use of a capital to risk asset ratio. Seeing the imprecision of this simple ratio, the New York Federal Reserve Bank in the U.S. proposed the ABC (Analysis of Bank Capital) ratio in the 1950s to recognize the different levels of risk in the bank's asset portfolio.

Since that time regulation in the U.S. has moved back and forth, proposing simple ratios with regulatory discretion, then moving to more complex ones with greater attention to some notion of portfolio risk.

Academic reaction to this regulatory procedure emphasized the crudeness of this process. Kahane (1977) and Koehn and Santomero (1980) develop an argument, known as the risk-shifting hypothesis. Banks that are forced into lower leverage will attempt to shift assets into higher risk categories in an effort to achieve an adequate return on equity. The net result is both a reduction of the return on equity and an increase in the riskiness of the underlying asset portfolio. Whether the result is an increase in the bank's failure exposure is a debatable issue. If risk aversion by bank decisionmakers is low and/or if the opportunity set available to bank investment does not substantially reward risk-taking, then such shifting tends to increase the risk of insolvency. The opposite would result under alternative conditions.

This result is caused by the combination of risk aversion on the part of decisionmakers, deposit insurance which results in the mispricing of liabilities, and limited liability for equity holders. The result is robust, except in the case where banks always and everywhere attempt to hold the riskiest portfolio allowed by law. At first, this view was met with skepticism both in the industry and in the academic literature. However, it became increasingly apparent that banks have been circumventing capital ratio requirements through a series of devices which include off-balance sheet activity, and declining asset quality.

Recognizing this clear trend toward increasing riskiness, regulators have recently proposed a shift toward a risk related system of capital adequacy BIS (1988). According to the approach developed by the bank assets are placed in several risk categories and assigned a risk weight to determine the minimum amount of equity capital which should be maintained against them. The plan is to be implemented in the U.S. and Europe, as well as Japan in two stages beginning in 1990 and becoming fully operational in December 1992. The new plan attempts to explicitly recognize the different risk characteristics of individual assets, and suggests that minimum required levels of bank equity capital depend on the riskiness of the asset portfolio.

The goal of the risk-related capital system is to require banks to use more capital to finance risky projects and to allocate capital to the support of off-balance sheet activities. The plan is thus specifically designed to counteract the asset reshuffling caused by binding capital regulation, (see Keeton (1989) for discussion). In addition, the new schedule may be viewed as an attempt to reduce the implicit increase in deposit insurance exposure associated with the risky bank's asset portfolio choice.

The idea is simple, yet elegant. Conceptually it is sound. However, it has two failings. First, the implications of such a system, even if it is accurately and exactly implemented, is a substantial shift in the flow of funds. Second, the current system is neither accurate nor exact.

To see both of these points, let us suppose that we wish to derive an optimal risk-related capital standard. How should it be done? As has been shown by Kim and Santomero (1988), one would attempt to require that the bank allocate capital to any asset in direct relationship to the net addition of that asset to the riskiness of the bank portfolio. In essence, therefore, an optimal weighting system charges for bearing risk.

Some would object to the word "charges" above. The bank is not charged; it is merely required to hold additional capital. However, if this is equity capital, the additional allocation of capital which is associated with the addition of a risky asset to the portfolio effectively increases the hurdle rate that must be achieved to maintain the market value of equity. In this sense it is truly a "charge." Such a capital allocation system will have a substantial impact on the bank's view of relative (net) prices of particular assets and accordingly alter the bank's asset demands. Variations in the equity weight across assets effectively encourage or discourage bank activity in individual markets.

It could be argued that such a shift in incentives is exactly what a risk related capital system is intended to achieve. Banks should be discouraged from an over emphasis in risky activity. The latter is encouraged by the fixed rate deposit insurance subsidies, and capital regulation offsets these distortions as discussed in Keeton (1989). There is much truth to this position. However, one should remember that a central feature of the banking system is the availability of funds to both households and business ventures. It is for this reason that banks are held to be special in the view of some, such as Gertler (1988). One must be prepared for a redirection in their flow of capital to the investing sector if the incentives for such risk-taking are reduced, as Goodman and Santomero (1986) point out in some detail. While such a realignment of risktaking incentives may be appropriate, given the recently observed level of risk in the banking industry which exploits the current insurance scheme, it strikes at the heart of our current presumptions about the role of banks in allocating credit within our society. If the funding of entrepreneurial activity along the lines suggested by Bernanke and Gertler (1989) is a casualty of regulation, it is perhaps not worth the price.

An ideal capital regulation system such as characterized above, even if desirable, however, is not likely to be the outgrowth of the current form of risk-related capital regulation. The current system is a highly imprecise, and at times totally deficient. Interest-rate risk is totally absent from this system. Book value accounting on both sides of the balance sheet remains part of the general accepted accounting practices. Credit risk is treated in the most arbitrary fashion. Finally, in the U.S. capital regulation has been extended to the holding company structure which reverses the trend towards allowing banks further autonomy in their umbrella financial entities that has been occurring for two decades in the United States.

This movement to regulate the entire holding company within which a commercial bank functions should not be taken lightly. The U.S. has long struggled with a specialized bank charter while international banks elsewhere moved toward or have been operating with the benefits of a universal banking franchise. These advantages of foreign bank structure appear substantial, as indicated in Herring and Santomero (1990). The American use of bank holding company structure for bank-related activity has been used to obtain many of these advantages of an expanded banking charter, even if they are obtained in a convoluted and inefficient manner. The recent emphasis on "source of strength" within banking institutions and the regulatory call for "firewalls" will give the banking firm and its regulators the best of both worlds, some would argue. The recent move toward holding company capital, however, should be seen as a step in the wrong direction. Rather than isolating the banking unit with the financial firm, the recent move toward capital regulation at the holding company level increases regulatory oversight and involvement. From what has transpired before, this will inevitably lead to greater implicit controls and implicit guarantees. We are making the conglomerate banking firm more special when it should be made less. It will make U.S. regulators less willing to allow their banks to expand unencumbered by regulation and give European central banks reason for more oversight and potential involvement. In the end, it is likely to lead to an extension of the regulatory umbrella at a time when it should be substantially reduced.

The most difficult problem with the current capital system, however, is the arbitrary nature of its weighting system. In the guise of reasonableness, weight categories have been imposed upon the industry with no justification or rationalization. We have moved away from a single simple-minded capital to asset ratio regime to one in which we have a series of simple-minded ratios. Each category contains a wide variance of riskiness. Interested banks could clearly manipulate the system by choosing among assets within a given category in the same way they had under the previous regime. In addition, the true risk ordering of some assets crosses the boundaries of individual categories. In several important cases, assets in one category are less risky than assets in the next higher risk classification. This issue of risk ordering is more important now than ever before. As instruments become increasingly complex and banks are allowed broader latitude, the imprecision in this regulatory framework becomes even more relevant. This structure also causes some competitive issues to arise as well. To the extent that one banking franchise permits greater latitude in a particular weight category other institutions may find themselves increasingly disadvantaged.

Cross-correlation is also ignored. The ideal system outlined above and developed from standard finance theory, e.g., Merton (1972), looks at incremental risk contributions, not simply additive ones. It is as if we have forgotten the lessons of portfolio diversification and hedging associated with our recent Nobel Laureate Harry Markowitz.

Supporters of the present system will be quick to concede that the weighting system is not perfect. They will take the "reasonable man" approach, as in Cooke (1989) or Corrigan (1987 & 1990), arguing that it is a starting point and an improvement from the previous system. This In addition,line of argument is difficult to contest. However, it is fundamentally insidious. Whether we wish to admit it or not, we are setting up an asset allocation system. We are allowing political expediency to define capital weights and, therefore, changing the desirability, from the bank's point of view, of various asset categories. It is a short step from here to asset allocation. Europe has a long history of such programs, at times disguised as prudential regulation or preferential refinancing rates, as Langohr and Santomero (1985) report. Few in the United States would argue for a broad-based implementation of such a system and it seems to violate the spirit of 1992. Nonetheless, the arbitrariness of the current system makes it quite attractive and more likely as we move into the future.

In short, the current system needs work. Resources ought to be spent on deriving optimal weights, if the current structure is to remain, rather than institutionalizing the existing rules and regulations. Some academic work has moved in this direction with work on off-balance sheet risk, e.g., Hull (1989), but more needs to be done. If better estimates are not obtainable from subsequent research, one should seriously question the advisability of the current *ad hoc* structure. At the very least, justification for existing weights should be provided.

6. ALTERNATIVES TO EFFICIENT CAPITAL REGULATION

Given the above, it can be argued that the current state of capital regulation is indeed not optimal. Difficult conceptual issues remain in deriving and estimating an exact weighting system. Further, there appears little interest in such exactness. Therefore, it seems appropriate to consider the question of whether or not alternative mechanisms exist to achieve the same end. Four proposals are currently receiving considerable attention. Let us consider the merits of each in turn.

Firstly, some have suggested that the exploitation of deposit insurance can be minimized by a structural change in the industry. Several experts have suggested that the banking firm be split up into two entities, i.e., a general financial firm, and a "narrow bank." The former would be an unconstrained financial firm. The latter would contain safe assets or at least easily verifiable assets which secure insured deposits. This proposal has been offered by Litan (1987) and the Brookings Task Force (Benston et al, 1987). Given the comments above concerning the holding company structure, it should be clear that there is much to recommend this proposal as a way to reduce insurance fund exposure. However, the reality of the political process is that such a radical shift in structure is unlikely and the Central Bank is equally unlikely to be willing to distance itself from the broader banking firm's activity. Even if these problems could be overcome, it should be clear that this solution is not perfect. Such a structural alteration would accentuate the complexity of organizational design that has become the hallmark of U.S. banking structure, without addressing the fundamental issue of the riskiness of American banks. In Europe developments are going in the opposite direction. As Herring and Santomero (1990) discuss at some length, the narrow bank proposal or some variant thereof, such as securing deposits through pledging of assets, may protect the deposit insurance fund but does not deal with bank riskiness itself. If the sole concern over the health of the banking firm is the security of insured deposits, then a "narrow bank" proposal would achieve this end. On the other hand, if the objective of capital regulation is the stability and efficiency of the banking system per se, because of its role in the financial markets, then the "narrow bank" remedy is not the ideal solution.

The second proposal, which does address the bank stability issue itself, centers on the capital ratio per se. As noted above, if banks are sufficiently capitalized, the benefits from deposit insurance mispricing are minimal. Therefore, it has been argued by Benston and Kaufman (1988) and Keeley and Furlong (1990) that banks should be encouraged to have large capitalization rates, and be allowed to engage in a full range of banking activity. There is much to recommend this proposal, too. However, it is not clear that it is a stable solution to the current debt-equity situation. Given the increasing competitiveness of the financial markets and the inherent benefit of debt, such proposals might suggest overcapitalization relative to optimal capital structure. This would result in an inferior industry structure and a relative decline of the banking sector to the benefit of other financial service competitors. While one may not decry the evolutionary decline of one subsector of the industry relative to another, unilateral changes in regulation should not be the motive force behind such evolutionary movements. Therefore, action in the direction of substantial increases in capital ratios should be prudently taken. Rose (1990) has made similar arguments.

Benston and Kaufman (1988) respond that banks could satisfy capital requirements with subordinated debt. This then would add the discipline of uninsured investors but also retain the tax benefits of debt securities. In essence, what is being proposed is *not* an increase in capital ratios, but a decline in the insured liability ratio. To the extent that secondary debt holders believe the disclaimers of the regulators, this might have the desired effect. However, there is little evidence to suggest that claims of no insurance coverage would be credible in the marketplace. In fact, existing studies of market discipline do not substantiate the claim that subordination will result in sizeable and well-behaved premiums associated with the risk of failure (Avery, Belton and Hanweck, 1988, or Gorton and Santomero (1990). Presumably this is the result of the historically accurate presumption of regulatory leniency on the part of investors. However, market perception may be changing. As major institutions in the U.S. and elsewhere have experienced asset quality declines, their debt has recently taken a substantial loss (American Banker, 1990). The market may be reassessing the vulnerability of subordinate debt to loss as well as the likelihood of real large bank failures.

A third alternative to the current dependence on capital regulation is a change in the much-discussed and now-institutionalized "too big to fail" doctrine. This approach to the handling of the regulation of large banks, although it is not clear how large one has to be, is under increasing attack. Even as some are questioning this doctrine, e.g., Seidman, (Atkinson, 1990), it should be observed that this policy causes a substantial increase in the benefits associated with leverage. Large banks in both the United States and all the major OECD countries can not fail according to current policy and, therefore, all their liability holders are de facto insured by federal regulators. This fact of life inevitably implies that many banking firms have a clear incentive to exploit their regulatory umbrella. Unquestionably, the "too big to fail" doctrine which attempts to minimize the distortion associated with dealing with an institution in crisis has accentuated the current banking problems.

As regulators debate rescinding this policy, this discussion itself has caused substantial revaluations of both the market value of bank equity, and the yield requirements of issues facing potential loss. Given the competitive nature of the markets in which banks operate, extreme care must be employed in the process of this debate. Simply put, bank debt and equity issues can not afford to sacrifice a substantial amount of stability and efficiency in the name of governmental dialogue to update regulatory policy toward insured institutions. At some point, prudent bankers may find that the costs of the bank charter outweigh its benefits, leaving only the aggressive members of their community in the industry.

What are the alternatives to implicit guarantee systems? There appear to be two. One could be the de facto guarantee of the entire banking firm, or the industry for that matter, so as to quell the most recent turmoil. It would appear, however, that there is little interest in this idea. Yet, this is the path upon which the Federal Reserve has embarked with its recent move to regulate total holding company activity. A preferable alternative is to withdraw from such activity explicitly and publicly, and restrict regulatory oversight to the banking unit of the holding company. This could be coupled with an opening up of banking-type activity to all financial firms via banking subsidiaries that are easily identifiable and regulated by existing rules and regulations. This approach (recently attributed to Toffler in Layne, 1990) seems preferable.

Finally, a fourth proposal for change has centered around the coupling of capital regulation with variable-rate deposit insurance. The argument has been made that fixed-rate insurance is the fundamental cause of bank risk-taking, as it prevents market discipline and does not price the risk borne by the insurer as in Kane (1985). Accordingly, over the last decade variable-rate deposit insurance schemes have been offered as a way to offset this adverse incentive problem. Mayer (1965) was the first to propose this, but work has advanced this idea to a potential reality as in Pennacchi (1987), Ronn and Verma (1986 and 1989) among others.

However, it should be clear that appropriate pricing of deposit insurance is an identical problem to optimal capital regulation. In the former, one needs an actuarial estimate of the riskiness of various components of the portfolio so as to price them. In the latter, one wishes to do the exact same thing so as to require capital that is consistent with the fixed-price deposit insurance program. This was the fundamental insight of Sharpe (1978). Either approach, if properly conceived and applied, will lead to appropriate risk incentives in the banking firm. However, if deposit insurance is implemented in a similar *ad hoc* fashion to risk-related capital, it is likely to further obscure market prices and efficient risk allocation. The cliche is, "two wrongs don't make a right." On the other hand, if deposit insurance pricing can be made more practical than capital regulation, it should be considered as a viable alternative. This may indeed be the case in light of the aforementioned research, as deposit insurance pricing may be implementable from financial market data, rather than balance-sheet risk judgments. At the very least, it should be given consideration on grounds of feasibility.

7. CONCLUSION AND IMPLICATIONS OF REGULATORY COMPETITION

Banks are complex firms in a highly competitive market. They perform needed services which include asset creation, payment system clearings and risk-pooling. Because of their importance, they have been given a special place in the regulatory environment and the benefit of deposit insurance. Both regulation and insurance substantially alter the market signals facing the firm. In an effort to prevent them from exploiting their position, regulators have long proposed some risk-limiting schemes such as: subjective regulation, asset restrictions and capital requirements. Given the presumed externalities provided by the industry, concerns for its health have led public policy makers to foster the notion of risk control of the banking sector. Over the last decade interest in subjective regulation and asset restrictions has waned as the externality of those regulatory devices has been observed. This has left capital regulation to be actively pursued both in the United States and to varying degrees around the world.

However, accurate capital regulation is very difficult. It requires substantial energy and exactness to efficiently offset the adverse incentives of deposit insurance without making the banking firm uncompetitive. Over the last several decades, we have moved from simple regulation to more and more complex structures. However, complexity does not imply precision. The current system, worked out within the BIS complete with *ad hoc* weights and subjective evaluation of various asset categories, is clearly not first best. Regulators must decide whether they want a serious pricing system or a politically subjective one. If they seek the former, more resources should be used to accurately estimate appropriate weighting schemes to offset adverse incentives in the current system. Such estimates could be used either for optimal capital or for variable-rate deposit insurance. The former reduces the risk exposure of the banking firm and the industry and therefore has some desirable characteristics. The latter explicitly prices risk and encourages the portfolio manager to reduce the underlying risk itself. Whether such estimates are feasibly in a political environment is another question. In the private sector, actuarial risk-taking by private insurers would, over time, generate efficient prices. Such efficiency cannot be assured in a governmental system. However, many have argued that some form of government involvement in the bank insurance system is essential, as no private insurer is large enough to credibly represent itself as guarantor.

The current posture vis-a-vis bank regulation in the EC surrounding the implementation of the Second Banking Directive is little better. Regulatory competition is an important principle within the 1992 process. Within the EC each country will be free to set regular capital requirements subject to a minimum as developed within BIS. In addition, each country will be able to insure deposits held by all banks in that country according to current plans. Will this regulatory competition provide regulators with incentives to approach an efficient regulatory system? This appears unlikely. Capital requirements regulated on a home country basis seem to provide incentives for regulators not to exceed the common minimum requirements. At the same time, if deposit insurance is regulated on a host country basis, then banks located in certain countries may have an advantage in attracting deposits. Thus, there seems to be a strong tendency towards minimizing capital requirements, while competition on deposit insurance will enable countries to differentiate insurance coverage.

Some will argue that, for the reasons listed above, an optimal capitalization system will never evolve. They, therefore, propose the dismantling of such risk-related systems in favor of either a new holding company reality or overcapitalization to minimize adverse incentives. While both approaches represent sound lines of reasoning, they each have a price. The first would require a discrete structural change in the industry and its stated regulatory umbrella. The latter may require a substantial equity infusion into the banking industry or a decline in industry assets to achieve high capital ratios. Failing to do either leaves the regulator with the difficult task of arriving at a reasonably accurate risk-weighting system to be used in either capital regulation or deposit insurance for the banking industry. None of the options are easy.

FOOTNOTE

This paper was written while the author was a Visiting Scholar at the Federal Reserve Bank of Philadelphia. An earlier version of this paper was prepared for the Board of Governors of the Federal Reserve System presentation in March 1990.

REFERENCES

American Banker (1990), May 12.

Atkinson, W. (1990), "Pressure Mounts for International Deposit Coverage," American Banker, September 27.

Avery, R.B., T. M. Belton, and M. A. Golaberg (1988), "Market Discipline in Regulating Bank Risk: New Evidence From Capital Markets", Journal of Money, Credit, and Banking, 20 November, 597-610.

Bank for International Settlements (1988), "International Convergence of Capital Measurement and Capital Standards," July.

Benston, G. J., and C. W. Smith, Jr. (1976), "A Transaction Cost Approach to the Theory of Financial Intermediation." Journal of Finance, 31, May, 215-31.

Benston, George, et al.(1987), <u>A Blueprint for Restructuring America's Financial Institutions</u>, Brookings, Washington, D.C.

Benston, G., R. Eisenbeis, P. Horvitz, E. Kane and G. Kaufman (1986), <u>Safe and Sound Banking: Past, Present and Future</u>, MIT Press, Cambridge, MA.

Benston, G. J. and G. G. Kaufman (1988), <u>Risk and Solvency Regulation of Depository Institutions: Past Policies and Current Options</u>, Salomon Brothers Center for the Study of Financial Institutions, New York, Monograph 1988-1.

Bernanke, B. and M. Gertler (1989), "Agency Costs, Net Worth, and Business Fluctuations," <u>American Economic Review</u>, 79, March, 14-31.

Black, F. (1975), "Bank Funds Management in an Efficient Market," <u>Journal of Financial Economics</u>, 2,323-339.

Board of Governors of the Federal Reserve System (1990), <u>Flow of Funds Accounts</u>, First Quarter.

Buser, S., A. Chen, and E. Kane (1981), "Federal Deposit Insurance, Regulatory Policy, and Optimal Bank Credit," <u>Journal of Finance</u>, 36, March, 51-60.

Campbell, T. and W. Kracaw (1980), "Information Production, Market Signalling, and the Theory of Financial Intermediation," <u>Journal of Finance</u>, Vol. 35, September, 863-82.

Chandler, L. V., and S. M. Goldfeld (1977), <u>The Economics of Money and Banking</u>, Harper and Row, New York.

Cooke, P. (1989), "Recent Developments in the Prudential Regulation of Banks and the Evolution of International Supervisory Regulation," Joint Universities' Conference on Regulating Commercial Banks, Australian Experience in Perspective, August.

Corrigan, E. G. (1987), "Financial Market Structure: A Longer View," Federal Reserve Bank of New York <u>Annual Report</u>, 1-10.

_____ (1990), "Perspectives on Payment System Risk Reduction," in <u>the U.S. Payment System: Efficiency, Risk and the Role of the Federal Reserve</u>, D. Humphrey, (ed.), Kluwer Academic Publishers, Boston.

Crouchy, M. and D. Galai (1986), "An Economic Assessment of Capital Requirements in the Banking Industry," <u>Journal of Banking and Finance</u>, 10, June, 231-42.

Diamond, D., and P. Dybvig (1983), "Bank Runs, Deposit Insurance, and Liquidity," <u>Journal of Political Economy</u>, 91, 401-419.

Diamond, D. (1984), "Financial Intermediation and Delegated Monitoring," <u>Review of Economic Studies</u>, 51, July, 393-414.

_____ (1989), "Reputation Acquisition in Debt Markets", <u>Journal of Political Economy</u>, Vol. 97, No. 4, August, 828-862.

Fama, E. F. (1970), "Efficient Capital Markets: A Review of Theory and Empirical Work, <u>Journal of Finance</u>, 25.

_____ (1980), "Banking in the Theory of Finance", <u>Journal of Monetary Economics</u>, 6, January, 39-57.

Fama, E.F. (1985), "What's Different About Banks?", Journal of Monetary Economics, 15, January, 29-30.

Flannery, M. J. (1985), "A Portfolio View of Loan Selection and Pricing," Handbook for Banking Strategy, R. Aspenwall and R. Eisenbies (ed.), J. Wiley & Sons.

_____ (1989), "Capital Regulation and Insured Banks' Choice of Individual Loan Default Risks," Journal of Monetary Economics, 21, 235-258.

Furash, E. (1987), "Make Your Bank a Special Place," Texas Banking, January.

Furlong, F. and M. Keeley (1987), "Bank Regulation and Asset Risk," Federal Reserve Bank of San Francisco Economic Review, Spring, 20-40.

Gertler, M. (1988), "Financial Structure and Aggregate Economic Activity: An Overview," Journal of Money, Credit, and Banking, 20, August, 559-596.

Goodman, L. and A. Santomero (1986), "Variable Rate Deposit Insurance: A Reexamination," Journal of Banking and Finance, 10, June, 203-218.

Gorton, G. and A. Santomero (1990), "Market Discipline and Bank Subordinated Debt," Journal of Money, Credit, and Banking, 22, February, 119-128.

Greenbaum, S.I. and A.V. Thakor (1987), "Bank Funding Modes: Securtization versus deposits." Journal of Banking and Finance, 11, No. 3, 379-402.

Greenspan, A. (1990), "Testimony Before Congressional Banking Committee", July 12.

Hart, O. and D. Jaffee (1974), "On the Application of Portfolio Theory to Depository Financial Intermediaries," Review of Economic Studies, 41, January, 129-147.

Herring, R. and P. Vankudre (1987), "Growth Opportunities and Risk-Taking by Financial Intermediaries," Journal of Finance, 42, July, 583-600.

Herring, R. J. and A. Santomero (1990), "The Corporate Structure of Financial Conglomerates," Journal of Financial Services Research, December.

Hull, J. (1989), "Assessing Credit Risk in Financial Institutions Off-Balance Sheet Commitments," Journal of Financial and Quantitative Analysis, December.

Jensen, M. C. and W. H. Meckling (???), "Theory of the Firm: Managerial Behavior, Agency Costs, and Ownership Structure," Journal of Financial Economics, No. 3, 305-360.

Kahane, Y. (1977), "Capital Adequacy and the REgulation of Financial Intermediaries," Journal of British Finance, No. 2, 207-217.

Kane, E. (1985), The Gathering Crisis in Federal Deposit Insurance, MIT Press, Cambridge, MA, 1985

Karaken, J.H. and N. Wallace (1978), "Deposit Insurance and Bank Regulation: A Partial Equilibrium Exposition," Journal of Business, 51, 413-488.

Keeley, M.C. and F.T. Furlong (1990), "A Reexamination of Mean Variance Analysis of Bank Capital Regulation," Journal of Banking and Finance, 14, March, 69-84.

Keeton, W.R. (1989), "The New Risk-Based Capital Plan for Commercial Banks," Federal Reserve Bank of Kansas City Economic Review, December, 40-60.

Kim, D. and A. Santomero (1988), "Risk in Banking and Capital Regulation," Journal of Finance, 43, December, 1219-1234.

Klein, M. (1973), "The Economics of Security Divisibility and Financial Intermediation," Journal of Finance, September.

Koehn, M. and A. Santomero (1980), "Regulation of Bank Capital and Portfolio Risk," Journal of Finance, 35, December, 1234-1244.

Langohr, H. and A. Santomero (1984), "The Impact of Equity in Bank Portfolios," Proceedings of a Conference on Bank Structure and Competition, Federal Reserve Bank of Chicago, April.

_____ (1985), "Commercial Bank Refinancing and Economic Stability: An Analysis of European Features, Journal of Banking and Finance, December.

Layne, R. (1980), "In Toffler's Crystal Call, Banks Have Rough Future", American Banker, October 25, 2.

Leland, H. and D. Pyle (1977), "Informational Asymmetries, Financial Structure and Financial Intermediation," Journal of Finance, 32, May, 371-387.

Litan, R. (1987), What Should Banks Do?, Brookings, Washington, D.C.

Marcus, A. (1984), "Deregulation and Bank Financial Policy," Journal of Banking and Finance, 8, 557-565

Mayer, T. (1965), "A Graduated Deposit Insurance Plan," Review of Economics and Statistics.

Merton, R.C. (1972), "An Analytic Derivation of the Efficient Portfolio Frontier," Journal of Financial and Quantitative Analysis, December, 1851-72.

_____ (1977), "An Analytic Derivation of the Cost of Deposit Insurance and Loan Guarantees: An Application of Modern Option Pricing Theory," Journal of Banking and Finance, 1, June, 3-11

_____ (1978), "On the Cost of Deposit Insurance when There are Surveillance Costs," Journal of Business, 51, July, 439-452.

Mester, L. (1990), "Traditional and Non-traditional Banking: An Information Theoretic Approach," Federal Reserve Bank of Philadelphia Working Paper 90-3.

Miller, M. (1977), "Debt and Taxes," Journal of Finance, 32, May, 261-275.

Miller, M. and F. Modigliani (1961), "Dividend Policy, Growth, and the Valuation of Shares," Journal of Business, 34, October, 411-433.

Modigliani, F. and M. Miller (1958), "The Cost of Capital, Corporation Finance, and the Theory of Investment," American Economic Review, 48, June, 261-297.

Orgler, Y.E. and R. A. Taggart, Jr. (1983), "Implications of Corporate Capital Structure Theory for Banking Institutions," Journal of Money, Credit and Banking, May, Vol. 15, 212-21.

Penati, A. and A. Protopapadakis (1988), "The Effect of Implicit Deposit Insurance on Banks' Portfolio Choices with an Application to International 'Overexposure'," Journal of Monetary Economics, 21, 107-126.

Pennacchi, G. (1987), "A Reexamination of the Over-(or Under-) Pricing of Deposit Insurance," Journal of Money, Credit, and Banking, 19, August, 340-360.

_____ (1988), "Loan Sales and the Cost of Bank Capital," Journal of Finance, 43, June, 375-396.

Ronn, E. and A. Verma (1986), "Pricing Risk-Adjusted Deposit Insurance: An Option-Based Model." Journal of Finance 41, September, 871-95.

_____ (1989), "Risk-Based Capital Adequacy Standards for a Sample of 43 Major Banks," Journal of Banking and Finance, 13, 21-29:

Rose, S. (1990), "Why Banking is a Zero-Sum Game," American Banker, August 21.

Ross, S. A. (1973), "The Economic Theory of Agency: The Principal's Problem", Papers and Proceedings of the American Economic Association, 85, May, 134-39.

Santomero, A. (1983), Current Views of the Bank Capital Issue, Association of Reserve City Bankers, Washington, D.C.

_____ (1984), "Modeling the Banking Firm," Journal of Money, Credit, and Banking, 16, November, 576-616.

_____ (1986), "How Bankers Can Bank on the Future," Issues The Journal for Management, PA International, London.

_____ (1989), "The Changing Structure of Financial Institutions," Journal of Monetary Economics, 24, September.

_____ (1988), "The Intermediation Process and the Future of the Thrifts," Expanding Competitive Markets and the Thrift Industry, 13th Annual Conference of the Federal Home Loan Bank of San Francisco.

_____ (1991), "The Evolving View of Banking Theory and Regulation," Capital Markets' Recent Developments, Informacion Comercial Espanola.

Sealey, C. W. (1983), "Valuation, Capital Structure and Shareholder Unanimity Depository FinancialIntermediaries," Journal of Finance, 38, June, 857-71.Schaefer, Sherrill, "A Revenue-Restricted Cost Study of 100 Large Banks," Federal Reserve Bank of New York, February 1990.

Sharpe, W. (1978), "Bank Capital Adequacy, Deposit Insurance, and Security Values," Journal of Financial and Quantitative Analysis, 13, November, 701-718.

Smith, B. D. (1984), "Private Information, Deposit Interest Rates, and the Stability of the Banking System." Journal of Monetary Economics, 14, November, 294-318.

Smith, P.F. (1971), Economics of Financial Institutions and Markets, Richard D. Irwin, Inc., Homewood, IL.

Williamson, S.D. (1986), "Costly Monitoring, Financial Intermediation and Equilibrium Credit Rationing," Journal of Monetary Economics, Sept, Vol. 18, No. 2, 159-180.

Financial Regulation and Monetary Arrangements after 1992
C. Wihlborg, M. Fratianni and T.D. Willett (Editors)

4 The Structure and Future of the Insurance Market

Göran Skogh

Department of Economics, School of Economics and Management, Lund University, P.O. Box 7082, S-220 07 Lund, Sweden

1. INTRODUCTION

It is no easy task to forecast the development of insurance in Europe after 1992. One reason is the lack of an institutional theory of insurance. The traditional theory of risk-aversion and risk-pooling does not give much guidance on these matters - it explains why risk-averse individuals demand diversification, but it has little to say about the institutions in financial markets or about the details of insurance contracts.

The institutional theory of financial intermediation first discussed by Benston and Smith (1976) and by Leland and Pyle (1977) has been applied mainly to banks.[1] Skogh (1991) shows that this theory provides a fruitful framework for the study of the insurance industry as well. Before discussing the future of the insurance market in Europe we will summarize the generalized institutional theory and use it as a framework for the discussion of the future common European insurance market.[2] First we present the institutional theory of financial intermediation. Next we discuss certain common features of bank guarantees together with various insurance policies. A general conclusion is that collateral, guarantees and insurance may be complements. The differences between guarantors and creditors carrying credit risk and insurers are due to the type of risk (e.g. insolvency, fire, transport or third party liability) and customers in which they specialize.[3] Thereafter I discuss the future European insurance market.

2. THE INSTITUTIONAL APPROACH TO BANKING

The institutional approach to financial intermediation presumes the existence of transactions costs (Benston and Smith, 1976). Namely, if no transaction costs were present, borrowers and lenders could transact directly and avoid the costs of intermediation. Leland and Pyle (1977) distinguish between direct transaction costs (costs of identifying lenders and borrowers and of administering the transaction of financial assets) and costs due to asymmetric information.

Leland and Pyle demonstrate the importance of informational asymmetries in a model of capital structure and financial equilibrium in which entrepreneurs seek to finance projects, the true qualities of which are known only to entrepreneurs. An entrepreneur's willingness to invest own funds in the project serves as a signal of project quality (Spence,

1974). As a consequence, the market value of the firm increases with the share of the firm held by the entrepreneur.[4]

Leland and Pyle also suggest that, in a world of asymmetric information and economies of scale, one might expect to observe organizations that gather and sell information. However, the properties of information may make it difficult for firms to profit from obtaining and selling information directly to investors or creditors. One reason is that some information is transaction-specific and hence is not easily traded (Williamson, 1979). For instance, the creditor in the Leland and Pyle example may have a long-term relation (repeated dealings) with the entrepreneur, which gives the creditor a comparative advantage in supervising the entrepreneur - an advantage not easily transferred to others. Another reason is that information is a public good; a firm selling information may therefore not be able to appropriate enough of its value to cover the costs of obtaining it. Reliability of the seller is a third obstacle to direct sales of information. Specifically, it may be difficult for potential buyers to distinguish good information from bad. This is the problem of Akerlof (1970); under it, the price of information should reflect average quality, and firms that expend resources to collect information may end up with losses.

These informational obstacles may be overcome if the information-gathering firm becomes an intermediary, using its specialized information to choose the assets it holds. The problems of transaction specificity, appropriability, and reliability are solved to the extent the firm's information is captured indirectly by the return it earns on its portfolio.

3. SECURITY BY COLLATERAL, GUARANTEES AND INSURANCE

3.1 Collateral

We argue that the institutional approach summarized above can be applied also to insurance. The differences between banks, guarantors, and insurers are due to the type of risks and customers in which they specialize. The approach can also explain the demand for combinations of financial services including collateral, guarantee and insurance.

To simplify the understanding we consider first a situation in which two traders, A and B contract on a risky project. The problem is of quite general nature. We may think, for instance, of an investment in which A is the entrepreneur and B is the creditor. Alternatively, we may think of sharecropping. Yet a third possibility is that A produces and markets a dangerous good to B, who is the buyer. In this section we couch the narrative in the dangerous good case.

Asymmetric information prevails in that B cannot identify precautions and safety controls taken by A. To establish an incentive for A to care, A is made liable of accidents. A financial problem arises because of the risk, and because the collectable assets of A are limited. The limited collectability reduces the incentive to take care. Hence an inefficiency arises when liability is limited or the claim cannot be collected.

We assume that A and B are risk-neutral. The assumption simplifies the analysis and emphasises the difference between the current theory and the traditional approach to insurance.

The collectable amount depends, among other things, on competing claims at a loss. Other claims may have a higher legal priority. The expected collectable amount also depends on costs of collecting claims. These costs may be high, for instance, if A and B are strangers that do not expect to trade with each other again; in such cases, A would have no incentive to compensate B ex post for a loss. The level of legally enforceable liability may also be unclear and the liable party may be hard to find. Indeed, A may sometimes be able to avoid paying damages even if A has substantial assets.

The parties may therefore end up with a project of low value, or with no contract and hence no project at all. A way out of the dilemma may be for A to offer collateral, that is, an asset reserved to ensure payment. "Collateral" in this sense should be interpreted broadly. For instance, a home mortgage effectively provides collateral. The purpose of collateral is to increase the expected collectable amount.[5] Collateral that increases the collectable amount increases the value of the project. If the collectable amount is increased to the level where all potential claims are fully compensated the precautions taken by A will be optimal.

3.2 Guarantees

A guarantee is a contract that transfers a risk to an external risk-carrier known as a guarantor (G). Contracts often require guarantees and/or collateral. This section compares a guarantee with collateral - a guarantee can increase the value of a contract in much the same way as collateral does.

One reason why a guarantee may increase the value of a project is that G may be able to collect more from A than B (the victim) can. For instance, G may be specialized in claims collection. G may also be able to collect more from A if G has a long-term relation to A, which B does not have. Assume, for instance, that A and B do not trade repeatedly. A would than have no incentive to compensate B voluntarily, which can make the collectable amount small. G, on the other hand, may be able to extract more from A because G trades repeatedly with A. Hence, the guarantee has the same function as collateral - it increases A's expected costs and thus the level of care taken by A.

Another reason why a guarantee may increase the value of the project is that G has some information about A that B does not have. We assume asymmetric information in that A but not B knows the care taken by A. It is conceivable, however, that some third party knows something more about A's behavior. The third party may be a business partner, a relative, or a bank that knows A relatively well and has information about A's business. Assume that G is this third party. Assume also that G is able to price marginal changes in the control taken by A. In this case, the guarantor may steer A's choice of care.

In sum, a guarantee may increase the value of a project if the guarantor has a comparative advantage in claims collection or specific information that enables the guarantor to influence that care be taken. A guarantee also can be seen as an alternative to repeated dealings - repeated dealings do not solve the credibility problem if the expected value of continued trade remains small relative to the claim of a loss.[6]

3.3 Insurance

An insurance contract is very close to a guarantee. In fact, the guarantee above is equivalent to an insurance contract in which A pays a premium and the insurer compensates for losses. To increase the value of the project, the insurer must have a comparative advantage in collecting claims and/or must have some information on the care taken by A. Insurers also gather information on the expected loss and on the control taken. In a perfect world in which the insurer knows the marginal impact of the control, the insurer can steer A's behavior by conditions in the policy and by varying premiums (Shavell 1979).

The demand for a transfer of the risk to an external guarantor/insurer arises because the potential loss is large and because the insurer/guarantor has a comparative advantage in obtaining information about the risky project and about the party that directly controls the value of the project. Risk-aversion does not change this result. When the liable party is riskaverse, the guarantee/insurance has the joint benefit of increasing the value of the project and eliminating the disutility due to risk bearing.

4. SPECIALIZATION IN CERTAIN RISKS AND CUSTOMERS

4.1 Creditors and Equity-holders

All projects include many risks that influence the expected value of a project, and there are usually large losses that one single party is not able to cover. When contracting on the liablities the parties must therefore distribute risks on various risk-bearers. We argue that risks will be accepted by the party specialized in the specific type of risk.

In addition, the risk-bearer must be credible. There must be no doubt that the risk-bearer has sufficient funds to indemnify the loss, and the parties must trust that the risk-bearer fulfills commitments.

A guarantor must be relatively well informed about the credit risk and/or have a comparative advantage in the collection of claims. This helps explain why banks often act as guarantors. Banks usually have sufficient funds to cover losses, and banks may be able to diversify risks by choices of portfolios. As a creditor, a bank can collect from the debtor to the limit set by bankruptcy. The creditor is also a residual claimant if the debtor becomes insolvent and thus the creditor has an incentive to gather and use information to steer the debtor's activities. The behavior of the debtor may be influenced, for instance by varying interest rates and amortization schedules. The bank may also require that the customer's books be audited and that the bank be represented on the board of the debtor's firm.

The information collected by the guarantor appears to be transaction-specific. The issuing of guarantees is therefore primarily a small-scale business. The guarantor may be a local bank, an employer, a relative, or some other party with specific local or personal information about the debtor and also with some power to collect claims. This may partly explain why banks often specialize in dealing with specific customers such as households, farmers, or branches of industries.

Note that the equity of a firm has roughly the same function as a guarantee. If A is an entrepreneur with limited assets and hence liability, the value of a project may increase if equity is added, as in Leland and Pyle (1977). If the entrepreneur adds equity, this equity functions like collateral. If external stock-holders add to equity, they act as guarantors of the liabilities of the entrepreneur.[7] To increase the value of the firm, the external equity-holders typically require influence on the behavior of the entrepreneur, as it is done through voting rights and through transactions in the stock market (Jensen and Meckling, 1976).

4.2 Property and Liability Insurance

Let us now compare the banking industry with the property and liability insurance industry. The industries differ in important respects even though both industries provide financial intermediation. Banks specialize in various business risks that are usually not insured by property and liability insurance firms. Moreover, while the comparative advantage in bearing credit risks appears to be due to specific (small scale) information on customers and their businesses, property and liability insurers appear to utilize economies of scale by specializing in a specific risks such as fire, storm, traffic accidents, and third party liability.

A characteristic of such risks is that there are a large number of low probability loss-events. The traders and/or guarantors in a given commercial business usually have little detailed information on such risks. The existence of a separate property and liability insurance industry appears to be partly due to economies of scale in the gathering of information on such low probability events. By insuring a large number of similar projects, the insurer obtains information on the actuarial relation between damages, the presence of safety devices, levels of deductibles, and costs of various claim settlement procedures. To capture most of the value from gathering actuarial information, it is helpful to keep the information secret and/or to have a large market share. The insurer also needs to be large enough to diversify the risks it holds. The size of the immediate pool is not decisive, however, when re-insurance is available.

Accident risks involving water, storm, traffic, and fire have much in common; their claims-adjustment procedures are similar. The common features and similarities in claims adjustment are an important source of economies of scale. It is thus not surprising that these risks are often insured by the same insurer. It is often advantageous to transact a whole bundle of contingencies to the insurer by the purchase of a single property and liability policy, because this reduces contracting costs.

The reliability problem also appears to help explain why insurers accept such risks and thus act as intermediaries. For instance, assume that a risk-management expert sells information directly to A and B on how to draw up a contract. The reliability of information provided by the risk-management expert may be low because of the low probability of each event, which makes it difficult to assess the information. The risk-manager may therefore signal quality by accepting the risk. This might involve payment to the risk-manager of an ex ante premium that covered expected claims, but such a contract is in essence an insurance contract.

A risk-manager who does not want to become a residual claimant must signal reliability in some other way. One possibility may be to sell information repeatedly to a limited number of customers such as to large firms with a relatively large number of similar accidents, or to insurers that are able to judge the quality of the information.

4.3 Trade-Credit Insurance

It is also of interest to compare guarantors and trade-credit insurers.[8] Both cover credit risks but the two industries differ considerably. The trade-credit industry is organized on a large scale, often with only a few firms in each country, while many guarantors are smaller firms or individuals. Moreover, trade-credit insurers typically insure all of a firm's customer-claims, while the guarantor selects specific credit risks to cover. Here we provide a tentative explanation of these differences.

In most manufacturing industries, payment is made some time after delivery with a credit length varying from several weeks to a year or more. If the selling firm is unable to separate good and bad risks and thus charges the same (average) risk premium for all post-payments, the firm may end up with losses. The selling firm may in principle collect information to ferret out such bad risks. However, many selling firms are specialized in other activities and have limited experience with credit-risk assessments. Credible guarantors who are willing to cover risks at reasonable costs might not be available, especially if: (i) claims are relatively small; (ii) there are many customers; and/or (iii) customers are unknown, which may be the case, for instance, with exports.

Exposure to trade-credit risk may also induce a desire to pool. Pooling may be simple if the selling firm is a publicly traded corporation with diffuse ownership; owners can then merely adjust their portfolios. The same is true if the portfolio of claims of customers consists of many relatively small and independent claims. Pooling may be difficult, however, if customer claims are large and/or dependent. Small firms with large customer claims and firms with risk-averse owners (or employees) who are unable to diversify risks may therefore demand external pooling.

Scale economies stem from the public-good nature of information. The insolvency risk of one firm is of interest to all of its creditors, so a large insurance firm insuring several creditors of each debtor/buyer will receive a greater return to information on a debtor than would a small insurer. Such information may be purchased by the trade-credit insurer from local guarantors with specific information about debtors.

Another source of scale economies is from possible adverse selection by the insured. That is, the seller may have information about the insolvency risks of its customers that is not available to the insurer. It may therefore be profitable for the seller to insure only bad risks. To reduce this adverse selection, insurers typically require that the seller not exclude any part of its trade-credit portfolio from insurance (Karrer, 1957). The insurer may, however, exclude some risks from insurance coverage.

The different sources of scale economies and the benefits of joint production of pooling, risk-assessment, and claims-collection appear to explain the concentration and specialization in the trade-credit-insurance industry. In many countries, there is one or only a few large trade-credit insurers (Briggs & Edwards, 1988). Internationally, trade-credit insurers cooperate via the International Credit Insurance Association. They exchange credit information, they cooperate in claims collection services, and they reinsure.

The trade-credit-insurance industry covers credit risks only, which is in contrast to property and liability firms that supply policies that cover a variety of accident risks. Karrer (1957) explains this by the specific nature of credit risks as compared with accident risks. However, within the credit risk business there are no sharp borders. Trade-credit insurers often act also as guarantors of various industrial projects, here in competition with banks. Some trade-credit insurers also sell credit information and claims collection services separately.

Separate rating bureaus, risk-managers, and claims collectors sell information on credit risks, partly in competition with insurers, and partly with insurers as customers. Journals publish easy to collect information. A reason why there is a market for such publicly accessible information may be that firms can sort, present, and interpret publicly available information in a way that is valuable to specific readers or customers. In the US, there are large rating bureaus with well established reputations. The explanation may be that separate functions like risk-assessment, lending, collection, and risk-bearing can be separated by a specialized firm, and that a reputation can be established without being an intermediary.

4.4 Life Insurance

The specific nature of mortality and disability risks may for the same reason account for the separation of life insurance into a separate line of business. One obstacle that is encountered in the assessment of mortality rates is that of asymmetric information. The insured often knows more than the insurer does about his/her own health status. This asymmetry increases when the insured person gets older. As long as the insured is relatively young, expected claims may be calculated from observable factors such as age, sex, health characteristics etc, which explains why mostlife-insurance and pension-schemes are based om long-term contracts. The long-term contracts contribute to the accumulation of a large fund, which is normally administered by the insurer and controlled by the authorities.

Claim settlement is simple relative to property and liability insurance. There is usually no question regarding whether a person is dead or has reached a certain age. Hence, there would not seem to be any considerable transaction-specific considerations in claim adjustment as, for instance, there are in the case of fire or liability insurance. The actuarial information on death rates is mainly of a public good nature, which indicates certain economies of scale. Moreover, the demand for similar policies by a large number of persons explains why large insurers produce highly standardized life-insurance policies.

The seller or broker of life insurance obtains, on the other hand, highly private information about the customer. Hence there would appear to be considerable scale diseconomies in marketing and distribution, which may explain the existence of more or less independent sellers and brokers operating on a small scale.

5. THE FUTURE

The institutional theory presented above is supported by the fact that the financial industry is organized in branches such as guarantors (banks) covering business risks, credit insurance, property and liability insurance and life-insurance. This structure is about the same in all market-oriented systems, independent of the regulatory system in a specific country. Hence the informational asymmetries related to the risk in question appear to have an important explanatory value.

This tends to suggest that types of business such as credit, property and liability, and life insurance will remain after the introduction of a common regulatory system in Europe. Basic functions such as risk-assessment and claims adjustment will presumably also be jointly produced as before. This is not to say that these different types of insurance services will be organized in the same legal entities as before. There is a large number of possible combinations of ownership, joint-ventures, and other contractual arrangements in a market where branches are separated by regulation.

Note that economies of scale in specific parts of the financial service industry is not a sufficient condition for a movement towards an industry where these are only very large firms. Scale economies may be utilized by contract. Re-insurance represents, for instance, a well established method of utilising the scale economies in pooling. Similarly, standardized distribution net-works can be organized by joint-ventures, and standardized contracts and the gathering of public actuarial information may be produced by branch organizations. Hence there are grounds to believe that specialized independent, small and medium sized firms will continue to co-exist with large conglomerates.

Presumably we will see substantial changes in future distribution and marketing systems. There is a trend towards most simplified and standardized forms of distibution. Travel agencies sell travel and traffic insurance over the counter together with tickets, while banks sell life insurance by the distribution of simple forms. In many situations, however, the financial decision is complicated. An industrial investor, or a household planning over its life-cycle may consider loans secured by collateral, risky loans, guarantees, together with savings and insurance for the above reasons. The customer therefore demands qualified and transaction-specific advice. The financial distribution system will be organized to meet this demand.

This does not mean that all financial services must be sold and produced by the same intermediary. The custom-related distribution and marketing systems are often separated from the large risk-bearing firms. This may be due to the prevalence of diseconomies. When selling insurance to a household, the adviser/insurer obtains access to private information and must therefore have a personal relation to the customer. Similarly, the party taking a credit risk needs custom-specific information.

Advisory services and marketing may be provided by independent brokers, by agents for one or several intermediaries, by local subsidiaries, or by sales departments fully integrated within the financial intermediary. The independent broker is able to make a free choice among the products of the market, while an agent may have the benefit of using, for instance, the distribution network of a bank. A problem for the broker or consultant may be the need to appear reliable. The agent of an intermediary or an integrated sales department is, on the other hand, biased in favor of his own firm.

A conclusion which may be drawn is that the general industry structure will presumably not be changed by the harmonized regulations within Europe. The different categories of business will remain, and the changes in ownership structure and distribution systems will continue, independently of the EC directives.

The early, and so far most far-reaching, directives towards an internal European insurance market concern re-insurance, co-insurance and the insurance of large risks. However, these parts of the insurance business have been international for decades. It is thus not surprising that the member States could reach an agreement in these areas. On the other hand, the impact of the directive is not very great. Reaching agreements on the directives concerned with mass risks has been shown to be more complicated, partly because consumer property and liability as well life insurance have been protected nationally.

National legislation and a number of obstacles to a free market in financial services will nevertheless continue to exist. However, in the long run, it will presumably become a reality. What will then happen? The huge demand for similar consumer policies, and the economies of scale in standardization indicates that we will end up with home, liability, traffic and life policies harmonized with EC legislation. The policies will thus to a large extent become European, while the marketing and claims adjustment will remain national. Scale economies will be utilized in large European firms, while the sales and claims adjustment activities may remain in small or medium size firms, either as intermediaries or consultants and brokers who do not themselves bear any risk.

6. CONCLUSION

The different firms and types of business in the financial service industry differ due to the risks and customers in which they specialize. The presence of scale economies versus diseconomies appears also to be related to risks and customers. The transaction-specific information held by guarantors cannot easily be traded, which may explain why guarantors usually operate as an intermediary, and on a small scale in their contacts with customers. The property and liability insurance industry specializes, on the other hand, in accident risks. Economies of scale in the gathering of information on the low- probability events insured by property-liability firms partly explains the relative large scale of such firms. The trade-credit insurance industry is also primarily a large-scale business. The trade-credit insurer utilizes scale economies in the gathering of general credit-risk information on a large number of debtors. Life-insurers, on the other hand, specialize in the assessment of mortality risk and in the administration of large funds. The public nature of actuarial information and the huge demand for similar contracts give rise to considerable economies in this part of the business.

We expect the structure of the insurance industry not to change, at least as far as the risk-assessment and claims-settlement is concerned. The co-existence of large concerns selling several various financial services, medium size intermediaries and small firm will continue. Future distribution systems will presumably be segmented. One part will be strongly standardized and simplified, while another part will be oriented towards customers who need specific advice on complicated financial matters that often include collaterals, guarantees and insurances. The transaction specific nature of these services suggests that it will remain decentralized.

The creation of an internal European market will be of minor importance for the re-insurance and large risk - markets which are already international. The impact will be larger in the consumer insurance markets where we will presumably create highly standardized European insurance policies, marketed and claims-adjusted in national markets.

FOOTNOTES

1. E.G. Stiglitz and Weiss (1981), Diamond (1984), Diamond and Dybvig (1986) and Fama (1990), Smith and Warner (1979) and Mayers and Smith (1981, 1982, 1987) and Main (1982,1983) compare insurance with other forms of financial intermediation. They argue that risk-aversion alone cannot explain the corporate demand for insurance. They suggest that the comparative advantage of the insurance industry is in claims and administration services and in assistance on safety and maintenance projects. Skogh (1989a) argues that contractors' transaction costs may be a rationale for insurance. Mian and Smith (1989) study the management of trade credits, the demand for credit, factoring, and credit insurance. Goldberg (1988) treats collateral, guarantees, and insurance as alternatives in a discussion of accountants' liability.

2. "The Geneva Papers on Risk and Insurance" has given the permission to summarize Skogh (1991).

3. The analysis is limited to risk-bearing, although most financial intermediaries produce other services as well.

4. Informational asymmetries thus explain why the value of a firm varies with the debt-equity ratio. This is in contrast with the result of Modigliani and Miller (1958), who showed that the financial structure of a firm

has no impact on the firm's value, given a capital market without direct transaction costs or asymmetric information.

5. Collateral may not only increase the collectable amount but also the probability that a given amount can be collected. However, as we assume risk neutral traders, only the expected collected amount matters here.

6. Note that the argument for a guarantee is similar to the argument for vicarious liability in tort-law (Sykes, 1984, and Shavell, 1986). That is, a "judgement-proof" problem arises when a party that has been found legally liable is unable to pay fully the claim. Someone else - for instance, an employer - may then be held vicariously liable. This can be efficiency-increasing because the employer observes the employee continuously and has power to reward or to dismiss the employee. Parents are for the same reason often liable for damages caused by their children. Similarly, professional associations and branch organizations with the power to exclude and control members may be willing to guarantee the services of their members (Skogh, 1989b). Such transfers or risks to third parties that may influence the behavior of the liable party are common.

7. The liability of stock-holders in corporation is obviously limited to the value of equity.

8. Factoring is nearly the same as trade-credit insurance, if defaulted claims are not recoursed to the creditor. Such non-recourse factoring is relatively frequent in the US (Mian and Smith, 1989).

REFERENCES

Akerlof, G. (1970), "The Market for 'Lemons': Qualitative uncertainty and the market mechanism", Quarterly Journal of Economics, Vol 84, 488-500

Alchian, A.A., and H. Demsetz (1972), "Production, information costs, and economic organization", American Economic Review, 62 December): 777-95.

Benston, G.J. and C.W. Smith Jr. (1976), "A Transactions Cost Approach to the Theory of Financial Intermediation", The Journal of Finance, vol.31, no 2, 215-231

Benston, G.J., G.A. Hanweck and D.B. Humphrey (1982), "Scale Economics in Banking: A Restructuring and Reassessment", The Journal of Money, Credit and Banking, 14:4, 435-456.

Briggs, D and B. Edwards (1988), Credit Insurance. How to reduce the risks of trade credit, Woodhead-Faulkner.

Diamond, D.W. (1984), "Financial Intermediation and Delegated Monitoring", Review of Economic Studies, Vol LI, 393-414.

Diamond, D.W. and P.H. Dybvig (1986), "Banking Theory, Deposit Insurance and Bank Regulation", The Journal of Business, vol. 59, no.1, 55-68.

Faith, R.L. & R.D. Tollison (1981), "Contractual Exchange and the Timing of Payment", Journal of Economic Behaviour and Organization, Vol 1, 325-342.

Fama, E.F. (1990), "Contract Costs and Financing decision", The Journal of Business, No 1:2, 75-91.

Goldberg, V. (1988), "Accountable Accountants: Are Third-Party Liability Necessary?" The Journal of Legal Studies, vol 17, 295-311.

Jensen, M.C & W.H. Meckling (1976), "Theory of the Firm: Manageral Behaviour, Agency Costs and Ownership Structure", Journal of Financial Economics, no 3, 305-60.

Karrer, H. (1957), <u>Elements of Credit Insurance</u>. An International Survey. Sir Isaac Pitman & Sons, Ltd, London.

Leland, H. & Pyle, D. (1977), "Informational Asymmetries, Financial Structure, and Financial Intermediation", <u>Journal of Finance</u>, Vol 32, 371-387.

Main, B.G. (1982), "Business Insurance and Large, Widely-held Corporations", <u>The Geneva Papers on Risk and Insurance</u>, 237-247.

Main, B.G. (1983), "Why Large Corporations Purchase Property/Liability Insurance", <u>California Management Review</u>, Vol. XXV, no. 2, 84-95.

Mayers, D. and C. W. Smith Jr. (1981), "Contractual Provisions, Organizational Structure, and Conflict Control in Insurance Markets", <u>Journal of Business</u>, Vol 54, no. 3, 407-34.

_____ (1982) "On the Corporate Demand for Insurance", <u>Journal of Business</u>, Vol 55, no. 2, 281-95.

_____ (1987) "Corporate Insurance and the Underinvestment Problem", <u>The Journal of Risk and Insurance</u>, no. 1, 45-54.

Mian S.L. and C.W. Smith Jr. (1989), Accounts Receivable Management Policy : Theory and Evidence. The University of Rochester. Workingpaper No. MERC 88-02.

Modigliani, F. and M. Miller (1958), "The Costs of Capital, Corporation Finance and the Theory of Investment", <u>American Economic Review</u>, 48:333-91.

Shapiro, C. (1983), "Optimal Pricing of Experience Goods", <u>Bell Journal of Economics</u>, no. 14, 497-507.

Shavell, S. (1979), "On Moral Hazard and Insurance", <u>Quarterly Journal of Economics</u>, no 93, 541-562.

_____ (1986), "The Judgement Proof Problem", <u>The International Review of Law and Economics</u>, 45-58.

_____ (1987), <u>An Economic Analysis of Tort Law</u>, Harvard University Press.

Skogh, G. (1989a), "The Transactions Costs of Insurance: Contracting Impediments and Costs", <u>The Journal of Risk and Insurance</u>, 726-732.

_____ (1989b), "Professional Liability Insurance in Scandinavia. The Liability of Accountants, Barristers and Estate Agents", <u>Geneva Papers on Risk and Insurance</u>, 360-370.

----- (1991), "Insurance and the Institutional Economies of Financial Intermediation", <u>The Geneva Papers on Risk and Insurance</u>, 59-72.

Smith, Jr., C.W. and J.B. Warner (1979), "On Financial Contracting. An Analysis of Bond Covenants", <u>Journal of Financial Economics</u>, 117-61.

Spence, M.A. (1974), <u>Market Signaling: Informational Transfer in Hiring and Related Screening Processes</u>, Harvard University Press, Cambridge, Mass.

Stiglitz, J.E. and A. Weiss (1981), "Credit Rationing in Markets with Imperfect Information", <u>American Economic Review</u>, Vol 71, no. 3, 393-410.

Sykes, A. O. (1984), "The Economics of Vicarious Liability", <u>The Yale Law Journal</u>. Vol 93: 1197, 1231-1280.

Williamson, O.E (1979), "Transaction-Cost Economics: The Governance of Contractual Relations", <u>Journal of Law and Economics</u>, Oct.

Part Two

Investment Banking and the Industrial Sector

Financial Regulation and Monetary Arrangements after 1992
C. Wihlborg, M. Fratianni and T.D. Willett (Editors)
© 1991 Elsevier Science Publishers B.V. All rights reserved

5 The European Market for Mergers and Acquisitions

Roy C. Smith and Ingo Walter

Leonard N. Stern School of Business, New York University Salomon Center, 100 Trinity Place, New York, N.Y. 10006, USA

1. INTRODUCTION

In 1985 the EC Commission announced its 1992 single market initiatives. To a significant extent, these initiatives - which had been promised at the inception of the Europe Common Market about 30 years earlier but never implemented - were the result of growing confidence among European statesmen that deregulated private-sector economic activity could produce superior growth performance among the EC countries than would continuation of direct intervention by government in markets. Enthusiasm spread quickly into the private sector, where emphasis was given to cutting costs, increasing productivity, and improving profit performance. The 1992 initiatives further encouraged the European private sector to invest in the infrastructure necessary to service a unified single market, and many companies began or accelerated programs of expansion through acquisition of other companies in Europe. The result has been a period of unprecedented, continuing and extraordinary growth in merger and acquisition (M&A) transactions in Europe in the latter half of the 1980s, one that promises to continue through the 1990s.

This period coincided with one of great industrial restructuring in the United States as well, and of rapidly growing U.S. foreign direct investment by European and Japanese corporations. It reflected efforts by companies in global industries exposed to substantial international competition to improve their own competitive performance, and to better position themselves in the principal markets for their products and services in the United States, Europe and Asia. In this sense, the late 1980s reflected extraordinary corporate realignments on the part of companies from all three regions.

The most active area for this sort of corporate restructuring has been inside the United States, where more than $1 trillion of disclosed merger and acquisition activity involving more than 6,000 transactions occurred between 1985 and 1989. The U.S. surge actually began in about 1981, rising in volume and numbers throughout the period to reach a peak in 1988 (the year in which the $25 billion RJR-Nabisco LBO transaction was announced). The volume of completed intra-U.S. transactions declined by 30 percent in 1989, and the data for 1990 reflected a substantial further decline - partly because of the discontinuation of large junk bond-financed LBOs. The intense M&A activity in the United States during the 1980s represented the fourth merger boom of the twentieth century. During the earlier booms (1898-1904, the 1920s, and the 1960s) there had been somewhat parallel activity in the United Kingdom, indicating a degree of international involvement and spillover, but the absence of similar M&A deal-flow in continental Europe and Japan - neither of which had any history or experience with such market-driven transactions - impeded a broader spreading of such transactions. The U.S. merger boom of the 1980s did, however, ignite a substantial global response, one that appeared to be continuing in Europe even after the boom in the United States had subsided.

This paper considers developments in European industrial restructuring and M&A activity since 1985. It begins with a section on the principles of industrial restructuring, in which conventional theories and economic fundamentals are reviewed, and the impact on the current environment of freer, more intensive competition on a global basis is considered. Similarities to the industrial restructuring occurring somewhat earlier in the United States are examined as well.

We continue with a discussion on the emerging takeover process in Europe. In this context, we examine the EC regulations regarding anti-competitive combinations, the emerging rules and practices by which M&A transactions are conducted, and the use of "free market" devices to execute transactions.

There follows an analysis of the patterns of European M&A activity for the period 1985-1990. It includes M&A activity by industrial sector, by country and region, by type of transaction (in particular, the acquisition of "stakeholdings," or partial ownership positions), and by form of initiation (agreed vs. opposed). The effects of LBOs and related financial restructuring, and the extent of the use of financial advisers - in each case as compared to U.S. reference levels - are also examined.

Statistical analysis of available M&A information is drawn from a database of merger and corporate transactions that is more extensive than those previously offered, especially with respect to European transactions. Nevertheless, the transaction values of a substantial number of transactions that have been identified are not disclosed. Our analysis is based on disclosed transaction values only, which we believe account for the vast majority of total transactions, and therefore provide a representative picture of the activity we are describing.

The paper concludes with a prognosis for the future of the European market for corporate control.

2. PRINCIPLES OF REGIONAL INDUSTRIAL RESTRUCTURING

Assuming it is unimpeded by anticompetitive distortions in the markets for goods, services and factors of production, regional economic integration can create static as well as dynamic gains for the participating economies. The static gains relate to its impact on efficiency in resource allocation, and are reflected in the level of real output and income. The dynamic gains relate to the its impact on the rate of growth in output and income, through accelerated capital formation, technological change and other elements imbedded in the production function. The EC 1992 initiatives are presumed to entail both static and dynamic gains of this nature, as was the original movement toward economic union anchored in the 1957 Treaty of Rome (European Communities, 1988).

2.1 Conventional Theories
The conventional theory of economic integration is largely associated with neoclassical and factor-endowments trade models in which the underlying economic adjustments work through arm's length trade linkages rather than movements of productive factors. The

supposition is that low-cost suppliers supplant high-cost suppliers as markets for goods and services are opened, and shifting trade shares drive resource-allocation patterns in markets for productive factors and at the same time alter underlying incentive structures to produce more rapid growth through accelerated capital formation and technological change (Balassa, 1961). In fact, much international and interregional economic restructuring occurs through the movement of factors of production, notably capital in the form of foreign direct investment, and through transfers of proprietary technology - especially when technology transfers via intrafirm control linkages prove to be more efficient than via such other interfirm linkages as licensing. The theory of the multinational firm addresses such issues (Dunning, 1981).

Economic restructuring via intrafirm linkages can take a number of forms. These may involve vertical integration as well as horizontal and conglomerate mergers and related equity transactions. Relative production costs, technology advantages and market logistics may prompt a firm in one country to establish or expand an affiliate in another country, for example. Or two independent firms may establish a strategic alliance involving joint marketing or R&D activities. Or two independent firms may acquire minority equity stakes in each other, cementing such an alliance and enhancing the intrafirm character of transactions between them. Or one firm may acquire another - either on an agreed or hostile basis - taking the form of foreign direct investment and leading to subsequent intrafirm transactions between the two countries. This may prompt restructuring of production and marketing logistics of the combined firm, and possibly the disposition of non-strategic assets. Opposed takeover attempts may in the end be unsuccessful, yet nevertheless lead to substantial restructuring by the target firm and produce significant changes in its domestic and international activities.

There are thus a number of alternative routes to economic restructuring within the context of regional economic integration initiatives, of which M&A transactions are only one - in particular reallocation of production among existing firms as demise of less-competitive firms, as well as foreign direct investment in local markets by firms home-based in other member countries or in third countries. One reason why M&A transactions might be chosen as the restructuring vehicle has to do with capital market inefficiencies. Market capitalization of target firms may be low relative to the cost of reproducing the productive assets de novo. Alternatively, target firms may be taken over by lower-cost suppliers from abroad, raising rates of return on capital across the industry. Still another alternative would be that firms engage in M&A activity to increase their market power and control over prices, and thereby increase their excess returns.

2.2 Economic Fundamentals of Restructuring

Applying the theory of economic integration to the removal of nontariff market-access distortions in Europe is straightforward (Walter and Smith, 1989). There are shifts in transactions from high-cost, relatively inefficient domestic producers that continued to enjoy a protected national market within the EC to low-cost suppliers located in other European countries. Output shifts toward the low-cost, high-quality suppliers and ultimately approaches some free-trade optimum within the integrated region. Efficiency in resource allocation is enhanced, real incomes increase, and consumers benefit from a broader choice among competing products and services - the classic "positive production and consumption effects" of regional free trade, usually reflected in a disproportionate expansion of interregional trade and specialization (Vanek, 1965).

But regional integration, by definition, involves an element of discrimination against external suppliers as well, and it is possible that some transactions will shift from low-cost vendors outside the region to relatively higher-cost and less efficient suppliers in participating countries. To the extent that this occurs, production will be reallocated from low-cost to high-cost suppliers internationally. From a global standpoint, productive efficiency will suffer. For their part, consumers may be prevented from fully communicating their preferences to non-member suppliers, and suffer from a narrowing of their range of choice among competitive sources worldwide. Such "negative consumption and production effects" of regional free trade tend to depress the volume of trade of the participating countries with nonmembers by diverting it to producers in other member states. Thus, trade partly changes direction and becomes increasingly inward-oriented; production becomes more "regionalized" within the confines of the free-trade zone.

The "static" structural effects of the EC 1992 initiatives form a balance between the positive and negative production and consumption effects. This issue can equally be restated in terms of the classic "trade diversion" versus "trade creation" arguments (Balassa, 1961). The less inward-looking and protectionist the EC proves to be in the 1990s and beyond, the more the positive static effects (trade creation) are likely to outweigh the negative static effects (trade diversion).

Besides its static effects on underlying economic structures, regional trade liberalization can yield significant growth-related gains as well. If the most competitive suppliers have free access to regional markets, only the fittest will continue to prosper after an initial period of economic restructuring (Scitovsky, 1958). Consequently, productive assets - capital, natural resources, and labor - will undergo continuous redeployment to those sectors in which they obtain the highest returns. National economies obtain maximum economic gains from high-growth sectors by securing assured access to markets in partner countries, while imports from these same countries progressively "weed out" decaying domestic sectors and release productive resources for alternative uses. In the process, firms will seek enhanced economies of scale and economies of scope linked to effective internal market size, even as rates of capital formation, human resource development, technological change and entrepreneurial activity accelerate.

One should thus distinguish between once-and-for-all increases on output attributable to regional integration and sustained increases in the *rate* of output growth. M&A transactions relate to both of these dimensions, although the latter may be more arguable than the former.

2.3 Intensified Competition and Diminishing Public Subsidies

Intensified competition among existing or newly-entering firms will force each of them to become more cost-effective. Economies of scale will be important in some sectors of manufacturing at the plant level and in distribution, and possibly in R&D activities. Diseconomies of scale and unrealized economies of scope will likewise make their appearance in a number of sectors, creating a need for subsequent restructuring through breakups and dispositions. Clearly, there will be winners and losers in the kind of industrial restructuring that must come if the economic gains from the creation of a single market in Europe are to be realized. There will also be significant social costs associated with market-driven economic restructuring. Yet, these costs may well be once-and-for-all in nature, and could pale by comparison to the present value of the expected future economic performance gains at any but the lowest of social discount rates.

With greater governmental focus on competitive viability and fiscal pressures, the subsidization of European industry should decline as a consequence of the EC 1992 initiatives and remaining capacity in traditionally subsidized sectors will involve enhanced levels of production or product technology. Nevertheless, a number of politically sensitive sectors will continue to receive public subsidies and/or protection for the foreseeable future, alongside concessionary financing for certain industries deemed technologically important - possibly in the context of Europe-wide strategic alliances and government-fostered "Euro-champions". There also remains the danger of protectionism affecting various economic sectors at the regional level, applied under pressure to replace previous national protectionist measures, as well as possible tolerance of Euro-cartel formation and continuation of sectoral subsidies not aimed at promoting economic restructuring.

3. EVOLUTION OF THE TAKEOVER PROCESS IN EUROPE

Measured against static and dynamic efficiency benchmarks, M&A activity invariably presents a complex picture. Bringing transactions inside the firm that involve high market transaction costs represents a clear gain. So does realization of available scale and scope economies. Firms of large size may undertake incremental R&D activities that would not otherwise be possible. On the other hand, M&A activity may also lead to monopolization of markets and hence resource misallocation, although the literature suggests that relatively small efficiency gains can easily offset even significant increases in monopoly power (Scherer, 1980; See also the Eckbo paper in this volume).

There is always a tradeoff between static and dynamic gains, on the one hand, and reduction in competition on the other, that must be considered in assessing the impact of M&A activity in Europe and in formulating and executing competition policy. According to one study (European Communities, 1989) the more rapid is the growth of market demand, the lower are entry and exit costs, and the more open the regional economy (i.e., the larger the share of imports in total consumption and exports in total production), the more likely it will be that M&A activity will be beneficial for allocative efficiency and growth.

Caves (1990) has argued that conventional wisdom linking the 1992-related market liberalizations to a wave of mergers and acquisitions lacks transparency. He examines two alternative models. The "strategic" model is based on oligopolistic market structures that respond to the expanded set of opportunities created by a single market. The "factor transfer" model is based on the substitutability between trade and capital flows, so that firms can take advantage of the enlarged market either through exporting or through acquisition of production and distribution facilities in the target markets. The first of these models would be consistent with a "bunching" of M&A activity around actual or perceived increases in market competition, while the second would not. Caves' analysis of U.S. cross-border merger data basically supports the second model, with little evidence of bunching around periods of increased competition, and concludes that even patterns of horizontal mergers pose no specific threat to monopolization of markets in the case of EC economic restructuring.

3.1 Use of Free Market Devices

As discussed in the previous section, M&A activity can be broken down into unopposed (friendly) and opposed (hostile) transactions. In the former case, the boards of two firms exercising their fiduciary roles find it in the mutual interest of their respective shareholders to engage in a full legal merger (e.g., through an exchange of shares), a full takeover of the shares of one firm by the other, or the unilateral or reciprocal acquisition of equity stakes. In the "opposed" case the board of the target firm rejects the transaction, which is nevertheless attempted (successfully or unsuccessfully) by the other firm on a hostile basis. The economic fundamentals of the latter, in terms of their impact on the shareholders of both firms, is the focus of the market for corporate control.

Since the values concerned inevitably are *ex ante*, the argumentation is by definition normative in nature. Management of the predator firm will tend to point to the static and dynamic gains it expects to achieve - usually related to reduced transactions costs, scale and scope economies in production, distribution, R&D, etc. - as well as market-share advantages, as reflected in the premium it is willing to pay for the target's shares relative to the market price. Management of the target firm will tend to refute these advantages, or will point to a series of steps it is intending to take designed to bring about the same gains without sacrificing the firm's independence - e.g., rationalizing production and distribution, share repurchases and increased leverage in the firm's capital structure, non-strategic dispositions, and the like. To the extent that it can defeat the predator by non-market devices, management entrenchment practices may succeed in thwarting the interests of the shareholders of both firms. Typical non-market techniques include restriction of shareholder rights anchored in company bylaws and appeals for external intervention on antitrust or other regulatory grounds. It may also appeal to shareholders directly in a proxy battle - arguing for example that long-term shareholder interests are better served by continued independence despite the foregone control premium. Or it may engage in greenmail - buying back shares from a hostile bidder at a premium to the prevailing market price - in which case there is a transfer of the control premium to the shareholders of the predator firm at the expense of the shareholders of the target firm.

3.2 EC Competition Rules and M&A Clearance Procedures

A key issue regarding EC economic restructuring through M&A transactions involves competition rules at the national and Community level under Articles 85 and 86 of the Treaty of Rome, administered by Directorate General IV (Sullivan & Cromwell, 1989). These govern clearance of M&A transactions within the Community.

The Commission's approach has been to provide informal clearance as expeditiously as possible, in order not to interfere unduly in market-driven transactions yet subject deals to careful scrutiny whenever there are serious doubts about a transaction's competitive impact. If a merger or takeover seems acceptable on a preliminary basis, the Commission may issue a "letter of comfort," indicating that the transaction can proceed, but at the principals' own risk pending a final determination of the competitive implications. If not, objections will be spelled out immediately and possibly cause the transaction to be called-off. The issuance of a comfort letter based on formal notification of the transaction and subsequent clearance occur at Commission meetings held weekly. Formal proceedings take four months, based on assignment of a "rapporteur" who tests the transaction's impact against EC competition criteria by drawing on the Commission's industry and competition expertise. (For greater detail, see Walter & Smith, 1989.)

Any reservations are set forth in a "statement of objection" provided on a confidential basis to the bidder and preventing the Commission from introducing new objections at a later time. The intention to approve a transaction despite anti-competitive implications under Article 85 of the Treaty of Rome must be published in the Official Journal of the EC, with opportunity provided for interested parties to comment. Commission procedures are thus open to third-party complaint and further argument on the part of the principals, as well as changes in the nature of the transaction in order to achieve compliance with EC competition rules, pending a final determination, which can only be overturned by the European Court of Justice. Any opponent and third-party views and counter-arguments by the transaction's principals are recorded by the rapporteur during this procedure, and combined with independent market and other technical information.

All of this is checked for fairness by an experienced "hearing officer" with independent access to the EC Commissioner for Competition Policy. Following translation of the case into the nine EC languages, the case is considered by the Advisory Committee on Restrictive Practices and Dominant Positions, composed of national anti-trust officials, and passed back to EC Director-General (DG) IV. The rapporteur then writes an official recommendation based on the accumulated evidence which provides the basis for the Commission's decision.

Following extended negotiations, EC industry ministers in December 1989 agreed that the Commission would have the authority to approve or block a merger or takeover solely on competitive grounds based principally on the interests of consumers - not on criteria related to economic or technology argumentation such as the desirability of "Euro-champions." However, they failed to agree on the minimum size transactions that would require vetting on the part of the Commission. There was general agreement that mergers or acquisitions falling below ECU 2 billion (in terms of global sales of the combined firms) would not require approval and that those exceeding ECU 5 billion would require such approval, but there was no agreement as to where between these two values the threshold should lie. At the high end, the Commission would have to deal with perhaps 50-60 transactions annually.

The argumentation generally pitted the United Kingdom, which favored a high threshold, against the smaller EC countries without well-established competition regulation interested in having the EC take a more active role in this respect. In the process, compromise was achieved between the British desire for "one-stop" vetting by the Commission against German Kartellamt concerns about loss of sovereignty regarding large M&A transactions. Eventual M&A criteria might also include "block exemptions" for relatively small two-party M&A cases, strict time limits would be fixed for the resolution of national versus EC disputes, and "legitimate interests" under which national authorities can continue to interfere, ought to be fairly well defined.

A transparent EC policy on mergers and acquisitions will be a valuable contribution to economic efficiency - based on policy clarity, expeditious review and pre-clearance procedures.

3.3 Emerging EC Takeover Rules

Besides competition rules, the European market for corporate control remains extremely fragmented, ranging from a relatively efficient, transparent and market-linked structure in the United Kingdom to those of Germany and Switzerland characterized by serious obstacles to takeover activity. Such obstacles are related for example to the traditional conduct of business in these countries (such as relationships with universal banks) and the relatively small number of publicly traded companies, as well as to "artificial" obstacles intended to impede unwanted bids for corporate control (see Walter and Smith, 1989). In December 1988 the EC Commission put forward a draft directive to harmonize takeover rules throughout the EC, containing three major provisions.

First, under the draft directive companies that offer to buy more than 30 percent of the voting shares in a target company must launch a bid to buy all of the voting shares. A basic principle of the proposed EC takeover rules would be that all shareholders should be treated equally, and shareholders would have from four to 10 weeks to submit their acceptance under any takeover bid.

Second, companies that launch takeover attempts would have to state their intentions about the target firm's future activities, including the work force, as well as financial structure and debt levels. The latter was aimed specifically at LBO deals.

Third, certain anti-takeover defenses would be prohibited, including "exceptional operations" diluting shareholder value in the context of a takeover bid - e.g., some types of "poison pills" such as giving friendly buyers the right to buy stock at a conceccionary price in the event of a hostile takeover attempt. Share sales without agreement of existing shareholders would likewise be prohibited.

A recent study proposed a number of benchmarks against which future EC rules on takeover activity should be measured (Booz Allen, 1990). These include (1) majority shareholder control, specifically with respect to takeover defenses; (2) periodic review and majority shareholder vote on control restrictions such as pre-emptive rights; (3) ban on self-control through company-owned and affiliate-owned shares; (4) shareholder equality of treatment in dividend policy, preferential share price offers, information disclosure and related aspects of takeover activity that may be unfair, enforced by stock exchange authorities; (5) full disclosure of management accounts, shareholder agreements, identity of large shareholdings, and free access to shareholder lists; and (6) common policies toward takeovers by non-EC companies to take into account takeover rules in their respective home countries.

Corporate restructuring in the EC has always reflected the fundamental differences that have existed in the member countries' financial systems. In much of continental Europe, corporate finance has traditionally been heavily bank-oriented, with financial institutions having universal banking powers heavily engaged in corporate lending as well as equity investments for their own and fiduciary accounts. Such a pattern provides banks with both non-public information and (indirectly and through external board memberships) potential influence over management decisions involving corporate restructuring activities. Firms that do not meet bank performance expectations find themselves under pressure to restructure - activity that may be initiated, orchestrated and implemented by the banks (Rybczynski, 1989). Indeed, continental European banks have historically had to carry out industrial restructurings in the absence of well-functioning capital markets in the past, following periods of war or economic collapse, and so are accustomed to this role.

In the United States and the United Kingdom, on the other hand, banks have not had a comparable tradition in corporate finance, and capital markets have played a constructive role in industrial development for well over a century. Corporate debt financing has relied much more heavily on the securities markets, with debt-holders exerting limited influence on managerial decisions, and public equity holders exposed to the agency costs associated with management pursuing interests other than those which would maximize the value of their shareholdings. At the same time, accounting and disclosure standards are such that the financial affairs of public companies are relatively transparent, while banks under the Glass-Steagall provisions in the United States and pre-Big Bang restrictions in the United Kingdom were limited in their ability to exert influence on management even remotely comparable to that of some of their continental European counterparts. Consequently, changes in corporate control have been exerted by the capital market, often through hostile takeovers by unaffiliated parties that lead (if successful) to changes in corporate ownership and control. Even if unsuccessful, existing management may engage in corporate restructuring activity not dissimilar to what an unaffiliated acquirer would do.

The merits and demerits of the two systems have been widely debated. Bank-oriented systems are often said to be less crisis-prone, to favor long-term as opposed to short-term views in corporate decision-making, and to provide superior continuous monitoring of corporate performance leading to preemptive structural adjustment. Market-oriented systems are often credited with greater efficiency, financial innovation and dynamism, superior resistance to inherent conflicts of interests among the various stakeholders involved, and (through better transparency) less susceptibility to major uncorrected industrial blunders. On the other hand, they are alleged to be prone to short-term myopia.

In the 1990s there is likely to be some degree of convergence between the two approaches. Financial liberalization and wider use of the securities markets by continental European corporations, together with increasingly performance-oriented portfolio management on the part of mutual funds, insurance companies and other institutional investors is leading to a gradual shift away from bank finance, and the appearance of unwanted takeover attempts through acquisition of shareholdings by unaffiliated (often foreign) investors. At the same time, easing of bank activity-limits in the United Kingdom and the United States is beginning to allow them to play a larger role in industrial restructuring transactions, and to exploit some of the information and relationship advantages they have as lenders.

4. THE GLOBAL AND EUROPEAN M&A ENVIRONMENT

Table 1 shows 1985-89 completed merger and corporate restructuring transactions in the United States, transactions involving U.S. and non-U.S. corporations, transactions outside the United States, and the global volume of such transactions. This table, derived from the Securities Data Corporation mergers and corporate transactions 1990 database, demonstrates the extent to which M&A transactions have indeed become international. In 1985, for example, domestic U.S. transactions accounted for 85 percent of global M&A activity; by 1989 this had declined to 53 percent. U.S. domestic transactions accounted for less than half of total world-wide activity in 1990.

Cross border transactions involving U.S. companies grew by a factor of 4.3 during the 1985-1989 period - one in which U.S. domestic M&A volume essentially remained static - with 82 percent (by volume) of the cross-border transactions representing sales of U.S. companies to non U.S. buyers. Transactions entirely outside the United States grew the most rapidly of all - from $16.3 billion (82 disclosed transactions) in 1985 to $115.3 billion (1459 disclosed transactions) in 1989, a 7.1-fold increase over the five year period.

Table 1
Volume of Completed International Merger and Corporate Transactions[a,b]
United States (1985-90)
(In Millions of U.S. Dollars)[c]

TOTALS YEAR	DOMESTIC U.S.		CROSS-BORDER U.S.						OUTSIDE U.S.		GLOBAL	
			Buyer From U.S.		Seller From U.S.		Total Cross-Border					
	(#)	($M)	(#)	($M)	(#)	($M)	(#)	($M)	(#)	($M)	(#)	($M)
1985	804[d] (868)	192,863.2	25 (57)	3,854.9	76 (106)	9,999.1	101 (163)	13,854.0	143 (106)	20,721.3	1,048 (1,137)	227,438.5
1986	1,178 (1,288)	203,985.7	39 (50)	2,918.4	164 (144)	31,126.8	203 (194)	34,045.2	296 (203)	38,728.9	1,677 (1,685)	276,759.8
1987	1,311 (1,311)	205,814.3	52 (189)	8,492.5	187 (135)	36,940.3	239 (224)	45,432.8	586 (366)	86,602.5	2,136 (1,901)	337,849.6
1988	1,580 (1,249)	294,429.7	81 (127)	6,687.6	247 (175)	61,450.9	328 (302)	68,138.5	1,452 (858)	124,230.1	3,360 (2,409)	486,798.3
1989	1,872 (1,705)	244,793.3	149 (213)	25,336.3	405 (236)	52,393.2	554 (449)	77,729.5	1,832 (1,575)	203,032.9	4,258 (3,729)	525,555.7
1990	1,304 (1,943)	76,965.9	126 (210)	20,084.8	339 (273)	32,521.7	465 (483)	52,606.5	1,738 (1,367)	149,001.7	3,507 (3,793)	278,574.1
TOTALS 1985-90	8,049 (8,364)	1,218,852.1	472 (746)	67,374.5	1,418 (1,069)	224,432.0	1,890 (1,815)	291,806.5	6,047 (4,475)	622,317.4	15,986 (14,654)	2,132,976.0

DATA: Securities Data Corporation, Mergers and Corporate Transactions database.

a. Completed transactions include: mergers, tender-mergers, tender offers, purchases of stakes, divestitures, recapitalizations, exchange offers and LBOs.
b. The volume data are classified according to the announcement date of a transaction -- not taking into consideration when a transaction is completed.
c. Million dollars of purchase price -- excluding fees and expenses -- at current exchange rates. The dollar value includes the amount paid for all common stock, common stock equivalents, preferred stock, debt, options, assets, warrants, and stake purchases made within six months of he announcement date of the transaction. Liabilities assumed are included if they are disclosed in press releases or newspaper articles.
d. Number of completed transactions with undisclosed dollar values.

Of the M&A transactions outside the United States for the 1985-1989 period, $196.4 billion, or 60 percent, were intra-European. An additional $156 billion (80 percent of the intra-European total) involved Europe/non-Europe transactions - a significant part of which undoubtedly is also reflected in the U.S. cross-border data. Intra-European transactions increased by a factor of 9 during the period, Europe/non-Europe deals (in which 72.6 percent of the transactions by volume involved European acquisitions of non-European corporations) grew 5.4 times, as shown in Table 2.

Table 2
Volume of Completed International Merger and Corporate Transactions[a,b]
EUROPE (1985-90)[c]
(In Millions of U.S. Dollars)[d]

YEAR	INTRA-EUROPEAN TRANSACTIONS (#)	($M)	EUROPE/NON-EUROPE TRANSACTIONS					
			Buyer From Europe (#)	($M)	Seller From Europe (#)	($M)	Total Cross-Border (#)	($M)
1985	72 [e](43)	10,613.7	45 (46)	6,267.4	29 (44)	2,342.3	74 (90)	8,609.7
1986	195 (101)	18,985.2	106 (66)	18,631.7	44 (36)	6,082.5	150 (102)	24,714.2
1987	416 (220)	48,965.3	132 (75)	28,161.4	63 (82)	12,314.6	195 (157)	40,476.0
1988	1,091 (613)	78,996.0	209 (139)	38,389.0	133 (138)	13,566.8	342 (277)	51,955.8
1989	1,359 (1,037)	121,030.3	306 (167)	40,129.7	212 (284)	25,091.8	518 (451)	65,221.5
1990	1,151 (781)	80,450.0	223 (157)	38,259.9	250 (285)	37,580.1	473 (442)	75,840.0
TOTALS 1985-90	4,284 (2,795)	359,040.5	1,021 (650)	169,839.1	731 (869)	96,978.1	1,752 (1,519)	266,817.2

DATA: Securities Data Corporation, Merger and Corporate Transactions database.

a. Completed transactions include: mergers, tender-mergers, tender offers, purchases of stakes, divestitures, recapitalizations, exchange offers and LBOs.
b. The volume data are classified according to the announcement date of a transaction -- not taking into consideration when a transaction is completed.
c. The region includes Eastern European countries.
d. Million dollars of purchase price -- excluding fees and expenses -- at current exchange rates. The dollar value includes the amount paid for all common stock, common stock equivalents, preferred stock, debt, options, assets, warrants, and stake purchases made within six months of he announcement date of the transaction. Liabilities assumed are included if they are disclosed in press releases or newspaper articles.
e. Number of completed transactions with undisclosed dollar values.

European corporations were demonstrably entering the M&A field more aggressively, with transaction volume growing far more rapidly than anywhere else in the world, during the 1985-1989 period. This expansion was occurring simultaneously on two fronts -- within Europe and in other regions of global importance to European corporations, mainly the United States.

The data suggest that an M&A boom has indeed taken hold in Europe (Cf. Walter and Smith, 1989). This boom appears to involve acquisitions between companies within individual European countries, between companies in two European countries, and between companies in European and non-European countries. The development, we believe, is the result of (a) an overdue need for industrial restructuring in Europe similar to that experienced in the United States, (b) the special motivations associated with the 1992 single market initiatives, (c) the availability of adequate financial resources, (d) the increasing liberalization of capital markets in Europe, and (e) the transfer to Europe of much of the M&A knowhow that accumulated in the United States during the 1980s.

Although it is difficult to predict how long the growth in European M&A volume will continue. Apart from recession-induced declines it appears that - barring any unexpected reversal of government policies affecting market-driven transactions, or a long-term reversal of economic prospects in Europe - there remains a great deal more to be done. Most of the M&A activity in Europe during the period 1985-1989 (about 58 percent by volume) has involved United Kingdom corporations which have a long history and familiarity with such transactions. French and Italian corporations (together accounting for 22 percent of intra-European transaction volume) have been the next most active M&A participants, followed by German corporations which - despite the size of the German economy - accounted for only 4.9 percent of intra-European transaction volume during 1985-1989.

There are a variety of differences between the structures of business enterprises within Europe. Many enterprises, including numerous very large ones, are not organized as publicly-owned limited liability corporations. A recent study for the DG-XV of the EC Commission shows, for example, only 54 percent of the top 400 EC companies are quoted, versus 99 percent in the United States (Booz Allen, 1990). Out of the top 100 domestic companies, 67 are quoted in the U.K., 56 in France, 45 in Germany and less than a third in all other EC countries. Furthermore, the study reports, in the three largest EC economies, only a relatively minor share of the domestic GNP can actually be "accessed through public takeovers." (Booz Allen Acquisition Services, 1990).

Nor do many of the continental European countries have a tradition of, or substantial experience with, market-driven internal (i.e., domestic) M&A activity. As a result, only a comparatively small percentage of enterprises in continental European countries have so far participated in such transactions. As more of them do participate, and the benefits of doing so become more visible (such as utilizing an efficient market for corporate control to dispose of shares in family owned or closely-held businesses that have limited liquidity), participation in M&A activity should continue to increase. There thus exists a substantial potential for future M&A transactions, especially in continental Europe. This potential has already begun to show itself in the rapid rates of growth in such transactions originating on the Continent.

Table 3
Rankings of Industry Groups of U.S. and European M&A Seller Companies by SIC Code[a,b]
(1985 - 90)
(In Millions of U.S. Dollars)[c]

SELLER SIC	DESCRIPTION	U. S. TRANSACTIONS			EUROPEAN TRANSACTIONS		
		RANKING[d]	NUMBER	VALUE[c]	RANKING	NUMBER	VALUE
28	CHEMICALS & ALLIED PRODUCTS	1	438	141,401.9	5	200	23,412.8
13	OIL & GAS EXTRACTION	2	438	85,754.7	4	100	29,852.5
48	COMMUNICATIONS	3	492	83,786.7	31	61	3,418.4
20	FOOD & KINDRED PRODUCTS	4	262	80,710.1	1	243	50,716.4
36	ELECTRONIC & OTHER ELECT.EQUIP	5	508	77,061.3	6	220	21,130.3
60	DEPOSITORY INSTITUTIONS	6	741	65,390.8	2	113	33,454.3
35	INDUSTRIAL MACHINERY & EQUIP.	7	553	57,919.3	15	235	9,611.7
53	GENERAL MERCHANDISE STORES	8	98	45,250.7	18	31	8,057.8
27	PRINTING & PUBLISHING	9	284	44,616.4	11	180	13,617.2
37	TRANSPORTATION EQUIPMENT	10	197	40,012.1	7	144	20,704.4
78	MOTION PICTURES	11	125	39,022.6	42	42	2,044.2
73	BUSINESS SERVICES	12	480	35,098.8	13	304	11,949.6
38	INSTRUMENTS & RELATED PROD.	13	370	34,697.2	35	89	3,070.4
21	TOBACCO PRODUCTS	14	12	33,140.8	57	4	560.7
61	NONDEPOSITORY INSTITUTIONS	15	148	31,954.6	22	54	5,647.9
54	FOOD STORES	16	102	30,315.3	14	38	10,141.3
49	ELECTRIC,GAS & SANITARY SERV.	17	198	30,127.6	12	52	13,396.5
70	HOTELS & OTHER LODGING PLACES	18	150	29,126.9	20	98	6,487.8
63	INSURANCE CARRIERS	19	267	27,193.1	3	86	30,610.2
32	STONE, CLAY & GLASS PRODUCTS	20	131	26,452.0	21	107	6,079.0
26	PAPER & ALLIED PRODUCTS	21	92	24,242.3	8	112	17,276.6
30	RUBBER & MISC. PLASTIC PROD.	22	143	24,165.3	36	104	2,980.8
58	EATING & DRINKING PLACES	23	138	23,383.1	33	72	3,401.4
33	PRIMARY METAL INDUSTRIES	24	176	23,316.1	23	125	5,030.4
40	RAILROAD TRANSPORTATION	25	52	23,218.2	66	1	24.1
45	TRANSPORTATION BY AIR	26	118	22,700.2	34	28	3,188.0
80	HEALTH SERVICES	27	203	20,827.9	52	32	1,149.1
65	REAL ESTATE	28	162	19,025.4	9	182	17,105.4
34	FABRICATED METAL PRODUCTS	29	199	18,031.6	17	158	8,065.6
62	SECURITY & COMMODITY BROKERS	30	148	16,055.8	16	120	9,225.7
23	APPAREL & OTHER TEXTILE PROD.	31	84	15,750.8	40	54	2,212.0
10	METAL MINING	32	68	14,455.6	25	13	4,584.0
59	MISCELLANEOUS RETAIL	33	133	12,799.4	38	57	2,506.4
87	ENGINEERING & MGMT. SERVICES	34	214	11,725.6	37	181	2,512.0
22	TEXTILE MILL PRODUCTS	35	90	11,061.8	32	95	3,410.9
51	WHOLESALE TRADE-NONDURABLE	36	118	10,545.1	24	127	4,622.5
50	WHOLESALE TRADE-DURABLE GOODS	37	203	9,100.1	19	245	6,849.8
75	AUTO REPAIR, SERV. & PARKING	38	28	8,803.3	46	24	1,721.2
64	INSURANCE AGENTS,BROKER.& SERV	39	22	7,569.7	43	35	2,033.6
67	HOLDING & OTHER INV'T. OFFICES	40	149	6,794.9	10	99	15,173.3
42	TRUCKING & WAREHOUSING	41	52	6,587.6	44	29	1,871.8
46	PIPELINES, EXC.NATURAL GAS	42	21	6,157.3	68	3	22.6
29	PETROLEUM & COAL PRODUCTS	43	43	5,238.9	30	20	3,494.1
79	AMUSEMENT & RECREATION SERV.	44	57	5,102.3	29	40	3,568.9
56	APPAREL & ACCESSORY STORES	45	58	4,979.3	54	22	833.9
39	MISC.MANUFACTURING INDUST.	46	88	4,925.2	53	58	1,019.2
25	FURNITURE & FIXTURES	47	59	4,916.3	56	42	631.5
24	LUMBER & WOOD PRODUCTS	48	50	4,622.4	41	37	2,077.4
12	COAL MINING	49	42	3,905.1	59	11	380.5
57	FURNITURE & HOMEFURNISH.STORES	50	50	3,816.2	28	33	3,768.2
44	WATER TRANSPORTATION	51	42	3,698.4	27	46	3,820.4
52	BUILDING & GARDEN MATERIALS	52	31	3,520.9	55	14	672.3
14	NONMETALLIC MINERALS-EXC.FUELS	53	26	3,503.5	60	15	312.8
8	FORESTRY	54	19	2,275.4	72	2	6.3
1	AGRICULTURAL PRODUCTION-CROPS	55	23	2,225.9	45	12	1,734.7
15	GENERAL BUILDING CONTRACTORS	56	52	1,993.2	39	71	2,225.5
2	AGRICULTURAL PROD.-LIVESTOCK	57	8	1,942.5	74	1	0.1

Table 3 (Cont.)
Rankings of Industry Groups of U.S. and European M&A Seller Companies by SIC Code[a,b]
(1985 - 90)
(In Millions of U.S. Dollars)[c]

SELLER DESCRIPTION	U. S. TRANSACTIONS			EUROPEAN TRANSACTIONS		
SIC	RANKING[d]	NUMBER	VALUE[c]	RANKING	NUMBER	VALUE
55 AUTO DEALERS & SERV.STATIONS	58	20	1,787.5	47	43	1,648.7
47 TRANSPORTATION SERVICES	59	23	1,590.7	50	32	1,340.1
31 LEATHER & LEATHER PRODUCTS	60	28	1,535.7	49	31	1,351.0
0 UNKNOWN	61	39	1,480.3	51	49	1,299.0
16 HEAVY CONTRUCTION-EXC.BUILDING	62	25	1,358.8	48	24	1,548.7
72 PERSONAL SERVICES	63	24	1,028.1	58	37	460.3
41 LOCAL & PASSENGER TRANSIT	64	3	509.0	67	5	22.9
89 SERVICES, NEC	65	7	439.8	63	3	117.0
7 AGRICULTURAL SERVICES	66	2	404.1	69	2	21.5
83 SOCIAL SERVICES	67	9	360.1	64	3	67.1
82 EDUCATIONAL SERVICES	68	9	322.4	61	12	165.9
17 SPECIAL TRADE CONTRACTORS	69	15	253.8	26	44	4,261.7
76 MISC.REPAIR SERVICES	70	7	171.3	71	4	8.7
9 FISHING, HUNTING & TRAPPING	71	1	27.0	65	2	31.6
91 EXEC., LEGISLATIVE & GENERAL	0	0	0.0	70	1	10.2
88 PRIVATE HOUSEHOLDS	0	0	0.0	62	1	152.9
81 LEGAL SERVICES	0	0	0.0	73	1	4.9

DATA: Securities Data Corporation, Mergers and Corporate Transactions database.

a.   Completed transactions include: mergers, tender-mergers, tender offers, purchases of stakes, divestitures, recapitalizations, exchange offers and LBOs.
b.   The volume data are classified according to the announcement date of a transaction -- not taking into consideration when a transaction is completed.
c.   Million dollars of purchase price -- excluding fees and expenses -- at current exchange rates.
d.   Ranking is based on total dollar value of target industry.

Table 4
Rankings of Industry Groups of U.S. and European M&A Buyer Companies by SIC Code[a,b]
(1985 - 90)
(In Millions of U.S. Dollars)[c]

SELLER SIC	DESCRIPTION	U. S. TRANSACTIONS			EUROPEAN TRANSACTIONS		
		RANKING[d]	NUMBER	VALUE[e]	RANKING	NUMBER	VALUE
67	HOLDING & OTHER INV'T. OFFICES	1	2,310	346,867.1	1	631	64,462.8
28	CHEMICALS & ALLIED PRODUCTS	2	327	94,062.3	2	256	49,938.9
13	OIL & GAS EXTRACTION	3	340	76,617.0	6	119	26,715.0
48	COMMUNICATIONS	4	385	65,744.0	23	56	6,334.2
60	DEPOSITORY INSTITUTIONS	5	641	61,679.2	4	138	37,364.7
27	PRINTING & PUBLISHING	6	199	43,109.3	8	188	18,191.0
20	FOOD & KINDRED PRODUCTS	7	198	40,453.7	3	248	44,135.5
35	INDUSTRIAL MACHINERY & EQUIP.	8	339	38,425.1	15	249	9,581.1
36	ELECTRONIC & OTHER ELECT.EQUIP	9	283	38,037.6	7	231	26,315.9
37	TRANSPORTATION EQUIPMENT	10	135	37,735.8	9	110	15,594.9
21	TOBACCO PRODUCTS	11	13	35,455.0	55	4	427.1
38	INSTRUMENTS & RELATED PROD.	12	217	30,423.6	35	68	3,285.9
63	INSURANCE CARRIERS	13	246	28,478.9	5	151	30,029.7
62	SECURITY & COMMODITY BROKERS	14	273	24,144.7	10	220	14,829.0
53	GENERAL MERCHANDISE STORES	15	57	22,437.4	26	25	4,825.6
61	NONDEPOSITORY INSTITUTIONS	16	125	19,769.7	41	35	2,342.4
78	MOTION PICTURES	17	97	19,735.2	31	27	4,106.6
49	ELECTRIC, GAS & SANITARY SERV.	18	171	19,287.1	24	38	5,853.2
40	RAILROAD TRANSPORTATION	19	34	18,351.5	66	1	78.4
73	BUSINESS SERVICES	20	259	16,854.6	14	204	9,611.9
45	TRANSPORTATION BY AIR	21	64	16,812.0	37	20	2,697.4
26	PAPER & ALLIED PRODUCTS	22	81	15,200.6	19	74	7,515.9
33	PRIMARY METAL INDUSTRIES	23	104	14,294.2	17	145	8,078.0
32	STONE, CLAY & GLASS PRODUCTS	24	85	12,727.9	12	144	12,492.6
54	FOOD STORES	25	46	11,840.2	34	20	3,643.6
10	METAL MINING	26	52	10,594.8	22	29	6,430.4
34	FABRICATED METAL PRODUCTS	27	97	10,522.4	32	110	4,038.2
70	HOTELS & OTHER LODGING PLACES	28	57	9,815.9	18	89	7,561.1
65	REAL ESTATE	29	107	9,608.8	30	121	4,592.0
30	RUBBER & MISC. PLASTIC PROD.	30	77	8,706.2	20	87	6,955.5
24	LUMBER & WOOD PRODUCTS	31	29	7,049.2	36	33	3,262.9
80	HEALTH SERVICES	32	126	6,882.0	49	21	963.9
58	EATING & DRINKING PLACES	33	65	6,619.5	16	62	8,736.6
23	APPAREL & OTHER TEXTILE PROD.	34	37	5,851.5	33	55	3,694.8
64	INSURANCE AGENTS,BROKER.& SERV	35	15	5,200.8	27	36	4,801.8
51	WHOLESALE TRADE-NONDURABLE	36	74	5,102.8	13	135	12,389.0
59	MISCELLANEOUS RETAIL	37	64	4,992.4	40	35	2,349.9
50	WHOLESALE TRADE-DURABLE GOODS	38	98	4,982.9	29	184	4,655.9
0	UNKNOWN	39	47	3,726.7	50	31	941.4
15	GENERAL BUILDING CONTRACTORS	40	32	3,589.7	28	82	4,751.6
39	MISC. MANUFACTURING INDUST.	41	45	3,200.6	57	32	326.3
87	ENGINEERING & MGMT. SERVICES	42	87	2,784.8	21	204	6,707.4
12	COAL MINING	43	27	2,690.3	45	15	1,108.3
52	BUILDING & GARDEN MATERIALS	44	11	2,059.8	63	6	139.2
22	TEXTILE MILL PRODUCTS	45	38	1,993.8	42	73	1,875.9
46	PIPELINES, EXC. NATURAL GAS	46	17	1,975.2	0	0	0.0
42	TRUCKING & WAREHOUSING	47	23	1,901.7	59	12	271.8
29	PETROLEUM & COAL PRODUCTS	48	18	1,824.1	39	25	2,428.7
75	AUTO REPAIR, SERV. & PARKING	49	9	1,791.4	56	15	333.3
44	WATER TRANSPORTATION	50	23	1,758.0	25	57	5,170.2
25	FURNITURE & FIXTURES	51	23	1,438.9	54	28	763.3
56	APPAREL & ACCESSORY STORES	52	22	1,355.4	43	18	1,505.9
47	TRANSPORTATION SERVICES	53	10	1,218.2	52	22	777.4
79	AMUSEMENT & RECREATION SERV.	54	22	1,187.6	47	23	1,025.4
14	NONMETALLIC MINERALS-EXC.FUELS	55	9	1,107.0	62	10	150.1
41	LOCAL & PASSENGER TRANSIT	56	6	934.5	0	0	0.0
55	AUTO DEALERS & SERV.STATIONS	57	9	774.8	61	26	211.1
8	FORESTRY	58	5	731.1	38	19	2,540.7

Table 4 (Cont.)
Rankings of Industry Groups of U.S. and European M&A Buyer Companies by SIC Code[a,b]
(1985 - 90)
(In Millions of U.S. Dollars)[c]

SELLER SIC	DESCRIPTION	U. S. TRANSACTIONS			EUROPEAN TRANSACTIONS		
		RANKING[d]	NUMBER	VALUE[c]	RANKING	NUMBER	VALUE
82	EDUCATIONAL SERVICES	59	11	600.9	58	6	273.7
72	PERSONAL SERVICES	60	16	573.1	51	59	871.0
16	HEAVY CONTRUCTION-EXC.BUILDING	61	14	550.1	44	37	1,357.7
1	AGRICULTURAL PRODUCTION-CROPS	62	12	432.3	53	7	769.0
83	SOCIAL SERVICES	63	9	353.4	69	1	1.3
31	LEATHER & LEATHER PRODUCTS	64	8	326.3	11	29	13,162.0
9	FISHING, HUNTING & TRAPPING	65	3	272.1	67	2	58.4
57	FURNITURE & HOMEFURNISH.STORES	66	14	263.7	48	22	1,009.6
17	SPECIAL TRADE CONTRACTORS	67	11	96.8	46	34	1,053.7
2	AGRICULTURAL PROD.-LIVESTOCK	68	1	88.0	0	0	0.0
96	ADMIN. OF ECON. PROGRAMS	69	2	70.0	0	0	0.0
86	MEMBERSHIP ORGANIZATIONS	70	3	49.9	0	0	0.0
76	MISC.REPAIR SERVICES	71	3	20.0	65	7	79.6
89	SERVICES, NEC	72	2	11.8	68	2	8.1
81	LEGAL SERVICES	73	1	1.0	0	0	0.0
95	ENVIRONMENTAL HOUSING/QUALITY	74	1	1.0	0	0	0.0
94	ADMINIST. OF HUMAN RESOURCES	0	0	0.0	60	1	234.2
7	AGRICULTURAL SERVICES	0	0	0.0	64	1	90.0

DATA: Securities Data Corporation, Mergers and Corporate Transactions Database.

a. Completed transactions include: mergers, tender-mergers, tender offers, purchases of stakes, divestitures, recapitalizations, exchange offers and LBOs.
b. The volume data are classified according to the announcement date of a transaction -- not taking into consideration when a transaction is completed.
c. Million dollars of purchase price -- excluding fees and expenses -- at current exchange rates.
d. Ranking is based on total dollar value of acquiring industry.

5. SIMILARITIES BETWEEN EC AND U.S. RESTRUCTURING

The economics of European industrial restructuring are certain to be highly country- and industry-specific, especially at a time of rapid technological change and changing market characteristics, both of which affect firms' ability to exploit economies of scale and scope - with the most dramatic impact being felt among the most highly regulated sectors. Labor-intensive manufacturing activities should be subject to relocation to low-wage areas, including Eastern Europe, Southern Italy, Spain and Portugal. Capital-intensive activities should see rationalization and consolidation across Europe's industrial heartland -- the United Kingdom, Belgium, the Netherlands, France, Germany and Northern Italy and possibly, in time, Eastern Europe as well - accompanied by both horizontal and vertical integration within and between firms in efforts to exploit available scale and scope economies. This will include elimination of duplicative production facilities. In some sectors, only the largest players will remain competitively viable. In others, there is ample room for smaller specialized or regional firms drawing on location-specific or technology-specific advantages.

European economic restructuring in the 1990s is likely to be similar to the restructuring that occurred in the United States in the 1980s, likewise propelled by intense international competition, with similar "global" industries most intensively involved in the process. Since competition for the domestic market in the United States is interregional, coupled to free inter-regional flows of productive factors, limited government subsidization and relatively transparent and benign antitrust policy, U.S. economic restructuring to a significant extent occurred at the corporate level through M&A transactions. There is evidence that the parallelism in U.S. and European restructuring has indeed been the case, and that the industries most intensively involved in restructuring in Europe have been the same ones that experienced restructuring in the United States during the 1980s. Table 3 ranks 1985-1989 U.S. and European merger transaction volume by the industry of selling companies. Table 4 does the same for the industry of buying companies. In each table approximately 70 industries (classified by two-digit SIC codes) were designated.

Table 5 indicates the Spearman rank correlations of U.S. and European industry involvement in M&A activity during the period. They show a high degree of rank correlation of industry participation in M&A transactions from the two regions, for both buyers and sellers.

Table 5
Pearson Correlation of U.S. and European Industries
Participating in M&A Transactions[a]
(1985 - 90)

| | | | EUROPEAN INDUSTRIES | | | |
| | | | BY SIC OF BUYER | | BY SIC OF SELLER | |
			# OF DEALS	$ VOLUME	# OF DEALS	$ VOLUME
U. S.	# OF DEALS	r	0.8241	0.7556	0.7068	0.6480
I		N	(66)	(66)	(70)	(70)
N D U S		P[b]	0.000	0.000	0.000	0.000
T R	$ VOLUME	r	0.7975	0.7828	0.5600	0.6911
I E		N	(66)	(66)	(70)	(70)
S		P	0.000	0.000	0.000	0.000

DATA: Tables 3 and 4.

a. Correlation coefficients are based on the number of transactions and the dollar volume of U.S. and European industries (2-digit SIC codes).
b. One-tailed significance.

Table 6
Correlations of Top 25 Industry Group of U.S. and European M&A Seller Companies by SIC Code[a,b] (1985 - 90)
(In Millions of U.S. Dollars)[c]

| SELLER | | U.S. TRANSACTIONS | | | | EUROPEAN TRANSACTIONS | | | |
| | | M&A DATA[d] | | WEIGHTED DATA[e] | | M&A DATA | | WEIGHTED DATA | |
SIC	DESCRIPTION	Ranking	Value	Ranking	Value	Ranking	Value	Ranking	Value
28	CHEMICALS & ALLIED PRODUCTS	1	141,401.9	18	0.105446	5	23,412.8	20	0.030091
13	OIL & GAS EXTRACTION	2	85,754.7	21	0.081345	4	29,852.5	17	0.040148
48	COMMUNICATIONS	3	83,786.7	23	0.077395	31	3,418.4	23	0.012822
20	FOOD & KINDRED PRODUCTS	4	80,710.1	16	0.128462	1	50,716.4	7	0.069992
36	ELECTRONIC & OTHER ELECT.EQUIP	5	77,061.3	13	0.135284	6	21,130.3	11	0.054298
60	DEPOSITORY INSTITUTIONS	6	65,390.8	12	0.136250	2	33,454.3	13	0.043750
35	INDUSTRIAL MACHINERY & EQUIP.	7	57,919.3	24	0.070932	15	9,611.7	14	0.043188
53	GENERAL MERCHANDISE STORES	8	45,250.7	15	0.131128	18	8,057.8	18	0.036403
27	PRINTING & PUBLISHING	9	44,616.4	11	0.168481	11	13,617.2	5	0.102694
37	TRANSPORTATION EQUIPMENT	10	40,012.1	22	0.079541	7	20,704.4	12	0.054268
78	MOTION PICTURES	11	39,022.6	7	0.295346	42	2,044.2	1	0.154181
73	BUSINESS SERVICES	12	35,098.8	2	0.589276	13	11,949.6	4	0.118980
38	INSTRUMENTS & RELATED PROD.	13	34,697.2	14	0.133104	35	3,070.4	6	0.089242
21	TOBACCO PRODUCTS	14	33,140.8	17	0.118048	57	560.7	24	0.004179
61	NONDEPOSITORY INSTITUTIONS	15	31,954.6	10	0.170675	22	5,647.9	10	0.058849
54	FOOD STORES	16	30,315.3	4	0.572038	14	10,141.3	8	0.067953
49	ELECTRIC,GAS & SANITARY SERV.	17	30,127.6	25	0.040683	12	13,396.5	16	0.041511
70	HOTELS & OTHER LODGING PLACES	18	29,126.9	1	0.823017	20	6,487.8	3	0.125778
63	INSURANCE CARRIERS	19	27,193.1	20	0.086315	3	30,610.2	15	0.041698
32	STONE, CLAY & GLASS PRODUCTS	20	26,452.0	6	0.436271	21	6,079.0	21	0.028368
26	PAPER & ALLIED PRODUCTS	21	24,242.3	19	0.099758	8	17,276.6	2	0.135760
30	RUBBER & MISC. PLASTIC PROD.	22	24,165.3	3	0.573737	36	2,980.8	22	0.020309
58	EATING & DRINKING PLACES	23	23,383.1	5	0.502557	33	3,401.4	9	0.065004
33	PRIMARY METAL INDUSTRIES	24	23,316.1	9	0.184456	23	5,030.4	19	0.035052
40	RAILROAD TRANSPORTATION	25	23,218.2	8	0.189221	66	24.1	25	0.000000

DATA: Securities Data Corporation, Mergers and Corporate Transactions database.

a. Completed transactions include: mergers, tender-mergers, tender offers, purchases of stakes, divestitures, recapitalizations, exchange offers and LBOs.

b. The volume data are classified according to the announcement date of a transaction -- not taking into consideration when a transaction is completed.

c. Million dollars of purchase price -- excluding fees and expenses -- at current exchange rates.

d. Ranking is based on total dollar value of the target industry.

e. Ranking is based on the annualized M&A dollar volume of the target industry weighted by the market capitalization value of its corresponding industry. Market capitalization values are as of December 30, 1988 for Western European industries and as of March 15,1990 for U.S. industries. Market capitalization values for U.S. industries were calculated using (at around) 70% of total market capitalization which corresponds to at around 7.2 percent of all listed domestic companies. Market capitalization values for Western European industries were calculated using (at around) 70% of total market capitalization (excluding Greece, Portugal and Luxembourg) which corresponds to at around 25 percent of all listed domestic companies.

Table 7
Correlations of Top 25 Industry Group of U.S. and European M&A Buyer Companies by SIC Code[a,b]
(1985 - 90)
(In Millions of U.S. Dollars)[c]

SELLER SIC	DESCRIPTION	U.S. M&A DATA[d]		U.S. TRANSACTIONS WEIGHTED DATA[e]		EUROPEAN M&A DATA		EUROPEAN TRANSACTIONS WEIGHTED DATA	
		Ranking	Value	Ranking	Value	Ranking	Value	Ranking	Value
67	HOLDING & OTHER INV'T. OFFICES	1	346,867.1	1	11.017720	1	64,462.8	1	0.358427
28	CHEMICALS & ALLIED PRODUCTS	2	94,062.3	18	0.070144	2	49,938.9	8	0.064182
13	OIL & GAS EXTRACTION	3	76,617.0	17	0.072677	6	26,715.0	18	0.035928
48	COMMUNICATIONS	4	65,744.0	23	0.060729	23	6,334.2	21	0.023759
60	DEPOSITORY INSTITUTIONS	5	61,679.2	10	0.128516	4	37,364.7	13	0.048864
27	PRINTING & PUBLISHING	6	43,109.3	7	0.162790	8	18,191.0	4	0.137187
20	FOOD & KINDRED PRODUCTS	7	40,453.7	21	0.064388	3	44,135.5	9	0.060910
35	INDUSTRIAL MACHINERY & EQUIP.	8	38,425.1	24	0.047058	15	9,581.1	15	0.043051
36	ELECTRONIC & OTHER ELECT.EQUIP	9	38,037.6	19	0.066777	7	26,315.9	7	0.067623
37	TRANSPORTATION EQUIPMENT	10	37,735.8	16	0.075016	9	15,594.9	17	0.040876
21	TOBACCO PRODUCTS	11	35,455.0	11	0.126291	55	427.1	24	0.003183
38	INSTRUMENTS & RELATED PROD.	12	30,423.6	12	0.116710	35	3,285.9	6	0.095506
63	INSURANCE CARRIERS	13	28,478.9	15	0.090396	5	30,029.7	16	0.040907
62	SECURITY & COMMODITY BROKERS	14	24,144.7	6	0.198745	10	14,829.0	3	0.145202
53	GENERAL MERCHANDISE STORES	15	22,437.4	20	0.065019	26	4,825.6	22	0.021801
61	NONDEPOSITORY INSTITUTIONS	16	19,769.7	14	0.105593	41	2,342.4	20	0.024407
78	MOTION PICTURES	17	19,735.2	9	0.149368	31	4,106.6	2	0.309734
49	ELECTRIC, GAS & SANITARY SERV.	18	19,287.1	25	0.026044	24	5,853.2	23	0.018137
40	RAILROAD TRANSPORTATION	19	18,351.5	8	0.149559	66	78.4	25	0.000000
73	BUSINESS SERVICES	20	16,854.6	2	0.282973	14	9,611.9	5	0.095704
45	TRANSPORTATION BY AIR	21	16,812.0	4	0.215899	37	2,697.4	14	0.048380
26	PAPER & ALLIED PRODUCTS	22	15,200.6	22	0.062551	19	7,515.9	10	0.059060
33	PRIMARY METAL INDUSTRIES	23	14,294.2	13	0.113083	17	8,078.0	12	0.056288
32	STONE, CLAY & GLASS PRODUCTS	24	12,727.9	5	0.209920	12	12,492.6	11	0.058298
54	FOOD STORES	25	11,840.2	3	0.223420	34	3,643.6	19	0.024414

DATA: Securities Data Corporation, Mergers and Corporate Transactions database.

a. Completed transactions include: mergers, tender-mergers, tender offers, purchases of stakes, divestitures, recapitalizations, exchange offers and LBOs.

b. The volume data are classified according to the announcement date of a transaction -- not taking into consideration when a transaction is completed.

c. Million dollars of purchase price -- excluding fees and expenses -- at current exchange rates.

d. Ranking is based on total dollar value of the target industry.

e. Ranking is based on the annualized M&A dollar volume of the target industry weighted by the market capitalization value of its corresponding industry. Market capitalization values are as of December 30, 1988 for Western European industries and as of March 15,1990 for U.S. industries. Market capitalization values for U.S. industries were calculated using (at around) 70% of total market capitalization which corresponds to at around 7.2 percent of all listed domestic companies. Market capitalization values for Western European industries were calculated using (at around) 70% of total market capitalization (excluding Greece, Portugal and Luxembourg) which corresponds to at around 25 percent of all listed domestic companies.

Of course, such rankings may well be affected by the absolute size of the various industries themselves, so that "larger" industries will be subject to the higher levels of M&A activity than smaller industries. In order to adjust for this, each industry was weighted by the industry's market capitalization at the end of 1988 (for the European countries) and March 1989 (for the United States). The respective rankings for the top 25 2-digit SIC industries for seller and buyer industries are presented in Tables 6 and 7.

Table 8 presents the Pearson correlation coefficients for buyer and seller transactions for the United States and Europe, respectively regarding the top 20 and 25 industries. The correlation coefficients are high and significant on the buyer side, which is consistent with the notion that the same kinds of economic pressures underlying economic restructuring are active in both regions.

Table 8
Pearson Correlation of Weighted Values of U.S. and European
Industries Participating in M&A Transactions[a]
(1985 - 90)

	BY SIC OF BUYER		BY SIC OF SELLER	
	TOP 20	TOP 25	TOP 20	TOP 25
r	0.6917	0.6924	0.5687	0.3425
N	(20)	(25)	(20)	(25)
r	0.6917	0.6924	0.5687	0.3425
P[b]	0.0007	0.0001	0.0089	0.0094

DATA: Tables 6 and 7.
a. Rank correlation coefficients are based on the annualized M&A dollar volume of the buying (target) industry
    (2-digit SIC codes) weighted by the market capitalization value of its corresponding industry.
b. One-tailed significance.

6. PATTERNS OF EUROPEAN M&A ACTIVITY, 1985-89

The patterns of intra-European M&A activity for the 1985-1989 period can be observed by sorting transactions by the nationality of buyers and sellers for each of the years in the data series, presented in Table 9. The average annual rate of growth of all intra-European M&A volume was an exceptionally high 120.4 percent. U.K. activity in the European merger marketplace was by far the greatest - 64.1 percent of all reported intra-European transactions involved British seller companies - although cross-country comparisons may be distorted by differences in premiums paid, on which no data are available. British seller volume grew at an average annual rate of 65.7 percent, consistent with the overall intra-European growth rates; transactions involving British sellers to British buyers grew at a somewhat slower rate of 59.8 percent during the period.

French and Italian companies, however, were acquiring other European companies (including British companies) at a much more rapid pace. Especially active on the buy-side in the intra- European market, French buyer-transactions grew at a rate of 465 percent per annum, and purchases by Italian companies grew at 111 percent annually during the same period. French buyers acquiring French companies totaled $13.7 billion (out of a total of $26.7 billion of French intra-European acquisitions) during the five- year period, and reflected an annual growth rate of 373 percent. Italian companies acquired other Italian companies worth $13.9 billion during the period, a growth rate of 112 percent per annum.

Although much less active in intra-European volume terms during the period ($9.7 billion), German companies (whose rate of growth in intra-European buyer transactions was 50.8 percent annually during 1985-1989) substantially lagged British, French, and Italian acquirers. German sell-side activity grew even more slowly, showing a growth rate of only 26.6 percent per annum. It is evident that it has become much easier for French and Italian companies to use the merger market for seller-initiated transactions than it has been for German companies, which have been perhaps the least accustomed to domestic M&A activity among all of the major home-countries of companies engaging in European mergers and acquisitions. Sellers from these four countries made up about 86 percent of aggregate intra-European transaction volume during the period; German sellers accounted for only 2.7 percent of all seller activity.

Also, in many continental European countries there are structural and/or regulatory barriers to takeover activity, such as control over voting rights, privileges granted to management to take actions without shareholder approval, and restrictions on the availability of material information. These barriers are sufficient in some countries (especially Switzerland, Germany, The Netherlands and France) to preclude most hostile takeover attempts. In general, these barriers are being dismantled, although gradually. In some cases, contested transactions have succeeded despite them, such as the Credit Suisse acquisition of Bank Leu. The barriers do not, of course, prevent a defender's board from finally coming to agreement with a pursuer, nor do they prevent a pursuer from going public with proposals for a friendly takeover at a fair price to shareholders, who in turn are free to exert pressure on the defenders. Even in Switzerland where shares owned by foreigners can be denied voting rights by unilateral management action, proposals direct to shareholders offering a high price for the stock of a company - subject to the condition that management register all the shares - would be taken very seriously.

European companies frequently enter into strategic alliances with other companies in an effort to secure many of the benefits of an acquisition without incurring all of the costs, financial and otherwise. Such alliances have been seen as characteristic for European companies, reflecting cultural patterns with a strong traditional base as well as the fact that those controlling a substantial minority investment often may be able to control the company itself. In such cases the level of investment needed to achieve effective control of the business and assets of a company may be comparatively small.

In the United States, on the other hand, and in the United Kingdom to a somewhat lesser extent, minority interests can be difficult to manage. If a company has a minority interest outstanding, such shareholders may institute litigation to ensure that their rights are not infringed, or that the value of their investments are not diminished by actions taken by controlling stockholders. Minority shareholders have for many years received the protection of the courts from inappropriate loss of rights or values. For example,

Table 9
Volume of Completed Intra-European M&A Transactions by Country
(1985-90)
(In Millions of U.S. Dollars)

COUNTRY OF BUYER COMPANY		U.K.	FRANCE	ITALY	GERMANY	OTHER EUROPEAN	TOTALS BUYER
			COUNTRY OF SELLER COMPANY				
U.K.	1985	8,363.9	0.0	0.0	0.0	12.2	8,376.1
	1986	12,401.1	23.8	0.0	1.0	70.0	12,495.9
	1987	29,859.4	124.5	125.9	216.5	520.5	30,846.8
	1988	39,537.9	1,172.8	480.8	201.6	1,012.3	42,405.4
	1989	54,204.9	1,261.3	290.2	361.9	3,125.3	59,243.6
	1990	19,790.5	2,406.7	114.9	528.5	3,316.1	26,158.7
	TOTAL	164,157.7	4,991.1	1,011.8	1,309.5	8,056.4	179,526.5
	CGR	18.8%					25.8%
FRANCE	1985	0.0	10.7	0.0	0.0	0.0	10.7
	1986	5.9	222.0	520.0	0.0	32.1	780.9
	1987	1316.6	1,674.4	207.3	0.0	0.0	2,198.3
	1988	3,137.0	7,355.1	35.7	310.2	1,056.2	11,894.2
	1989	5,211.9	15,145.6	602.4	1,989.7	3,331.9	26,281.5
	1990	3,129.6	9,078.0	3,042.4	358.5	4,089.6	19,698.1
	TOTAL	11,801.0	33,485.8	4,408.7	2,658.4	8,508.8	60,863.7
	CGR		285.2%				349.8%
ITALY	1985	16.8	0.0	165.0	0.0	0.0	181.8
	1986	0.0	0.0	1,199.4	129.0	0.0	1,328.4
	1987	0.0	20.4	7,876.3	0.0	1,050.8	8,947.5
	1988	0.0	325.0	1,314.2	429.3	887.7	2,956.2
	1989	7.9	294.4	7,007.8	63.1	0.0	7,373.2
	1990	55.4	237.6	5,310.4	500.6	347.6	6,451.6
	TOTAL	80.1	877.4	22,873.1	1,122.0	2,286.1	27,238.7
	CGR			100.2%			104.2%
GERMANY	1985	0.0	0.0	0.0	895.5	445.0	1,343.5
	1986	425.0	0.3	887.4	980.0	0.0	2,292.7
	1987	159.6	330.6	0.0	425.6	0.0	915.8
	1988	59.2	154.0	866.1	2,227.3	39.8	3,346.2
	1989	817.8	1,341.3	37.5	2,221.3	1,475.3	5,893.2
	1990	934.8	2.2	53.2	988.9	1,301.5	3,280.6
	TOTAL	2,396.4	1,828.4	1,844.2	7,741.6	3,261.4	17,072.0
	CGR				1.9%		19.5%
OTHER EUROPEAN	1985	209.2	0.0	0.0	0.0	492.4	701.6
	1986	828.6	0.0	0.0	0.0	1,258.7	2,087.3
	1987	558.5	169.1	0.0	239.0	5,090.3	6,056.9
	1988	7,489.1	1,028.6	2,391.7	0.0	7,384.6	18,394.0
	1989	1,759.6	3,975.1	305.9	826.6	15,371.6	22,238.8
	1990	5,778.8	1,201.0	233.1	2,607.7	15,040.4	24,861.0
	TOTAL	16,623.8	6,373.8	3,030.7	3,673.3	44,638.0	74,339.6
	CGR					98.1%	104.1%
TOTAL SELLERS	1985	8,589.9	10.7	185.0	898.5	949.6	10,613.7
	1986	13,660.6	246.1	2,607.7	1,110.0	1,360.8	18,985.2
	1987	30,894.1	2,319.0	8,209.5	881.1	6,661.6	48,985.3
	1988	50,223.2	10,035.5	5,188.5	3,168.4	10,380.4	78,996.0
	1989	62,002.1	22,017.7	8,243.8	5,462.6	23,304.1	121,030.3
	1990	29,689.1	12,927.5	8,754.0	4,984.2	24,095.2	80,450.0
	TOTAL	195,059.0	47,558.5	33,188.5	16,504.2	66,751.7	359,040.5
	CGR	28.2%	313.5%	121.3%	40.9%	90.9%	49.9%

DATA: Securities Data Corporation, Mergers and Corporate Transactions database.

multiple-plaintiff (class action) suits are permitted in the United States, which means that the slightest perceived irregularity will almost assuredly provoke a lawsuit against controlling shareholders. For this reason, few controlling shareholders in the United States wish to leave minority interests outstanding for any length of time.

In the United States also, many companies have experienced joint shareholding arrangements with partners which were unwound after a few years. Either the two parties did not share the same expectations, or shoulder the burdens of the venture equally, or business or personnel changes took place that altered the importance of the venture in one or both parties' minds. Very few partnership arrangements of this sort last very long, but for many individuals contemplating new challenges, it is tempting to think that one can face those challenges best with a like-minded partner.

Table 10
Partial Ownership Positions as a Percentage of
All Completed U.S. and European M&A Transactions[a,b]
(1985 - 90)
(In Percentage Terms)[c]

YEAR	U. S.[d] SELLER	EUROPEAN SELLER[e]		INTRA-EUROPEAN DEALS[f]	
		UNITED KINGDOM	REST OF EUROPE	UNITED KINGDOM	REST OF EUROPE
1985	5.820%	15.494%	22.410%	5.598%	23.024%
1986	14.591%	9.770%	43.234%	6.266%	36.827%
1987	12.651%	40.712%	4.888%	31.807%	3.357%
1988	9.582%	27.279%	35.701%	13.590%	28.549%
1989	20.909%	26.866%	33.124%	30.019%	28.081%
1990	13.391%	21.333%	22.120%	17.448%	17.107%
AVERAGE 1985-90	12.824%	23.576%	26.913%	17.455%	22.824%

DATA: Securities Data Corporation, Mergers and Corporate Transactions database.

a. Partial ownership positions involve open or privately negotiated stake purchases of stock or assets.
b. Data include only completed transactions. Data are classified according to the announcement date of a transaction -- not taking into consideration when a transaction is completed.
c. Percentage values denote the fraction of total transaction volume which involves partial stakes.
d. Completed partial stakes as a percentage of total dollar volume of completed M&A transactions in which the seller is a U.S. company.
e. Completed partial stakes as a percentage of total dollar volume of completed M&A transactions in which the seller is a European company -- i.e., when the seller is a U.K. company or when the seller is a European company different from the U.K.
f. Completed partial stakes as a percentage of total dollar volume of completed M&A transactions in which the buyer and the seller are European companies.

Table 10 shows attempted partial ownership positions as a percentage of all attempted U.S. and European M&A transactions. As expected, the incidence of these transactions is relatively small in the United States, where they accounted for 10 percent or less of all transactions in each year since 1985, and averaged 5.5 percent for the entire 1985-1989 period.

In Europe, the use of partial ownership positions differs significantly between the U. K. and continental European transactions. The incidence of stakeholdings in the United Kingdom has been relatively small, but larger than in the United States - averaging between 12 percent and 8 percent, depending on whether the acquirers (including U.S. acquirers) of U.K. partial ownership positions were more easily persuaded that partial ownership was the right way to take over a British company than were European acquirers, although there are insufficient data to allow more than speculation on this point.

With respect to continental Europe, a much higher incidence of partial ownership is evident, averaging between 24 and 26 percent of all European transactions for the 1985-89 period. It may be, however, that the rate of partial ownership transactions in the rest of Europe has begun to decline, as difficult managerial lessons are learned from experience in stakeholdings.

Another European notion about M&A activity is that hostile transactions - often viewed as an unwelcome creation of overly aggressive Anglo-Saxon bankers and entrepreneurs, have little role to play in continental Europe. Certainly, the prevalence of hostile deals flourished in the United States and the United Kingdom, where they accounted for an average of 18 percent and 29 percent to total attempted transactions by volume, respectively, during the 1985-1989 period. This was a time when hostile bids were relatively easy to arrange and finance, and were therefore in especially active use in these two countries particularly for larger sized transactions. In the case of both the United States and the United Kingdom, however, after 1987 the level of hostile activity declined considerably.

Table 11 illustrates the patterns of hostile offers for U.S., U.K. and continental European companies. American companies, although rarely employing hostile bids when acquiring firms abroad, were frequently targets of hostile bids from non-U.S. companies, especially British companies. The U.K. experience was roughly the same in cross-border transactions, whether U.K. companies were acquirers or targets. Continental European companies, on the other hand, experienced a much lower incidence of hostile activity, averaging 8.8 percent of all intra-European transactions, although the data also indicate an increase in hostile activity after the de Benedetti raid on Société Générale in 1988. Transactions over $50 million in size show roughly the same share of hostile activity as do all transactions reflected in Table 11, except that U.S. hostile bids for companies in continental Europe drop from 34.2 to 23 percent.

There are at least two reasons why continental European companies are becoming more willing to resort to hostile bidding techniques, despite their traditional reluctance to do so.

First, many larger European companies have either participated in (or observed closely) takeover activity in the United States or the United Kingdom and have become sufficiently familiar with takeover practices to consider importing them back to their home countries.

Table 11
Unsolicited or Hostile Offers as a Percentage of All Completed
U.S. and European M&A Transactions[a,b]
(1985 - 90)
(In Percentage Terms)[c]

	UNITED STATES			INTRA-EUROPEAN TRANSACTIONS			
				UNITED KINGDOM			
	U.S.	CROSS-BORDER[e]			U.K. / REST OF EUROPE[g]		REST OF[h]
YEAR	DOMESTIC[d]	U.S. BUYER	U.S. SELLER	DOMESTIC[f]	U.K. BUYER	U.K. SELLER	EUROPE
1985	9.983%	0.000%	16.168%	71.800%	0.000%	0.000%	4.889%
1986	5.823%	0.000%	15.781%	7.615%	0.000%	20.786%	0.000%
1987	3.513%	2.120%	9.859%	22.274%	0.000%	0.000%	0.000%
1988	21.617%	2.025%	29.914%	17.227%	7.658%	60.663%	4.310%
1989	3.797%	0.000%	2.888%	13.754%	0.000%	0.000%	11.140%
1990	0.000%	0.000%	0.000%	6.586%	0.000%	0.000%	0.118%
AVERAGE 7.456% 1985-90		0.691%	12.435%	23.209%	1.276%	13.575%	3.410%

DATA: Securities Data Corporation, Mergers and Corporate Transactions database.

a. Hostile offers are defined as those transactions in which the acquiring company proceeds with its offer against the wishes of the target company's management.
b. Data include only completed transactions. Data are classified according to the announcement date of a transaction -- not taking into consideration when a transaction is completed.
c. Percentage values denote the fraction of total transaction volume which involves hostile offers.
d. Completed hostile deals as a percentage of total dollar volume of completed M&A transactions in which both buyer and seller are U.S. companies.
e. Completed hostile deals as a percentage of total dollar volume of completed M&A transactions in which either the buyer or the·seller is a U.S. company and the counterpart is a non-U.S. company.
f. Completed hostile deals as a percentage of total dollar volume of completed M&A transactions in which both buyer and seller are U.K. companies.
g. Completed hostile deals as a percentage of total dollar volume of completed M&A transactions in which either the buyer or the seller is a U.K. company and the counterpart is a Continental European company.
h. Completed hostile deals as a percentage of total dollar volume of completed M&A transactions in which both buyer and seller are Continental European companies.

Second, capital market activity in Europe has increased substantially in volume and sophistication, so that funds are available to entrepreneurs seeking to launch takeovers and institutional investors have come to understand the pros and cons of takeovers better and to behave more objectively than they did in the past. The greatest progress in breaking through takeover barriers have been achieved in France, Italy and Spain where, as noted earlier, aggregate growth in M&A activity has been the highest in all of Europe.

Table 12 draws a similar comparison for LBO penetration in the United States, the United Kingdom and continental Europe. Whereas the U.S. level of activity has begun to drop off at the end of the period (after achieving a peak of 31 percent of all attempted

transactions in 1988), the United Kingdom and the rest of Europe have experienced
significant increases in LBOs, where the $20 billion Hoylake (Sir James Goldsmith and
others) bid for BAT (British American Tobacco) industries in 1989 was especially
prominent.

Table 12
Leveraged Buyouts as a Percentage of
All Completed U.S. and European M&A Transactions[a,b]
(1985 - 90)
(In Percentage Terms)[c]

YEAR	U. S.[d] SELLER	EUROPEAN SELLER[e]		INTRA-EUROPEAN DEALS[f]	
		UNITED KINGDOM	REST OF EUROPE	UNITED KINGDOM	REST OF EUROPE
1985	13.520%	5.613%	0.000%	0.966%	0.000%
1986	16.436%	2.373%	1.038%	3.691%	0.000%
1987	17.326%	5.360%	0.618%	6.924%	0.646%
1988	25.817%	6.769%	3.622%	9.668%	3.214%
1989	11.104%	9.764%	2.473%	13.965%	2.374%
1990	7.320%	4.456%	1.862%	11.884%	1.713%
AVERAGE 1985-90	15.254%	5.723%	1.602%	7.850%	1.325%

DATA: Securities Data Corporation, Mergers and Corporate Transactions database.

a.   Leveraged buyout (LBO) is defined as a transaction in which an investor group, investor, or
     investment/LBO firm acquires a company, taking on an extraordinary amount of debt, with plans to repay
     the debt with funds generated from the company or with revenue earned by selling off the newly acquired
     company's assets. An acquisition is considered an LBO if the investor group includes management or if
     newspaper articles or press release describe the transaction as a buyout.
b.   Data include only completed transactions. Data are classified according to the announcement date of a
     transaction -- not taking into consideration when a transaction is completed.
c.   Percentage values denote the fraction of total transaction volume which involves LBOs.
d.   Completed LBOs as a percentage of total dollar volume of completed M&A transactions in which the
     seller is a U.S. company.
e.   Completed LBOs as a percentage of total dollar volume of completed M&A transactions in which the
     seller is a European company -- i.e., when the seller is a U.K. company or when the seller is a European
     company different from the U.K.
f.   Completed LBOs as a percentage of total dollar volume of completed M&A transactions in which the
     buyer and the seller are European companies.

Transactions over $50 million in size show basically the same pattern of activity. The
significance of the table is in the fact that LBOs are occurring in continental Europe at
all (where they accounted for about 6 percent of intra-European M&A activity in 1988
and 1989), and that such transactions have been growing in recent years. Even such a
complex free-market device as the LBO can be put to use in continental Europe once the
financing is available and investors understand its uses and drawbacks.

Table 13
U.S. and European Corporate Use of Financial Advisers as a Percentage
Of All Completed Merger and Acquisition Transactions[a]
(1985 - 90)
(In Percentage Terms)[b]

| YEAR | U.S. SELLER | ADVISER TO BUYER FREQUENCY[c] | | | | | ADVISER TO SELLER FREQUENCY[d] | | | |
| | | EUROPEAN SELLER | | INTRA-EUROPEAN DEALS | | U.S. SELLER | EUROPEAN SELLER | | INTRA-EUROPEAN DEALS | |
		UNITED KINGDOM	REST OF EUROPE	UNITED KINGDOM	REST OF EUROPE		UNITED KINGDOM	REST OF EUROPE	UNITED KINGDOM	REST OF EUROPE
1985	17.270%	36.583%	100.000%	33.391%	89.412%	18.561%	12.871%	0.000%	3.843%	0.000%
1986	15.734%	54.895%	97.380%	39.801%	78.550%	31.198%	10.468%	2.620%	10.669%	0.881%
1987	12.361%	50.282%	56.128%	41.846%	42.351%	33.708%	16.959%	5.490%	17.956%	3.551%
1988	18.116%	40.093%	65.827%	33.988%	44.714%	23.006%	9.077%	19.200%	10.469%	8.409%
1989	19.017%	39.988%	67.923%	40.074%	57.901%	27.270%	15.895%	24.080%	15.875%	17.153%
1990	16.422%	67.433%	63.153%	54.175%	54.002%	38.094%	10.066%	7.513%	12.204%	3.930%
AVERAGE 1985-90	16.487%	48.212%	75.069%	40.546%	61.155	28.640%	12.556%	9.817%	11.836%	5.654%

DATA: Securities Data Corporation, Mergers and Corporate Transactions database.
a. Data include only completed transactions. Data are classified according to the announcement date of a transaction -- not taking into consideration when a transaction is completed.
b. Percentage values denote the fraction of the total number of transactions which involves the presence of financial advisers.
c. Presence of financial advisers to the buying company as a percentage of the total number of attempted M&A transactions.
d. Presence of financial advisers to the selling company as a percentage of the total number of attempted M&A transactions.

Table 13 (a) and (b) compares the use of financial advisers in M&A transactions by companies from the United States, the United Kingdom and the rest of Europe. Here, we see relatively high usage of advisers by U. S. and U.K. companies, which have learned that it is nearly impossible to be assured of the highest price (if a seller) or the most effective tactics (if a buyer) without such services. Continental Europeans show a less frequent usage of advisers on average.

7. CONCLUSION

Based on the analyses in this paper, we can draw the following conclusions pertaining to the future of European economic restructuring through M&A transactions:

1) A merger boom has indeed begun in Europe, and is being regarded as beneficial to industrial corporations (both those owned by the private sector and those still owned by governments) seeking restructuring for the purpose of enhancing their competitive performance in what are now global industries, and by investors seeking liquidity and greater value-realization of longstanding holdings. Some disruption of established relationships and entitlements can be seen to result from increased M&A activity, but there is little evidence to date of either public or institutional resistance to the level of activity attained, nor of extreme behavior on the part of the principals engaged in restructuring that might attract increased regulation in the future. At the same time, there is a growing recognition that clear rules of procedure, and suitable powers of enforcement must be put into place in order to prevent possible abuses.

2) The user-benefits of a global or European market for corporate control are considerable. In many parts of continental Europe, businesses are owned by individuals, proprietorships, partnerships, or closely held corporations. Such owners have lacked liquidity in their holdings and thus have been restricted in distributing wealth to successive generations of their families, or in being able to sell out at the end of their active years. In the past, such owners have had to accept low prices for their businesses in a sale to a competitor, to a bank, or to the market in a limited "going-public" transaction. More recently, as a result of privatization issues, increasing deregulation, growing trading volumes and enhanced liquidity - in part due to investments from the United States and Japan - European equity markets have become much more active, efficient (in the sense of competing-away corporate control premiums) and transparent. With this has come the possibility of selling businesses at prices attuned to the public equity markets plus, as has long been the practice in the United States and the United Kingdom a substantial control premium. Thus the market for corporate control has attracted numerous owners of businesses seeking buyers. There is reason to believe that once this pattern of transactions has become established in Europe, as it has in the United States and the United Kingdom, it will become a permanently operating market.

3) Buyers too have become important users of the market, especially those larger European corporations looking for strategic additions to their businesses in anticipation of the liberalization in 1992, or for other reasons. Many continental buyers have gained substantial experience in acquiring companies in the United States and in the United

Kingdom, and have become comfortable operating in other countries. Moreover, many have found a growing number of experienced advisers to assist them in affecting complicated transactions, and a substantial access to needed capital. Successful buyers attract other companies from their industries as emulators.

4) Both buyers and sellers are benefitting from better understanding of company valuations, financing techniques, and the opportunity to dispose of businesses that no longer fit strategic objectives. Much greater financial flexibility has been developed. Sellers of businesses, in particular, have benefitted from tactics designed to utilize auction processes in order to increase selling prices. Buyers have benefitted from the increasing opportunity to make offers directly to shareholders, even if such offers are opposed by the board of directors of the companies concerned.

5) The extraordinary volume of transactions after 1985, relative to prior levels of activity, indicate that the market for corporate control has begun to generate its own attention, attract infrastructure to support future growth, players of all sorts (advisers, bankers, strategic consultants, lawyers, etc.) who will attempt to stimulate transactions, as well as a new breed of financial entrepreneur who can be expected to create and exploit profit opportunities from the scene.

6) These factors, taken together, suggest the development of an exceptional amount of momentum in the merger market in Europe, one that will assist in its further expansion, until such time as a substantial proportion of large businesses, especially those intending to operate on regional or global bases, have been restructured and corporate control values have found equilibrium levels. Perhaps the process, coming as it does to Europe for the first time, could last a decade or more.

In essence, market-driven economic restructuring is linked to profit motives that have been stimulated by the EC 1992 initiatives to trigger a variety of transactions that involve corporate equity. These transactions may be aimed at more efficient deployment of economic resources and capturing available economies of scale and economies of scope under intensified competitive pressure, and/or rent-seeking under market structures altered by the new rules of the game. They may involve financial restructuring within the firm itself, buying part or all of another firm, or selling the firm in order to execute strategies felt to be competitively viable. Much of this activity is captured in the M&A transactions-flow reviewed in this paper, which is likely to intensify further in the 1990s. Liquefying the market for corporate control is likely to be of lasting benefit for the efficiency and growth of the European regional economy.

REFERENCES

Balassa, B. (1961), Economic Integration, Homewood, Ill.: Richard D. Irwin.

Booz Allen Acquisition Services (1990), Study on Obstacles to Takeover Bids in the European Community Paris: Booz Allen.

Caves, R.E. (1990), "Corporate Mergers in International Economic Integration," Paper Presented at CEPR /Instituto Mobiliare Italiano Conference on European Financial Integration, Rome, 22- 23 January.

Commission of the European Communities (1988), "The Economics of 1992," European Economy, No. 35 (Cecchini Report), Office des Publications des Communautes Europeennes, Luxembourg, March.

Commission of the European Communities (1989), "Horizontal Mergers and Competition in the European Community," European Economy, No 40, Office des Publications des Communautes Europeennes, Luxembourg, May.

Doukas, J. and N. Travlos (1988), "The Effect of Corporate Multinationalism on Shareholders' Wealth: Evidence from International Acquisitions," Journal of Finance, December.

Fleuriet, M. (1989), "Mergers and Acquisitions: The French Experience," Chase Manhattan S.A. (mimeo.). Paris.

Dunning, J.H. (1981), International Production and the Multinational Enterprise, Allen & Unwin, London.

Jacquemin, A. (1987), The New Industrial Organization, Oxford University Press, Oxford.

Kay, J. et al. (1989), 1992: Myths and Realities, Centre for Business Strategy, London Business School, London.

Lipsey, R.G. (1960), "The Theory of Customs Unions," Economic Journal, September.

Peltzman, S. (1977), "The Gains and Losses from Industrial Concentration," Journal of Law and Economics, No. 28.

Porter, M.E. (1980), Competitive Strategy, Free Press, New York.

Rybczynski, T (1989), "Corporate Restructuring," National Westminster Bank Review, August.

Scherer, F.M. (1980), Industrial Market Structure and Economic Performance, Rand McNally, Chicago.

Scitovsky, T. (1958), Economic Theory and Western European Integration, Allen & Unwin, London.

Sleuwaegen, L. and H. Yamawaki (1988), "The Formation of the European Common Market and Changes in Market Structure and Performance," European Economic Review, No. 32.

Smith, R.C. and I. Walter (1991), "Industrial Restructuring in Europe and the Market for Corporate Control," in Cool,K., D. Neven and I. Walter (Eds.), Industrial Restructuring in Europe, Macmillan, London. Reprinted in "Economic Restructuring in Europe and the Market for Corporate Control," Journal of International Securities Markets, Winter 1990.

Smith New Court (1988), Europe and the Takeover Game, Smith New Court, London.

Sullivan & Cromwell (1989), "An Overview of the Competition Law of the European Community," Memorandum, Sullivan & Cromwell, New York.

Walter, I. and R. C. Smith (1989), Investment Banking in Europe: Restructuring for the 1990s, Basil Blackwell, Oxford.

Vanek, J. (1965), General Equilibrium of Economic Integration, Harvard University Press, Cambridge, Mass.

Financial Regulation and Monetary Arrangements after 1992
C. Wihlborg, M. Fratianni and T.D. Willett (Editors)
© 1991 Elsevier Science Publishers B.V. All rights reserved   123

6 Mergers, Concentration, and Antitrust

B. Espen Eckbo

Faculty of Commerce, University of British Columbia, Vancouver, B.C.,
Canada V6T 1Y8

1. INTRODUCTION

In 1988, the value of public acquisitions in Britain was some $34 billion, up from $24 billion the previous year.[1] In France, merger activity jumped 72 percent, from 884 takeovers in 1987 to 1,522 in 1988. As emphasized by Smith and Walter elsewhere in this volume, this trend is expected to continue as the European nations integrate their financial markets, further lowering the cost of financing industrial restructuring by merger.

Expectations of a large-scale restructuring has also brought pressure to introduce a more restrictive antitrust policy towards horizontal mergers. The purpose of this chapter is to review the likely efficiency of such constraints, as judged by the North-American experience. This comparison is particularly relevant because the policy debate within the EEC to a large extent uses U.S. antimerger policy as a model of reference. Moreover, there is a high degree of correlation between acquisition-intensive industries in Europe and North America. For example, Smith and Walter show a Pearson correlation of .8 between the two-digit SIC industries of acquiring firms in Europe and USA in the 1980's (whether based on the number of transactions or transaction volume), with a corresponding correlation of .7 for the industries of acquired firms.

Historically, European antitrust authorities have elected to monitor an industry's product price while encouraging firms to select the optimal size. The underlying philosophy is that if supracompetitive pricing can be avoided through direct monitoring, there is little need for consumers to worry about firm size or industry concentration *per se*. In contrast, U.S. antitrust authorities have elected to constrain firm size *ex ante* by placing ceilings on the level of industry concentration and market shares of merging firms.[2]

These two diverging antitrust philosophies have substantially different implications for the amount of resources needed for effective enforcement, as well as for the social cost of the implicit constraints on productive activity. Shifting antitrust enforcement, from an *ex post* analysis of anticompetitive effects to an *ex ante* assessment of the likelihood a merger will reduce competition, means that the regulatory agencies forego the benefit of the larger and more complete data set available *ex post*. As a result, an *ex ante* enforcement policy places particularly strong demands on the theoretical model used to separate anticompetitive from socially efficient takeovers *ex ante*.

Thus, a central issue is to what extent existing theoretical models of market power lead to a precise identification of truly anticompetitive mergers. U.S. antitrust authorities' reliance on structural standards for selection of merger cases is rooted in the "market concentration doctrine", one of the oldest and most controversial propositions in industrial economics. This doctrine, which is an implication of oligopoly models in the tradition of Cournot ([1838] 1927) and Nash (1950), holds that the level of industry concentration is a *reliable* index of the industry's market power.

The market concentration doctrine has been criticized on both theoretical and empirical grounds. For example, the oligopoly framework behind the doctrine explicitly rules out potential competition, as well as important dynamic aspects of changes in market structure. Competitive pressures cause firms to specialize their productive skills and resources, which in turn leads to increased concentration whenever the resulting cost-advantage increases optimal firm size. Thus, one can view the degree of industry concentration as an index of *competition* (through resource specialization) as well as of monopoly power, in which case a deconcentration policy forces a costly, suboptimal duplication of otherwise efficiently allocated corporate resources.

These two conflicting views of the causal links between competition and concentration can only be resolved through systematic empirical evidence. The central empirical implication of the market concentration doctrine is that relatively high levels of industry concentration will be associated with relatively large industry-wide monopoly rents.[3] Following Bain (1951), numerous studies have examined this proposition by estimating the cross-sectional correlation between accounting measures of industry profits and the level of industry concentration.[4] However, although this correlation is indeed typically found to be positive, it could also simply reflect inter-industry differences in risk or average costs of production.[5] Thus, this type of evidence does little to resolve the basic issue concerning the true causal link between competition and concentration.

Furthermore, with the level of aggregation involved in the empirical measures of profitability, and since merger is only *one* particular route to increased concentration, cross-sectional estimates of the correlation between concentration and industry average accounting profits provide little – if any – basis for determining an optimal public policy towards mergers. For this purpose one needs systematic evidence on the relationship between changes in industry concentration and firm profitability, based directly on the history of merger activity. Some first evidence of this type is presented by Eckbo (1985) based on mergers in the U.S. industrial sector and is extended here. No evidence to support the central predictions of the market concentration doctrine in the context of horizontal mergers is uncovered.

Since 1950, the U.S. antitrust authorities have filed more than 500 antitrust complaints against firms involved in mergers, on the grounds that these mergers would "substantially lessen competition". More then 80 percent of these complaints resulted in forced divestiture or cancellation of the proposed transaction.[6] A central issue in the antitrust debate concerns whether this strong level of enforcement activity, despite its costs, substantially benefits consumers by *deterring* a significant number of anticompetitive mergers from being proposed. Proponents of the deterrence argument implicitly assume that such anticompetitive mergers would indeed take place in an *unregulated* environment. In this chapter, I also discuss some evidence on the industry valuation effect of horizontal mergers in such an unregulated economy (Canada). The empirical results fail to support the deterrence argument.

The chapter is organized as follows. Section 2 describes an econometric model of horizontal mergers, the empirical methodology, and the results of the estimation. This section merges the data in Eckbo (1985) with recent methodological developments in

Eckbo, Maksimovic and Williams (1990). Section 3 contains large-sample evidence based on Canadian mergers. During the sample period, the Canadian mergers took place without any significant antitrust constraints, much as in Europe, which makes a Canada-U.S. comparison particularly interesting from a European perspective as well. Finally, since the restructuring of European corporations is expected to promote merger activity in the *financial* as well as in the industrial sector, I review in section 4 some recent results concerning U.S. bank mergers presented by James and Wier (1987), based on closely related empirical methodology. Section 5 concludes the chapter.

2. INDUSTRY WEALTH EFFECTS OF U.S. HORIZONTAL MERGERS

2.1 Predicted Impact on Rival Firms' Stock Prices

Let AR_j be the abnormal stock return to firm j as a result of the public announcement of a merger proposal. As in Eckbo (1985), the focus is on the bidder, the target and a portfolio of non-merging rivals in the industry of the merging firms. The stock price reactions of the rival firms are of particular interest since the effect of the merger on product prices will tend to cause a revaluation of the rival firms in the direction of the product price change. Thus, under market power theories, the merger, by reducing the number of independent producers, is expected to cause a marginal increase in the degree of cartelization of the industry. The resulting price umbrella benefits rival firms as well as the merging firms themselves.

Alternatively, under productive efficiency arguments, mergers occur to take advantage of a lower-cost production technology, and the merger gains are in the form of increased infra-marginal rents.[7] The effects on the rivals of a merger that lowers the costs of the merging firms will tend to reduce the value of the rivals. However, if the new technology can be imitated by rivals, or if the merger signals that a particular industry-specific resource has increased in value, the market value of the rivals may rise.

Figure 1 illustrates two possible scenarios where the net impact of an efficient merger on the market value of the merging firms' product market rivals is either negative or positive. Assume the merger is scale increasing, producing a rightward shift in the merging firms' supply curve. The industry of the merging firms is assumed to be perfectly competitive and, in figure 1(a), infra-marginal firms earn rents. The increased scale of the merging firms translates into a rightward shift in industry supply (S_T shifts to S_T'), and causes the product price to fall from P to P'. If it is prohibitively expensive for the rivals to copy the new cost-reducing technology,[8] then area DBC in figure 1(a) is internalized by the merging firms while the rivals lose their share of area PABP' to consumers (who also gain area BAC).

If, on the other hand, valuable technological information is leaked out to the industry during the merger negotiations, then rivals can do better by imitating the new cost-saving production technology. Such imitation activity might require merger among rival firms, or the rivals might compete for resources (such as employees) presently under the control of the bidder and target firms. Depending on the ability of the rivals to rapidly adopt the new technology, the present value of the benefits from imitation can outweigh the costs of the merger-induced drop in the product price.

If there are only a few efficient imitators in the industry, then the merger-induced wealth effect on the rivals *as a group* will continue to be negative. However, as illustrated in figure 1(b), an efficient merger can also cause the rival firms as a group to be better off. In figure 1(b), PCD is the pre-merger supply of the merging firms. The industry consists of PR/PC identical firms earning zero infra-marginal rents at the premerger product price P. Potential entrants are less efficient than existing producers, as reflected in the upward sloping industry supply curve beyond point R. Suppose the merger leads to a scale-preserving shift in the cost curve of the merging firms from PCD to ABD. If there is no dissemination of information necessary for the rivals to copy the new technology, then the market value of the rivals remains unchanged. At the other extreme, with instant and perfect imitation throughout the industry (including potential entrants), the post-merger industry supply curve becomes S_T' and the new product price P'. In this case, the rivals earn post-merger rents equal to the area UTR'B. With less than perfect and instant imitation the present value of the rents are smaller but may still be non-negative.

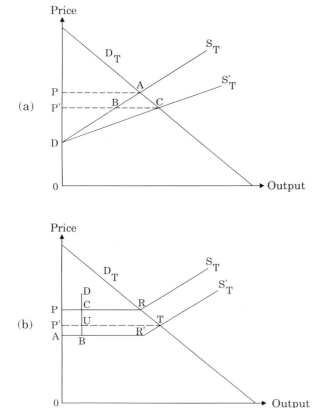

Figure 1 Examples of product market effects of efficient merger

In sum, while the collusion hypothesis predicts a positive impact on rival firms of a collusive, anticompetitive merger, an efficient merger can have either a positive or a negative wealth impact on rivals. These predictions can be further strengthened by considering industry factors which are likely to impact the merger-induced wealth effects differently under the two classes of hypotheses.[9]

2.2 A Cross-sectional Model of Merger Gains

The principal focus of the subsequent empirical tests is on the estimated value of the vector of parameters ϕ in a structural model $x_j\phi$ designed to explain the cross-sectional variation in firm j's abnormal return caused by the public announcement of a merger proposal. That is,

$$AR_j = x_j\phi + e_j, \quad j = 1,...,N, \tag{1}$$

where the residual e which is a summary statistic for variables that are omitted by the econometric model but publicly available to participants in the capital market and therefore reflected in the abnormal return AR_j, is assumed to satisfy

$$E(e_j) = 0, \quad E(e_j^2) = \sigma^2, \quad E(e_j e_{j'}) = 0 \text{ for } j \neq j'.$$

The cross-sectional model is estimated for pairs of bidder and target firms as well as for portfolios of non-merging rivals.

The following variables are used to define the econometric model:

$$x_j\phi \equiv \phi_0 + \phi_1 \ln(V_B / V_T)_j + \phi_2 NR_j + \phi_3 CR_j + \phi_4 dCR_j, \tag{2}$$

where V_B and V_T are the market values of the bidder and target firms, NR is the number of non-merging rival firms in the industry of the horizontal merger, and CR and dCR are the pre-merger level of and merger-induced change in industry concentration.

There are several reasons why one might expect the merger-induced wealth effect to depend on the characteristics in (2). If the sources of merger benefits are industry specific, then the number of rival firms in the industry may dictate the relative bargaining power of the bidder and target firms. For example, if the non-merging rival firms are predominantly substitute targets, then one would expect ϕ_2 to have a positive value for bidder firms and negative for target firms. If industries with a relative large NR tend to use resources commonly used in other industries as well, then the *sum* of the gains to bidder and target firms is predicted to be negatively correlated with NR, reflecting the generally low level of infra-marginal rents (including those arising from merger) in competitive industries.

Furthermore, if high industry concentration tends to be the result of high entry barriers, then CR is inversely related to the elasticity of industry demand.[10] A low demand elasticity accentuates the product price impact of a given merger-induced change in industry supply. Thus, if a merger is designed to adopt a scale-increasing new production technology, then the resulting product price decrease is predicted to be relatively large in industries with high concentration. Since the private value of the scale increase is decreasing in this product price decrease, one would therefore also expect to find $\phi_3 < 0$ if the mergers in the sample are predominantly of the scale-increasing, efficient type. Vice versa, if the effect of the merger is to reduce output, either through a collusive anti-competitive agreement or through scale-reducing new technology, then the value of a given output reduction is higher in industries with relatively inelastic demand. Thus, if the mergers are predominantly of the output-reducing type, one would expect to find $\phi_3 > 0$.

An analogous argument holds for the merger-induced change in concentration dCR. While the pre-merger level of concentration (CR) captures the cross-sectional effect of a given change in industry output, the merger-induced change in concentration is a proxy for the scale of the output change. This is perhaps most obvious in the classical dominant firm or price-leader model. To illustrate, suppose that the bidder firm is part of a coalition of producers who determines the industry's product price by unilaterally restricting output, letting the rival "fringe" firms taking full advantage of the output restriction. In the presence of entry barriers, it may pay the coalition to buy up one or more of the fringe firms in order to restrict output and raise the product price further. In the price-leader model, it is easily shown that, *ceteris paribus*, the increase in the industry's price that results from the purchase of one of the fringe firms is an increasing function of the market share of the target.[11]   Thus, if the mergers are predominantly anticompetitive, one expects $\phi_4 > 0$.   On the other hand, if the merger is of the scale-increasing type, dCR will reflect the magnitude of the scale increase. Again, for a given elasticity of industry demand, the larger the scale increase, the larger the product price drop and, *ceteris paribus*, the lower the private value of the scale-increasing technology. Thus, one expects to see $\phi_4 < 0$ if the sample of mergers are predominantly of the efficient, scale-increasing type.

Finally, the model includes the natural log of the relative size of the bidder and target firms, $\ln(V_B/V_T)$. A merger between relatively equal-sized firms represents a relatively large change for *both* firms, and may therefore be expected to generate larger gains. Moreover, a given dollar gain translates into a relatively small percentage return to relatively large bidders. Thus, the precision of the estimated gain is also lower for relatively large bidders since the normal variation in equity value is greater, relative to a given dollar gain. The relative size variable will reflect this property of the data.

2.3 A Consistent Estimator for the Cross-Sectional Model

Eckbo, Maksimovic and Williams (1990) argue that, for discrete non-repetitive corporate events, standard OLS and GLS estimation of models such as (5.1) can be inconsistent with rational expectations made by market participants. To see why, suppose it is common knowledge that managers of the bidder firm initiate a merger only after receiving a private signal η_j which indicates that the event has a positive value, i.e., such that

$$x_j\phi + \eta_j \geq 0$$

As a result, when the (unanticipated) event occurs, the market uses its knowledge of managers' incentives to impound into the firm's stock price the following expected return,[12]

$$E(AR_j /\eta_j > -x_j\phi) = x_j\phi) = x_j\phi + E(\eta_j /\eta_j > -x_j\phi). \tag{3}$$

In other words, when inferring the value of the event, the market uses its knowledge that managers decide to undertake the corporate event only if $x_j\phi + \eta_j > 0$. In effect, the market's inference truncates the residual term η_j that measures the value of managers' private information. This truncation is ignored if the econometrician elects to estimate equation (1) (whether using OLS or GLS). In the latter case, the non-linear expectational term in equation (3) ends up in the error term ε_j in equation (1), causing the estimated parameter values to be inconsistent.

Eckbo-Maksimovic-Williams construct a consistent estimator for the case where $\eta_j \sim N(0,\omega^2)$, where the private signal is independent across sample firms. In this case, a consistent specification of the cross-sectional model is

$$AR_j = x_j\phi + w \frac{n(x_j\phi/\omega)}{N(x_j\phi/\omega)} + \zeta_j, \tag{4}$$

where $n(\cdot)$ and $N(\cdot)$ represent the standard normal density and distribution functions evaluated at $x_j\phi/\omega$ and ζ_j is assumed to satisfy

$$E(\zeta_j) = 0, \quad E(\zeta_j^2) = v^2, \quad E(\zeta_j\zeta_{j'}) = 0 \quad j \neq j'.$$

The vector ϕ and the parameter ω in (4) are estimated using non-linear maximum-likelihood.

While, in this framework, the *bidder* is the one that receives the private signal and therefore initiates the merger, I also use the non-linear model (4) when the dependent variable is the abnormal return to targets or to non-merging rivals. The purpose of this is twofold: First, the bidder's private information, which is partly revealed through the merger proposal, may have value implications for the target and the rivals as well, in which case OLS or GLS again produces a truncation bias. Second, since the parameter ω represents the standard error of the private information, its estimated value should be non-negative. Thus, evidence of a significantly negative value of ω would suggest that the model is misspecified.

2.4 Adjusting for the Effect of Antitrust Regulation

The cross-sectional model (4) assumes that the proposed merger will go through. However, a proposed horizontal merger may be challenged – and possibly blocked – by antitrust authorities. The effect of this possibility on the proposal-induced abnormal stock return is analyzed explicitly in Eckbo (1985) and Eckbo, Maksimovic and Williams (1990) and is repeated here.

Let p_{rj} be the probability that the antitrust regulator decides to challenge the case, and let p_{cj} be the probability that the (independent) court decides in favour of the regulator. Both the regulator and the court have access to the public information x_j. Suppose the regulator decides to challenge the merger if the value of $x_j\phi_r + \eta_r \geq 0$. Furthermore, suppose that the court will block the merger if $x_j\phi_c + \eta_c \geq 0$. If the private information received by the merging firm, the regulator and the court (i.e., η, η_r, and η_c) all are normally and independently distributed random variables, then $p_{rj} = N(-x_j\phi_r/\hat{\alpha}_3)$ and $p_{cj} = N(-x_j\phi_c/\hat{\alpha}_c)$, where ω_r and ω_c are the standard errors of the regulator's and the court's private information, respectively. Below, these probabilities are estimated using probit analysis.

The merger proposal now has three possible outcomes: (1) No challenge with probability $1-p_{rj}$, (2) an unsuccessful challenge (no court conviction) with probability $p_{rj}(1-p_{cj})$, and (3) a successful challenge (court conviction) with probability $p_{rj}\, p_{cj}$. Assume a challenge imposes a legal cost on the merging firms equal to a proportion c of the merger gains. As a result, conditional on the public information x_j, the market reaction to the merger proposal can be written as

$$E(AR_j/\eta_j > -x_j\phi) = (1-p_{rj}\, p_{cj})[x_j\phi + \omega\, \frac{n(x_j\phi/\omega)}{N(x_j\phi/\omega)}] - p_{rj}c. \tag{5}$$

The conditional expectation (5) is used in the following cross-sectional regression analysis.

2.5 Data and Parameter Estimates

The main focus of this section is on the 80 horizontal challenged mergers compiled by Eckbo (1985). These mergers were proposed between 1963 and 1981, and either the bidder or the target firm was listed on the New York or the American Stock Exchange at the time of the proposal. Table 1 lists central characteristics of these 80 cases. The rival firms are identified as stock-exchange listed members of the industry listed in the antitrust complaint as the industry "threatened" by the allegedly "anticompetitive" merger.[13] The mean number of rivals per merger is 5, the mean four-firm concentration ratio is 59 percent, and the mean change in the industry's Herfindahl index (the proxy for dCR in the cross-sectional regression) is 3.3 percent.[14]

Table 2 shows the average abnormal stock return (CAR) over the 7-day window (day -3 through day 3) centered on the day of the announcement of the merger proposal in the Wall Street Journal.

For each firm in the average, $CAR_j = 7AR_j$, where the daily abnormal return parameter AR_j is estimated directly from the following market model:[15]

$$r_{jt} = \alpha_j + \beta_j r_{mt} + AR_j\, d_{jt} + e_{jt}, \tag{6}$$

where r_{jt} and r_{mt} are the continuously compounded rates of return on firm j and the value-weighted market portfolio of all stocks traded on the New York- and the American Stock Exchanges over day t; the dummy variable d_{jt} is 1 if day t is within the event period $[-3,3]$ and 0 otherwise. The estimation starts on day -200 and ends on day 3.

Table 1

The number of rival firms per merger (NR), values (V) and market shares (S) of the bidder and target firms, four-firm concentration ratio (CR), and merger-induced change in the Herfindahl index (dCR) for the total sample of 80 horizontal mergers challenged under Section 7 of the Clayton Act, 1963-1981.[a]

Variable	Mean	Median	Minimum	Maximum
NR	4.80	3.00	1.00	29.0
V_B ($mill.)	1,544	452	10.0	23,555
V_T ($mill.)	471	101	1.0	9,470
CR (percent)	58.6	59.0	5.00	99.0
S_B (percent)	14.8	12.0	0.1	60.0
S_T (percent)	12.8	9.0	0.2	47.0
dCR (percent)	3.3	1.0	0.02	24.2

[a] Source: Eckbo (1985). The concentration ratio CR is measured as a percentage for the major 4-digit SIC industry of the target. The number of rivals NR are the number of non-merging firms in the major 4-digit SIC industry of the target that are listed on the NYSE or the ASE. The values V are the natural log of the maximum of the book value of the firm's assets and the market value of its equity (if listed). dCR is twice the product of S_B and S_T. S_B is available for 72 of the 80 cases, and S_T (and therefore dCR) for 64 of the 80 cases, respectively.

The average CAR is 1.01 percent for bidder firms, which is significantly greater than zero at a 5 percent level of confidence. The average target firm realizes a highly significant CAR of 11.5 percent, with an average CAR to equal-weighted pairs of bidder and target firms of 6.4 percent. Finally, the average rival firm portfolio realizes a CAR of 0.5 percent, statistically significant at a 5 percent level.

Table 3 shows the results of the probit regression used to estimate the probability of a challenge, p_{rj}.[16] As expected, the estimated probability increases with the concentration ratio CR and decreases with the number of rival firms NR. The value ratio has no significant impact. A similar regression for the probability that the challenge would be successful (p_{cj}) produced only insignificant results. Thus, the sample proportion of successful challenges (52/80) is used to estimate p_{cj} for all j.

With these estimates of CAR_j, p_{rj}, and p_{cj}, it is possible to run the full cross-sectional regression of model (5). The results are shown in table 4. The estimation, which treats the proportional court cost c as a constant equal to 0.01, shows several interesting results. The regression with the equal-weighted sum of the gains to bidder and target firms is significant and indicates that the gains increase with CR but decrease with dCR. The value of ω is positive and significant, which is consistent with the proposition that the average merger proposal announcement conveys private information to the market concerning the true value of the merging firms.

Table 2

Summary of regression results for cumulative abnormal returns (CAR)

Summary of regression results for the model:

$$r_{jt} = \alpha_j + \beta_j \, r_{mt} + AR_j \, d_{jt} + e_{jt}.$$

The variables r_{jt} and r_{mt} are the continuously compounded rates of return on firm j and the value-weighted market portfolio over day t. The dummy variable d_{jt} is *1* if day t is within the pre-specified event period and *0* otherwise. The event period is day -3 through 3 relative to the announcement at day 0 of the proposed merger in the Wall Street Journal.[a]

Horizontal	Average CAR (percent)	
Challenged Mergers	Sample	7-day window
1963-81	size	-3 through 3
Bidders	67	1.01 (1.85)
Targets	43	11.46 (12.55)
Equal-weighted pairs of bidders and targets	37	6.41 (10.71)
Equal-weighted portfolios of rival firms	80	0.48 (2.01)

[a] Source: Eckbo (1985). AR_j is the average daily abnormal return over the 7-day event period and $CAR_j = 7AR_j$. The numbers in parentheses are z-values. For large sample sizes J the statistic $z \equiv (1/\sqrt{J}) \sum_j (AR_j / \sigma_{AR_j})$ is approximately normally distributed, where σ_{AR_j} is the standard error of the OLS estimate of the abnormal return parameter AR_j. The 80 portfolios of rival firms (one for each of the 80 horizontal mergers) contain a total of 384 individual rivals.

Table 3
Results of probit model for horizontal mergers being challenged by the government

Estimated coefficients of the probit model generating the probability p_{rj} that a horizontal merger proposed by firm j will be challenged by the government. Sample of 80 horizontal challenged and 116 horizontal unchallenged mergers, 1963-1981.[a]

Sample Size		Independent Variables				
yes	no	Constant	CR	NR	$\ln(V_B/V_T)$	χ_2 statistic
80	116	-1.170	0.031	-0.040	-0.068	45.2[b]
		(-3.67)	(6.01)	(-2.77)	(-1.04)	(3df)

[a] The independent variables are defined in table 1. The outcomes of all challenged cases are discussed in the Appendix of Eckbo and Wier (1985). "Yes" indicates the merger was challenged.

[b] Significant at the 1 percent level.

The regression with the abnormal returns to rival firms as dependent variable is statistically insignificant. The only significant parameter value is for the variable dCR and indicates that the higher the increase in industry concentration caused by the merger, the *lower* the wealth impact on non-merging industry members.

These results do not, of course, support the market concentration doctrine. As discussed above, a horizontal merger produces a measurable change in the industry's level of concentration, dCR, as well as a change in the risk-adjusted present value of industry rents that is directly associated with the concentration change, i.e., the CAR to rival firms. Under the market concentration doctrine, this change in industry rents should, *ceteris paribus*, be positively correlated with the change in concentration, which is contradicted by the negative impact of *dCR* in table 4. Note also that the insignificant impact of the level of concentration, CR, fails to support the proposition that a merger is more likely to have anticompetitive effects the greater the *pre*merger value of industry concentration, an assumption underlying the U.S. Department of Justice's Merger Guidelines.

Since a significant part of the data on market shares and concentration was collected using sources related to the challenged cases, the rejection of the market concentration doctrine evident in table 4 is unlikely to be explained by an excessive level of aggregation in the measures of these industry characteristics: The enforcement agencies frequently use a definition of the relevant "endangered" product market that contains only a few closely related products. Second, since the value of CR ranges from a low of 5 percent to a high of 99 percent (table 1), the rejection of the market concentration doctrine hardly reflects the possibility that the respective product markets were monopolized *prior* to the merger (despite the government challenge). Third, the explicit estimation of the probability of a government challenge (p_r) helps correct for the effect of the antitrust "overhang" which impacts the announcement-induced abnormal stock returns. Further evidence on the likely importance of such an "overhang" is given in the subsequent section.

Table 4
Estimated contributions to CAR to bidders, targets and rival firms

Estimated coefficients ϕ, ω in non-linear cross-sectional models with announcement-induced abnormal stock returns *(CAR)* to bidders, targets and rival firms in horizontal mergers as dependent variables, 1963-1981.[a]

$$CAR_j = (1 - p_{rj} \, p_{cj})[x_j \phi + \omega \frac{n(x_j \phi / \omega)}{N(x_j \phi / \omega)}] - p_{rj} c + \zeta_j, \qquad j = 1 \ldots N.$$

			Explanatory Variables				
Constant	$\ln(V_B/V_T)$	NR	CR	dCR	$\hat{\omega}$	χ^2 statistic

			I. Equal-Weighted Pairs of Bidder and Target Firms (N=31)				
0.241	-0.257	-0.025	0.019	-0.079	0.022	25.21[b]
(0.60)	(-2.52)	(-1.74)	(3.98)	(-2.47)	(7.18)	(4df)

			II. Equal-Weighted Portfolios of Rival Firms (N=69)				
0.100	-0.014	-0.004	0.0007	-0.002	-0.0001	4.3
(1.42)	(-0.97)	(-0.97)	(0.66)	(-2.08)	(-0.68)	(4df)

[a] The dependent variable is defined in table 2 and the explanatory variables in table 1. Numbers in parentheses are asymptotic *t*-values. In this non-linear model, standard OLS estimates of the coefficients are used as initial (starting) parameter values, with the regression standard error from the OLS regression as the initial value for ω. The estimated probabilities $\hat{p}_{rj}$ (from table 3) and $\hat{p}_{cj}$ ($= 52/80$ for all j) are here treated as constants. The value of c, the cost of going to court, is also treated as a constant with a value of 0.01. The normal distribution is approximated to five digits.

[b] Significant at the 1 percent level.

It follows from the discussion earlier in this section that the evidence in table 4 is consistent with the efficiency hypothesis, i.e., the proposition that the horizontal mergers in the sample were expected to result in a more efficient allocation of corporate resources *regardless* of the level and change in industry concentration. Most important, however, is the fact that the evidence systematically rejects the antitrust doctrine, even for values of CR and dCR which, over the past four decades, have been considered critical in determining the probability that a horizontal merger will have anticompetitive effects.

3. ANTITRUST DETERRENCE AND HORIZONTAL MERGERS IN CANADA

While the U.S. has a long history of strict enforcement of antitrust laws regulating merger activity, horizontal mergers in Canada have taken place in a virtually unrestricted legal environment. The lack of an antitrust "overhang" in Canada makes it interesting to compare the wealth effects of horizontal and non-horizontal mergers in this country.

3.1 Data

In this section I focus on the 247 horizontal and 626 non-horizontal mergers and acquisitions in mining and manufacturing industries compiled by Eckbo (1986). In this sample of 873 cases, a 'horizontal' merger is defined as a merger in which the bidder and target firms have at least one overlapping 4-digit SIC code describing the firms' major productive activity. A non-horizontal merger is one where this condition is not satisfied, given that information on the respective firms' SIC codes is available in sources such as Scott's Industrial Index, Dun and Bradstreet's Canadian Key Business Index, and Standard and Poor's Register of Corporations, based on the year prior to the year of the merger announcement.

The sample period in Eckbo (1986) is 1964 through 1983, and the mergers and acquisitions in that sample were identified using the Merger Register compiled by Consumer and Corporate Affairs Canada.[17] For each merger, the Register records the identity of the bidder and target firms, the newspaper in which the merger is announced, and a short summary of the major activity of the two firms involved. The sampling procedure in Eckbo (1986) requires that the bidder or the target firm is among the firms on the University of Laval monthly stock return data tape (covering Toronto Stock Exchange listed firms). Furthermore, a case is included in the sample only if the month and year of the merger announcement in the press is documented in the Merger Register, and if there is sufficient share price information on the Laval tape to perform the regression analysis.

In order to produce a data base of industry rivals, 4-digit SIC codes were allocated to as many TSE-listed (Laval-tape) firms as possible using information in the industry manuals listed above. For each of the 873 horizontal and non-horizontal firms, a list was generated containing all firms on the Laval tape whose 4-digit SIC code overlapped with the target's own major 4-digit code.[18] This initial list of rival firms is then reduced to those firms which, according to the product-specific information listed in the industry manuals, have a substantial product overlap with target. In other words, the rivals are essentially selected on a 5-digit SIC level of accuracy. Finally, if markets are regional rather than national, then firms having regional sales that do not overlap substantially with the target's sales region are also eliminated.

This procedure yielded one or more rival firms for 116 of the horizontal and 89 of the non-horizontal mergers in Eckbo (1986). The number of rivals per merger ranges from 1 to 34 (mean 9) for horizontal mergers, and from 1 to 33 (mean 7) for non-horizontal mergers. As shown in table 5, the industries with the largest number of mergers are oil and gas extraction (SIC 13, 24 horizontal and 11 non-horizontal cases), food and kindred products (SIC 20, 22 horizontal and 10 non-horizontal cases), printing and publishing (SIC 27, 13 horizontal and 13 non-horizontal cases), and lumber and wood products (SIC 24, 9 horizontal and 6 non-horizontal cases).

Table 5
Horizontal and non-horizontal mergers by industry

The number of horizontal and non-horizontal mergers, classified by the first two digits of the bidder and target firms' major four-digit SIC codes. Sample drawn from Eckbo (1986), 1964-83.[a]

	Major 2-digit SIC industry	Number of Mergers	
		Horizontal	Non-horizontal
10	Metal mining	6	4
13	Oil and gas extraction	24	11
15	General Construction	1	0
20	Food and kindred products	22	10
22	Textile mill products	3	2
23	Apparel and other textile products	1	0
24	Lumber and wood products	9	6
25	Furniture and fixtures	4	4
26	Paper and allied products	6	2
27	Printing and publishing	13	13
28	Chemicals and allied products	5	12
29	Petroleum and coal products	1	1
30	Rubber products	1	2
32	Stone, clay and concrete products	6	3
33	Primary metal industres	1	3
34	Fabricated metal industries	6	10
36	Electronic machinery	5	4
37	Transportation equipment	1	2
39	Miscellaneous manufacturing	1	0
10-39	All industries	116	89

[a] The sample in this table consists of all horizontal and non-horizontal cases in the data base compiled by Eckbo (1986) for which it was possible to identify at least one industry rival whose shares were trading at the Toronto Stock Exchange at the time of the merger announcement.

3.2 Industry Wealth Effects

Figure 2 and table 6 show the wealth effects of the horizontal and non-horizontal mergers. Figure 2 is included to show that the merger announcement indeed appears to represent a significant news-event, a crucial assumption underlying the methodology described in this paper. Figure 2 plots the monthly abnormal stock returns to bidder and target firms, cumulated over month -12 through month +12 relative to the month of the merger announcement.[19] The pattern seen in Figure 2 is as expected if the merger news is fully impounded in stock prices by the end of the announcement month (month 0). The curves indicate that the merger announcement itself has a large and significant impact on stock returns, with prior rumors and speculations most likely accounting for the systematic rise in stock prices in the few months prior to the press announcement of the merger.

Table 6 lists the abnormal returns to bidder, target as well as to equal-weighted portfolios of rival firms in month zero. First, the results do not indicate that bidder and target firms involved in horizontal mergers perform significantly better than firms in non-horizontal mergers. The 77 target firms in horizontal mergers earn average abnormal returns of 3.7 percent over month 0, while the corresponding performance of the 139 targets in non-horizontal mergers is 2.9 percent, both numbers statistically significant. Furthermore, the 215 bidder firms in horizontal mergers earn significantly positive average abnormal returns of 0.9 percent over month 0, while the corresponding performance of non-horizontal bidders is 1.3 percent.

The results in table 6 for the rival firms are particularly interesting. The announcement-month average abnormal return to the 116 portfolios of rivals of horizontal mergers is *negative* while the corresponding performance of rivals on non-horizontal mergers is *positive*; -1.5 vs. 2.4 percent, respectively. Both numbers are statistically significant on a 5 percent level of confidence. The negative rival firm performance in the sample of 116 horizontal mergers rules out collusion and dominant-firm market power arguments as explanations for the average gains realized by the merging firms in this category of mergers. The negative rival firm performance is consistent with the hypothesis that the market expects the horizontal merger to place the rival firms at a competitive disadvantage in product markets. This competitive disadvantage possibly is the result of an expected increase in the rate of output by the merged firm, with the associated downward pressure on the industry's product price, lowering the expected profits to rival firms. The expected downward pressure on the product price is consistent with the average horizontal merger in the sample being efficient, and inconsistent with market expectations that the merger would have collusive anticompetitive effects.

The rival firm performance in the sample of 89 non-horizontal mergers is positive and of a magnitude similar to the average performance of target firms in this merger category. Since non-horizontal mergers do not lead to anticompetitive effects, the positive rival performance most likely reflect dissemination of valuable information caused by the merger announcement. As discussed above, this information possibly includes opportunities for rival firms to improve the efficiency of their own operations, or the merger may signal an increase in the demand for resources commonly owned by firms throughout the industry of the target firm.

Table 6
Summary of regression results for CAR of target, bidder and rival firms

Summary of regression results for the model:

$$r_{jt} = \alpha_j + \beta_{j}r_{mt} + AR_j d_{jt} + e_{jt},$$

where the variables r_{jt} and r_{mt} are the continuously compounded rates of return on firm j and the value-weighted market portfolio over month t; the dummy variable d_{jt} is 1 if t is the month of the first public announcement of the merger, and zero otherwise. Sample of Canadian mergers, 1964-1983.[a]

Firm type	Average CAR (percent)	
	Horizontal[b]	Non-horizontal
Target firms[c]	3.7	2.9
	(2.0;77)	(4.0;139)
Bidder firms[c]	0.9	1.3
	(2.0;215)	(2.6;562)
Rival firms[d]	-1.5	2.4
	(-2.1;116)	(1.8;89)

[a] The numbers in parentheses are z-values and the sample size N. For large sample sizes J, the statistic $z \equiv (1/\sqrt{J})\sum_j (AR_j / \sigma_{AR_j})$ is approximately normally distributed, where σ_{AR_j} is the standard error of the OLS estimate of the abnormal return parameter AR_j.

[b] A 4-digit horizontal merger is one where the bidder and target firms have at least one overlapping 4-digit SIC code describing their major productive activity. The z-statistic has a standard normal distribution. Thus, z-values of 2 or greater indicate statistical significance on a 1 percent level of confidence.

[c] This is the number of firms identified in Eckbo (1986).

[d] The sample is restricted to those 4-digit horizontal and non-horizontal mergers in Eckbo (1986) for which it was possible to identify at least one industry rival listed on the Toronto Stock Exchange. For each merger, the rivals are combined into an equal-weighted portfolio before estimating the abnormal return to the rivals of that merger. The total number of rivals in the sample of 116 horizontal mergers is 1044 (an average of 9 rivals per merger), while in the sample of 89 non-horizontal mergers the total number of rivals is 623 (an average 7 rivals per merger).

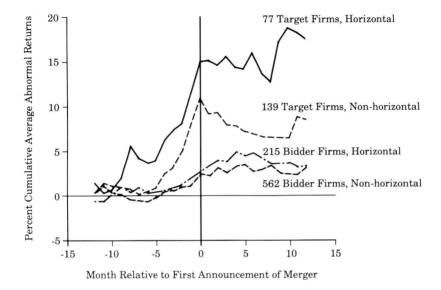

Figure 2 Monthly abnormal returns relative to the merger announcement. Canadian sample

4. HORIZONTAL MERGERS IN THE BANKING SECTOR

The analysis thus far has been focusing on horizontal mergers between industrial companies. In a recent study, James and Wier (1987) provide estimates of the merger-induced abnormal stock return to bidder firms in horizontal mergers between U.S. banks from the period 1972-1983. The authors argue that existing public regulations of the entry conditions in the banking sector possibly affect the competitiveness of the banking industry. With this in mind, they examine whether bidder gains are due to industry-wide rather than purely firm-specific factors. Evidence that bidder gains are in part driven by industry-wide factors is a necessary implication of the market power hypothesis.

The regulations governing the banking sector also simplifies the identification of rivals, industry concentration, and market shares. Thus, their study to some extent eliminates possible measurement errors inherent in a study based on industrial firms. James and Wier document significantly positive gains of 1.1 percent to the average bidder firm in a sample of 60, and show that this gain depends on the number of potential bidders and alternative targets in the banking industry. As a proxy for potential bidders they use banks larger than the acquired bank in the geographical region where current federal and state bank regulations permit acquisitions. Their proxy for alternative targets is based on banks in the above geographical region belonging to the same size class as the acquired bank.

The number of alternative targets is shown to have a positive impact on the gains to acquiring banks, while the gains are negatively related to the number of potential bidders.

This is consistent with the hypothesis that bidder gains from bank mergers emanate from resources owned to some extent by other banks as well. Thus, there is competition both on the target and on the bidder side of the horizontal transaction. A related interpretation can be given to the evidence in table 4 above: The gains to equal-weighted pairs of bidders and targets in horizontal industrial mergers is negatively related to the number of rival firms in the industry and positively related to the degree of industry concentration. Since target percentage gains are typically much larger than the percentage gain to bidders (table 2), the equal-weighted sum is primarily driven by the target gains. Thus, the results in table 4 are consistent with the proposition that the relative bargaining power of the target is stronger in industries with fewer rivals.

James and Wier further ask the question of whether the common industry factor generating bidder gains is reflecting increased market power as the number of independent banks is reduced. They reject this hypothesis based on two results: (1) The gains to bank bidders appears negatively correlated with the change in the market share caused by the merger, and (2) they fail to find a positive impact of the bank merger on the rivals of the merging firms. The first result is consistent with the finding in table 4 above: Gains to bidders and targets in horizontal mergers between industrial firms is negatively correlated with dCR, the change in the industry's Herfindahl index.

The second finding of James and Wier is also consistent with the results of table 4: The abnormal stock returns to rivals of horizontal mergers between industrial firms appears unrelated to industry concentration and possibly negatively related to dCR. In sum, the earlier conclusions with respect to industrial mergers appears to carry over to mergers in the banking sector as well.

5. CONCLUSION

Mergers and acquisitions are essentially a mechanism by which firms can quickly enter or exit an industry. Instead of wasting resources duplicating the production technologies already existing in an industry, the new entrant can focus on reallocating existing resources to a higher-valued use. The existence of a corporate control market effectively puts a ceiling on the degree of inefficiency that can develop within an industry. Furthermore, since the costs of a takeover, such as fees to lawyers and consultants, normally do not increase in proportion to the size of the firm being taken over, this entry mechanism works equally well in industries with relatively large production units as in industries characterized by small firms.

Given the social importance of the takeover market, one must carefully consider the cost/benefits of implementing a more restrictive antitrust policy towards horizontal corporate combinations. This chapter evaluates this issue based on the history of antitrust enforcement activity and horizontal mergers in North-America. The North-American experience is particularly relevant because of the high correlation between the acquisition-intensive industries in Europe and the U.S./Canada, and because the current policy debate within the EEC to a large extent uses U.S. antitrust philosophy as a model of reference.

The accumulated evidence on U.S. antitrust enforcement rejects the hypothesis that the typical challenged horizontal merger would have been anticompetitive if allowed to go through. Using recently developed econometric techniques, I fail to uncover evidence which supports the market concentration doctrine underlying current antitrust policy towards merger.

Second, I document evidence that horizontal mergers in Canada's unregulated environment on average produce a significantly *negative* impact on the stock prices of industry rivals, while no such negative price reaction is found for non-horizontal mergers. This is inconsistent with the proposition that strict antitrust laws are likely to deter a significant number of truly anticompetitive mergers. The deterrence proposition implies that there should be evidence of anticompetitive mergers in an unregulated environment, which the Canadian evidence fails to support.

Third, the lack of evidence in favor of the market power hypothesis/market concentration doctrine carries over to horizontal mergers in the banking sector. In sum, it is becoming ever more clear that the market power hypothesis rests on an extremely weak empirical foundation in the context of horizontal corporate combinations. As a consequence, the principle of applying rigid structural standards for evaluating the competitive effects of mergers is likely to entail a substantial social cost in terms of reduced incentive to undertake socially desirable, efficient acquisitions. This principle also carries with it the risk that special interest groups, including those representing relatively inefficient producers and/or a rigid work force, will succeed in taking advantage of the regulatory process.

FOOTNOTES

1. Source: <u>Acquisitions Monthly</u>, various issues

2. In the Department of Justice Merger Guidelines of 1968, the critical aggregate market shares vary according to the four-firm market concentration between two firms each having 4 percent of the sales in a market with a four-firm concentration ratio of 75 percent or more was likely to be challenged. The 1982 Merger Guidelines use the Herfindahl Index of concentration and are somewhat less restrictive than the old guidelines, but their focus is also on market structure. Note that the government does not strictly adhere to its own guidelines: Rogowsky (1982) finds that 20 percent of the mergers challenged under the 1968 guidelines actually fell below the guidelines, and one-third of these were found in violation of Section 7 of the Clayton Act.

3. A closely related but less general prediction is that high levels of concentration will be associated with relatively high, supracompetitive product prices. Although evidence of supracompetitive pricing is sufficient to conclude that market power is present, it is clearly not necessary: monopoly rents can also be generated by means of collusion on non-price variables, by monopolizing inputs, or by sophisticated price discrimination schemes that need to be evident through the observed product price.

4. For a survey of the literature on the "structure-conduct-performance" paradigm, see e.g. Weiss (1974).

5. Brozen (1970), Demsetz (1973), Peltzman (1977), and Carter (1978) present evidence supporting the theory that industry concentration is predominantly a result of the expansion of relatively cost-efficient producers. The issue of cross-industry variation in risk is not explicitly addressed in this literature.

6. See Eckbo and Wier (1985). The government's high success rate in terms of blocking the challenged mergers is not surprising. Under U.S. antitrust laws, a potential threat to competition constitutes a (civil) offense, and it is not necessary to prove a horizontal relationship between the bidder and target firms. Furthermore, anticipated economic efficiencies are not a defense against the illegality of a merger that may "substantially lessen competition".

7. Realizing techological complementarities, replacing inefficient management teams and organizations, reducing agency costs associated with the incentive to appropriate quasi-rents created by large sunk costs, exploting unused corporate income tax credits and reducing bankruptcy costs are frequently cited examples of this broad class of theories.

8. For example, the new techology may be perfectly and costlessly patentable, or the resources needed to duplicate it may be owned exclusively by the merging firms.

9. Note that the impact of an efficient merger is unambiguous if one were to examine the change in the market value of "upstream" sellers of inputs or "downstream" buyers of the product of the merging firms' industry. Efficient mergers will not cause a decline in the value of these two categories of firms. Data on upstream and downstream firms are, however, difficult to obtain. Thus, the focus on the horizontal rivals.

10. For example, a high degree of resource specialization may prevent rapid entry of new firms in response to the existence of rents in the industry. Such an industry will tend to have relatively few firms and, given the uniqueness of the product, few substitutes and a low elasticity of industry demand.

11. In the dominant firm pricing model, $(p-mc)p = s^{-1}[e_d + (1-s)e_f]$, where p is the product price, mc is the sum of the marginal costs of the firms in the coalition, s is the market share of the price leader, and e_d and e_f are the numerical values of the price elasticities of industry demand and fringe firm supply. Note that one could also use Stigler's (1964) oligopoly model to justify the prediction in the text. In Stigler's framework, the success probability of a collusive agreement is inversely related to the number of firms in the industry. The fewer the firms, the lower the costs of policing the cartel agreement and the closer the price will be to the single-firm monopoly level.

12. Eckbo, Maksimovic and Williams (1990) also discuss the case where the event is partially anticipated by the market.

13. See Eckbo (1983, 1985) for further details, and Eckbo and Wier (1985) for empirical results based on a study of the rival firms identified by the antitrust agencies as relevant industry members. The empirical results appear to be largely insensitive to the choice between the two alternative sets of rival firms.

14. dCR is computed as twice the product of the market shares of the bidder and target firms, which equals the change in the industry's Herfindahl index given the merger. While data on four-firm concentration ratios is generally available, the source of the information on market shares is case-related court records and publications.

15. As estimated in (6), Ar_j is the average daily abnormal return to security j over the 7-day event window.

16. The unchallenged horizontal mergers needed for this regression are from Eckbo (1985).

17. This data source contains a total of 9294 corporate acquisition bids announced between January 1945 and December 1983, of which 7559 were announced after January 1964. The Register has been maintained by the Department of Consumer and Corporate Affairs since 1960. It attempts to record all reported mergers in industries subject to the Combines Investigation Act. Accordingly, until the 1976 amendment of the Combines Investigation Act, firms in most of the service sectors of the economy were excluded from the register. Furthermore, the Merger Register depends on news-coverage of merger by the major financial news media, including daily and financial newspapers, trade journals, business magazines and other publications in Canada, the United States and Britain.

18. In horizontal mergers, this 4-digit SIC code also overlaps with the bidder's major industry code.

19. Monthly stock returns (from the University of Laval data tape) are used in the absence of a machine-readable data source covering daily stock returns for the firms over the 196483 sample period

REFERENCES

Bain, J.S (1951), "Relation of profit rate to industry concentration: American manufacturing, 1936-1940", Quarterly Journal of Economics 65, 293-324.

Brozen, Y.(1970), "The antitrust task force deconcentration recommendation", Journal of Law and Economics 13, 279-292.

Carter, J.R. (1978), "Collusion, efficiency, and antitrust", Journal of Law and Economics 21, 435-444.

Cournot, A.A. (1927), Researches into the mathematical principles of the theory of wealth, (New York: Macmillan), [1838].

Demsetz, H. (1973), "Industry structure, market rivalry, and public policy", Journal of Law and Economics 16, 1-9.

Eckbo, B.E. (1983), "Horizontal mergers, collusion, and stockholder wealth", Journal of Financial Economics 11, 241-273.

Eckbo, B.E. (1985), "Mergers and the market concentration doctrine: Evidence from the capital market", Journal of Business 58, 325-349.

Eckbo, B.E. (1986), "Mergers and the market for corporate control: The Canadian evidence", Canadian Journal of Economics 19, 236-260.

Eckbo, B.E., V. Maksimovic and J. Williams (1990), "Consistent estimation of cross-sectional models in event studies", Review of Financial Studies 3, 343-365.

Eckbo, B.E. and P. Wier (1985), "Antimerger policy under the Hart-Scott-Rodino Act: A reexamination of the market power hypothesis", Journal of Law and Economics 28, 119-149.

James, C.M. and P. Wier (1987), "Returns to acquirers and competition in the acquisition market: The case of banking", Journal of Political Economy 95, 355-370.

Nash, J.F. (1987), Equilibrium points in N-person games, Proceedings of the National Academy of Sciences of the U.S.A. 36, 48-49.

Peltzman, S. (1977), "The gains and losses from industrial concentration", Journal of Law and Economics 20, 229-263.

Rogowski, R.A. (1982), "The Justice Department's merger guidelines: A study in the application of the rule", unpublished paper, Federal Trade Commission.

Stigler, G.J. (1964), "A theory of oligopoly", Journal of Political Economy 72, 44-61.

Weiss, L.W. (1974), "The concentration-profits relationship and antitrust", in Industrial Concentration: The New Learning ed. H.J. Goldschmid, H.M. Mann, and J.F. Weston, (Boston: Little, Brown).

Financial Regulation and Monetary Arrangements after 1992
C. Wihlborg, M. Fratianni and T.D. Willett (Editors)
© 1991 Elsevier Science Publishers B.V. All rights reserved

Comment

Steven R. Weisbrod

Weisbrod Group Ltd, 114 East 32 Street, Suite 1306, New York, N.Y. 10016, USA

Professor Eckbo discusses the American anti-trust policy of preventing mergers that lead to increases in market concentration. He finds that this policy is more effective in reducing the number of efficiency enhancing combinations than in reducing the threat of monopoly. On the basis of this evidence, he argues that a common European anti-trust policy should regulate monopolistic pricing behavior rather than market structure. Policing prices would catch an actual monopolist in the act of monopolizing rather than impede economically efficient behavior as happens with structure regulation.

I am quite sympathetic to Professor Eckbo's criticism of structure regulation. As he points out, there are many factors in addition to market structure which affect the ability of a firm to exercise monopoly power, and there are many incentives to create large firms besides an attempt to monopolize a market. Hence, a policy of regulating structure is bound to be heavy handed. However, I am skeptical that a policy of price monitoring can be any less heavy handed.

The October, 1989 issue of the <u>Journal of Law and Economics</u> was dedicated to the problem of determining when pricing behavior can be interpreted as monopolistic. There are a number of pricing patterns which are consistent with both monopolistic and competitive pricing behavior. Making a distinction between the two requires a rather detailed understanding of the production function of the industry being challenged. Thus, the problem of isolating monopolistic pricing seems to be at least as difficult as judging whether a particular market structure is anti-competitive. Neither anti-trust policy can give an economist much confidence that its enforcement will increase consumer welfare.

Where it is hard to discern the economic benefits of a particular public policy, it usually pays to search for other interests at work influencing that policy. American anti-trust policy gives us ample opportunity to apply this rule. Examples can be found in applications of both price and market structure regulation. The first is illustrated by recent attempts to apply anti-dumping rules to international trade problems. The second can be observed in the regulation of the structure of the U.S. banking industry.

REGULATING PRICING BEHAVIOR OF FOREIGN FIRMS

Price monitoring has been given a new lease on life in American anti-trust policy as a result of the politics of the trade deficit. American firms which have been particularly hard hit by foreign, specially Japanese, competititon have complained that their foreign rivals are dumping to build market share. The U.S. has defined dumping as selling below average total cost. Policy makers have threatened that evidence of dumping will lead to restricted access to the U.S. market.

To prove the case of dumping, the U.S. government has hired accounting consultants to pour over the production costs of Japanese firms. Where it is found that they are producing below cost, the charge of dumping is applied. Policy makers do not take into account that it does not pay a firm with large fixed costs to cover all its expenses in every economic situation. Dumping has become a lightening rod for trade policy rather than an attempt to reduce the threat of monopoly in the U.S. marketplace.

REGULATING MARKET STRUCTURE IN BANKING

In banking, the U.S. has traditionally applied a very stringent market structure policy. Each state has had the authority to prevent banking organizations chartered in another state from opening banks within its boundaries. Each state has also had the authority to regulate the extent to which banks within its border are permitted to branch. Some states, such as Illinois, still forbid any bank branches. The results of this policy are well known. In 1987 there were over 14,000 banks.

The politics of this policy are also well known. Local politicians and their supporters have achieved a degree of control over bank policy to insure that local deposits are used in local projects. Small banks tend to be much more community oriented because powerful local individuals serve on their boards, and it is often too expensive to investigate credit opportunities outside their own markets.

The policy of local control is fading fast. All but five states changed their laws to permit some form of interstate banking within their borders during the 1980's. A large part of the reason for this change has been the realization that large banks can fail and that it is often difficult to find local purchasers for large banks. For example, no in-state purchaser could be found for large failed banks in the Southwest and Northwest. This led to changes in banking law in the states composing these regions and large increases in the share of assets in these states owned by out-of-state banking organizations.

A second reason for the change in the law has been pressure from regional banking organizations which grew large as states liberalized their branching laws in the 1980's. Contiguous states formed "regional compacts" permitting regional banking organizations to purchase banks in neighboring states on a reciprocal basis. These compatcs effectively excluded the large New York and California banks from entering markets in certain parts of the country. Regional banks have preferred to expand under regional compacts because this gives them the opportunity to grow without facing competition from large New York and California banks.

As a result of the liberalization of interstate branching restrictions in the 1980's, the share of banking assets held by the top 100 banking institutions in the U.S. rose from 50.2 percent in 1977 to 61.5 percent in 1987. However, the share of assets accounted for by the ten largest firms, all of which were headquartered in New York or California, actually declined slightly over the same period from 21.0 percent to 20.2 percent.

Armed with information provided by the large banks, Congress has noticed that U.S. banking organizations no longer dominate the list of the world's largest banks measured in terms of assets. It is concerned that restrictions which keep the large banks of New York and California from expanding into regional markets threaten the national interest.

Consequently, there is a push to permit, perhaps even encourage, the formation of large banks.

Removing geographic restrictions on U.S. bank expansion is certainly a positive development. However, it is by no means certain that this action will have the effect that Congress desires since it is not clear that New York and California banks would have expanded nationwide if state laws had permitted. Their stock prices are extremely depressed relative to strong regional banks, making it difficult for these banks to invest the capital necessary for nationwide expansion.

Some might claim that these low stock prices are the result of legislation restricting their entry into regional markets. This claim must be viewed somewhat skeptically in light of the fact that New York City banks have not even expanded into upstate New York, even though they have been permitted to do so for almost fifteen years. In California, which has had statewide branching since the early part of this century, the concentration ratio is falling faster than nay other state in the Union. In 1976 the five largest banks in California had 77.9 percent of total assets. In 1987 they had 66.9 percent of total assets.

It is very doubtful that the U.S. banking market will evolve into a nationwide market of a few large firms in the near future. The largest banks are not growing relative to other banks because their peculiar role of providing liquidity to large corporations and securities markets is becoming less important. There are no obvious economies of scale in retail banking under current service delivery technologies. Providing cash to consumers and small businesses has become the major function of banks. This is a very local matter, and will probably remain so until cash is replaced as the primary means of making small transactions. Thus, the large banks will probably have to purchase current local distribution systems if they are to expand nationwide. Based on current stock prices, this is going to be a long process.

The one factor that might encourage nationwide expansion, asset diversification across regional economies, is of no concern to depositors because of government insurance. If this protection is reduced as a result of the savings and loan scandals, it may be that some depositors will demand the safety of large, nationwide banks. However, two factors may reduce this demand: large banks do not have a good record of creating safety through diversification and securitization may replace nationwide banking as the solution to diversification.

The European parallel to the removal of interstate banking restrictions in the U.S. is, of course, the removal of international banking restrictions within the European Community. The U.S. experience indicates that this will not automatically create a few large retail banks that dominate the European market. Assuming that European retail banking, like U.S. retail banking, is a local affair centered around a branch network, Europe's major banks are going to have to face the same acquisition issues as their U.S. counterparts. One possible difference is that many large European banks have a stronger capital position than American large banks, making it easier for them to consolidate the market. Looking back on the U.S. experience, however, it seems doubtful that the large European banks will find an aggressive acquisition campaign worthwile. New York City banks did not venture upstate even when they had a relatively strong capital position, and large California banks were not able to hold the large market share they once had.

REFERENCES

Amel, D.F. and M.J. Jacowski (1989), "Trends in Banking Structure since the Mid-1970's", <u>Federal Reserve Bulletin</u>, March, 120-133

<u>The Journal of Law and Economics</u> (1989), Vol. XXXII (2) (pt.2), October

Financial Regulation and Monetary Arrangements after 1992
C. Wihlborg, M. Fratianni and T.D. Willett (Editors)
© 1991 Elsevier Science Publishers B.V. All rights reserved   149

7   Financial Institutions in a European Market for Executive Competence

Gunnar Eliasson

The Industrial Institute for Economic and Social Research (IUI), P.O.Box 5501,
S-114 85 Stockholm, Sweden

1. INTRODUCTION

The ongoing deregulation of financial markets in Europe will induce substantial development of financial institutions. It is too early to tell whether EC markets will become securitized to the same degree as in the USA and in the UK. Continental European financial structures are traditionally more bank-oriented, and the banks in many countries are by ownership or by personal connection heavily involved in industry.

The thesis of this paper is that the organization of financial markets plays an important role in the economic growth process by influencing the allocation of, and the trading in individual and team competence in top level corporate management.

Competence is traded in (1) Internal Labor Markets, (2) External Labor Markets and (3) the Mergers and Acquisitions (M&A) Market. Developments in EC after 1992 will influence the relative role of these markets. *First*, the international expansion of large firms is expanding the internal markets for high quality labor internationally. *Second*, improved external monitoring of high quality labor ("headhunting") is reducing the "lemon" characteristics of the external market for managerial talent, thus making firms increasingly exposed to being raided for such labor. *Third*, improved efficiency in the international M&A market enables firms to acquire teams with competence that cannot be subdivided into individual competence. I argue that the growth of internal markets for high quality labor will be the most important vehicle for diffusing industrial knowledge between nations, that will also exercise a significant influence on the distribution of comparative advantages.

Financial markets play an important role not only because they facilitate or hinder take-overs, mergers and acquisitions but also because they monitor competence in firms and individuals. In these markets information is evaluated and incentives are provided for all modes of trade in individual and team competence.

The paper proceeds as follows. In Section 2 I discuss in more detail the concepts of individual and organizational competence and their role in the growth process within an essentially dynamic Schumpetarian theory of the firm. The view of the sources of competitiveness presented here contrasts sharply with conventional economic thinking underlying "industrial targeting" and trade policy arguments. This argument is developed in Section 3, where the European policy perspective is introduced.

The efficiency of alternative modes for trade and allocation of competence in internal and external markets are discussed in Section 4. I return thereafter in Section 5 to the link between the institutional structure of financial markets and the allocation of competence in the growth process. Section 6, finally, contains conclusions for the policy maker fearing that Europe is lagging behind the USA and Japan in industrial development and growth.

2. ORGANIZATIONAL LEARNING AS THE SOURCE OF SUSTAINABLE COMPETITIVENESS IN FIRMS

Quality embodied in goods traded in international markets is becoming the mark of distinction of advanced manufacturing firms and the source of technological competition. Rate of return targets imposed on firms by internationally integrated financial markets is increasing the intensity of competition. Results are evaluated in the stock markets, which, while still largely local are increasingly opening up to international competition.

The source of competitiveness of the individual firm no longer rests on cheap labor and technology embodied in new machines. Textile manufacturers learned by experience long ago that when technology became embodied in tradable machines, their earlier unique source of competitiveness also became tradable.

The source of sustainable competitiveness is embodied in individual or team competence within a firm. Sustainability requires that competence includes ability to continuously upgrade and renew technological and managerial competence. These static and dynamic aspects of competence are in the following summarized in the concept of the firm's organizational knowledge base or its *organizational competence*. Eliasson (1990a,b) contains a systematic presentation and a definition of this concept.

The nature of firm knowledge or competence is highly complex and not naturally tradable in markets. Allocation of firm competence means allocating people or teams of people. The dynamic aspect of sustainable competence has at least two components; competence to create new knowledge (*innovation*) and competence to receive and accumulate new knowledge created elsewhere (*receiver competence*). The latter has been almost completely forgotten in the literature. I use the concept *organizational learning* to describe the upgrading and renewal of competence, including both innovation and receiver competence.

The economic growth process cannot be understood unless we understand how people with competence are organized as hierarchies of competent teams making up the intellectual superstructure of firms. The use of organizational competence to create synergies, or economies of scale or scope among input factors, has important implications for the firm's organization in relation to imperfections in the markets for financial resources, labor, capital and products.

Economic theory is gradually rediscovering the intellectual dimension of economic activity, emphasized some 150 years ago by John Stuart Mill (1848), but later forgotten. There is a new awareness about, for example, the joint production characteristics of on-the-job learning exemplified by Arrow (1962a) and Rosen (1972). The business administration literature has paid increasing attention to "unique knowledge" or "ownership specific assets" as the source of competitiveness of firms. Selznick (1957), Williamson (1975) and Pelikan (1989) are three examples.

Rosen (1982) observes how superior competence in hierarchical positions can add value to all other factors of production through scale and scope economies, leading to very high rewards to top managers. Romer (1986) shows how scale economies that originate in the application of knowledge (an externality), can still be compatible with an interior solution in the static general equilibrium model, as long as the accumulation of such knowledge is associated with strongly diminishing returns.

There is also a growing literature on managerial and work incentives and performance in, for instance Lazear (1981), Harris and Holmström (1982), Holmström and Ricart i Costa (1986), Baker, Jensen and Murphy (1988), Jensen and Murphy (1990) and Campbell, Chan and Marino (1989). Most of this literature is cast in the asymmetric information mold, assuming that the capacity to diffuse managerial competence directly as information through markets is possible but costly. Non-tradable competence, on the other hand is the raison d'être for the existence of the firm and the source of the rent it enjoys in the capital market. Managerial and, more broadly, organizational competence can, however, be traded indirectly in the M&A markets. Here I am particularly concerned with the potential for trade in organizational competence of the firm, especially organizational learning, the ability to constantly upgrade competence to sustain a superior rent earning capacity.

Competence for organizational learning is generally tacit and experimentally arrived at. Tacit implies that knowledge cannot be "blue-printed", but is embodied in individuals or teams. By definition it has no well defined reproduction value. Hence, it cannot be measured as other capital items. The stock-market would value it as the present value of its future rents. This market valuation, however, depends on the competence of market agents to assess the business situation of the firm. One cannot simply assume such markets to be perfect. This issue is discussed in Section 5.

Before turning to markets for indirect trade in organizational competence I contrast the above view of the firm and its source of competitive advantage with the conventional view providing the basis for industrial and trade policy.

3. ECONOMIC LEARNING IN AN INTERNATIONAL PERSPECTIVE - THE EUROPEAN POLICY CONCERN

3.1 The European Industrial Policy Argument

This section introduces the European industrial policy dimension. I begin with the misconceived economic argument behind "industrial targeting". In subsection 2 the requirements necessary to fulfill the vision of an advanced, dynamic European economy is discussed. Clearly organizational learning must provide the foundation for sustainable competitive advantages.

European industrial policy makers worry about export firms having difficulties providing jobs for blue collar workers. This tradition dates all the way back to the early seventies and it is reviewed in Eliasson (1984). At that time the advanced U.S. industrial technology was the source of concern. Today Japanese technology worries industrialists and policy-makers. This concern was one of the reasons quoted for the Europe 1992 initiative, a "policy instrument" aimed at revitalizing European industry. Similar concerns about deficient factory-based technology, loss of competitiveness of manufacturing industry and deindustrialization have been voiced over the last decade in the U.S. (Singh 1987, Seal

1990). Factory automation and more investment have become a frequently prescribed cure and economic arguments are made for "strategic targeting" of industrial and trade policy (see Dixit, 1987, Krugman, 1983).

Viewing tacit, team embodied knowledge accumulation as the source of firm competitiveness suggests that this orientation of policy thinking is misconceived. Inevitably, it takes us into a discussion of "industrial targeting". This concept is a polished-up version of the old "infant industry" argument rephrased on the basis of the so called "new international trade theory". It has been proposed as a protective device to shield U.S. firms from Japanese competition, while they achieve scale and work themselves up their learning curves, through R&D spending, notably on factory automation. The "medication" is expressed in hardware processing or production functions terms.

In the general learning context, including organizational learning as defined here such advice becomes outright misleading. Empirically, it runs contrary to the Swedish experience of the 80s. The successful, giant Swedish multinationals, operating in markets for mature, technologically mature products, dominating the domestic Swedish economy emerged, contrary to all expert opinions, out of the debris, and the worried debate of the economically disorderly 70's. They did not base their success on hardware performance. They were probably helped by the devaluations of the Swedish krona, but primarily they conceived a new strategy of merging innovative product development with large scale, global production and marketing in a free trade environment (Eliasson, Bergholm et. al. 1985). They have been joining the EC-economy on their own, not bothering to wait for Swedish policy makers to decide.

As observed by Carlsson (1979, 1989) these firms have concentrated in the areas where their competence is superior by international standards. They have (Eliasson 1986, 1987) positioned themselves in the 80s on "three competitive legs": global international marketing, domestically based development of products and an internationally flexible and streamlined production organization, not focusing on large plant size but applying organizational competence in product development, marketing, and production organization in many production units worldwide.

The critical question for sustainability of these advantages is, however, what enables these firms to upgrade and renew their advantages. This is the issue of organizational learning.

Rephrased in terms of the European or the U.S. "competitiveness" problem, the source of productivity growth is the acquisition and upgrading of human based competence. A pertinent question to ask is, if an industry or a firm has allowed its human competence base to deteriorate, what makes management and policy-makers believe - as the industrial targeting proponents implicitly assume - that it will be able to revitalize it? If competence exists, why has it not been put to use before? Why is there a problem to begin with? Can a problem really be solved by those who have created it? Traditional economic theory underlying industrial targeting does not address these questions.

A problem of national competitiveness in an industry, by definition, means that more competent producers are operating from a base in other nations. If firms and people can move freely in response to economic incentives there should be no such problem. The upgrading of local competence can be achieved partly by allowing other firms to establish production in the problem nation, or by foreign acquisitions of low grade firms in that nation. The markets in which tradability in competence is most open are the M&A markets. This is also where we observe exactly this action already taking place. If it is hindered, local firms fail or have to be protected by trade barriers, like Italian and French automobile manufacturers. If the concern of the laggard nation is the welfare of, and jobs for its people, irrespective of centralistic political concerns, industrial targeting does not solve a real problem, although it might be motivated by concerns about loss of national political control of the economy.

3.2 Europe 1992 and Organizational Learning

What are the prospects for creating a viable "market" for industrial competence in Europe. I will find the answer, first of all in the opening up of financial markets (compare with the Smith-Walter paper in this volume), transacting freely across borders in shares, but also in the spontaneous development of EC markets for high quality labor.

Adam Smith (1776) has often been represented in literature (see e.g. King 1977) as hostile towards the joint stock company, and, hence, by modern standards towards big business. Similarly, Schumpeter (1942), following up on the Smithian theme, voiced strong concerns about the scientific corporate machine, that could routinize industrial R&D and enjoy extraordinary economies of scale. Once it had achieved a competitive edge this R&D machine would become the winner that took over the market, very much as the static general equilibrium model predicts will happen when scale economies are achieved. This is a puzzling worry on the part of two economists of towering proportions that made path breaking contributions to the theory of economic growth. They have been represented in literature out of context, however.

As Anderson and Tollison (1982) observe from rereading Smith (1776), the main worry of the latter was how to check monopoly formation among joint stock companies without reducing the incentives for them to use superior innovative ability. For Adam Smith, the moving force behind economic growth and the creation of wealth differences between nations was the market regime, or more specifically the extent to which it allowed for free competitive entry. Neither Smith nor Schumpeter, or for that matter Marshall (1890) would have suggested, as Arrow (1962b) did, to socialize innovative activity and distribute its results free of charge.

In my perspective entry should be interpreted broadly as a major force behind organizational learning. Entry requires competence and manifests itself in many ways, through international trade competition and in the M&A markets. Above all, organizational learning to maintain a competitive edge, once acquired, requires continued direct participation in market competition with free entry and exit.

The global learning problem facing each firm and each nation can be illustrated within a simple model. In Figure 1 the competence structure in one country and industry at each point in time is represented by a "Salter curve" describing the productivity distribution of firms. Such distributions are usually thought of as linked to physical capital. I will link it to human-based competence, associated with firms, as in Eliasson and Lundberg (1990). Productivity may be measured by labor productivity as in Figure 1 or by total factor productivity.

Potential competition in a market is characterized by a set of potential distributions as in Figure 1, including entry by foreign firms to the left in the figure. Depending upon the openness of markets, the local, say French, market for cars might have not only local producers, but also foreign manufacturers positioned along the curves as in the far right diagram. The best producers may be closed out by trade restrictions, thus reducing potential competition in the domestic market. The best foreign producers might nevertheless establish themselves in the market through foreign direct investment, boosting the upper, left hand corner of the local Salter distribution through infusion of competence. Firms might merge and recombine across national borders, reallocating competence to appropriate places, thus changing the shape of Salter curves in different markets. Almost all of this change is accomplished through reallocations of human competence in individuals and teams, much of it through the intermediation of financial markets, and some of it through individuals moving inside firms or in the international labor market.

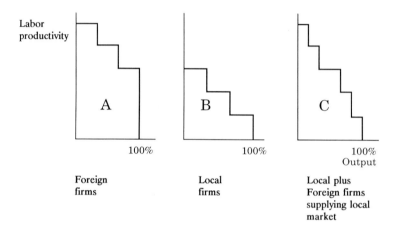

Figure 1 Market integration and Salter curves

If the supreme global performers on the far left in Figure 1 are shut out from a market through trade or establishment restrictions, then interior local producers may survive as in the middle diagram, leading to a welfare loss. The main point here is that the low end performers are also shut off from the learning experience of competing head on with the best global producers (Eliasson 1988c). In the longer run such policies, if enacted in a once rich nation, will be disastrous for productivity. In the longer term, when performance has been low for many years, and assets are cheap, these protected firms may be acquired by their competitors, then not for their competence, but rather for their acquirer to be able to take over their domestic market shares rapidly.

It is highly unlikely that even large political regions like the U.S. or Europe include the globally best performers in more than some markets. Other countries may have potentially promising candidates capable of learning if subjected to global competition with the best. Revitalizing Europe 1992 will have to allow for this competitive gamble and allow the market to select both the winners and the losers.

4. ORGANIZATIONAL LEARNING AND TRADE IN COMPETENCE

4.1 General Issues

The sustainability of a firm as a rent generating organization depends, as noted, on its ability to coordinate its internal activities efficiently at each point in time, and to organizationally learn efficiently over time. Firms that cannot balance these two tasks sooner or later fail and/or break up into smaller entities. The ability to achieve such viable integration of long-term (dynamic) and short-term (static) efficiency defines the organizational efficiency of the firm. This competence depends on how the steady filtering of competent people within the firm is organized and the ease by which new competence can be acquired in the market and integrated with the competent teams of the firm.

Trade and reallocation of competence discussed in this section can occur through:

1. *Internal labor markets* within a corporation
2. *External labor markets* for managerial competence
3. *The market for M&A*

While the first, internal market tends to strengthen the cohesive forces of a competent team, success in the other two markets requires receiver competence to work in favor of the firm. The acquisition of external competence can take place in external markets for labor and in the M&A market. Two different types of competence acquisition are involved and there is an apparent substitutability between the two. While acquisition of new competence in the labor market can be gradual without disrupting the organization of the firm, acquisitions of new competence in the M&A market can be swift, but also disruptive to the internal organization of the acquiring firm, often impairing its internal capacity to upgrade its competence in internal markets, and to keep the team together.

Two important aspects of competence allocation and organizational learning influence the relative efficiency of different modes for trade in competence. *First*, markets for competent labor may be imperfect, and the monitoring of competence characteristics costly. This explains the particular employer/employee relationships discussed within an asymmetric information, principal agent context by Greenwald (1986), Harris and Holmström (1982), Lazear (1981), and others. This problem becomes the dominant problem in establishing, running and reorganizing a firm with quality dominating all dimensions, and tacit knowledge being the typical competence characteristic. In brief, the market for the most critical quality input exhibits the characteristics of a market for lemons (Akerlof 1970). An important issue for alternative modes for trading in competence is the degree to which the lemon problem can be resolved.

The *second* important aspect of competence allocation is that experimental search becomes the optimal learning and allocation method for the firm due to the tacit nature of organizational competence. Experimental search requires an ability not only to coordinate, but also to identify mistakes early, and correct them efficiently (Eliasson 1988a,b). There are distinctly different characteristics associated with internal allocation of quality labor through the career and external allocation through the market.

4.2 The Internal Labor Market - The Career

The expansion of large firms (MNCs) internationally is expanding the internal markets for high quality management internationally, contributing to a more efficient international diffusion of industrial competence. The merger of ASEA and Brown Bovery provides interesting illustrations. The organization of the internal labor market, very much determines the capacity of the firm to earn a rent. As a consequence its effectiveness is part of the firm's organizational competence that is evaluated in financial markets.

The importance of the internal career is most obvious in large firms, notably in the large U.S. firms, with an internal educational organization to support the career. This formal organization is less extensive in European firms of similar size.

Since the method to identify talent and competence is experimental, the internal labor or career market carries a definite advantage from the point of view of monitoring career candidates for quality, compared to hiring in the external market. Internal recruitment, on the other hand, narrows the degree of variation in talent and experience compared to what is offered in the external market. This handicap can to some extent be overcome in large firms, notably large international firms. It is my conviction that the international integration of internal firm labor markets will constitute the most important internationalization of the markets for executive competence. Although in the short run M&A markets, and internal markets can be seen as substitutes, they are in the longer run complementary, since the organization of effective, internal and international markets is a reason for, and a consequence of M&A activity.

The development of markets for executive talent is illustrated by Glete (1989) who observes that executive labor markets were very thin in Sweden during the first half of the 20th century. Hence, very much as among specialized crafts, "manager dynasties" developed, the executive competence being passed on within families. As a result the resistance to changes in the orientation of the firm was great and monitoring of efficiency by owners was difficult. The prestige of executive managers was great. Tradability in and transferability of executive competence increased during the course of the 20th century, through the development of a career market in large firms and through the improved efficiency of external markets as well as through the links between financial institutions and corporations in, so called, *industrial bank groups*.

Glete (1989) studied the Wallenberg industrial bank group in particular. Such industrial bank groups do not build on risk diversification but on the organizational technique of earning a rent from allocating and integrating competence efficiently and also from achieving financial scale. Such groups incorporate a "quasi"internal market for very high level executive competence. It runs across several firms operating in many lines of business, with both domestic and foreign subsidiaries, offering a wide diversity of "corporate cultures", including a well rounded experience in international banking. Since such groups recombine all the time through acquisition and divestment of parts of firms, or entire firms, it is obvious that the internal labor market of such loosely structured groups perform a labor quality allocation function similar to that of a more decentralized M&A market of the Anglo Saxon type. We return to this comparison when discussing financial market organization in Section 5.

An internal "career-market" for managerial and other types of competence requires investment of firm-specific resources in individuals. Highly efficient external labor markets implies high potential mobility and a trade-off between efficient internal and external allocation mechanisms for competence. As Lazear (1981) notes, there are contracts with delayed compensation schemes that can "tie" the individual to the corporation, but, since "slave contracts" are illegal, the characteristics of external markets for top-level competence requires discussion.

4.3 Changing the Mind of the Firm through Competence Hiring in External Labor Markets

The large internal pool of career candidates is the benefit of the large firm, and increasingly the large international firm. To acquire human talent the small firm normally has to reach out into the external labor market, at significantly higher search costs. If a (small) domestically based firm wants to go international the experience needed to do this successfully is usually not available inhouse. Even a big firm may have to reach out to acquire knowledge, when "it realizes" that its current competence base has grown too limited or obsolete. It is a common experience that a corporate organization problem can rarely be solved by the same group of people who allowed it to arise. The viability of a strong and capable owner is created by his or her mandade *to change the mind of the top competent team* through the removal of the existing team.

In interviews with top executives in large Swedish firms about such competence matters, the presence of directors from many other firms and close ties within an industrial bank group have been stressed. The capacity of the Board to overcome the inbreeding of competence common in closed and tightly run corporations has often been mentioned. Meyerson (1991) analyzes these issues in more detail.

Obviously, the trade in highly individualized and tacit human competence in open markets entails substantial transactions costs to overcome asymmetric information. "Traders" of various kinds have to be involved to reduce the risk of catching a high cost "lemon". The most common "trading institutions" are the "educational institutions" in the beginning of a candidate's career as emphasized, for example, by Sicherman and Galor (1990). "Old friends networks", "mentors" and other institutions have been created to establish the reputation needed for a viable trade in human embodied competence. As noted, the loosely structured industrial bank group arrangements can be seen as a "quasi"-internalization of market transactions in managerial talent.

The new emerging traders in corporate talent, who may play a significant future role in the international talent trade, are the "headhunting firms". Headhunting is still a costly search activity reserved for the exclusive few. But such search is gradually becoming more systematically organized, allowing also for systematic knowledge accumulation within the search firms themselves. An internationalization of headhunting activities can be discerned, as noted by Jones (1989) and the exclusive nature of this activity will certainly break down national political and cultural barriers to executive mobility if the commercial incentives are sufficiently strong. An expansion of headhunting activities is clearly a substitute for internal markets in multinational firms.

Increased efficiency of internal organizational learning will make the firm a more attractive object for external talent raiding. External raiding requires a matching receiver competence, however. IBM did not succeed in incorporating Rolm competence into its organization. AT&T has not been all that successful in making marketing people hired from IBM successful in the AT&T environment. The acquisition of Sculley of Apple from Pepsi Cola by the headhunting firm Heidrick & Struggles, has, however, so far been claimed to be a success according to Jones (1989). The headhunting firm Boyden, scored a similar success finding Geneen for ITT in 1959. The mixed record of headhunting indicates that external markets cannot become a perfect substitute for internal career markets. Thus, incentives for firms to invest in competence development will remain. The risks associated with such investments increase, however, as external market agents become increasingly efficient in identifying internally developed talent. A career at

Electrolux has been quoted several times in my interviews as "the best management education available in Europe".

4.4 Markets for M&A Activity

The third mode for trade and reallocation of organizational competence is M&A activity. Smith and Walter document the importance of this mode in an international context in this volume. The major advantage of M&A activity in my context is that it enables tacit knowledge and competence embodied in teams, as opposed to individuals to be reallocated. Like trade in external labor markets the effectiveness of this mechanism for allocation requires receiver comptence in both the acquiring and the acquired firm.

The rationale behind competence trade through M&A activity is either that the acquiring firm is seeking an infusion of team competence or that it has competence that can be applied in another firm.

It was noted above that internal markets, external labor markets, and M&A activity can be seen as substitutable modes for reallocation of competence and organizational learning. In the longer run internal markets and M&A activity are also complements. The diverse, international firm probably offers the best internal, educational environment for executive competence. The most important complementarity between internal and external labor markets, on the one hand, and M&A activity on the other, arises as a result of M&A activity in the market for corporate control. Here the connection with financial markets and markets for competence and organizational learning is established.

The organizational knowledge base of the firm and its rent-earning ability is evaluated in financial markets. These markets signal information to incumbent management teams about the limits of their competence. They also provide incentives for the reallocation of organizational competence in firms. The effectiveness of markets for corporate control in performing this signalling and incentive functions, however, depends on their institutional structure. We turn to this issue next.

5. FINANCIAL MARKET INSTITUTIONS AND THE ALLOCATION OF COMPETENCE

5.1 Alternative Institutional Structures

Dahmén (1988) observed that each firm, as well as each bank internally performs the same three traditional functions of the credit market

1. short-term lending (classical banking)
2. long-term investment financing (the capital market)
3. venture financing ("innovation")

Depending upon circumstances these three financing functions are performed in different mixes between the firms, the banks and the market. Sometimes all three "activities" are incorporated within large corporate hierarchies. Sometimes they are mostly performed in the market without the intermediation of banks. An intermediate form, sometimes called "industrial banks", or "industrial bank groups" of firms, more or less intimately tied to a bank through joint ownership arrangements were more common in the past. They still exist in Germany. In Sweden such groups are still functioning to some extent, although banks are not allowed to own corporations. Bank control of corporations is achieved through strong personal ties, common board members, and unequal voting rights.

An efficient integration of all three activities - short term, long term and innovative - in the same monolithic organization of a large firm is very difficult, perhaps impossible. A conservative management style geared to short-term profit targeting tends to dominate at the expense of long-term innovative performance. The fragmented organization of many small firms in an efficient financial market, on the other hand, while perhaps innovative, normally lacks the benefits of large scale production and of efficient monitoring of venture activities.

The industrial banking group has sometimes been seen as the optimal organizational design to cope with the balancing of long and short term factors and the efficient monitoring of borrowers by, for example, Dahmén (1988), Eliasson (1990a), and Glete (1989). The ultimate controller of such groups has been the active owners who have taken on both the long-term responsibility and the ultimate selection of top competent people. Political concerns about the scope of individual or family wealth needed to support such a capitalist organization of the economic system and concerns about industrial concentration and monopoly formation have made it difficult in the last few decades to maintain this organization in many countries. In deregulated financial markets parts of such banking groups, often based on minority positions, have become exposed to take-overs. This threat is especially strong when the group allocates its resources and talent towards long-term ventures with delayed pay-offs relative to preferences revealed in stock market prices. Increased securitization of the international financial system therefore represents a consequence of deregulation that "threatens" the traditional industrial group with a bank at the center.

Rybczynski (1988) argues that in the securitized financial system

- rate of return monitoring and comparison of corporate activities become more efficient with improved information technology
- competitive entry and exit of financial institutions are facilitated, and
- exit of inefficient institutions is more efficiently enforced.

These mechanisms make it easier for investors to act rapidly, supplying finance to good prospects or pulling finance out of defunct operations from a distance. In the securitized market a larger number of agents are operating in the financial system, increasing the opportunities to obtain financing on a good, but risky idea. The junk bond market in the U.S. is one example of the changing performance characteristics of the financial system that directly influences the structure of the production system through the M&A market. The important question is whether Europe will experience a development similar to the U.S.

The "softening" of manufacturing is another factor that facilitates competence mobility. Technology is moving increasingly in favor of smaller scale and more reliance on knowledge-based service production. As pointed out by Rybczynski (1988) such activities widen the competence gap between producers/investors and suppliers of finance, and require a new, more venturelike organization of financial markets. Rybczynski (1988) argues that the securitization of financial markets will facilitate the transition into a knowledge-based service economy, through integration of the knowledge allocation and financing functions through a multilayered, fragmented structure of specialist intermediaries thus reducing problems of asymmetric information while simplifying M&A and the financing of risky projects.

5.2 Does the Market Give the Firm Time to Learn?

The industrial banking group was, and may still be an efficient way to integrate the long-term innovative and the short-term operational functions within the same group, since organizational learning can proceed through quasi-internal markets for different types of competence. The weakness of this organization is that, without the threat of take-overs of parts of the group based on market valuation, competence development goes in the direction determined by a few dominant owners.

In the securitized system, on the other hand, M&A activity is more prevalent with the consequence that corporate structures are less stable and more threatened by potential M&A activity. The efficiency of organizational learning and the reallocation of competence therefore depends more on incentives provided by the two external modes of trading in competence. Incentives for individuals to invest in competence development depends on the returns that can be obtained in external labor markets, while owners of firms would invest in organizational learning if the M&A market provides a satisfactory return on such investment.

Do labor and financial markets *give the firm time to develop an efficient organizational knowledge base,* or is the securitization creating "markets failures" in the long run? The detachment of financial agents in the market system from direct involvement in production decisions means that less effort and less competence are put to use by owners to actually remedy a distressed corporate situation. Owners sell off and leave rather than solve the problem.[1] The industrial bank organization took care of the long term in the past. Rybczynski (1988) argues that in the securitized system competition will see to it that if there is a long-term merit to a project there will be some, among a large number of financial intermediaries, who understand that. The critical counterarguement would be that project evaluation requires evaluation of competence that is inherently tacit. Therefore the relevant information of insiders within the competent team of the business organization, required for competent valuation of the firm, cannot be available in the market (Eliasson 1988b, 1990a).[2] If such insider competence is not allowed to influence the market valuation of the firm its assets will be undervalued and outsiders without the necessary competence to understand the organizational learning process would be able to take control and interrupt the organizational learning process, hence reducing the knowledge capital residing in the group as a whole. The market would not give the firm time to learn. To achieve the previous efficiency of long-term organizational learning compensatory mechanisms would have to exist to acquire the necessary competence externally through direct hiring in the labor market and/or through acquisition of competent teams in the M&A market. Empirical evidence would suggest that firms lack the *receiver competence* for such external learning. Its tacit character may even make it impossible to acquire externally (Eliasson 1990a,b).

Some additional observations can be made about the securitized market oriented system. The more innovative a firm, the larger its propensity to fail and the more important that institutions exist that can understand the innovation potential and take on the long term risks needed in the financing of innovative activity. The developed securitized system will in principle be able to spread the financial risks and (through its diversity) mobilize the necessary evaluation competence. However, the greater the ambition to aim for the small probability of a large success, the more important it is for the innovator to be able to appropriate its innovation rent, i.e. to prevent imitations and to prevent the financial system from appropriating too large a share of the rent from a successful innovation. These observations point to the growing importance of large scale organizational technique in creating, protecting and rapidly commercializing innovations in advanced industrial nations, while at the same time effectively minimizing the incurred experimental costs, i.e. the costs of mistakes. The latter corrective function is only efficiently accomplished through competition in financial markets, and the securitized market should be most efficient in that respect.

However, in so far as it is true that the creative, innovative activity cannot be efficiently organized within large firms with the financial capacity to pursue long term goals, a particular organizational structure must develop in advanced industrial nations which both effectively promotes innovative work in small firms and effectively cashes in on innovations through rapid, large scale commercialization. Such firms, to succeed in the longer term must also possess a competence to identify and correct mistakes faster than the market does it. U.S. manufacturing firms seem to have been slow in learning this competence, being the first to be hit by early securitization of financial markets. Since securitization is such a strong force it will also unavoidably be forced upon the European financial systems, making it even more imperative that European firms and markets rapidly build the organizational competence to effectively cope with both innovation and large scale commercialization.

One solution could be that small firms specialize in innovations. The innovative firm is then acquired in the market by a large firm that is specialized in bringing innovations from the pilot to large industrial scale. In the small scale end of the innovative activity large learning costs will be incurred through frequent failure. Expected returns on innovative activity must then be very high to compensate for the risk. The bulk of resource use, including large scale risktaking will be managed in the large corporation with an entirely different organizational technique. Again, this requires the *receiver competence* to implement the new innovative competence in an entirely different production environment. Even though, as mentioned above, there may be principal obstacles to merging two very different tacit competence cultures successfully, without an extended learning period, it has been done. In fact, Japanese and Swedish firms have appeared as very successful organizers in the second, large scale end, drawing heavily on the generous output of the U.S. research establishment, to the detriment of a less implementation competent U.S. manufacturing industry. The future viability of the innovative machine of a country will, then, depend on the development of efficient competitive markets for financing of such innovative output, allowing the innovators to survive through capturing a sufficiently large part of the value they create (Eliasson 1986).

6. CONCLUSION

The initial question asked was what are the economic consequences of financial market developments for a European market for executive competence. The task has been to define the nature of this competence and the way it can be diffused through markets. The impact of financial market developments on organizational learning including both the creation of new competence (innovation) and of the receiver competence to accommodate external knowledge determines how the new vision of a dynamic Europe will be realized.

The central problem addressed is what effects the securitization of European financial markets will have on industrial structure. The conclusion is that the force of securitization imposed from international financial markets is too strong to be countered by policy, and it should not be, since securitization carries with it many beneficial effects. There is, however, the risk that securitization will force a break up of certain corporate structures, like industrial bank groups, that have successfully promoted internal organizational learning and the long term perspective in Europe, notably in West Germany and in Sweden.

One question is whether this has implications for financial market regulation. Yes, it has. One implication is that the existence of such innovative combinations of firms and financial institutions in a securitized financial system requires that the market be capable of informal evaluation of assets, such that market values of competence be kept sufficiently high to avoid destructive raiding. This requires the presence of active insiders in the market (Eliasson 1990a) and the first task for the European regulator is to avoid importing U.S. insider regulation to Europe. It may also be wise to allow a certain measure of unequal voting rights and to taylor the rules regulating the interests of competent financial institutions and firms carefully. Europe in fact offers a large variety of such rules to learn from, before hasty regulation is introduced.

The policy problem facing politicians turns out *not* to be a national problem, and *not* even a European problem. The solution lies in diffusing the national definitions of economies. Europe is probably too narrow a definition of a successful economic area because the organizational competence residing within it is not sufficient to match the corresponding competence of the U.S. and Japanese firms universally. Hence, opening up Europe to the globally best performers in each field is the best way to an efficiently specialized Europe. Another critical problem is whether European firms possess the receiver competence needed to acquire lacking knowledge efficiently. If not, it maybe necessary to call in the Japanese and the U.S. firms to invest in Europe and to infuse their knowledge in their European subsidiaries. It may be instructive to recall that this is exactly what the Swedish king did in the 17th century, when he realized that Sweden lacked the manufacturing competence needed for industrial development in those days to create a viable arms manufacturing industry. The king created the incentives needed to induce competent entrepreneurs and skilled workers to move to Sweden, notably from Wallonia.

FOOTNOTES

1. Other arguments for a short-term bias in decentralized makers characterized by asymmetric information is found in, for instance, Stein (1988).

2. Human capital theory suffers from the same problem. With tacit knowledge embodied in individuals or teams (firms) stable earnings functions do not exist and external market valuation of capital becomes imperfect.

REFERENCES

Akerlof, G.A., (1970), "The Market for "Lemons": Qualitative Uncertainty and the Market Mechanism", Quarterly Journal of Economics, Vol. 84 (August), 488-500.

Anderson, G.M. and R.D. Tollison (1982), "Adam Smith's Analysis of Joint-Stock Companies", Journal of Political Economy, Vol. 90 (December), 1237-1256.

Arrow, K.J. (1962a), "The Economic Implications of Learning by Doing", Review of Economic Studies, Vol. 29 (June), 155-173.

_____ (1962b), Economic Welfare and the Allocation of Resources for Inventions; in Nelson, R (ed), 1962, Rate and Direction of Inventive Activity: Economic and Social Factors, NBER, Princeton University Press, Princeton.

Baker, G.P., M.C. Jensen, and K.J. Murphy (1988), "Compensation and Incentives: Practice vs. Theory", Journal of Finance, Vol. XLIII, No. 3 (July), 593-615.

Barnard, C.H. (1938), The Functions of the Executive, Harvard University Press, Cambridge Mass. & London, England.

Campbell, I.S., Y.S. Chan, and A.M. Marino (1989), "Incentive Contracts for Managers who Discover and Manage Investment Projects", Journal of Economic Behavior & Organization, No. 12, 353-364.

Carlsson, B. et al. (1979), Teknik och industristruktur - 70-talets ekonomiska kris i historisk belysning, IUI and IVA, Stockholm.

Carlsson, B. (1989), "The Evolution of Manufacturing Technology and its Impact on Industrial Structure", Small Business Economics, Vol. 1, No. 1, 21-37.

Carmichael, L. (1983), "Firm-Specific Human Capital and Promotion Ladders", Bell Journal of Economics, Vol. 14, No. 1 (spring), 251-258.

Dahmén, E. (1988), Entrepreneurial Activity, Banking and Finance, Historical Aspects and Theoretical Suggestions, IUI Working Paper No. 209, Stockholm.

Dixit, A. (1987), "Strategic Aspects of Trade Policy", in Bewley, T. (ed.), Awareness in Economic Theory, Cambridge University Press, Cambridge.

Eliasson, G. (1976), Business Economic Planning - theory, practice, and comparison, John Wiley & Son.

_____ (1984), "The Micro-Foundations of Industrial Policies", in Jacquemin, A. (ed.), European Industry: Public Policy and Corporate Strategy, Oxford University Press.

_____ (1986), Innovative Change, Dynamic Market Allocation and Long-Term Stability of Economic Growth, IUI Working Paper No. 156, to be published in David and Dosi, (eds.), Innovation and the Diffusion of Technology, Oxford University Press, Oxford. Forthcoming.

_____ (1987), Technological Competition in The Experimentally Organized Economy, IUI Research Report No. 32, Stockholm

_____ (1988a), "Schumpeterian Innovation, Market Structure and the Stability of Industrial Development", in Hanusch, H. (ed.), Evolutionary Economics, Applications of Schumpeter's Ideas, Cambridge University Press.

_____ (1988b), "Ägare, entreprenörer och kapitalmarknadens organisation - en teoretisk presentation och översikt" in Örtengren, J. et al., Expansion, avveckling och företagsvärdering i svensk industri, IUI, Stockholm.

_____ (1988c), The International Firm: A Vehicle for Overcoming Barriers to Trade and a Global Intelligence Organization Diffusing the Notion of a Nation, IUI Working Paper No. 201, Stockholm.

_____ (1990a), "The Firm as a Competent Team", Journal of Economic Behavior & Organization, Vol.13, No. 3 (June), 275-298.

_____ (1990b), Business Competence, Organizational Learning and Economic Growth, paper presented to the 1990 Joseph A. Schumpeter Society Meeting, Virginia, USA, June 3-5, 1990. Also as IUI Working Paper No. 264.

Eliasson, G., F. Bergholm, E.Ch. Horwitz, and L. Jagrén, (1985), De svenska storföretagen - en studie av internationaliseringens konsekvenser för den svenska ekonomin (The Giant Swedish Multinationals - a study on the consequences for the Swedish economy of Business internationalization), IUI, Stockholm.

Eliasson, G. and O. Granstrand (1985), Venture Capital and Management - a study of venture development units in four Swedish firms, mimeo, IUI.

Eliasson, G. and L. Lundberg (1990), The Creation of the EC Internal Market and Its Effects on the Competitiveness of Producers in Other Industrial Economies; in Siebert, H. and Mohr, J.C.B. (eds.), The Completion of the Internal Market Symposium 1989. Also as IUI Booklet No. 263, Stockholm.

Glete, J. (1989), "Long-term Firm Growth and Ownership Organization", Journal of Economic Behavior & Organization, Vol. 12, No. 3 (December).

Granstrand, O. and S. Sjölander (1990), The Acquisition of Technology and Small Firms by Large Firms. Paper presented at the IUI Conference "Markets for Innovation, Ownership and Control", Saltsjöbaden, Stockholm, 1988. Published in Journal of Economic Behavior and Organization Vol. 13, No. 3 (June).

Greenwald, B. (1986), "Adverse Selection in the Labor Market", Review of Economic Studies, Vol. 53, 325-347.

Harris, M. and B. Holmström (1982), "A Theory of Wage Dynamics", Review of Economic Studies, Vol.XLIX, 313-333.

Holmström, B. and J.E. Ricart i Costa (1986), "Managerial Incentives and Capital Management", Quarterly Journal of Economics, Vol. CI, Issue 4, November.

Jensen, M.C. and K.J. Murphy (1990), "Performance Pay and Top Management Incentives", Journal of Political Economy, Vol. 98, No. 2 (April), 225-265.

Jones, S. (1989), The Headhunting Business, Macmillan, London.

King, M. (1977), Public Policy and the Corporation, Chapman and Hall, London.

Krugman, P.R. (1983), Targeted Industrial Policies: Theory and Evidence; Industrial Change and Public Policy symposium sponsored by the Federal Research Bank of Kansas City.

Lazear, E.P. (1981), "Agency, Earnings Profiles, Productivity and Hours Restrictions", American Economic Review, Vol. 71, No. 4, 606-620.

Locke, R.R. (1989), Management and Higher Education since 1990 - The Influence of America and Japan on West Germany, Great Britain and France, Cambridge University press, Cambridge, New York etc.

Marshall, A. (1890), Principles of Economics, Macmillan, London.

Meyerson, E. (1991), Recruitment Processes for Leadership, Internal Dynamics and External Control, forthcoming doctoral thesis 1991, IUI Stockholm.

Mill, J.S. (1948), Principles of Political Economy with Some of Their Applications to Social Philosophy, London.

Murnane, R.J. and R.R. Nelson, (1984), "Production and Innovation when Techniques are Tacit: The Case of Education", Journal of Economic Behavior & Organization, Vol. 5, Nos. 3-4 (Sept.-Dec.).

O'Brian, D.P. (1990), "Marshall's Industrial Analysis", Scottish Journal of Political Economics, Vol. 37, No.1 (Febr.).

Pelikan, P. (1989), "Evolution, Economic Competence, and the Market for Corporate Control", Journal of Economic Behavior & Organization, Vol. 12, No. 3 (December), 279-303.

Pratten, C. (1976), A Comparison of the Performance of Swedish and UK Companies, Cambridge University Press, Cambridge.

Ricart i Costa (1988), "Managerial Task Assignment and Promotion", Econometrica, Vol. 56. No. 2, (March) 449-466.

Romer, P.M. (1986), "Growth Based on Increasing Returns and Long-term Growth", Journal of Political Economy, Vol. 94, No. 5 (October), 1002-1037.

Rosen, S. (1972), "Learning by Experience as Joint Production", Quarterly Journal of Economics, Vol. LXXXVI, No. 3, (Aug.), 366-382.

_____ (1981), "The Economics of Super Stars", American Economic Review, Vol. 71, No. 5.

_____ (1982), "Authority, Control and The Distribution of Earnings", Bell Journal of Economics, (Autumn), 311-323.

Rybczynski, T. (1988), Innovative Activity and Venture Financing; Access to Markets and Opportunities in Japan, the U.S. and Europe, IUI Working Paper No. 216, Stockholm. Forthcoming in Eliasson, Day, and Wihlborg (eds.) Markets for Innovation. Ownership and Control, IUI.

Schumpeter, J. (1942), Capitalism, Socialism and Democracy, Harper & Row, New York.

Seal, W.B. (1990), "Deindustrialization and Business Organization: an institutionalist critique of the natural selection analogy", Cambridge Journal of Economics, Vol. 14, 267-275.

Selznick, P. (1957), Leadership in Administration, Harper & Row, New York.

Sicherman, N. and O. Galor (1990), "A Theory of Career Mobility", Journal of Political Economy, Vol. 98 No. 1, 169-192.

Simon, H.A. (1955), "A Behavioral Model of Rational Choice", Quarterly Journal of Economics, Vol. 69, 99-118.

Singh, A. (1987), "Manufacturing Deindustrialization", in Eatwell, Milgate and Newman (eds.) The New Palgrave, Macmillan, London, 301-307.

Stein, J., (1988), "Takeover Threats and Managerial Myopia", <u>Journal of Political Economy</u>, Feb., 61-80.

Smith, A., (1776), <u>An Inquiry into the Nature and Causes of the Wealth of Nations</u>, Modern Library, New York 1937.

Spence, M. (1973), "Job Market Signaling", <u>Quarterly Journal of Economics</u>, Vol. 87 (Aug.), 355-379.

Stafford, I.P. and M.O. Stobernack (1989), <u>Manufacturing Wages and Hours: Do Trade and Technology Matter</u>? Mimeo, Department of Economics, University of Michigan and Technische Universitet, Berlin.

Williamson, O.E. (1975), <u>Markets and Hierarchies: Analysis and Antitrust Implications. A Study in the Economics of Internal Organization</u>, Free Press, New York.

Financial Regulation and Monetary Arrangements after 1992
C. Wihlborg, M. Fratianni and T.D. Willett (Editors)
© 1991 Elsevier Science Publishers B.V. All rights reserved

Comment

Niels Chr. Nielsen

Institute of Finance, Copenhagen School of Economics and Business Administration,
Rosenørns allé 31, DK 1970 Frederiksberg C, Denmark

Eliasson's paper addresses a number of important issues and makes a number of important observations. The lack of focus can, however, also be considered a weakness of the paper. In particular, since there already exists basically a free "European market for executive competence", what is it that makes the situation after 1992 so different? The paper provides more challenges for future research than it answers questions.

The main proposition is that the market for managerial competence - in a European context - will improve after 1992. Three reasons for this are provided. First, the international expansion of individual companies will generate an internal international "labor market". And internal markets function better than external markets (fewer externalities and market failures, fewer information problems, etc.). Second, the increased international monitoring (e.g. head hunting) will reduce market failures. Third, financial arbitrage (i.e. the market for corporate control) by selling and buying companies, mergers and acquisitions, take-overs (friendly or hostile), management and leveraged buy-outs, etc. will result in a better performance of the market for managerial competence.

These suggestions are not substantiated by much empirical evidence although, ultimately, their validity is an empirical issue. Even without the empirical evidence, some scepticism seems warranted. In the following, the main emphasis will be on the third suggestion, i.e. the importance of the growing market for corporate control.

It is true that some companies are becoming larger and more international. But it is also true that other companies are becoming smaller. MBO (Management Buy Out), LBO (Leveraged Buy Out) and spin-offs are daily phenomena on the international financial scene.

There has been a large number of "performance examinations" of M&A activities. The generel wisdom is not quite clear. Measured in terms of rate of return on shares, the stock holders of target companies appear on average to be among the winners. There is fairly strong evidence that these shareholders gain 20-30% in share values, the exact gain depending on a number of factors (such as the relative size of the companies, whether the take over is friendly or hostile, etc.).

There is no strong evidence, however, that the stockholders of the company taking over make a profit on average. They might win or they might loose, but the average gain appears to be close to zero. M&A-activities appear to be more in the interest of the management than in the interest of the shareholders in the company taking over another company.

Some of the companies that appear to have been doing best in the 1980s are companies that have been "growing smaller" by eliminating none-core business. Hence, although there are clear economies of scale in many industries, it is by no way a general phenomenon that companies are growing larger.

It is true, as suggested by Eliasson, that the market for corporate control can be considered a market for "managerial competence". Managerial teams are available in the market, and companies do compete to get the best managerial team for their specific kind of business. For example, Lichtenberg and Siegel (1987) show how by selling and buying plants a better matching of management and production units is obtained. At least they hypothesize that this is the likely explanation for the observed increase in productivity for individual plants when ownership is changed.

The market for corporate control is not very well understood, and there are a number of reasons why it might not work well as a market for managerial competence. As observed by Grossman and Hart (1980) there is a "free rider" problem. Further, there is a problem of asymmetric information ("lemon problem"), since companies for sale are most likely to be low in quality. This problem of asymmetric information is not easy to solve. In a horizontal take-over, for example, the company taking over will not be allowed access to all relevant information unless it is totally committed to complete the take-over. But it would not commmit itself without having all relevant information, implying that the take-over always will be a matter of good faith combined with "shooting in the dark".

There is also some evidence that managerial compensation depends more on size than on performance, implying that managers have an incentive to increase the size of "their" firm, even if it happens at the cost of the shareholders. This argument runs contradictory to the argument that mergers and acquisitions and take-over threats are means to solve managerial problems. To state briefly, it is not clear whether M&A-activities are a result of or a solution to an agency problem.

Similarly, diversification (i.e. conglomerates) might be attractive in the short run for risk-averse managers, but there is not much evidence that shareholders in the long run will gain from it.

There seems to be an immense growth in different kinds of "defense arrangements" which, if anything, cause a deterioration of the market for corporate control and results in a stronger position for management vis-à-vis shareholders. The result is a less efficient market for managerial competence.

Defense arrangements are primarily a protection of management. It could be argued that in some cases they might even benefit the shareholders by having a positive influence on the final price offer in a take-over situation. It should be without doubt, however, that they have a negative impact on the efficiency of the market for managerial competence.

To understand the market for corporate control requires a thorough explanation why corporate raiders and others active in the take-over business are able to bid a higher price than the existing shareholders and/or the existing management. And a convincing explanation of how the values and cash flows necessary to justify the higher price-bid are created.

This again requires a better understanding of managerial compensation schemes and how these compensation schemes relate to managerial productivity as well as a better understanding in general of the relationship between wages and productivity. It seems apparent that there are huge short term discrepancies between wages and productivity. One extreme case is the Japanese life-long (implicit) employment contract with employees expecting later to be "compensated" for being underpaid in their earlier working life. Another extreme is the saying about American journalists, that "you are as good as your latest article", implying that you are always paid exactly your marginal product.

European compensation schemes are probably closer to the Japanese system than this conventional picture of salaries for American journalists, implying that there are always potential gains from breaching of trust and breaching of implicit contracts, as pointed out by e.g. Schleifer and Summers (1988). Without a much better understanding of these processes it is very difficult to form hypotheses about the relation between the market for corporate control and the market for executive competence. In addition, we lack knowledge about how the market for corporate control will develop in the future.

The growing number of MBOs and the increased use of stock-options as incentive devices for top management indicate that monitoring and agency costs tend to be pretty high.

It is interesting to observe that there are surprising (?) differences across countries when it comes to M&A-activities, MBOs, LBOs, take-overs and similar activities in the market for corporate control. The activity level has been high in Anglo-Saxon countries and Sweden and much lower in Central Europe.

It is also interesting to observe that the group of highest paid CEOs apparently can be divided into two groups: Those who benefit from an extraordinary good performance and those who make all their money from an awful performance, by golden parachutes, poison pills and similar arrangements.

REFERENCES

Grossman, S.J., and O.D. Hart (1980), "Takeover Bids, the Free-Rider Problem, and the Theory of the Corporation", Bell Journal of Economics, 11, 42-64.

Lichtenberg, F. R., and D. Siegel (1988), Principles of Financial Management, Prentice Hall, New Jersey.

Schleifer, A. and L. H. Summers (1988), "Breach of Trust in Hostile Takeovers", Chapter 2 in A. J. Auerbach, ed., Corporate Takeovers: Causes and Consequences, Chicago, The University of Chicago Press,.

Part Three

Barriers to Capital Mobility and Financial Intermediation

Financial Regulation and Monetary Arrangements after 1992
C. Wihlborg, M. Fratianni and T.D. Willett (Editors)
1991 Elsevier Science Publishers B.V.

8 Market Segmentation and 1992: Toward a Theory of Trade in Financial Services

John D. Montgomery

Division of International Finance, Board of Governors of the Federal Reserve System, Washington, DC 20551, USA

1. INTRODUCTION

The effect of the creation of a single European market for the services of banks and other financial intermediaries depends on the economic role that these intermediaries play. Standard theorems of gains from international trade may not apply to financial services. This paper concentrates on banks and similar lending institutions[1] and argues that the structure of banking markets are quite different from the markets for goods which standard trade theory treats. In particular, markets for some banking services appear to be fragmented geographically, and it is in these services that the value-added of banks may be the highest. This fragmentation implies that the market for financial services may never approximate the geographically integrated market assumed by trade theory.

In order to consider the effect of regulatory changes such as the EC's Second Banking Directive, it is necessary to have a framework consistent with recent literature. A number of recent papers have argued that financial intermediaries are an efficient response to asymmetric information between borrowers and lenders (see Diamond (1984), Williamson (1986) and Boyd and Prescott (1986)). Another strand of the literature, starting with Bernanke (1983), argues that bank failures, by damaging credit relationships, may have real economic effects. Both areas of literature are surveyed by Gertler (1988). More recently, a series of empirical studies, starting with Fazzari, Hubbard and Petersen (1988), have found that investment is sensitive to the cash-flow of a firm and that this sensitivity tends to increase for smaller and newer firms, as well as for those without strong ties to financial intermediaries.

The theoretical portion of the literature cited above tends to be quite abstract and, as it stands now, not well suited to considering the issues in the structure of banking markets. This paper represents a first step toward developing a framework that is consistent with recent theoretical and empirical literature and that can also explain the forms that banking markets take. I argue that to do so it is necessary to take into account the fact that the markets for some banking services may be geographically segmented. I also present some evidence on the segmentation across regions of the Italian banking market. Italy is chosen because data are available both on regional bank interest rates and on regional capital flows.

Montgomery (1990) argues that banks with local market power may cause reduced capital mobility between regions. This decreased capital mobility results from two factors: first, banks have market power in local deposit markets, which gives them access to a supply of cheap funds; second, lending in a locality is more efficiently done by locally based intermediaries. Lending between regions will therefore tend to take place between intermediaries, which is costly because of agency problems.[2] It follows from this argument that the extent to which the liberalization of the European capital market equalizes the cost of capital across countries may depend on the structure of financial intermediation in Europe.

Section 2 of this paper discusses the economic basis for financial intermediation and the effect this has on analyzing trade in financial services. A distinction is drawn between services that can be efficiently offered across international borders (except possibly for regulatory reasons) and services where local presence gives an intermediary a substantial cost advantage. I argue that the second pattern may be applicable for the services where intermediaries' economic role is the greatest. When such local advantages exist, imperfect competition is likely, which makes the case for cross-border expansion of intermediaries unclear.

Section 3 presents an empirical analysis of market segmentation in the Italian market. Data on regional interest rates and interregional capital flows is examined for the 1981-1984 period. The analysis provides evidence of the presence of either imperfect mobility of capital between regions or local market power of intermediaries - the two elements of the environment postulated in Montgomery (1990). The sensitivity of this analysis to econometric issues and idiosyncrasies of the Italian system is discussed.

Section 4 discusses the effects of cross-border expansion of banks and thus the effects of the Second Banking Directive when there is market segmentation. The consolidation of banks from different local markets into multi-regional and multi-national banks may contribute to increased mobility of capital between regions. It may also reduce the likelihood of bank failure and therefore reduce the need for authorities to monitor bank behavior as part of the supervisory process. On the other hand, such a consolidation, by reducing the number of participants in the market, is likely to decrease competition for the banking services that can be provided across borders. Its effect on competition within local markets is uncertain. This section also discusses the possible effects of changing technology of information processing.

Section 4 concludes with a brief discussion of the policy implications of this work. A central message of this paper is that a model of a unified geographical capital market may be unsatisfactory for both positive and normative analysis, since markets for loans and possible other services of financial intermediaries appear to be geographically fragmented, at least for some classes of borrowers. I also suggest avenues for further research.

2. THE ECONOMICS OF TRADE IN FINANCIAL SERVICES

The economic effect of a liberalization in the cross-border activities of financial intermediaries depends both on the nature of the liberalization and on the economic basis for financial intermediation. A fundamental distinction is between banking services that can readily be offered at a distance and those that require a presence near the user of the service.[3]

For those services that can be offered at a distance, a framework similar to that used to analyze trade in goods can be used. Absent market power or externalities, the standard theorems of trade theory are applicable, and free trade is likely to be optimal.

Comparative advantage will depend either on relative factor endowments or on differences in production technologies.

As long as perfect competition holds in the market for international banking services, the case for government intervention will be rather weak, although an exception may be made because of safety and soundness issues. Authorities may wish to prevent some international banking transactions because of the risk of bank failure posed by such transactions. Banks in most wealthy countries have implicit or explicit deposit insurance, usually provided by the government. This insurance may, through the familiar moral hazard channel, induce bankers to take on more risk than is socially optimal, because the cost of deposit insurance is insensitive to additional risk.

Absent such an externality, however, the presumption must be that international banking transactions can only increase welfare and should therefore be permitted. This conclusion need not carry through if banks are imperfectly competitive. Then, depending on the exact circumstances, a host of policies may enhance national or even international welfare, although as has been shown by the literature on trade under imperfect competition, the case for government intervention is still far from straightforward.

One case where imperfect competition might be economically justified is if there are significant increasing returns to scale in banking. Then, banking services will be concentrated in large firms which deal with many customers, both domestic and foreign. The problem with this justification, however, is that such increasing returns to scale have been very difficult to identify in banking. For example, Benston, Hanweck, and Humphrey (1982) find in U.S. banking data for 1978 that no significant economies of scale are obtained for banks past the small threshold of $25 million in deposits.[4]

Although the foregoing has considered trade in financial services across international borders, it may be more important to focus on the cross-border expansion of banks. Many banking services are offered by banks (or bank branches) located in the same country, and often in the same region and town, as the banks' customers. Thus borrowers obtain loans through their local loan officer and savers deposit their money at their local teller window (or ATM). Most international capital transactions take place between two banks rather than between banks and non-bank customers.

Recent economics and finance literature suggests that the way in which these banking services are offered is of great importance to a national economy. Relationships between banks and borrowers are part of the productive capital of an economy, because they are the result of a long-term process of information acquisition. For example, Bernanke (1983) finds that disruptions in bank credit worsened the Great Depression in the United States. Fazzari et al. (1988) provide evidence that small firms are more prone to the informational constraints that lead to a role for financial intermediaries. These firms tend to use bank financing more than larger firms, and they also tend to retain more of their earnings.

Whited (1990) finds that the borrowings of U.S. firms whose debt is rated by a bond rating agency appear to be less constrained than those firms without bond ratings. This suggests that firms about which information is widely and cheaply available (those followed by bond-rating agencies) face lower financing costs than those on which information is not easily obtained. This second type of firm is likely to have to borrow through a financial intermediary; the wedge in costs suggests both that financial intermediation plays an important economic role and that it is imperfect.

Hoshi, Kashyap and Scharfstein (1991) find that investment in Japan is more sensitive to liquidity for firms that are not members of industrial groups than for those firms that are members of these groups and that therefore have close ties to large banks. They argue that this evidence is consistent with the hypothesis that monitoring by banks overcomes asymmetric information problems that would otherwise require companies to finance investment internally.

This literature suggests that transactions between banks and customers may be the result of costly and irreversible investment in information acquisition by the parties involved in the transaction. If these transactions also are significantly less costly when done at short range, then not only will markets be segmented, but it may be difficult for new bank entrants to gain access to these markets. Evidence that such barriers are high can be seen by the fact that multinational banks wishing to enter into a new market frequently buy existing banks in that market rather than set up their own branches from scratch. Since the availability of credit and the return on savings are crucial economic variables, the nature of the geographically segmented financial markets may have a significant impact on economic welfare in different regions or countries.

Trade in financial services in this context is a different issue than in the world of cross-border transactions described above. It is likely that the market for financial services, at least for those purchased by smaller agents without good access to liquid securities markets, will be segmented into geographically separated markets. These individual markets are likely to be characterized by imperfect competition between a small number of firms. In fact, existing theoretical studies of financial intermediation as a response to informational costs (especially Diamond, 1984 and Williamson, 1986) predict unlimited increasing returns to scale for financial intermediation, due to gains from diversification. Given the fact that most geographical markets have more than one bank, it seems clear that some cost must increase with bank size. The optimal scale of a bank is uncertain, but if it is large relative to a particular geographical market, this fact, along with the barriers to entry posed by long-term relationships, means that geographical markets will be characterized by small numbers of imperfectly competing banks.

A foreign bank can enter such a domestic market in one of two ways: first, it can lend to or borrow from local intermediaries; second, it can open a branch or subsidiary in the local market, which can then build relationships and enter into the set of transactions best done locally. The first of these options is open to a bank as long as there are no legal restrictions on international capital transactions; analytically, this case is similar to the case of dealing with cross-border transactions between banks and non-banks. By adopting principles of regulatory harmonization and mutual recognition, the EC Second Banking Directive facilitates the second option; see Key (1989) for a discussion. A bank may expand into a foreign country either by opening new operations or by purchasing an existing intermediary. The implications of this expansion are discussed in Section 4.

3. EVIDENCE FROM ITALY

The gains and losses to opening a country's financial markets to outside financial intermediaries depends on the degree to which the market is localized, as discussed in the previous section, versus the degree to which the location of the intermediary providing the service is irrelevant. In this section, I provide evidence from Italian banking data that the market for bank lending is localized. The concept of local will be taken to be the region of the country; our data for Italy distinguishes twenty such regions. This section provides evidence that one of two types of localization exists: either some local borrowers prefer to borrow from local intermediaries, who in turn exercise a significant degree of market power over those borrowers, or else the flow of funds between regions is imperfect, perhaps due to agency costs in interbank transactions, as discussed in Montgomery (1990).[5]

Previous work in this field is scarce, but includes the study by Neumark and Sharpe (1989), who use data from U.S. metropolitan areas. They concentrate on the deposit side of the market and find that deposit interest rates are more sensitive to money market interest rates in banking markets that are less concentrated. This is evidence in favor of the view that financial services are to a significant extent localized markets and that the competitive structure of banks in local markets affects the effective interest rates faced by individuals in these markets.

Both the U.S. market examined by Neumark and Sharpe and the Italian market examined in this section are markets in which legal restrictions exist (or did exist during the period from which the data are taken) on the ability of banks to expand geographically. As discussed in Montgomery (1990), multi-regional banks, by increasing interregional capital movements, may reduce some of the inefficiencies associated with the localization of banking. However, it is not evident that inefficiencies connected with interregional capital flows should disappear nor is it evident that local market power should be eliminated. It would therefore be useful to run tests similar to Neumark and Sharpe or to the one conducted in this section on data from countries where banking is dominated by nationwide banks with branches in many localities.

3.1 A Theoretical Framework

This sub-section discusses a simple theoretical framework with which to analyze local market power of banks and the degree of capital flows between regions. The case where banks have local market power will be treated as if a region has only a single monopolist bank. On the other hand, the case in which there exists perfect competition will require only that banks act as price-takers; I do not impose a zero-profit condition on banks, because there may exist fixed entry costs that render ex post profits positive. The price-taking condition allows for such fixed entry costs as long as profits are zero for entrants.

The following two simple assumptions will be maintained throughout this analysis: First, the demand for bank loans in a particular region is a decreasing and linear function of the interest rate charged on loans. Second, the supply of deposits from a particular region is an increasing and linear function of the interest rate paid. The assumption on the direction of these relationships is innocuous, but the linear nature of these relationships is a simplification. These relationships can be written in inverse form:

$$R_L = a - bL, \tag{1}$$

and

$$R_D = c + dD. \tag{2}$$

Equation 1 is the inverse demand curve for bank loans in a region, where a and b are positive parameters, R_L is the interest rate charged on bank loans, and L is the real volume of loans made. Equation 2 is the inverse supply curve for bank deposits in a region, where c and d are positive parameters, R_D is the interest rate paid on deposits, and D is the volume of deposits. In the analysis to follow, a and c will be assumed to vary across regions, while b and d will be assumed fixed, which simplifies the analysis.

A regional bank may also borrow from other banks. On a regional basis, borrowing by banks from other banks in the same region will net out, meaning that net interbank borrowing must be from outside the region. Denote funds borrowed this way by B, which can also be negative if a bank takes in more local deposits than it makes local loans. The bank's budget constraint requires that B = L - D; bank equity capital is lumped in with borrowed funds.

If funds are perfectly mobile between banks in different regions, the bank should be able to borrow as much as it wishes at a fixed interest rate. There are two exceptions to this, but neither exception will affect the analysis of this section. The first exception is if the region were a large portion of total capital markets, in which case the cost of funds would increase with the amount borrowed. But in this case, under perfect capital mobility, the cost of funds would still be the same in all regions in a given time period, which is sufficient for the analysis carried out here.

The second exception is that the riskiness of the bank may vary with the quantity it borrows. It is important in this context to distinguish between the riskiness of an individual bank and the riskiness of the entire banking sector in a particular region. There is no reason to expect the riskiness of a bank to increase as it borrows more. Models such as Diamond (1984) and Williamson (1986) predict that as banks become larger, they become more diversified and their risk of failure decreases. Alternatively, it could be argued that less responsible or less risk-averse bankers both borrow more and make riskier lending decisions, possibly because they expend less effort on evaluating loan applicants. Some individual banks would be quite likely to have a reputation for being riskier or more irresponsible than others, but for this fact to affect the results of this paper, these characteristic would have to vary systematically across regions. It also requires that these banks can obtain more funds despite a reputation for not carefully evaluating potential borrowers. Bankruptcy risk is also unlikely to rise with the amount borrowed, since I am allowing B to consist of both debt and equity,[6] so that the debt-equity ratio and therefore bankruptcy risk should be unrelated to B.

Even if the riskiness of a particular bank might increase with the amount it borrows, lenders to the region where that bank is located need not lend through that particular bank, unless the bank had some particular advantage in the region that could not be duplicated by other banks. If that were the case, then capital would in fact be imperfectly mobile between regions, for reasons of financial structure similar to those discussed in Montgomery (1990).

If funds are imperfectly mobile across regions, then the bank faces an upwardly sloping supply curve for funds. The reasons for such a slope may be agency costs (as discussed in Montgomery (1990)), transactions costs, or non-diversifiable, region-specific risk. Of these, transactions costs seem the least plausible; it seems unlikely that transactions costs could be high enough to account for a significantly upwardly sloping supply schedule. Non-diversifiable risk could account for such an upward slope, especially if Italian capital markets were effectively cut off from foreign capital markets during the period of this study (1981-1984), which would have reduced diversification opportunities. The inverse supply curve for funds borrowed is

$$R_B = e + fB \tag{3}$$

where e and f are positive parameters, B is the quantity of funds borrowed interregionally, and R_B is the interest rate at which the funds are borrowed.

In all cases discussed below, it is assumed that the representative regional bank is a price-taker on the interregional market. Although a bank may be large in its own local market, it is always assumed to be small in the interregional market.

In the derivations that follow, b, d, and f are assumed fixed, while a, c, and e vary. Since this paper focuses on cross-sectional variation, variation in e will not be of interest, since e will be the same for every region. In one of two sets of regressions run in this paper, I will use time dummies to control for the effect of e, which can vary over time; the other set of regressions uses the spread between the regional bank lending interest rate and the national treasury bill rate instead of the level of the bank lending interest rate as the left-hand side variable, as a more parsimonious way to control for e. Denote the variance of a as σ_a^2, the variance of c by σ_c^2, and the covariance of a and c as σ_{ac}. I will derive the $\mathrm{cov}(R_L, B)$ for the four separate cases: the different possible combinations of perfect local competition vs. local market power and of perfect interregional capital mobility vs. imperfect regional capital mobility.

It is assumed throughout that banks are on their respective supply and demand curves. This assumption precludes the type of credit rationing discussed by Stiglitz and Weiss (1981). In their model, the interest rate charged by banks might not vary with the amount lent, because of asymmetric information between borrowers and banks, when banks have a limited supply of funds available. Such a partial equilibrium model, with the supply of funds to the bank not modeled, is not directly reconcilable with the analysis of this paper, but is unlikely to change the main results.[7]

This analysis also excludes other possible heterogeneity in borrowers, for example the fact that different regions have borrowers of differing riskiness, who will therefore borrow at different nominal rates even if there is perfect interregional capital mobility and perfect competition among banks within a region. This heterogeneity presumably accounts for some of the variation of R_L across regions, but there is no reason to expect that this variation will be systematically related to B.

In the rudimentary model sketched above, the structure of financial intermediation along two dimensions. First, either competition within regions is perfect or banks wield market power within the region. Second, funds are either perfectly or imperfectly mobile between regions. In what follows, I will sketch out the implications of the four possible combinations of these hypotheses for the correlation of regional interest rates R_L and regional borrowings B from other areas.

Case 1: Perfect regional competition and perfect interregional capital mobility.
A regional bank acts as a price taker on all markets. R_B is fixed, and the same for all regions. Bank profits are given by

$$\pi = LR_L - DR_D - BR_B \tag{4}$$

and are maximized subject to the constraint

$$B + D = L. \tag{5}$$

Price-taking behavior implies $R_B = R_L = R_D,$[8] and loans L and deposits D are determined by the demand and supply schedules (1) and (2). B is given by L - D and will be affected by interregional variations in a and c. Since R_L is constant across regions (because R_B is fixed), R_L will not depend on a or c and will therefore be uncorrelated with all region-specific variables.

Case 2: Perfect regional competition, but imperfect interregional capital mobility. Regional banks solve the same constrained optimization problem (4) and (5), but in equilibrium B is determined by the inverse supply schedule (3). When these equations are solved for B and R_L, they yield

$$R_L = \frac{adf + bcf + bde}{bf + df + bd},$$

and

$$B = \frac{ad + cb - e(b+d)}{bf + df + bd}.$$

Case 3: Regional market power, but perfect interregional capital mobility.
I confine my attention to the case of a regional monopolist. In this case, the regional bank no longer takes R_L and R_D as given when maximizing profit (4), but instead considers the interaction of interest rates and quantities given by the demand and supply curves (1) and (2). In this case, the solution for R_L is

$$R_L = \frac{a}{2} + \frac{1}{2} R_B,$$

where R_B is constant across all regions, and the solution for B is

$$B = \frac{ad + bc - (b+d)R_B}{2bd}.$$

Case 4: Regional market power and imperfect interregional capital mobility.
In this case, the regional bank acts as a monopolist toward local depositors and borrowers, and although the bank is still a price taker on the interregional market, now the supply of interregional funds is upward sloping. The solution for R_L is
and the solution for B is

$$R_L = \frac{a(2bd+bf+2df)+cbf+2ebd}{2(2bd+bf+df)} \; ,$$

$$B = \frac{ad+bc-e(b+d)}{2bd+bf+df} \; .$$

These four cases give the expected correlations between interregional borrowings B and the interest rate of bank loans R_L. In the null hypothesis of perfect regional competition and perfect interregional capital mobility, there should be no correlation between these two variables. In the other three cases, which comprise different alternative hypotheses with varying combinations of imperfectly mobile capital between regions and banks with local market power, there should be a non-zero correlation between B and R_L. Furthermore, if innovations (c) in the supply of deposits are controlled for, it can be shown that this correlation should be positive.

The intuition for this positive correlation is straightforward. A change in a represents a shock to the demand curve for loans facing the bank. This has two effects. The first effect stems from the imperfect immobility of capital, which implies that the supply of funds to the bank is upward sloping (the supply of local funds is always upward sloping), so that the marginal cost of funds is increasing with the quantity borrowed. If, for example, a increases, meaning the demand for loans increases, then bank lending will tend to increase. But this increases the funds banks use and therefore the marginal cost of those funds, so that the bank's new optimum implies a higher marginal revenue than before. For the competitive bank, this marginal revenue is simply R_L, while for the monopolistic bank, the marginal revenue is $2R_L - a$; in either case, a higher marginal cost, brought on by greater borrowing (both locally and interregionally) requires a higher R_L.

The second effect arises if the bank exercises market power. Then as the demand curve for loans shifts, the profit-maximizing bank will tend to take some of that shift in a quantity shift and some in a price change. The quantity change affects borrowing (from both sources if capital is imperfectly mobile and interregionally if capital is perfectly mobile), and the price shift refers to a change in R_L.

The empirical analysis in this section will use total interregional borrowings as a proxy for interregional bank borrowings. In a world where financial intermediaries are the most efficient means for channeling funds from savers to investors and where financial transactions are more costly with distance, most interregional transactions will take place between financial intermediaries (or between branches of the same intermediaries). The fact that some transactions do not take place through intermediaries should not bias the results of this analysis, which depends on there being no correlation between borrowings and regional interest rates under the null hypothesis. The reason for this is that there is no *a priori* reason to expect the volume of transactions that do not take place through an intermediary to behave systematically so as to cause total borrowings to be spuriously correlated with interest rates on bank loans, when there is no correlation between bank borrowings and interest rates. I consider the effects of this and other possible sources of measurement error in the appendix.

The analysis uses several different controls for deposit supply. Supply of deposits should be correlated with income of residents in a region. One control used is therefore per capita income of a region; income is scaled by population in order to approximate deposit supply relative to lending opportunities, which will generally also increase with population and other measures of size of the region. Income suffers from the drawback, however, that it may endogenously depend on local interest rates; another control used is spending of governments (at all levels) in the region, with investment spending excluded. This measure, also expressed in per capita terms, has a better claim on exogeneity than income does. Both of these measures, however, may also be imperfect controls because they may also cause shifts in the demand for banks loans (a) as well as shifts in the availability of funds to banks (c). In the appendix, I also carry out a thorough analysis of the consequences using different controls.

3.2 Data and Implementation

The data are in a panel of annual observations over 4 years (1981-1984) and 20 regions. All data used in this study come from Italian government sources. Annual interest rates on bank lending is the average of quarterly regional observations from a table "Distribuzione per Regione ed Area Geografica dei Tassi d'Interesse sui Prestiti in Lire" in the Banca d'Italia (1985).[9] These interest rates are on short-term loans to households and non-financial enterprises, including non-profit institutions. Data on regional net imports, regional GDP, and regional government spending come from Istituto Centrale di Statistica (1986); the data are in 1970 prices (billions of lira). Regional net imports are the net inflow of goods from all other areas, including other regions of Italy. Regional population figures, used to compute per capita income, come from the 1981 Census, as reported in Istituto Centrale di Statistica (1988). Consumer price indices are published by the Banca d'Italia in its 1985 annual report; the base year is 1980 = 100. Interest rates are converted to ex post real interest rates using consumer price inflation over the following year.[10]

The interest rate spread is calculated by subtracting the interest rate of Italian Treasury bills from the interest rate on regional bank loans. The Treasury bill rate is an average of monthly observations on three-month bills at primary market auctions. This data also comes from the Banca d'Italia.

In the theoretical discussion above, no distinction was made between stocks and flows. Banks in Italy are prohibited from making all but a small number of long-term loans (see Price Waterhouse (1988, p. 108)). All other lending must not exceed a term of 18 months; the data used in this paper is on the short-term loans. Thus most but not all of a bank's loans will be turned over each year, so that the data I am using comes close to being the interest rate on the entire stock of loans, but with new loans weighted somewhat more heavily.

The analysis will be done for both flow and stock measures of borrowings. For the flow measure, I will use regional net imports. This is related to net borrowings by the following identity:

$$NM = B + FI + T,$$

where NM are net imports, B new borrowings from other areas, FI net factor income received from other areas, and T unilateral transfers from other areas. The presence of factor income and transfers means that net imports measure new borrowings with error, a fact that may bias the coefficient of NM. Another problem with this measure is that factor income and transfers may affect the volume of deposits in a region. Both of these points are discussed in more detail in the appendix, but they suggest that the results using flows must be interpreted with some caution, since they may be tainted by measurement error.

The stock measure is less subject to measurement error, in that it is possible to take into account those factor payments that represent interest payments on previous borrowings. The stock of borrowings is the region's net debt to the outside world and is equal to the sum of previous flow borrowings plus the accumulated interest on these flows. This measure can be derived as follows. First, decompose factor income in period t into non-capital factor income Y_t^F less interest on the region's net debt position D_{t-1}:

$$FI_t = Y_t^F - rD_{t-1}.$$

Net debt evolves according to

$$D_t = D_{t-1} + \left(NM_t + rD_{t-1} - Y_t^F - T_t\right).$$

Backwards substitution yields

$$D_t = D_0 (1+r)^t + \sum_{i=1}^{t} \left((1+r)^{t-i} NM_i\right) - \sum_{i=1}^{t} \left((1+r)^{t-i} \left(Y_i^F + T_i\right)\right).$$

In this expression, net debt in period t is represented as the sum of the initial net debt in some period 0 (grossed up by subsequent interest payments on this debt) and subsequent borrowings (also grossed up by subsequent interest). The subsequent borrowings are separated into a weighted sum of net imports, which we observe, and a weighted sum of transfers and non-capital factor income, which will be subsumed into the error term. In this paper, $t = 0$ represents 1980 and $t = 1$ through $t = 4$ represents 1981 through 1984, the sample periods. Since a stock measure for D_0 does not exist, this component will be approximated by a region-specific fixed-effect that is constrained to grow by the real interest rate each year. This term will enter the regression the regression separately from the $(\Sigma \ (1+r)^{t-i} NM_i)$ term. The interest rate will be approximated as a real interest rate of either 0 or 5 % per year. This is an approximation in that only under the null hypothesis of perfect capital mobility should the interest rate be the same across regions. Since I have allowed for interest payments, the error term in the stock regressions will include only factor payments on non-capital factors, particularly labor, and unilateral transfers. Thus we have substantially reduced the measurement error inherent in the flow measure and can expect more accurate results with this stock measurement.

The data are scaled to prevent differences in size of region from having an effect. The income and government spending measures used to control for deposit supply are regional per-capita income (regional GDP divided by regional population) and regional per-capita government spending (regional government spending divided by regional population). Regional borrowings, both in the stock and in the flow cases, are scaled by dividing by regional GDP. Units for the data are as follows. Borrowings are expressed as a percentage of income. Interest rates and interest rate spreads are expressed as annual percentage rates. Per capita income and per capita government spending are both in terms of thousands of 1970 lira.

3.3 Empirical Results

The data decisively reject the null hypothesis. The regressions using the flow measure of borrowings are reported in Tables 1 and 2. All regressions employ ordinary least squares. Table 1 uses the lending interest rate as the left-hand side variable, while Table 2 uses the spread between the lending interest rate and the interest rate on Italian Treasury bills.

Table 1
Flow Version
Regressions on lending interest rate

	(1)	(2)	(3)	(4)	(5)
Borrowings	0.0174	0.0173	0.0175	0.0331	0.0335
	(0.0056)	(0.0056)	(0.0057)	(0.0040)	(0.0040)
Income	-0.7744	-0.7725	-0.7708	-	-
	(0.2108)	(0.2110)	(0.2117)		
Government Expenditure	-	-	-	-0.3553	
				(0.3025)	
Constant	7.6256	7.6235	7.6235	6.4041	6.4951
	(0.3519)	(0.3521)	(0.3532)	(0.1241)	(0.1461)
1982 Dummy	1.2787	1.2788	1.2916	1.2744	1.2764
	(0.1602)	(0.1603)	(0.1619)	(0.1730)	(0.1726)
1983 Dummy	3.6793	3.7042	3.6748	3.6940	
	(0.1602)	(0.1624)	(0.1609)	(0.1730)	(0.1726)
1984 Dummy	3.4228	3.4228	3.3729	3.3947	3.4018
	(0.1604)	(0.1605)	(0.1771)	(0.1730)	(0.1727)
Income Growth	-	-	0.0210	-	-
			(0.0068)		
R^2	0.917	0.918	0.918	0.902	0.904

(Standard errors in parentheses. Columns 1,3, 4 and 5 for full sample (80 observations); Column 2 omits Lazio, 1983.)

Table 2
Flow Version
Regressions on interest rate spread

	(1)	(2)	(3)
Borrowings	0.0248	0.0366	0.0369
	(0.0075)	(0.0050)	(0.0051)
Income	-0.5856	-	-
	(0.2804)		
Government Expenditure	-	-	-0.2881
			(0.3831)
Constant	5.0608	4.1329	4.2095
	(0.4516)	(0.0823)	(0.1312)
R^2	0.436	0.405	0.409

Interest rate spread is bank lending rate minus Italian treasury bill rate.
(Standard errors in parentheses.)

In both tables, Column 1 reports the basic regression of the interest rate variable on regional net borrowings and regional per capita income. Annual dummy variables are added in Table 1 to control for the fact that the overall level of interest rates may vary from year to year due to factors not specific to any particular region. The interest rate spread provides the same correction, so that dummies are not used in the regressions reported in Table 2. The spread regression therefore has more degrees of freedom. Standard errors of the coefficient estimated coefficients are in parenthesis. All coefficients are significantly different from 0 at the 1% significance level, except for the coefficient on income in Table 2, which is only marginally significant. In both cases, the coefficient on borrowings is significantly positive, which rejects the hypothesis outline in Case 1 above, that of perfect interregional capital mobility combined with perfectly competitive behavior within regional banking markets.

This regression was redone in Table 1 after omitting an apparent outlier, the 1983 observation for Lazio, for which net imports differed radically from other years. The results with this omission, reported in Column 2, are almost identical to those above. The results obtained above do not, therefore, appear to be the work of an outlier.

Productivity shocks may affect interest rates and borrowings. Since productivity shocks may affect different industries to different degrees, regional average interest rates may differ for reasons of aggregation across industries at the same time that borrowings differ across regions. Such productivity shocks are difficult to observe, at least without disaggregated, industry-level data. In the context of the appendix, this implies a non-zero $\sigma_{\in \eta}$. In the event this induced a positive $\sigma_{\in \eta}$, R3 would be violated and the coefficient on B might be positive even under the null hypothesis. One way to control for this problem is to observe that productivity shocks that increase borrowings are likely to be correlated with income growth. I have therefore added income growth to the regressions on the lending interest rate reported in Table 1, in an attempt to control for the effects of productivity shocks. The growth rate used is $ln(Y_t/Y_{t-1})$, where Y_t is current year's income. This regression is reported in Column 3 above. The coefficient on income growth is significant, but it does not affect the coefficient on borrowings much. The results in this paper therefore do not appear to be a spurious consequence of productivity shocks, although if better measures of productivity shocks became available, it would be important to retest this conclusion.

Results using government expenditure instead of total income as a control for deposit supply are reported in Column 5 of Table 1 and Column 3 of Table 2. In both of these regressions the coefficient on borrowings is positive and highly significant. Government spending, however, is significant in neither regression.

Finally, regressions without controls (Column 4 of Table 1 and Column 2 of Table 2) have a highly significant and positive coefficient on borrowings. All of the results reported in Tables 1 and 2 reject the null hypothesis of perfect regional competition and perfect interregional capital mobility.

Table 3
Stock Version
Regressions on lending interest rate; Assumed real return: 0%

	(1)	(2)	(3)
Debt Stock	0.0089	0.0092	0.0119
	(0.0024)	(0.0023)	(0.0024)
Income	1.6226	-	-
	(2.4723)		
Government Expenditure	-	-	-26.8471
			(9.0742)
Constant	2.9019	5.9078	11.7832
	(4.5849)	(0.2098)	(1.9956)
1982 Dummy	1.2620	1.2436	1.4055
	(0.1169)	(0.1129)	(0.1191)
1983 Dummy	3.6205	3.5915	3.9233
	(0.1237)	(0.1149)	(0.1555)
1984 Dummy	3.2345	3.2638	3.7811
	(0.1274)	(0.1187)	(0.2072)
R^2	0.970	0.969	0.974

(Standard errors in parentheses. These regressions also include 19 regional dummies, corrected for accumulated interest payments. The coefficients on these variables are not reported.)

The results using the stock measure of borrowings are reported in Table 3, 4, 5, and 6. To conserve space, the coefficients on the regional dummies (corrected for accumulated interest payments) are not reported. In almost all of the stock regressions, the coefficient on borrowings is positive and significant at the 1% level. The exceptions to this are the two regressions that use income as a control and assume a 5% real rate of return, reported in Column 1 of Tables 4 and 6; although the estimated coefficient is positive in both cases, it is insignificant in Table 6 (with the spread as the left-hand side variable) and only significant at the 5% level in Table 4 (with the lending interest rate as the left-hand side variable). In all but one case, therefore, we can reject the case of perfect interregional capital mobility and perfect regional competition using the stock version as well.

The empirical results presented here show that external regional borrowings are significantly and positively correlated with the loan rate in a region, which demonstrates either that banks must have market power within regions or that interregional capital mobility is imperfect. This therefore shows that at least for the country and time period studied, the structure of the banking industry plays an important role in the allocation of funds within a region and across regions, and by extension across countries.

The foregoing analysis has assumed that interest rates are set by the interaction of profit-maximizing banks with markets. Banking markets are rarely that perfect, in that they are subject to widespread government restrictions and regulation. Italy is no exception to this, and financial markets there are affected by a number of government programs designed, for example, to channel funds to poorer areas. However, I have been unable to find any information which would lead to the belief that the results found in this paper are a spurious correlation due to some government program. In particular, there do not appear to be any restrictions that require a borrower to borrow from a local bank rather than a bank in a different locality.[11]

Italy does have a rather fragmented banking system. During the sample period, banks in large Italian cities were prohibited from opening branches in smaller localities. This paper therefore cannot directly answer the question of whether extensive branch banking, including multinational banking, is a more efficient way to organize capital markets. What I have shown is that in examining this issue, it is necessary to take into account the fact that banking tends to be localized, at least for some borrowers, and that local banking markets tend to be characterized by a significant degree of imperfect competition. Any theory of multi-regional banking must explain how the moving of market transactions into a corporate structure can affect the economic forces identified in this section.

Table 4
Stock Version
Regressions on lending interest rate; Assumed real return: 5%

	(1)	(2)	(3)
Debt Stock	0.0066 (0.0032)	0.0078 (0.0024)	0.0072 (0.0023)
Income	1.0438 (1.7628)	-	-
Government Expenditure	-	-	12.7298 (5.3501)
Constant	3.9809 (3.2897)	5.9250 (0.2041)	3.1206 (1.1949)
1982 Dummy	1.2175 (0.1155)	1.2196 (0.1147)	1.1655 (0.1126)
1983 Dummy	3.5270 (0.1188)	3.5381 (0.1166)	3.4284 (0.1212)
1984 Dummy	3.1139 (0.1625)	3.1781 (0.1203)	3.0065 (0.1362)
R^2	0.969	0.968	0.971

(Standard errors in parentheses. These regressions also include 19 regional dummies, corrected for accumulated interest payments. The coefficients on these variables are not reported.)

Table 5
Stock Version
Regressions on interest rate spread; Assumed real return: 0%

	(1)	(2)	(3)
Debt Stock	0.0148 (0.0034)	0.0160 (0.0033)	0.0113 (0.0036)
Income	4.5293 (2.8473)	-	-
Government Expenditure	-	-	19.9022 (7.2987)
Constant	-4.7832 (5.2830)	3.6084 (0.2886)	-1.0152 (1.7176)
R^2	0.734	0.722	0.754

Interest rate spread is bank lending rate minus Italian treasury bill rate.
(Standard errors in parentheses. These regressions also include 19 regional dummies, corrected for accumulated interest payments. The coefficients on these variables are not reported.)

Table 6
Stock Version
Regressions on interest rate spread; Assumed real return: 5%

	(1)	(2)	(3)
Borrowings	0.0040 (0.0039)	0.0126 (0.0034)	0.0095 (0.0031)
Income	5.7486 (1.6039)	-	-
Government Expenditure	-	-	25.4136 (5.9593)
Constant	-7.4291 (3.0117)	3.3258 (0.2840)	-2.3809 (1.3613)
R^2	0.787	0.740	0.802

Interest rate spread is bank lending rate minus Italian treasury bill rate.
(Standard errors in parentheses.)

4. FINANCIAL SERVICES WITH GEOGRAPHICALLY SEGMENTED MARKETS

4.1 The Applicability of the Empirical Evidence to Other Markets

The preceding section presented strong evidence for the segmentation of banking markets at the regional level for Italy. I also referred to evidence on geographical segmentation of the banking market in the United States (Neumark and Sharpe, 1989). Both of these studies demonstrate that location is economically significant in these two countries. In the United States, banks were shown to have market power in local markets for deposits. In Italy, banks either have local market power in loan markets or funds are imperfectly mobile between regions. In all of these instances, the structure of local banking markets matters economically, because local markets are at least partially shielded from outside competition.

Both of these studies examined rather idiosyncratic banking markets, and the question remains as to whether the results can be generalized. In both Italy and the United States, there have existed substantial restrictions on the geographical expansion of financial intermediaries. In both of these markets, banks are both more numerous and less diversified geographically than in many other industrialized countries. Italy has also had many special credit programs targeted to less prosperous regions. (Some of the restrictions on banking in Italy are discussed in Price Waterhouse (1988, pp. 67-68)). Neither of these tests therefore supply a perfect laboratory for examining the outcome of natural economic forces on the structure of financial intermediation. It is theoretically possible that countries with more diversified financial intermediaries, both geographically and in product lines, have a much more efficient system of moving capital from saver to borrower; this proposition remains untested. Regional data for other countries is difficult to obtain. Even if such data were available, it would in fact be difficult to test the effect of regionally diversified intermediaries on capital market efficiency. The equality across regions of interest rates charged by multi-regional banks, if such an equality were indeed found, cannot prove that those interest rates are efficient.

These two studies do demonstrate, however, that the structure of local financial markets matters for the efficient allocation of capital. It suggests that locally-based financial intermediaries, or locally-based branches or agents of larger intermediaries, serve important economic functions. One such function is the ability to monitor and evaluate borrowers more efficiently, especially small and medium-sized commercial borrowers, where information is not easily standardized. These functions are discussed Montgomery (1990), which suggests that long-term relationships between borrowers and lenders help to segment capital markets. Clearly, local intermediaries affect prices faced by their customers and the quantities available to them. If locally-based intermediaries did not contribute to economic efficiency, depositors and borrowers would deal with intermediaries outside their locales when local prices got out of line with prices in other locales.

I have concentrated on informational advantages possessed by local intermediaries in evaluating and monitoring local customers. This function provides a technological basis for examining the structure of markets for the services of financial services that is the same technological advantage used by Diamond (1984) and Williamson (1986) to demonstrate when financial intermediation is more efficient than direct dealings between saver and final borrower. I have not mentioned other advantages possessed by locally-based intermediaries that may account for some of the geographical segmentation found empirically. One of these is high search costs on the part of customers, which prevent their searching for better interest rates outside their locales when the number of intermediaries in that locale is restricted either by law or by economic forces. One problem with this story is that ways to ameliorate search costs, such as advertising, must be precluded.

4.2 The Advantages of Multi-Regional and Multi-National Banks

If financial markets are geographically segmented for technological (as opposed to regulatory) reasons, then multi-regional intermediaries can ease the movement of capital from one region to another, thus increasing capital market efficiency, but their effect on the competitiveness of regional capital markets is uncertain. Here I use "region" to denote the relevant geographically segmented market, which may vary greatly in size, depending on the type of transaction. Multi-national banks are clearly a variety of multi-regional bank.

Montgomery (1990) suggests that multi-regionals can move capital more efficiently between regions than can separate locally-based intermediaries. In that paper, capital that moves between regions does so at least partially through financial intermediaries, which are the most efficient way at least for smaller borrowers and lenders to deal with the world capital market. By taking what would have been an arms-length transaction into a corporate setting, contracting problems can at least partially be overcome. While separate intermediaries may find it necessary to deal via debt contracts (perhaps because of legal restrictions), a multi-regional offers implicit contracts to its employees that permit a richer structure of rewards, which in turn better induce local agents of these intermediaries to expend effort on monitoring and evaluating local borrowers. Thus multi-regional banks can, at least in theory, help increase the flow of capital from region to region and therefore reduce differences in cost of capital between regions.

The entry of a multi-regional might also enhance efficiency of intermediation within a regional market. For example, the new entrant may possess proprietary technology or techniques that enable it to perform banking functions more efficiently. It may also be better positioned to help residents of a region perform transactions with other regions, especially in the context of inter-regional trade. To the extent that customers with whom the multi-regional deals in other regions also have operations in the newly entered region, the multi-regional will have credit information on this customer that need no longer be duplicated by it and a regional intermediary.

However, the effect of the multi-regional on competition in a regional market is uncertain. As a larger corporation, the multi-regional is likely to be better able to withstand increased competition than regional banks. If these banks are forced to exit the market, the relationship capital built up by these exiting banks may be lost. Also, if the same set of multi-regionals operate in many different markets, opportunities for implicit price coordination may increase; if one bank deviates in a particular market, its rivals can punish it in other markets, which in turn can preserve an oligopolistic equilibrium.

Thus, while multi-regional intermediaries are likely to increase the mobility of capital between regions, they are not likely to eliminate the imperfect competition that appears to characterize regional financial markets.

4.3 The Effect of Changing Technology

It is a commonplace that computer and telecommunication are quickly causing vast changes in banking and other financial industries. Whether technological advantages will fully erode the market segmentation examined in this paper is unclear.

Such technology is certainly reducing the need for a local presence for a number of administrative tasks. It is less clear that electronic technology can remove the need for repeated human interaction for the core information-related tasks of evaluating and monitoring borrowers. This is most likely for easily standardized loans, such as consumer lending, or lending with stable and predictable collateral, such as home-mortgage lending. In fact, such loans are increasingly being disintermediated in the United States and to a lesser extent in Europe, although intermediaries typically still perform origination services. The meaning of mortgage securitization in the United States is clouded by an array of government guarantees that make it unclear whether the disintermediation would occur for purely economic reasons.

However, I have argued that developing information on small and medium-sized enterprises is one of the core roles played by financial intermediaries. This does not seem easily standardized and, although technology can certainly reduce the costs of such information processing, it is unlikely to replace human interaction and therefore the role of locally-based agents acting as financial intermediaries.

By providing easier means of financial control, technology may well improve the efficiency of the operation of multi-regional banks. It holds the promise of providing more up-to-date information on branch operations and therefore tightening control over branch operations. This increase in the flow of information may then help alleviate some of the agency problems that could exist within such a firm and thus increase the flow of funds within the organization from region to region.

4.4 A Framework for the Analysis of Financial Services

The evidence examined in this paper suggests that an empirically consistent framework for examining trade in financial services will have to take into account the need for the presence of factors of production, especially skilled labor, in the same country as the customers purchasing the financial services, at least for some of those services. The need for this presence is likely to cause geographical market segmentation. A firm from a foreign country wishing to "export" financial services will actually have to set up operations in the home country. If the segmented markets are imperfectly competitive, then the welfare effects of this entry are uncertain, especially if there are fixed costs to setting up in a local market and if existing firms choose to exit.

When analyzing financial services, it is necessary to distinguish two kinds of markets. The first is a cross-border market, in which, absent regulatory restraint, a firm can compete regardless of its physical location. The second is a localized market, in which a firm must locate factors of production, and in which services are not truly tradeable, although they can be sold by a multi-national firm. These are extremes, and the markets for most banking services fall somewhere in between. In some cases, a local presence may be needed, but that local presence may involve a fairly trivial expenditure, such as to satisfy legal requirements.

In both types of markets, the size of the fixed costs needed to enter may determine the degree of competition in the market. At the extreme, when fixed costs go to zero, the markets will, absent regulatory restraints, become contestable, and even in the presence of increasing returns to scale, pricing of services in those markets will be at the levels afforded by perfect competition. I have argued, however, that some important banking markets are characterized by high fixed entry costs, especially the costs of developing customer relationships.

Given these costs, a bank in one country wishing to enter the local market has three choices: (1) establish a presence in the market, but only as a way to compete more effectively in the market for cross-market services, such as transaction services provided to large multi-national services; (2) slowly build up the customer relationships needed to service smaller customers, where the value-added of financial intermediation is potentially high; (3) purchase an existing intermediary. In considering the effect of these actions, authorities should consider the effect of the new entrant on competition in the local market.

Given the nature of imperfect competition, sweeping conclusions about the costs and benefits of such competition should not be made. If the foreign bank enters by creating its own operations from scratch, then the concentration of the local market will over time be reduced, which should have beneficial welfare consequences, although this may eventually cause existing banks to exit the market. If such exit occurs because the foreign bank has a lower cost of funds, and thus was more able to withstand a period of intense competition, welfare in the local market may be impaired once other banks have exited, because the surviving banks will not need to pass on their lower cost of funds to their customers.

An entering bank may have lower cost of funds because it faces a different regulatory environment. The move to regulatory harmonization in the EC is likely to reduce such regulation-induced cost differentials within the EC, and in this sense has positive welfare consequences. However, the geographical fragmentation of capital markets documented in this paper may have deeper roots than government regulation, so that even with regulatory harmonization, banks may not be on an even footing in a particular local market, if their home country differs or if the extent of their other operations differs.

The case for a foreign bank buying a domestic bank is substantially weaker than for a foreign bank that creates its own operations from scratch. If both the acquiring foreign bank and the acquired domestic bank compete in the market for cross-border services, competition in that market is likely to be reduced. And the merger will not increase competition in the local market, because the number of banks has not increased.

This sub-section has discussed a framework for analyzing trade in financial services, especially banking. To the extent that other services require a local presence, as many certainly do, such a framework may be useful for them too. To formalize the notions discussed here, it will be necessary to combine theories of trade under imperfect competition with theories of the multinational firm. Applications to financial intermediation should also take into account the key role intermediaries appear to play in overcoming problems of asymmetric information.

4.5 Safety and Soundness

One of the major reasons for regulation of banks is the fear of the economic effects of bank runs, especially if those runs became contagious. Although explicit deposit insurance is not universal in industrialized countries, the lender-of-last-resort function exists at least in principle in all countries, in order to provide liquidity to banks under the threat of a bank run. When such assistance is also extended to insolvent banks, a widely recognized moral hazard problem exists, in that banks may have an incentive to take on excessive risks. Bankers can be dissuaded from taking these risks if the value of the bank charter is high enough (in the case a deposit insurance system) or if lender-of-last-resort assistance is given only at a high enough penalty rate. If the value of the bank charter is insufficient to prevent the bank's management from taking more than the optimal amount of risk, then supervision of the bank by authorities will be necessary. The case for supervision under a system without deposit insurance is less clear, but it may be argued that the supervisory process gives the regulator better knowledge of the bank assets that it may have to discount in an emergency, helping it distinguish insolvent banks from the merely illiquid.

A multi-regional bank may reduce both the risks of bank failures and the cost of such supervision by authorities. The multi-regional's presence in more than one market diversifies its income, so that a region-specific shock will be less likely to cause the bank to fail, since its revenue is diversified across different regions. Since the multi-regional bank (instead of the deposit insurer) now bears the cost of underperformance of a regional office, the multi-regional will have an incentive to replace with internal controls some of the tasks banks supervisors perform with more fragmented banks. The multi-regional will be induced to monitor its own locally-based employees, replacing some of the monitoring by government bank supervisors. The geographical integration of banks within a country is therefore a way of privatizing part of the government's task of bank supervision. When banks expand across international borders, however, the task of bank supervision becomes more difficult and must be coordinated between different countries.

5. CONCLUSION

This paper has argued that in analyzing the effects of EC integration on banking markets it is necessary to take into account the fact that banks and similar financial institutions play an important role in overcoming informational problems, especially in lending to borrowers other than governments and large corporate borrowers. It is also important to recognize that this function takes place at least partially in geographically segmented markets. Evidence was presented on geographical segmentation in Italy, which may accompany imperfectly competitive behavior within regional markets. This provides evidence for the environment assumed in Montgomery (1990) to motivate real barriers to capital mobility.

There is no clear evidence that this geographical segmentation of banking markets is an artifact of outmoded regulation and outmoded technology. It is probable that this segmentation is instead the result of a combination of the cost advantages that location apparently confers on financial intermediaries and market power derived from long-term customer relationships. There is no reason to believe that the consolidation of the local functions of banking into multi-regional and multi-national banks would eliminate this market power.

The primary policy message of this paper is that the gains from trade in financial services may not be well approximated by standard models of perfectly competitive trade in goods. Financial intermediaries operate in segmented, imperfectly competitive markets. While thus far we lack good models to address welfare questions in this framework, it is clear that governments should not presume that eliminating restrictions to cross-border expansion of financial intermediaries will lead to unambiguous welfare gains. Instead, authorities must pay close attention to competitive conditions in domestic markets for financial services. They should not assume that the elimination of barriers to capital movement and of restrictions on establishment of banks will lead to fully efficient capital markets.

In arguing that existing modes of analyzing financial intermediation may be inadequate, this paper may have raised more questions than it has answered. More research, empirical as well as theoretical, is clearly warranted on the structure of financial markets. One important area for research is on the role intermediaries play in moving capital from locale to locale. Another important goal for future research is to develop models of imperfect competition among financial intermediaries that incorporate an information-processing role for intermediaries.

APPENDIX: MEASUREMENT ERROR AND IMPERFECT DEPOSIT CONTROLS

The analysis of this paper consists of ordinary least squares estimation of the relationship

$$R_{it} = b_B B_{it} + b_G G_{it} + e_{it},$$

where R_{it} is either the lending interest rate or the interest rate spread, B_{it} is regional net imports, and G_{it} is either per capita regional income or per capita regional government spending.[12] This is not, however, a structural model, nor even a true reduced form in which the right-hand side variables are exogenous. Thus we must take some care in interpreting these regressions.

Suppose, without loss of generality, that we have the following three structural equations:

$$R = \alpha_1 a + \alpha_2 c + \epsilon$$
$$B = \beta_1 a + \beta_2 c + \eta$$
$$G = \gamma_1 a + \gamma_2 c + \psi$$

The subscripts have been suppressed on R, B, and G. The shocks a and c are as defined above in Section 3. The coefficients $\alpha_1, \alpha_2, \beta_1$, and β_2 take on various signs depending on which of the four theoretical cases is true. The values of γ_1 and γ_2 determine how good a control G is. Finally, ϵ, η, and ψ are additional sources of noise that is orthogonal to a and c.

Under these circumstances and suitable regularity conditions, it is straightforward to derive the probability limit of the b^*_B, the estimate of b_B:

$$plim\ b^*_B = \frac{1}{\Delta}\left[\left(\alpha_2\beta_2\gamma_1^2 + \alpha_1\beta_1\gamma_2^2 - \alpha_1\beta_2\gamma_1\gamma_2 - \alpha_2\beta_1\gamma_1\gamma_2\right)\left(\sigma_a^2\sigma_b^2 - \sigma_{ac}^2\right) + \Theta\right],$$

where σ_x^2 denotes the variance of any variable x and σ_{xy} the covariance of any two variables x and y. $\boldsymbol{\Theta}$ stands for a complicated expression that subsumes all the terms containing variances and covariances of the error terms ϵ, η, and ψ. Δ is given by

$$\Delta = (var\ B)(var\ G) - cov^2(B, G)$$

and can be shown to be positive. The sign of plim b^*_B therefore is the same as the sign of

$$\lambda = \left(\alpha_2\beta_2\gamma_1^2 + \alpha_1\beta_1\gamma_2^2 - \alpha_1\beta_2\gamma_1\gamma_2 - \alpha_2\beta_1\gamma_1\gamma_2\right)\left(\sigma_a^2\sigma_b^2 - \sigma_{ac}^2\right) + \Theta.$$

The null hypothesis in Case 1 above, that of perfect regional competition and perfect interregional capital mobility, implies that R is unrelated to the regional shocks *a* and *c*, so that the following restriction holds:

R1: $\alpha_1 = \alpha_2 = 0$.

In this case, λ reduces to

$$\lambda = \sigma_{e\eta}(var\ G) - \sigma_{e\psi}(cov\ (B,G)).$$

Under the null hypothesis, therefore, *plim b*$^*_B$ = 0, except for the influence of the measurement error terms. The assumption that one of these two terms, $\sigma_{e\psi}$, is zero is reasonable if G does not depend directly on the interest rate, which is more likely to hold when G is government spending than when G is income.[13] The restriction

R2: $\sigma_{e\psi} = 0$.

combined with R1 yields

$$\lambda = \sigma_{e\eta}(var\ G),$$

which has the same sign as $\sigma_{e\psi}$
  A simple argument demonstrates that if $\sigma_{e\psi}$ is not zero, it is likely to be negative, and that therefore, under R1 and R2,

$$plim\, b^*_B \leq 0.$$

This argument runs as follows. The measure used in this paper for B, regional net borrowings, is regional net imports, which are related to true regional net borrowings (i.e. the current account deficit) by the following identity:

$$B = B_T + FI + T,$$

where B_T is true regional borrowings and FI and T represent two error terms, net factor income and unilateral transfers. Now consider a shock e > 0 that drives up regional interest rates. Agents from other regions who lend money to the region receive a positive shock to the factor income they receive. Therefore net factor income FI received by the region drops. Since $\underline{\eta}$ is closely related to *FI + T*, this means that $\underline{\eta}$ and $\underline{e}$ are likely to be negatively correlated.
  This motivates the following restriction:

R3: $\sigma_{e\eta} \leq 0$.

Under the null hypothesis, that of perfect regional competition and perfect interregional capital mobility (given by R1) and the error term restrictions R2 and R3, we have

$$plim\, b^*_B \leq 0.$$

Under the alternative hypotheses embodied by Cases 2, 3, and 4 in Section 3, *plim* $b^{\bullet}_B$ conversely is likely to be positive. Consider, for example, the strong restriction

R4: $\gamma_1 = 0$.

This means that except for the error terms, G is a perfect control for c, the shock to deposit supply, since it does not depend on a, the shock to loan demand. Under R4 alone, λ reduces to

$$\lambda = \alpha_1 \beta_1 \gamma_2^2 \left(\sigma_a^2 \sigma_b^2 - \sigma_{ac}^2 \right) + \Theta_{R4},$$

where Θ_{R4} contains a subset of the error moments in Θ. It is easy to see that in all of the alternative Cases 2, 3, and 4, both α_1 and β_1 are positive. This implies that, except possibly for the noise term Θ_{R4}, *plim* $b^{\bullet}_B$ is positive.

An alternative strategy for dealing with the sources of error outlined above is to ignore controls altogether and to simply run the regression

$$R_{it} = b B_{it} + e_{it}.$$

Under R1 (the null hypothesis),

$$plim\ b^* = \frac{\sigma_{e\eta}}{var\, B}.$$

Combining R1 with R3, therefore implies

$$plim\, b^* \leq 0.$$

With no controls, $b^{\bullet}$ should be non-positive if the null hypothesis is true. In fact, however, in the empirical results presented, $b^{\bullet}$ is always significantly positive.

FOOTNOTES

This paper represents the views of the author and should not be interpreted as reflecting those of the Board of Governors of the Federal Reserve System or other members of its staff. I thank Maurizio Trifilidis for helping to obtain the data, Leonardo Bartolini and Anna Lusardi for translations, Sean Craig and Sydney Key for helpful discussions, and William Branson, Glen Donaldson, Jonathan Eaton, David Howard, Andrew Rose and conference participants at the Univeristy of Gothenburg, especially the discussant and the editors, for useful comments.

1. Through most of this paper, I will use the term bank to refer to an institution that performs the lending services that banks perform; the term should be understood to include various similar institutions that perform similar functions.

2. If these capital flows occur through debt placements, then they will take the form of standard interbank flows. With contracts restricted to debt, Montgomery's theory becomes a formalization of the credit limits and tiering of risks that are common in the interbank market.

3. This distinction in the general context of trade in services is discussed in McCulloch (1987) and in some of the references therein.

4. This study did not, however, consider the possibility suggested by the theoretical banking literature that larger banks should have a lower cost of funds because they are more diversified.

5. This phenomenon was probably accentuated for the data considered in this paper, since during this period, Italy had no centralized interbank market, but rather a system of negotiated, bilateral deals.

6. This is contrary to the assumptions of Diamond (1984) and Williamson (1986).

7. An exception would be if the following situation occurred: lenders were tiered into different risk categories, the optimal interest rates charged to different categories varied, and the total expected return on loans decreased as the interest rate increased (which would be possible if the bank had some market power over its borrowers). In this case, the demand for loans could appear to be upward sloping, since the loans with the highest expected return, which the bank would lend to first, would also have the lowest stated interest rate. In this case, the parameter b in the inverse loan demand schedule (1) would be negative.

8. This abstracts away from other variable costs, an abstraction that will not effect the correlations derived in this sub-section.

9. Interest rate data for the first quarter of 1981 was not available, so that the 1981 interest rate observation is an average of the second through the fourth quarter.

10. The purpose of this is to provide a more consistent scaling of interest rates from year to year. Nominal interest rates would give identical significance levels for the flow regressions, which employ time dummies as well, but not for the stock regressions. The possibility that inflaiton rates vary across regions introduces a possible source of measurement error for interest rates, which is analyzed in the appendix.

11. The fact that net regional capital flows in Italy contain substantial government transfers may lead to a moral hazard problem. If such funds passed through regional banks and if the central government did not control the use of the funds, banks might have an incentive to make riskier lending decisions than if it had more risk-sensitive private funding. (During the period examined by this paper, there was no formal deposit insurance system in Italy.) Riskier loans would have a higher probability of default and therefore a higher stated interest rate. This could make $\sigma_{\epsilon\eta}$ positive and induce a positive correlation between interest rates and borrowings. However, these transfers should primarily go to poorer regions, leading to a (negative) correlation between per capita income and interest rates. I have included per capita income in some of the regressions as a way to control for this effect. With this control, the coefficient on borrowings remains significantly positive.

12. As described in Section 3, all variables are expressed in real terms.

13. In some countries, expenditures of local and regional governments are often financed by borrowing and therefore regional government spending might depand on regional interest rates. This has not been the case in Italy since the 1970s, however; the deficits of local and regional governments are instead usually financed by transfers from the central government.

REFERENCES

Banca d'Italia (1985), Supplemento al Bollettino, Aziende di Credito, 38:42, Sept. 25.

Benston, G.J., G.A. Hanweck, and D.V. Humphrey (1982), "Scale Economies in Banking: A Restructuring and Reassessment", Journal of Money, Credit, and Banking, November, 14, 435-456.

Bernanke, B. S. (1983), "Nonmonetary Effects of the Financial Crisis in the Propagation of the Great Depression", American Economic Review, June, 73, 257-276.

Boyd, J. H. and E.C. Prescott (1986), "Financial Intermediary-Coalitions," Journal of Economic Theory, April 38, 211-232.

Diamond, D. W. (1984), "Financial Intermediation and Delegated Monitoring", Review of Economic Studies, 51, 393-414.

Fazzari, S.M., R.G. Hubbard, and B.C. Petersen, Bruce C. (1988), "Financing Constraints and Corporate Investment", Brookings Papers on Economic Activity, no.1, 141-195.

Gertler, M. (1988), "Financial Structure and Aggregate Economic Activity: An Overview", Journal of Money, Credit, and Banking, August, 20, 559-596.

Hoshi, T., A. Kashyap, and D. Scharfstein (1991), "Corporate Structure, Liquidity, and Investment: Evidence from Japanese Industrial Groups", Quarterly Journal of Economics, February, 106, 33-60.

Istituto Centrale di Statistica (1986), Annuario di Contabilità Nazionale, 14:2.

Istituto Centrale di Statistica (1988), Annuario Statistico Italiano,.

Key, S. J. (1989), "Financial Integration in the European Community", Board of Governors of the Federal Reserve System, International Finance Discussion Paper 349, April.

McCulloch, R. (1987), "International Competition in Services", NBER Working Paper 2235, May 1987.

Montgomery, J.D. (1990), "Financial Intermediation, Contracts and International Capital Mobility", Chapter 2 in Essays on Financial Intermediation and International Capital Mobility, unpublished Princeton University doctoral dissertation.

Neumark, D. and S.A. Sharpe (1989), "Market Structure and the Nature of Price Rigidity: Evidence from the Market for Consumer Deposits", Board of Governors of the Federal Reserve System, Finance and Economics Discussion Series 52, January.

Price Waterhouse (1988), The "Cost of Non-Europe" in Financial Services, Volume 9 of Research on the "Cost of Non-Europe". Basic Findings, Luxembourg, Commission of the European Communities.

Stiglitz, J. and A. Weiss (1981), "Credit Rationing in Markets with Imperfect Information", American Economic Review, June, 71, 393-410.

Whited, T. M. (1990), "Debt, Liquidity Constraints, and Corporate Investment: Evidence from Panel Data", Board of Governors of the Federal Reserve System, Finance and Economics Discussion Series 114, March.

Williamson, S.D. (1986), "Costly Monitoring, Financial Intermediation, and Equilibrium Credit Rationing," Journal of Monetary Economics, July, 18, 159-179.

Financial Regulation and Monetary Arrangements after 1992
C. Wihlborg, M. Fratianni and T.D. Willett (Editors)

Comment

Daniel Gros

Centre for European Policy Studies, Rue Ducale 33, B-1000 Brussels, Belgium

This paper opens a very interesting avenue for research by looking at the dispersion of interest rates inside a currency area. This research will become more important as interest rates become more closely linked in the EC. But as a discussant I will focus on what I consider the weak points of the paper.

The basic message of this paper is that financial intermediation requires specialised inputs (mainly to perform the necessary monitoring of lenders) so that it is not a perfectly competitive market. The empirical part of the paper provides evidence that interest rates inside a country can vary systematically across regions. This broad message is indeed reasonable. Who would deny that in order to evaluate and monitor small/medium sized firms (not to speak of households) in a given region it is necessary to acquire a lot of local information. But it is not clear to me whether accepting this idea leads to the theoretical model proposed by the author. Moreover, the empirical results provide only rather weak support for the theory since they can be explained in a number of other ways. In my comments I will therefore concentrate on these two points.

The author assumes that there are regional demand and supply schedules for bank deposits and lending. In doing so he must refer to the retail market since it is likely that a large interregional company will obtain exactly the same terms (for both borrowing and deposits) irrespectively of the location of the bank. FIAT would surely shift all its borrowing from Turin to Milan if it paid only "epsilon" more in Turin. Households and small enterprises are not able to do that because they are not known outside their region, so the model can apply only to this sector of the market.

The interesting question is, however, whether all banks in the country can get additional funds at the same price. Why not? As the author argues, the most plausible reason is region specific (non-diversifiable) risk. How could such a risk arise? Only if the local intermediary faces a risk of not being repaid, but this is exactly the reason why the local intermediary offers borrowers an upward sloping supply curve of funds.[1] Inside an interregional bank for example, there is absolutely no reason why headquarters should charge a local branch a different rate just because it has more business. This might be appropriate, however, if local managers do not evaluate and monitor local borrowers properly, i.e. if there are bank internal agency costs. How this would arise in practice and, therefore, why interregional capital mobility should not be perfect is never sufficiently explained.

In Italy, as in most other industrialised countries, there is an active inter-bank market through which, at least apparently, all banks can obtain funds at the posted market interest rates. Strong theory and empirical results are required to argue differently. Is there any evidence that perhaps some smaller banks do not have access to it? The author does not present any such evidence.

The empirical results show that the lending rate charged by banks in different regions to enterprises and households is a function of regional income per capita and regional net imports.

The author can claim that this supports his theory because his theory excludes "possible heterogeneity in borrowers" (p. 179); and I would add, he excludes heterogeneity in depositors as well. However, I regard this assumptions unacceptable in the context of the empirical part of the paper. Banks charge clearly different rates to different households because the probability of repayment is obviously a function of the income and wealth of the household. For this part of overall lending it is therefore apparent that one would expect a negative relationship between income per capita and the interest rate, which is what the author finds.

The important part of his findings is the fact that net regional imports are correlated with the interest rate. This variable need not have much to do with interregional "net bank lending". In Italy regional trade deficits are financed not by lending, but by unilateral transfers from the government and from private sources. There is no reason to presume that a constant proportion of these regional deficits are caused by capital flows, much less by bank lending. But there are a number of reasons why one would expect regions with a large deficit to have on average borrowers and depositors that differ from those in surplus regions. For example, the aid programme for the "Mezzogiorno" includes a substantial proportional subsidy on capital costs, which implies that firms will be less concerned about the interest rate they pay. One would therefore expect that the higher the transfers from this programme, i.e. the higher net imports, the higher should be the average interest rate in the region.

One could avoid this crucial problem by using the interest rate on one or several somewhat standardized securities e.g.:

i)   a mortgage covered by a certain percentage

ii)   loans to enterprises of a certain size

If this is impossible, it might be possible to use some crude indicators of the composition of the loan portfolio, such as households versus enterprises, and importance of loans that are subsidised.

Another, radically different, approach would be to look at investment/savings correlations that would provide some direct evidence for this theory of capital market segmentation.

The basic conclusion of the paper is that small borrowers have to rely even after 1992 on their local/regional intermediaries for funds. The consequences of 1992 might therefore be minor, since interregional or international banks will face the same problem of acquiring local information. This conclusion is difficult to quarrel with, but one does not necessarily need a theory of capital market segmentation to get to it.

In summary, the paper opens up an interesting direction for research, but more theory and evidence are required before this approach can be used for policy advice.

FOOTNOTE

1. It is obvious at this point that excluding the Stiglitz and Weiss (1991) story is not innocuous, because with credit rationing there would be no such supply schedule.

REFERENCE

Stiglitz, J.E. and Weiss, A. (1981), "Credit Rationing in Markets with Imperfect Information", <u>American Economic Review</u>, June.

Financial Regulation and Monetary Arrangements after 1992
C. Wihlborg, M. Fratianni and T.D. Willett (Editors)

9 Currency Substitution and Monetary Policy

Alberto Giovannini

Graduate School of Business, Uris Hall, Columbia University, New York, N.Y. 10027, USA

1. INTRODUCTION

The elimination of physical, technical, and fiscal barriers to economic integration in Europe will conceivably increase the integration of Europe's goods and financial markets a great deal. This process might have profound effects on the constraints faced by monetary authorities, and - as a consequence - on the conduct of monetary policy in Europe.

In this paper I discuss the sources and consequences of increasing "substitutability" among the currencies of the countries that participate in the process of European integration. Most of the academic work on the effects of currency substitution has concentrated on flexible exchange rates. The most notable result of the theoretical literature is that, in the presence of currency substitution exchange-rate fluctuations are substantially magnified (see, for example, Calvo and Rodriguez (1977) and Girton and Roper (1981)). Indeed, with perfect substitutability of currencies exchange rates can be indeterminate.[1] Studies of currency substitution under fixed exchange rates are, however, lacking.[2]

This paper's objective is to offer a survey of the research questions concerning the problem of currency substitution in Europe, rather than a specific theoretical or empirical analysis of any one of them. The questions for monetary theory raised by the process of European integration are numerous, and in some cases very hard: it is therefore useful to discuss them together in the attempt to build a chart of a rich and important research area. Section 3 discusses the effects of increased currency substitutability. Section 4 contains a summary and concluding observations.

2. SOURCES OF CURRENCY SUBSTITUTION

In order to discuss the sources of currency substitutability it is necessary to address the question of the value of different currencies coexisting in an integrated economy. Currency values are the sum of intrinsic values and the value of the monetary services they provide. Of course, the major difference between the current monetary system in Europe and the bimetallic standard of, say, the Latin Monetary union is that the current system is a *fiat* currency system: the intrinsic values of different currencies are zero.

Hence, in order to identify the causes of fluctuations in currency demands, we need to study the determinants of their monetary services.

A given currency performs two types of monetary services: it allows to carry out transactions *at any given point in time* with other agents (in that sense it is a *medium of exchange*), and it allows to *postpone transactions, i.e.* to carry value to the future (in that sense it is a *store of value*). The value of currencies is a sum of their medium of exchange and store of value functions. In what follows I will not make reference to the third traditional determinant of the monetary value of currencies - their "unit of account" function. This omission is largely due to ignorance on the economic effects of the unit-of-account services, despite a suspicion that in Europe the complications arising from the coexistence of difference units of measurement might be very important.[3] Also, the following discussion will be general, without explicitly referring to the exchange-rate regime in which different currencies coexist. Of course, the store-of-value services of different currencies - and therefore currency substitution - are affected in a major way by the exchange-rate regime.

2.1 Currencies as Media of Exchange

In modern societies, many transactions are settled with "cash" - banknotes or checks payable on sight. The use of cash in transactions can be required by law, as for example in the payment of taxes and the settlement of many other transactions with the government. However, the use of cash can also be preferable for its convenience, since other ways of settling transactions would in general require costly verifications of a counterparty's creditworthiness, or of the value of the goods or assets used in the exchange. Furthermore, other financial assets may be less readily "acceptable" than cash, or may have, as Tobin (1958) first suggested, more uncertain value than cash.

Technological progress in financial intermediation and deregulation of financial markets have eroded many of the advantages of cash versus other forms of settlement of payments, like bank credits. Yet these developments have not by any means eliminated the ability of central banks to control interest rates through the management of monetary aggregates: there still exists a reasonably stable demand function for money.[4] One should expect, however, that the wave of financial deregulation that will accompany the process of European integration, and the incentives to technological innovations to financial intermediaries arising from increased competition, will produce further instabilities in the *total* demand for money in Europe, independently of the coexistence of different currencies.

In monetary theory, the microeconomic underpinnings of money demand have often been expressed by postulating a *transactions technology*,[5] through which the purchase of goods is facilitated by the use of money. Such a transactions technology may be expressed as a term in the private sector's budget constraint, stating that the purchase of goods requires real resources, in amounts that are inversely related to the quantity of money used in the transactions. An extreme form of this technology is the so-called "Clower constraint", according to which money has to be used for *all* purchases of goods - the cost of purchasing goods without money is infinite. An intermediate case studied in the literature is discussed, among others, by Lucas (1984): the assumption in this case is that only a fraction of goods purchased (the "cash goods") need to be paid for with money, the other goods ("credit goods") can be paid for using (inside) credit.

The foregoing description of the most common justifications for the use of cash in private transactions suggests that similar effects must also explain why, in a world where many currencies coexist, one versus another currency is adopted to settle payments. The discussion of the determinants of private currency portfolios can be organized around two questions:

- Will national currencies tend to be used in "local" markets, and why?

- Can dominant currencies emerge, and how?

Will National Currencies Tend to be Used in Local Markets?
The discussion above has shown that a major determinant of the use of cash are transactions costs, that is the costs of providing the medium of exchange, and the costs of verifying its value. In an area characterized by multiple currencies, transactions costs also include the costs of changing one currency for another, and the costs of managing a cash portfolio which includes several different currencies. For given expected returns on different currencies (a concept that is discussed below in more detail), agents will therefore find it desirable to minimize the costs of currency conversion, by minimizing the diversification of their currency portfolios. These efforts will be fulfilled only if an agent's desire to hold a specific currency is consistent with that of its trading partners.

For these reasons we should expect that transactions costs maintain some "local" role for national currencies. This proposition is best explained by considering the structure of exchanges in an area like Europe. While there will be an increased number of transactions across individual states, it will still be the case that, for any average individual resident in an European country, most transactions will be carried out with other residents of the same country. Employers and employees are usually geographically close, and most purchases of consumption goods and services are made locally (indeed many services are considered "nontraded goods").[6] Given this structure of transactions, and the existence of "local" markets, we should expect that, in equilibrium, common currencies are used in local markets. The adoption of a common medium of exchange, even with no intrinsic value, is proven, for example, by Kiyotaki and Wright (1989).

But which currencies are chosen for the local markets? The choice of the currencies might be determined, exogenously, by legal restrictions. Many transactions carried out within national boundaries involve national governments: taxes are paid in cash, using only national currency. Transactions with national governments account for a large percentage of countries' national product, as well as for a large fraction of their money stock.

Table 1 reports the average ratios (in percent) of (annual) government receipts relative to the end-of-year money stocks in France, Germany and Italy. While the comparison of the stock of money with the flow of transactions is made difficult by the absence of information on the velocity of circulation of "government" money (the number of transactions per unit of time that make up government receipts), the table clearly indicates that the effects of government transactions on money demand is likely to be significant. Table 2 shows the importance of another legal determinant of the demand for money: required reserves at commercial banks. Required reserves can be as high as two-thirds of the stock of high powered money.

Table 1:
Government Receipts as Percent of Money Stock
Receipts Annual, Money Stock End of Year

Years	France	Germany	Italy
1952-1959	64	86	52
1960-1969	63	83	45
1970-1979	112	164	36
1980-1987	158	176	69

Source: International Financial Statistics. Government Receipts line 81; Money Stock line 34.

Table 2
Average Reserve Ratios, Reserves and High-Powered Money

Country	High-Powered Money (% of GDP)	Reserves (% of GDP)	Reserves/ Deposits
Portugal	14.8	5.8	5.8
Greece	18.3	8.4	17.3
Spain	19.8	12.3	20.5
Italy	17.5	11.8	18.7
France	6.3	2.0	5.2
Germany	9.4	3.6	6.8
United Kindgom	3.7	0.2	0.4
Belgium	8.2	0.4	1.1

Source: Giavazzi and Giovannini (1989).

Hence we have the second proposition: a significant fraction of local transactions are carried out with national governments; governments require the use of national currencies in transactions; governments also require financial intermediaries to hold national currencies as reserves against fluctuations of deposit liabilities. Hence national currencies will tend to be used in the countries where they are issued.

Will Dominant Currencies Emerge?

In the previous subsection we have established that national currencies will tend to circulate in local markets, and will tend to be used in transactions with governments and in purchases of nontraded goods and services. There are, however, a number of factors that tend to limit these phenomena, and are also associated with the convenience of using widely-circulating media of exchange.

These factors are: the *size of national economies*, the *transactions costs of individual currencies*, and the *economies of scale* in transactions services.

The size of national economies matters because the larger countries tend to have (in absolute terms) a larger volume of international transactions. In order to save in currency-conversions costs, the structure of payments will tend to match the structure of exchanges of these countries. This is the basic idea underlying the theory of "vehicle currencies" put forth by Krugman (1980). This effect might be magnified by the removal of constraints to bank competition, and the ensuing ability of commercial banks to issue checking accounts in other European currencies (a sort of retail Euromarket). The development of foreign currency deposits will prompt more aggressive reserve management by commercial banks, which will magnify the shifts in demand for transactions balances mentioned above.[7]

The tendency of large countries' currencies to be more in demand for payments in international trade will be balanced by the relative *costs of transactions* of the currencies available. Consider a European multinational corporation, trying to manage its own cash portfolio. The corporation will hold more cash balances in the currencies where business is more active, but only as long as these transactions balances will not be much more expensive than transactions balances in other currencies. The costs of transactions balances are the costs of clearing checks--the fees applied to check clearance, as well as the lags in transfer of funds for every check payment--and the costs of wire transfers, the costs of holding checking accounts--represented by the differential between interest paid on less liquid instruments like government securities and interest paid on checking accounts, and all the other charges applied by banks for executing payments on behalf of their customers.

Together with the external economies mentioned above in the use of a widely-circulating medium of exchange, there are also economies of scale in the transactions technologies used by banks. It is cheaper to operate a check clearing house characterized by very high volume than a small one, where the number of offsetting entries are limited; similarly, a higher volume will guarantee lower unit costs for wire transfers, and shorter delays in value dates; the decreases in unit costs of transactions with the increase in volume are also explained by the fact that very large volumes would justify investments in expensive and sophisticated technologies to operate them, like supercomputers. With increasing returns in the transactions technology the desired shares of individual currencies increase with their actual shares in the market. Under these conditions the presence of multiple equilibria is possible. The different equilibria will be characterized by the existence of different predominant currencies as media of exchange.

It is very difficult to determine the "critical mass" of a local market that justifies its own currency. The current 12 members of the European Community are countries of very different sizes, and wide-ranging degrees of openness. It is quite possible that, with high integration of goods and financial markets, and in the absence of constraints from regulators, a much smaller number of currencies would better facilitate transactions. The discussion of the previous sections has shown a way to extend the optimum-currency-area argument: increasing returns in transactions technologies and the external economies arising from the use of a common medium of exchange provide additional elements in the calculations of the gains from the adoption of a common currency.[8] Table 3 reports the averages (over the 1980--86 period) of the percent ratio of exports plus imports over GDP in the 12 EC countries. The table shows that 4 out of 12 countries have volumes of international trade that exceed the size of GDP. In those countries the efficiency gains from using a national currency might be very small, and would definitely decrease in the future. In the absence of resistance from national governments, and if the process of European integration continues, the currencies of those 4 countries might slowly lose importance. There are however no firm criteria to determine how many currencies will survive in Europe in the absence of regulatory interference - assuming, for example, that governments will remove legal tender rules, and accept any of the 12 currencies in payment of taxes. In particular, it is not known what would move the economy from one to the other of the multiple equilibria depicted in Figure 1. An answer to this question would have to rely on an empirical estimate of the effective private costs of switching one currency to another and of the information hurdles associated with the coordination problem.

Table 3
Openness of EC Member Countries

Country	Openness (% of GDP)
Belgium	132.9
Denmark	70.1
France	45.4
Germany	61.5
Greece	50.3
Ireland	111.8
Italy	42.6
Luxembourg	170.1
Netherlands	112.3
Portugal	72.9
Spain	40.3
United Kingdom	53.4

Notes: Exports plus imports as percent of GDP: averages 1980-86. Source: International Financial Statistics, lines 90c, 98c, 99c.

2.2 Currencies as Store of Value

Currencies are held not only for the transactions services that they provide in the present, but also for the transactions services they are expected to provide in the future: hence they provide also a *store of value* service. A currency's future transactions services depend both on its future purchasing power and its future medium-of-exchange services. Indeed, the value of a currency is equal to the present-discounted value of all future transactions services it is expected to perform - see Svensson (1985) and Giovannini (1989).

The expectations about the stream of future transactions services and purchasing power - which is itself determined by future exchange rates - affect the demand for different currencies. Transactions services are endogenously determined by the factors discussed above. Expectations depend on past experience, as well as on the public perceptions of the determinants of currency values and transactions services. As it often happens in economics, expectations can give rise to large fluctuations in currency demands, and can become self-fulfilling, even in the absence of any changes in fundamentals. The possibility that expectations become self-fulfilling is increased by the presence of multiple equilibrium shares of different currencies in private portfolios, arising from increasing returns in transactions technologies and from the external economies in the usage of a common medium of exchange.

The public's suspicion that governments are going to negatively affect the transactions services of certain currencies, either by preventing the development of efficient payments' clearing systems, or by limiting currency substitutability with regulations, or finally by inflating the currency, will prompt a quick fall in its demand in the foreign exchange markets, with an ensuing adjustment of either the exchange rate or foreign reserves of central banks.

The store-of-value services of different currencies are a function of the exchange-rate regime. Under credibly fixed exchange rates currencies must have identical store-of-value services in equilibrium and become perfectly substitutable as stores of value: see Giovannini (1990a). They do not necessarily need to be perfect substitutes as media of exchange. Under managed exchange rates parity changes are not ruled out, and phenomena like the above-mentioned self-fulfilling prophecies can occur. Whether currency substitution is higher or lower under managed rates than under fixed rates remains an open question that is beyond the scope of this paper. Fluctuations of currencies' store-of-value services also occur under floating exchange rates.

3. EFFECTS OF CURRENCY SUBSTITUTION

The discussion in the previous section has laid out the major determinants of the demand for different currencies in an economy where private agents are allowed to hold all of them in their portfolios. The next question regards the effects of the increased substitutability of European currencies on the equilibrium.

3.1 Hayek's Theory

One classic discussion of the effects of currency substitution is Hayek's (1976). Hayek shows that in a world where currencies were allowed to compete, that is in a world where currency substitution could occur, the monetary system would slowly converge to maximum efficiency. It would be characterized by stability of purchasing power of the different currencies, as well as the best technically feasible payments systems. Most monetary distortions would be eliminated by the progressive removal of national governments' monopolies in the issuance of currencies. In his work he puts forth a proposal which applies directly to the current debate in Europe. According to Hayek,

> "the countries of the Common Market [...] mutually bind themselves by formal treaty not to place any obstacles in the way of the free dealing throughout their territories in one another's currencies (including gold coins) or of a similar free exercise of the banking business by any institution legally established in any of their territories." (page 17)

The effect of the plan and the purpose of the proposal is

> "to impose upon existing monetary and financial agencies a very much needed discipline by making it impossible for any of them, and for any length of time, to issue a kind of money substantially less reliable and useful than the money of any other." (page 17)

The scheme of competing currencies is regarded by Hayek to be superior to the introduction of a common currency, for two reasons. Member countries would not agree on the policy to be pursued in practice by a common monetary authority; and it would be highly unlikely that, even in the most favourable circumstances, it would be administered better than the present national currencies. As Hayek puts it, "The advantage of an international authority should be mainly to protect a member state from the harmful measures of others, not to force it to join in their follies." (page 18)

> "The main advantage of the proposed scheme [...] is that it would prevent governments from 'protecting' the currencies they issue against the harmful consequences of their own measures, and therefore prevent them from further employing these harmful tools. They would become unable to conceal the depreciation of the money they issue, to prevent an outflow of money, capital, and other resources as a result of making their home use unfavourable [...] The scheme would, to all intents and purposes, amount to a displacement of the national circulations only if the national monetary authorities misbehaved. Even then they could still ward off a complete displacement of the national currency by rapidly changing their ways."

A recent proposal by the UK Treasury (1989) for economic and monetary union in Europe bears striking similarities to Hayek's views. According to the UK document:

> "the pressures on governments to keep down inflation and enhance the stability of currencies would be increased by the complete removal of all unnecessary restrictions on the use of Community currencies."(para. 21)

> "the costs and inconveniences of changing between Community currencies could be reduced further by tackling remaining barriers, including those affecting the development of appropriate technology, the use of relatively cheap and convenient means of payment." (para. 22)

> "Over time, all these measures would strengthen the process of convergence on price and exchange rate stability." (para. 23)

> "The ERM [Exchange-Rate Mechanism] will have become more stable as a result of a natural process" (para. 19)

> "The Delors Report was not asked to and did not set out the economic gains from such a move [the move to a common currency]. They are most unlikely to outweigh the political and economic risks" (para. 34)

> "The evolutionary approach maintains national monetary policies in the context of a strengthening ERM, and allows currencies to compete to provide the non-inflationary anchor in the European Monetary System." (para. 35)

The above paragraphs should have highlighted the extreme resemblance of the UK proposal to Hayek's theory. However Hayek's theory is a description of the effects of currency substitution in a world where, crucially, the regime of coexisting currencies under flexible exchange rates is to be maintained forever, because it provides the necessary competitive pressures that are needed to ensure the efficiency of the monetary system. The UK proposal, by contrast, was presented as an alternative to the Delors plan for economic and monetary union in Europe, and therefore it should presumably be a proposal of a strategy to achieve such a monetary union. The British proposal claims that (see above) a regime of competing currencies would "naturally evolve" into a monetary union. This natural evolution could be the one briefly considered by Hayek, the "displacement of the national circulations" that occurs "if the national monetary authorities misbehaved". But Hayek himself assigns a very small probability to this type of event, since its occurrence would eliminate the advantages of currency competition. The extinction of certain national currencies is equivalent - using an industrial organization analogy - to the evolution of a regime of monopolistic competition into a pure monopoly, and in Hayek's model it surely brings about a welfare loss. In summary, the UK Treasury has borrowed Hayek's theory to counter the Delors project, but appears to be consistent with Hayek's views only under the hypothesis that its main objective is forever to maintain in Europe a regime of different currencies coexisting under flexible exchange rates.

What would be the effect of competing currencies in a fixed-exchange-rates regime? Fluctuations of relative monetary services of different currencies would produce Gresham's Law in reverse: the "good" currency would drive out the "bad". This reverse Gresham's Law is due to the absence of any intrinsic value of currencies in the current monetary system. The original statement of Gresham's Law - the bad currency drives out the good - refers to the intrinsic values of currencies. When, for example, gold becomes more valuable in the industrial market, it tends to be withdrawn from monetary circulation to be sold in the industrial market: as a result the monetary circulation of the "bad" currency, silver, increases. In a world where currency values are only determined by the monetary services they provide, the increase of a currency's transactions services would prompt the private sector to purchase it at the official parity from the central bank in exchange for the bad one. Hence foreign exchange reserves at central banks will include increasingly large shares of the bad currency,[9] while an increasingly large share of the good currency will be in circulation.

Whether or not the predictions of the Hayek model on the effects of currency competition would go through under fixed exchange rate depends on the reserve arrangements among the monetary authorities that belong to the system. For example, if the rules are such that the scarce currencies can be borrowed freely from the central banks issuing them, there would be no guarantee that competing currencies under fixed rates would converge to maximum efficiency. Indeed, as I argued above, expected store-of-value services of different currencies will be equalized, and in that case central banks would have an incentive to export the inflation tax to their partners, and would induce, in equilibrium, an inflationary bias. Therefore under fixed exchange rates the properties of the equilibrium crucially depend on the rules governing the financing of balance-of-payments surpluses and deficits: the Hayek model does not necessarily apply. The model might however apply under a managed floating system like the current EMS, where expectations about currency changes can still be realized. As I discuss elsewhere, however (Giovannini, 1990d), the problems of credibility of the Delors plan are such that countries like Italy and the United Kingdom are forced to maintain very high domestic interest rates in order to stabilize their exchange rates relative to the mark. Currency competition might impose an upward bias on interest rates under managed floating.

The implicit model used by Hayek is one where governments force upon private citizens the use of national currencies in order to be able to extract from them more revenue from the inflation tax. To ensure a relatively large inflation tax base, governments resist innovations in the transactions technology, and effectively discourage technological progress in payments systems.[10]

Hayek's historical references provide support for this view, but also suggest that the current regime - at least among industrial countries - might be one where the revenue motive in monetary policy is largely absent, and authorities believe that the objective of insuring stability of financial markets has gained overriding importance. Stability in financial markets is important whenever interest-rate fluctuations have significant real effects. This occurs in models characterized by the presence of imperfect information, mentioned below.

If central banks are mostly concerned about financial markets' stability, then it is not clear that an increase in the substitutability of currencies would necessarily bring about a significant efficiency gain. Furthermore, Hayek's analysis neglects other determinants of the demand for different currencies on which I have devoted some discussion in sections 2 and 2.1.2. The conclusion of such discussion was that there are gains from the adoption of a common currency, which are associated with the transactions and informations costs of switching from one currency into another. These gains have to be added in the calculus of the costs and benefits of alternative monetary regimes. It might also be useful to consider the likelihood and effects of increased financial volatility associated with increased currency substitutability. I turn to this problem in the next section.

3.2 The Instability Hypothesis

A potential alternative to Hayek's currency-competition theory is the "instability hypothesis", stating that increased currency substitution brings about exchange-rate, price-level, and financial markets instabilities, with adverse effects. This hypothesis is not - to my knowledge - formally presented anywhere, although a number of papers have started to systematically tackle some of its aspects. Hence it does not represent a full-fledged alternative to Hayek's theory, despite the large and growing literature on financial markets' instability and imperfections. The purpose of this section is to highlight the most important theoretical questions raised by the "instability hypothesis" and to offer some elements that might be relevant in the construction of models that support it.

A higher degree of substitutability among currencies implies that the response of their relative demands to exogenous shocks is greatly magnified. This general proposition clearly surfaces in the work of Calvo and Rodriguez (1977) and Girton and Roper (1981). Kareken and Wallace (1981) have shown that in the limiting case, where the substitutability of currencies is perfect the nominal exchange rate is indeterminate.[11] These results, however, cannot provide specific guidance as to the economic effects of increased currency substitution: they naturally lead to the question of the behavior of *equilibrium* prices and exchange rates with increased currency substitution.

On the nature of equilibria with currency substitution work is much more scant. Recent papers by Weil (1990) and Woodford (1990) tackle this question using a family of general-equilibrium perfect-foresight models of economies populated by representative individuals. They consider the case where currency is used either because it is required to carry out purchases of goods and services, or because real money balances enter into agents' utility function. They show that the standard multiple-equilibria characteristics of monetary models are not ameliorated by increased currency substitution, and are often made worse. In particular they show that, with higher currency substitution, the emergence of hyperinflationary equilibria is more likely and that - in the case where expectations are slow to adjust to rationality - the convergence of expectations is further slowed down. These papers thus lead to the general conclusion that, indeed, higher currency substitutability leads to greater instability.

The welfare effects of this greater instability, however, are not studied in detail by these authors. In the simple Kareken-Wallace model, for example, the infinity of equilibria indexed by the exchange rate are all characterized by the same welfare level. Similarly, imploding or exploding paths often cannot be ruled out only because their effects on utility is not different from that of stable paths.[12] Intuitively, in the neoclassical family of models, we should expect that higher currency substitutability implies that large fluctuations in the values of different currencies in private portfolios do not have large welfare effects.

In order to determine whether the instability hypothesis can represent a valid alternative to Hayek's theory, it is thus necessary to include in equilibrium models the elements that will make exchange-rate and interest-rate fluctuations costly, and then to prove that the multiple-equilibria problems mentioned above still arise in these models. Below I limit myself to considering the first half of this program, that is the identification of the sources of costs of interest-rate fluctuations arising from swings in money demand.

The direct effects of fluctuations in currency demands are swings in liquidity in money markets, with ensuing swings in interest rates. The first problem raised by these shifts in liquidity has to do with the extent to which they can be reabsorbed through international financial intermediation. Work by Fazzari Hubbard and Petersen (1988), Montgomery (1988) and Branson (1990) has shown that a realistic geographical structure of costs of monitoring investments - such that investments can more easily be monitored by local intermediaries - gives rise to local financial markets, which by their nature are unable to completely diversify away idiosynchratic risks. For these reasons sudden shifts in currency demands might give rise to liquidity problems in local markets, and nonsynchronized interest-rate movements.

Why are these swings in liquidity dangerous? If these movements are of extreme proportions, they can give rise to financial crises. These phenomena can trigger failures of financial intermediaries and increase uncertainty in the marketplace.[13] The increase in uncertainty, in turn, exacerbates two typical problems of financial intermediation: adverse selection and credit rationing. Since lenders cannot perfectly assess the riskiness of borrowers, they charge interest rates that reflect their average assessment of the quality of loan projects. This means that high quality borrowers pay too high interest and low quality borrowers pay too low interest (the adverse selection problem). At the same time, lenders are likely to deny arbitrarily loans to good borrowers, since they cannot tell who are the borrowers with the riskiest investment projects (the credit rationing problem). The increase in uncertainty and interest rates during a financial crisis thus dries up lending and business investment, producing the conditions for a recession. A likely side effect is also a massive deposit withdrawal in the interbank market, caused by concerns about the liquidity and the viability of the banks themselves.

4. CONCLUSION

This paper has discussed the sources and effects of currency substitution, with special reference to the issues raised by the removal of controls on international capital flows, and on the holdings of foreign-currency checking accounts in Europe.

I have argued that despite these sweeping reforms of the financial markets, there are good reasons to expect a significant "local" component in the demand for national currencies, even independently of the remaining regulations, like those that require the payment of taxes using national currency. In general, multiple equilibria are likely to arise from the externalities generated by wider use of currencies as well as the increasing returns in transactions technology. Yet we do not know how easy it is for an economy to move from one to the other of these equilibria. I suspect that the coordination problem of these economy-wide movements might make them quite unlikely, in the absence of extreme instabilities.

Next I discuss two theories of the effects of increased currency substitution. The first is the classical Hayek (1976) parable, according to which - if exchange rates are floating and if different currencies coexist forever - currency substitution has desirable efficiency properties, since it limits governments monopoly power. This theory is correct only if governments' "misuse" their monopoly power by devoting part or the whole of their revenues to socially unproductive or undesirable uses. I also argue that in the absence of floating exchange rates the effects of currency competition might not be the desirable ones.

The alternative to the currency competition hypothesis is what I called the "instability hypothesis", which, however, has not been developed fully. According to this view, instabilities (like multiple equilibria) associated with higher currency substitution might have undesirable welfare effects. I argue that the most promising channel to generate these undesirable welfare consequences is the one of disintermediation coming from the effects of asymmetric information.

FOOTNOTES

The first version of this paper was presented at the CEPR meeting on *Managing Change in the EMS*, Ministerio de Economia y Hacienda, Madrid. I am grateful to Pamela Labadie and Mario Sarcinelli for discussions over successive versions. Any errors, opinions and omissions are my own.

1. See Kareken and Wallace (1981), Lapan and Enders (1983), and Nickelsburg (1984).

2. A first attempt to fill this gap is carried out in Giovannini (1990a,1990b).

3. Indeed, in Giovannini (1990c) I propose to deal directly with the unit of account problem, with a currency reform to set all bilateral rates in Europe equal to unity.

4. The adverb "reasonably" hides a wide divergence of experiences across European countries, including, for example, that of the F.R.G. (that has managed to successfully target M3 over the past several years) and that of the United Kingdom (that has changed its monetary targets a number of times, with mixed success).

5. See, for example, Marshall (1987). An explicit solution of the (partial equilibrium) problem of balancing transactions costs with the (foregone interest) cost of holding money was first studied by Baumol (1952).

6. The spreading of interstate mail sales in the USA might suggest that the geographical distribution of transactions could become more uniform, even though it is well known that the US experience is more driven by tax arbitrage incentives, than by lower transactions costs and search costs.

7. The response of regulatory authorities to this has not been seen yet. The second banking directive sanctions the removal of competitive barriers in the commercial banking industry, and will be part of national laws starting in 1993. There is no provision, in the directive, as to the currency of denomination of reserve requirements. It only assigns to the host country the responsibility to set liquidity ratios.

8. See also Bertola (1989) for a related set of arguments, based on the distortionary effects of mobility costs of goods and factors.

9. The good currency will become the scarce one among monetary authorities.

10. The revenue from the inflation tax is presumably devoted to nonproductive uses, otherwise this strategy could be perfectly justified in the context of an optimal taxation problem.

11. Kareken and Wallace consider a model where currencies only have a store-of-value function. Their result, however, would go through even if currencies provided transactions services. In Giovannini (1990a) I show that under fixed exchange rate that indeterminacy is reflected in an indeterminacy of the composition of central banks' foreign exchange reserves.

12. See for example the methods used by Obstfeld and Rogoff (1983).

13. For an illuminating analysis of the history of financial crises in the US, and the role of monetary authorities, see Mishkin (1990), whose basic approach is adopted here.

REFERENCES

Baumol, W.J. (1952): "The Transactions Demand for Cash: An Inventory Theoretic Approach," Quarterly Journal of Economics, 66, November, 545-556.

Bertola, G. (1989): "Factor Flexibility, Uncertainty, and Exchange Rate Regimes," in M. De Cecco and A. Giovannini (eds.) A European Central Bank?, Cambridge: Cambridge University Press.

Branson, W.H. (1990): "Financial Market Integration, Macroeconomic Policy and the EMS," CEPR Working Paper n. 385, March.

Calvo, G.A. and C.A. Rodriguez (1977): "A Model of Exchange Rate Determination under Currency Substitution and Rational Expectations," Journal of Political Economy, 85, 617-625.

Fazzari, S.M., R.G. Hubbard and B.C. Petersen (1988): "Financing Constraints and Corporate Investment," Brookings Papers on Economic Activity, 1, 141-195.

Giovannini, A. (1989): "Uncertainty and Liquidity," Journal of Monetary Economics, 23, n.2, March, 239-258.

Giovannini, A. (1990a): "Currency Substitution and the Fluctuations of Foreign-Exchange Reserves with Credibly Fixed Exchange Rates," mimeo, Columbia University.

Giovannini, A. (1990b): "Money Demand and Monetary Control in an Integrated European Economy," European Economy.

Giovannini, A. (1990c): "The Transition Towards Monetary Union," Essays in International Finance no. 178, November.

Giovannini, A. (1990d): "European Monetary Reform: Progress and Prospects," Brookings Paper on Economic Activity, 2, 217-292.

Girton, L. and D. Roper (1981): "Theory and Implications of Currency Substitution," Journal of Money, Credit and Banking, 13, February, 12-30.

Hayek, F.A. (1976): Denationalization of Money, London: The Institute of Economic Affairs.

HM Treasury (1989): An Evolutionary Approach to Economic and Monetary Union, London: HM Treasury, November.

Kareken, J. and N. Wallace (1981): "On the Indeterminacy of Equilibrium Exchange Rates," Quarterly Journal of Economics, 207-222.

Kiyotaki, N. and R. Wright (1989): "On Money as a Medium of Exchange," Journal of Political Economy, 97, 927-954.

Krugman, P. (1980): "Vehicle Currencies and the Structure of International Exchange," Journal of Money, Credit and Banking, 12, August, 513-526.

Lapan, H.E. and W. Enders (1983): "Rational Expectations, Endogenous Currency Substitution, and Exchange Rate Determination," Quarterly Journal of Economics, August, 427-439.

Lucas, R.E., Jr. (1984): "Money in a Theory of Finance," Carnegie-Rochester Conference Series on Public Policy, Vol. 21, Autumn, 9-46.

Marshall, D.A. (1987): "Inflation and Asset Returns in a Monetary Economy with Transactions Costs," Doctoral Dissertation, Carnegie Mellon University, November.

Montgomery, J. (1988): "Financial Intermediation, Contracts and International Capital Mobility," mimeo, Princeton University.

Nickelsburg, G. (1984): "Dynamic Exchange Rate Equilibria with Uncertain Government Policy," Review of Economic Studies, 509-519.

Svensson, L.E.O. (1985): "Money and Asset Prices in a Cash-in-Advance Economy," Journal of Political Economy, 93, no. 5, October, 919-944.

Tobin, J. (1958): "Liquidity Preference as Behavior Towards Risk," Review of Economic Studies, 65-86.

Weil, P. (1990): "Currency Competition and the Evolution of Multi-Currency Regions," presented at IMI-CEPR conference on European Financial Integration, Rome.

Woodford, M. (1990): "Does Increased Competition Between Currencies Lead to Price Level and Exchange Rate Stability?", presented at IMI-CEPR conference on European Financial Integration, Rome.

Financial Regulation and Monetary Arrangements after 1992
C. Wihlborg, M. Fratianni and T.D. Willett (Editors)

Comment

Michael Melvin

College of Business, Department of Economics, Arizona State University, Tempe, AZ 85287, USA

I welcome a survey of research questions related to European currency substitution. I believe that several events in the early 1980s turned our attention away from this potentially important issue. Articles by Cuddington (1983) and Bordo and Choudhri (1982) caused many people to question whether currency substitution (CS) was relevant. I believe that it is under certain circumstances. For instance, no one should believe that cross-ocean CS is important. Japanese residents do not demand dollar currency. But in border areas and regions characterized by high mobility of resources, cross-border tourism, and trade, we may expect CS to be relevant. I believe that Western Europe is one such area (see Melvin 1985).

Giovannini gives us an agenda for future work. I agree with every issue he raises. However, I should point out that some of the issues are difficult. For instance, the transactions demand for foreign currencies will be difficult to identify. We cannot look to data on bilateral trade volume because what is relevant is the currency used to invoice trade, and this can be very different than the reported trade volume between countries. For instance, the US dollar may be used as a vehicle currency between two countries for pricing trade that does not involve the United States. Furthermore, within a single nation, foreign money may serve a transactions function for domestic goods. The use of a parallel currency is more common in high-inflation situations (like Latin America), but it cannot be completely dismissed in border areas in more stable regions.

The store of value (or portfolio) demand is easier to approach. I have (in Kutan, Melvin, and Ormiston, 1990) looked at the stochastic dominance rankings across European currencies (including the ECU). As Farber, Roll, and Solnik (1977) found in the 1970s, one finds many ambiguous results in such analysis. By computing generalized stochastic dominance and varying the degree of risk aversion, Kutan, Melvin, and Ormiston find unique rankings for all currencies over reasonable ranges of absolute risk aversion. The idea of this approach is to answer the question, which currency would emerge from an open competition among European currencies from the view of an investor in each country (based on the realized distributions of returns over the past decade). For pure foreign exchange returns, the mark dominates. For uncovered Eurodeposit returns, the lira dominates. The ECU is ranked near the bottom of possible choices for the FX returns, and is near the top for the uncovered returns in Eurodeposits. This causes one to question the economic justification for the ECU as a single money for Europe (although I realize that on political grounds it may be the most reasonable choice).

An implication of a high degree of CS is exchange rate volatility. Attempts to follow independent monetary policies will generate large swings in exchange rates. This is one area where the criticism that floating exchange rates are "too volatile" is reasonable. I am pleased that Giovannini takes care to point out why exchange rate volatility could be harmful. Shifts in currency demand can cause liquidity and financial crises that could trigger recession. In extreme cases of very high substitutability, I could envision such results.

It is important to realize that with CS, pressure for fixed exchange rates comes from the market. It is not a discretionary political decision to unify monetary systems, but is forced by market pressures. With perfectly fixed exchange rates, it does not make sense to think of competing currencies. The governments make currencies perfect substitutes from the supply side. However, the potential for breaks in the exchange rate peg allow for competing currencies. I understand this to be the point Giovannini makes by saying that properties of the fixed exchange rate equilibrium depend on rules governing balance of payments surpluses and deficits.

REFERENCES

Bordo, M.D. and E. U. Choudri (1982), "Currency Substitution and the Demand for Money: Some Evidence for Canada", Journal of Money, Credit, and Banking, Feb., 14, 48-57

Cuddington, J.T. (1983), "Currency Substitution, Capital Mobility and Money Demand", Journal of International Money and Finance, March, 2, 111-133

Farber, A., R. Roll, and B. Solnik (1977), "An Empirical Study of Risk Under Fixed and Flexible Exchange", Journal of Monetary Economics, Supplement, 5, 235-265

Kutan, A., M. Melvin, and M.B. Ormiston (1990), "ECUs, Marks, Pounds, or Which Single Currency for Western Europe?", Working Paper, Arizona State University

Melvin, M. (1985), "Currency Substitution and Western European Monetary Unification", Economica, Feb. 52, 79-91

Part Four

Economics and Politics of the EMS

Financial Regulation and Monetary Arrangements after 1992
C. Wihlborg, M. Fratianni and T.D. Willett (Editors)

10 Fiscal Constraints and Incentives with Monetary Coordination: Implications for Europe 1992

Reuven Glick
Research Department, Federal Reserve Bank of San Francisco, 101 Market Street, San Francisco, Ca. 94105, USA

Michael Hutchison
Bank for International Settlements, Centralbahnplatz 2, CH-4102 Basle, Switzerland, and University of California, Santa Cruz, Ca. 95064, USA

1. INTRODUCTION

Recent plans by the member countries within the European Community (EC) to create a single integrated market by 1992 have raised questions concerning the appropriate conduct of fiscal policy in interdependent, open economies. There is little disagreement that this increased integration will necessitate coordination of monetary policies if European countries are to move closer to a longer-run goal of full monetary union, possibly with a common currency. However, the possible need to establish a community-wide fiscal policy stance through fiscal policy "harmonization" or coordination has only recently received much attention.

In order to progress smoothly toward an European Monetary Union (EMU), a greater degree of convergence in inflation rates, as well as closer coordination of monetary policies would appear desirable. This has important implications for fiscal policy. Most directly, it is clear that a reduction in monetary autonomy will affect the extent to which deficits can be financed via the creation of base money (seigniorage revenue). In addition, coordinated monetary policies may affect the magnitude and pattern of fiscal policy transmission across countries. Finally, coordination of monetary policies may affect the incentives fiscal policy makers face in setting policy. That is, given a new set of external constraints and institutional arrangements associated with a monetary union, governments may choose to alter the absolute level and time pattern of fiscal spending, as well as the choice between tax and debt finance.

A major issue concerning progress towards an EMU is the extent to which fiscal policies of member nations need to be aligned in order to allow smooth coordination of monetary policies and maintain exchange rate stability. It has been forcefully argued by some that fiscal convergence among the member states of the EC is desirable, and perhaps even necessary, if stability in exchange rates is to be established and a monetary union successful (Thygesen, 1989; CEC, 1989; Delors Committee, 1989).

Thygesen (1989), for example, states two concerns. First, widely divergent budget deficits or debt-to-income ratios in individual countries could threaten the fixity of exchange rates. This could arise because of the incentive individual countries face to lower the real value of these debts from additional inflation, and the recognition by the market that these incentives exist, at least until the credibility of the EMU is firmly established. Second, the creation of an EMU without explicit constraints on budget deficits could encourage an excessively lax aggregate fiscal stance. Since the need to be concerned with exchange rate pressures or large international reserve flows presumably would be reduced, the incentive for greater reliance on debt finance of existing budgetary deficits might increase. From this perspective, present divergences among EC countries in their existing fiscal deficit and debt positions, as well as in the extent to which monetization is relied upon in the financing of government expenditures, pose a concern.

For this reason the Delors Committee report, sponsored by the EC and issued in April 1989, suggests that certain binding rules should be imposed limiting the size of budget deficits in individual EC countries, as well as the degree upon which monetary financing can be relied.[1] More recently, the Governor of the Bank of France stated that monetary union implies strongly convergent fiscal policy (de Larosière, 1990). Moreover, a report by the Commission of the European Communities warns that "...prospective budgetary developments in most of the high deficit and public debt member countries contrast sharply with the needs arising from making a good start to the first stage of Economic and Monetary Union..." (CEC, 1989; p. 1), and goes on to urge countries towards greater coordination in fiscal policy and convergence of budgetary deficits to a lower level.

In contrast, other observers reject the view that a smooth transition to an EMU, and its functioning, require binding rules and procedures for budgetary policies. For example, in its study on a monetary order for the single European market, Germany's Board of Academic Advisers to the Federal Ministry of Economics states that "...in itself, a European monetary union does not require any formal restrictions on national autonomy in fiscal policy beyond the ban on central bank financing of state expenditure" (Watrin, 1989). The study argues that market pressures for fiscal convergence may be induced by the institutional shift to a monetary union. "The fact that one must pay interest and debts with money one cannot create oneself is the prime mover of discipline; it creates informal pressures towards a convergence in the form of sound fiscal conduct" (Watrin, 1989). This suggests that market discipline will be imposed on government borrowers, much as in a private setting. In support of this view, Eichengreen (1990) concludes that U.S. experience suggests that individual U.S. states, though implicitly members of a monetary union, still face rising costs of debt finance. Moreover, Fratianni and von Hagen (1990) and von Hagen (1990) argue that U.S. experience also indicates that formal fiscal restraints have done little to constrain the fiscal activities of individual states.

To shed light on these issues this paper explores the fiscal linkages between countries under different institutional economic policy arrangements. We begin by considering a two-country model where real and financial markets are completely integrated (a broad objective of the moves toward European economic integration), and nominal exchange rates are perfectly flexible. In this model linkages between the two countries are established through real interest rate equality and purchasing power parity. We then investigate the implications of institutional arrangements roughly corresponding to the increasing degree of monetary integration being proposed within the EC: (i) "irrevocably" fixed nominal exchange rates which tightly link price levels, and (ii) monetary policy coordination that constrains money growth rates. In the first case both monetary and fiscal policy instruments may be coordinated to achieve the price level (and exchange rate) target. In the second case, only the fiscal instrument is available for use. We show explicitly how these monetary arrangements affect the degree of fiscal independence as well as the behavioral incentives facing policy makers when setting fiscal policy, defined in terms of the level and time pattern of spending, and financing of expenditures. We do not dwell on the process through which these arrangements are achieved. Rather we treat them as given constraints on behavior. The results of this analysis provide insights into how the feasibility and desirability of pursuing divergent fiscal policies will change as monetary integration proceeds in the EC. Moreover, they shed light on the issue of whether the new incentives associated with institutional monetary arrangements would help to accomplish fiscal policy convergence in the EC.

Our analytical framework highlights the role of intertemporal budget constraints and maximizing private and public sector behavior in the context of a two-period, two-country framework. Following Frankel and Razin (1985, 1987), Greenwood and Kimbrough (1985), Djajic (1987), among others, we emphasize that private and public sector spending decisions are not independent events with a one-time outcome, but are multiperiod decisions linked across time through borrowing and lending. This framework considers policies in a general equilibrium setting with rational, forward-looking households and governments. Similarly to Tabellini (1988) and Masciandaro and Tabellini (1988), we incorporate monetary considerations by assuming real money balances enter household utility functions because of the liquidity services that they provide. Also, following the approach of these papers, we assume that fiscal policy is determined within the constraint of institutionally-given monetary arrangements. Unlike the latter papers, however, we focus on the interactions between institutional arrangements and policy in a two-country setting - the appropriate paradigm for economic integration among the larger countries in the EC.

The remainder of the paper is organized as follows. Section 2 presents an overview of existing fiscal policy stances, government debt positions, and the extent of monetary finance of fiscal deficits in the EC. Section 3 presents the two-country model and discusses the linkages between the two countries and the interdependence of fiscal policies. Section 4 considers the implications of institutional constraints associated with monetary integration for "feasible" fiscal policy. We show that the ability to maintain fiscal independence is reduced. In Section 5 we analyze "optimal" fiscal policy and discuss how monetary integration affects the incentives to pursue divergent fiscal policies. We demonstrate within our model that the incentive for fiscal divergences lessens with greater monetary policy coordination. A concluding section completes the paper.

2. FISCAL DIVERGENCES AND MONETARY FINANCE IN THE EC

Large divergences in budgetary deficit positions and marked differences in the extent to which EC countries rely on monetary finance of government deficits could pose a problem to the process of monetary integration. A number of measures may be employed to assess the extent of fiscal convergence and whether progress has been made in the consolidation of public finances. Perhaps the three most common measures are the trend in gross public debt, developments in actual budget balances, and developments in the budget balance emanating from changes in economic activity. As Tables 1 and 2 demonstrate, the existing fiscal divergences among the EC countries are in fact quite large and, by several measures, have increased in recent years.

Table 1
Gross Public Debt in Ten European Community Countries[1]
(Percentage of Nominal GNP/GDP)

	1982	1983	1984	1985	1986	1987	1988	1989	1990
Countries with debt below European Average in 1990									
Germany	39.5	40.9	41.5	42.2	42.4	43.8	44.2	43.1	44.6
France	40.1	41.4	43.8	45.5	45.7	47.5	47.4	46.9	46.7
United Kingdom	53.0	53.2	54.8	53.1	51.7	49.2	42.6	38.6	36.1
Spain	29.0	35.0	41.8	47.3	48.1	48.5	43.9	43.1	43.2
Denmark	53.0	62.6	67.0	65.7	59.3	56.9	55.7	54.9	55.3
Countries with debt above European Average in 1990									
Belgium	102.3	113.4	118.6	122.7	127.2	131.7	133.7	130.8	129.3
Greece	36.1	41.2	49.5	57.9	58.6	64.6	72.1	79.6	83.4
Netherlands	55.5	61.9	66.1	69.6	71.3	75.2	78.1	80.9	83.0
Italy	66.4	72.0	77.2	84.1	88.5	93.0	95.6	98.4	99.9
Ireland	92.2	104.7	113.4	117.5	132.8	135.2	134.1	125.1	117.7
European Average Debt	48.8	51.8	54.5	56.7	57.7	58.8	58.1	57.3	57.4

Source: OECD *Economic Outlook*, December 1990, Table 34.

[1]Figures for 1988 and 1989 partially estimated, figures for 1990 partially forecast. European average debt calculated at 1987 GNP/GDP weights and exchange rates.

The upper panel of Table 1 shows the gross public debt time profile of EC countries with debt below the European average in 1990, while the lower panel shows the remaining countries with much greater public debt levels. In the first group of countries, which includes Germany, France and the United Kingdom and represents some 70 percent of EC GDP, the gross public debt ratios in 1990 either were lower than previous years or roughly stable.[2] In contrast, the second group of countries has had less success in stabilizing debt ratios. Although the two countries with the highest debt ratios, Ireland and Belgium, have reduced their debt position somewhat in recent years, the other countries display continued rapid growth. Particularly rapid growth rates are evident in Italy and Greece. By this measure, divergences in debt positions generally have increased in recent years.

Table 2 shows the development of general government financial balances in ten EC countries between 1986 and 1990. The five countries in the upper (lower) panel correspond to those in Table 1 with relatively low (high) debt/GNP ratios. Financial balance levels and changes are reported.

Table 2
General Government Financial Balances in 10 European Community Countries[1]
(Percentage of Nominal GNP/GDP)

	Level			Changes	
	1986	1988	1990	1986-88	1988-90
Germany	-1.3	-2.1	-3.1	-0.8	-1.0
France	-2.7	-1.8	-1.2	0.9	0.6
United Kingdom	-2.2	1.0	0.1	3.2	-0.9
Spain	-6.1	-3.2	-3.2	2.9	0.0
Denmark	3.4	0.3	-1.3	-3.1	-1.6
Average[2]	-2.2	-1.3	-1.8	0.8	-0.4
Belgium	-8.9	-6.4	-5.9	2.5	0.5
Greece	-10.6	-15.3	-18.3	-4.7	-3.0
Netherlands	-6.1	-5.1	-5.5	1.0	-0.4
Italy	-11.7	-10.9	-10.0	0.8	0.9
Ireland	-11.6	-5.1	-1.7	6.5	3.4
Average[3]	-10.3	-9.4	-8.9	0.9	0.5
Average[4]	-4.5	-3.6	-3.7	0.9	-0.1

Source: OECD Economic Outlook, December 1990, Table 9

[1] Net lending (+) or net borrowing (-). 1990 values partly estimated. Average values calculated at 1987 GNP/GDP weight and exchange rates. Authors' calculation.
[2] Weighted average of Germany, France, U.K., Spain and Denmark
[3] Weighted average of Belgium, Greece, Netherlands, Italy and Ireland
[4] Weighted average of 10 countries listed above

Table 3
Monetary Finance in the EC

	Outstanding loans from central bank to general government[1]	Counterparts to changes in broad money stock[2]					Total money creation
		Lending to public sector	Net lending to private sector	Banks' non-monetary liabilities	Change in net external position	Other counterparts	
Belgium							
1985	5.2	16.3	3.4	-7.2	-6.3	0.7	6.9
1986	5.5	16.5	5.7	-4.2	-4.6	-0.6	12.8
1987	3.7	11.6	6.8	-3.6	-4.2	0.9	11.5
1988	3.2	7.1	10.3	-3.6	-7.5	0.2	6.5
Greece							
1985	12.4	26.5	12.9	-2.4	-11.3	1.1	26.8
1986	11.5	20.7	10.2	-4.3	-5.8	-1.8	19.0
1987	10.1	17.9	6.3	1.5	-1.4	0.9	25.2
1988	7.8	16.1	8.4	-1.0	2.1	-3.2	22.4
Spain							
1985	7.8	8.2	7.2	-2.2	0.5	-0.8	12.9
1986	5.0	5.8	8.3	-1.6	0.9	-1.2	12.2
1987	3.5	4.3	11.1	-3.6	2.9	-1.1	13.6
1988	2.4	3.2	12.7	-4.9	0.9	-1.6	10.3
Ireland							
1985	--	11.4	3.5	--	-11.0	1.5	5.4
1986	--	10.9	7.2	--	-18.8	-0.3	-1.0
1987	--	9.9	5.0	--	-1.1	-2.9	10.9
1988	--	0.5	13.3	--	-5.9	-1.6	6.3
Italy							
1985	6.6	7.8	6.8	--	-1.7	-1.8	11.1
1986	6.2	4.9	5.2	--	-0.5	-0.2	9.4
1987	6.7	5.0	4.1	--	0.2	-1.0	8.3
1988	6.4	2.8	7.5	--	0.1	-1.8	8.6
Portugal							
1985	--	13.6	17.1	-7.9	5.4	2.2	30.4
1986	--	12.3	16.8	-3.3	-0.7	-0.1	25.0
1987	--	12.0	3.8	-2.3	7.1	-2.8	17.8
1988	--	8.3	5.2	-2.2	6.9	-4.7	13.5

Source: CEC (1990, Table 2).

[1] As percent of GDP.

[2] As a percentage of broadly defined money stock outstanding at the beginning of the period. *Source:* CEC (1990, Table 3).

A tendency towards fiscal consolidation is clearly evident over the period 1986-1988 in both "high-debt" and "low-debt" countries. This process continued into 1989 as rapid growth in Europe and some structural reforms allowed declines in deficits as a percentage of GNP/GDP. Nonetheless, over the period 1986-1988 the improvement in the high-debt EC countries deficit positions was roughly the same as low-debt EC countries as a percent of GNP/GDP in absolute terms, at 0.9 and 0.8, respectively, and much lower when calculated relative to the level of the deficit. Over the period 1988-1990, the deficit positions of high-debt countries improved somewhat, while the low-debt countries deteriorated following a slowdown in growth in 1990 in the United Kingdom and the sharp rise in government expenditures in Germany associated with the unification and restructuring process.

On balance, however, no clear tendency toward a decline in the average budget deficit of the high-debt/high-deficit countries *relative* to the low-debt/low-deficit countries is discernable. In 1986, the weighted average deficit of the high-debt countries was 4.7 times greater than the low-debt countries, and was 4.9 times larger in 1990. Moreover, a recent study by the European Commission estimates that all of the improvement in overall deficit positions of EC countries with deficits greater than the EC average during the past five years is attributable to the impact of strong economic growth rather than significant budget reforms (CEC, 1989). The only notable exception in this respect is Ireland.

By these measures, relatively little progress toward fiscal convergence in the EC is discernable. As Dornbush (1989) points out, however, a measure of the budgetary position net-of-interest payments (the primary budget) suggests that EC fiscal deficits have declined and converged in recent years. The primary budgets of Belgium and Ireland were in substantial surplus in 1989, for example, following a sustained period of budget deficit reduction. Nevertheless, the actual financing demands of government are more closely related to actual government deficit positions than to the primary budget.

Monetary financing of fiscal deficits and how convergence in this area may be essential for further progress towards monetary integration in the Community is another important concern. Quantitative indicators of the importance of existing monetary financing policies are shown in Table 3 for the EC countries where this seems particularly relevant. The first column in the table shows that the share of outstanding loans from the central bank to the public sector as a percentage of GDP has fallen significantly in recent years. While it reached a low level in Belgium and Spain in 1988, it remained more substantial in Italy and Greece. The remaining columns, showing data on the development of the counterparts of the money supply, suggest that monetary financing of the public sector is still important, particularly in Belgium, Greece and Portugal. In addition, financing of the public sector via the banking sector is still important though its relative contribution to total money creation has declined since 1987.

Estimates of the degree of seigniorage - the degree to which current government expenditures are financed via the creation of base money (the issue of non-interest-bearing, or below-market interest-bearing, currency plus bank reserves) - vary widely within the EC. Table 4 presents recent "cash flow" estimates of seigniorage by Gros (1989), which shows that during the 1979-81 period it ranged from more than five percent of GDP for Portugal to zero percent for Germany. Together with the reduced monetary expansion and fall in inflation rates associated with participation in the EMS, however, the discrepancies in the shares of GDP that the fiscal authorities command through seigniorage has already been considerably reduced. Four of the five countries with the largest seigniorage in 1978-81 have substantially reduced this source of revenue as a percent of GDP by 1987.

Table 4
Seigniorage in the EC[1]
(Percentage of Nominal GDP/GNP)

	Average 1979-81	1982	1983	1984	1985	1986	1987
Portugal	5.29	5.86	2.70	0.63	1.07	1.62	2.74
Greece	2.28	3.39	-0.02	3.48	0.56	0.22	2.99
Italy	1.37	1.45	1.49	1.39	1.81	0.60	0.63
Spain	1.32	1.87	2.01	7.51	0.59	0.88	1.18
France	0.64	1.32	0.52	0.82	0.06	-0.25	0.33
Denmark	0.31	0.08	0.22	0.31	4.58	-2.39	-1.09
Belgium	0.22	0.00	0.32	0.06	-0.08	0.38	0.21
United Kingdom	0.19	0.19	0.12	-0.45	0.22	0.33	0.06
Ireland	0.10	0.20	0.52	0.16	0.24	0.08	0.56
Netherlands	0.07	0.48	0.78	0.41	0.28	0.26	0.73
Germany	0.00	0.48	0.50	0.35	0.30	0.56	0.83

Source: Gros (1989, Table 1)

[1] The figures represent a "cash flow" definition of seigniorage, i.e. the command over real resources obtained by the government by increasing the supply of currency in circulation plus increases in required reserves less interest paid on total required reserves

Nonetheless, significant differentials in the relative importance of seigniorage revenues remain and greater convergence will presumably be necessary if a smooth transition to the EMU is to be realized. In particular, inflation rates - and hence monetary growth rates and seigniorage revenues - will decline in several high-inflation countries. In this regard, Gros (1989) estimates seigniorage changes under assumptions that all EC members participate fully in the EMS by 1992, i.e., push down inflation rates to a common low level so as to maintain exchange rate parities fixed, and adopt common reserve requirements. Using this assumption and 1987 as a base year, he finds that government revenue from seigniorage will be reduced by 2 to 3 percentage points of GDP in Greece and Portugal and 1 to 2 percentage points in Italy and Spain by 1992.

Finally, Table 5 presents some comparative statistics on the relative size of base money in individual EC countries. Spain, Greece, Italy, and Portugal are the four countries for which the monetary base is largest as a percentage of GDP, with ratios ranging from 13.5 percent to 20.4 percent. These countries have a GDP share equal to roughly one-quarter of the EC total, but monetary base shares equal to almost double that amount. Again, it appears that considerable divergence exists among the EC countries in their reliance on monetary finance. The concern over EC divergences in this aspect of policy, as well as in budgetary deficit and debt positions, appears well founded.

Table 5
Monetary Base and GDP in the EC, 1988 (percent)

	Monetary Base/GDP	Share of GDP in EC	Share of Monetary Base in EC
Belgium	7.5	3.2	2.6
Denmark	3.7	2.3	0.9
France	5.8	20.0	12.5
Germany	9.9	25.3	26.9
Greece	14.9	1.1	1.8
Ireland	10.1	0.7	0.7
Italy	14.6	17.5	27.4
Netherlands	8.1	4.8	4.2
Portugal	13.5	0.9	1.3
Spain	20.4	7.2	6.0
United Kingdom	3.3	17.0	6.0
Total	9.3	100.0	100.0

Source: Padoa-Schioppi (1990)

3. MONETARY AND FISCAL LINKAGES IN A TWO-COUNTRY SETTING

This section develops a simple two-period, two-country model to explore the effects of increased integration and monetary policy coordination on the conduct of fiscal policy. This framework allows us to capture the flavor of international and intertemporal linkages within the simplest possible setting.

Households in each country are price takers in international goods and capital markets. It is assumed they produce and consume the same perfectly substitutable good. All borrowing and lending commitments are assumed to be fulfilled, ruling out defaults. Real interest rate equality links the capital markets, and purchasing power parity links nominal prices in goods markets internationally. Nominal money balances are assumed to be held only by local households.

The specification of the model below focuses on the domestic economy. The analogue expressions for the foreign country are introduced when appropriate.

3.1 Specification of the Model

The representative private household of the domestic country produces an exogenously given quantity of output Y_t and pays T_t lump-sum units of taxes in each period t ($t=1,2$). In addition, at the beginning of the first period ($t=0$) it holds exogenously given levels of nominal money balances, M_0, real domestic government assets, B_0, and real foreign assets, F_0. What is left over in the first period is consumed, lent to the domestic government or abroad, or spent on real money balances. In the second period, all lending is repaid and available resources are allocated to consumption or money holdings.

Accordingly, the household's first and second period budget constraints are:

$$C_1 + M_1/P_1 = Y_1 - T_1 - B - F + M_0/P_1 + (B_0+F_0) , \tag{1a}$$

$$C_2 + M_2/P_2 = Y_2 - T_2 + (1+r)(B+F) + M_1/P_2^e . \tag{1b}$$

where B and F denote (real) lending in period 1 to the domestic government and foreigners, respectively, that is repaid in full in period 2 at the same associated (real) interest rate r; C_t denotes consumption, M_t, nominal money balances, and P_t the price level in period t; and P_2^e, the expected price level for period 2 as of period 1. For simplicity of notation we do not time subscript lending variables and the associated interest rate in period 1 (B,F,r). The implied intertemporal budget constraint for the household is:

$$C_1+RC_2+(M_1/P_1)(1-R\pi_2^e)+R(M_2/P_2) = Y_1+RY_2-(T_1+RT_2)+M_0/P_1+(B_0+F_0) \equiv W, \tag{2}$$

where $R \equiv 1/(1+r)$ is the period 1 present value factor, $\pi_2^e \equiv P_1/P_2^e$ is the *inverse* of the expected inflation rate in period 2, and W denotes lifetime household real wealth as of period 1.[3]

While government spending, taxes, and money creation are given from the point of view of households, they are linked together by the following period government budget constraints:

$$G_1 + B_0 = T_1 + B + M_1/P_1 - M_0/P_1, \tag{3a}$$

$$G_2 + (1+r)B = T_2 + M_2/P_2 - M_1/P_2. \tag{3b}$$

It is assumed that the government faces the same interest rate as the private sector. The corresponding government intertemporal budget constraint is

$$G_1 + RG_2 + B_0 = T_1 + RT_2 + M_1/P_1 - M_0/P_1 + R(M_2/P_2-M_1/P_2). \tag{4}$$

To restrict the degrees of freedom in setting monetary and fiscal policies, it is assumed that the (gross) rate of money supply growth in the first period, M_1/M_0, is exogenously given at the level , and that a fixed proportion θ of government debt, $0<\theta<1$, is monetized in period 2:

$$R(M_2/P_2-M_1/P_2) = \theta B, \tag{5a}$$

$$R\left(G_2 - T_2\right) = -(1-\theta)B. \tag{5b}$$

The parameter θ may be interpreted as an institutional parameter reflecting the degree of fiscal "dominance," i.e. the extent to which the burden of satisfying the government's budget constraint falls on the monetary authorities (see Tabellini, 1988; Masciandaro and Tabellini, 1988). Thus a high value of θ indicates a high degree of debt monetization undertaken by the monetary authorities. It is assumed that θ is set exogenously either by domestic institutional conditions or, as we discuss below, by external institutional monetary arrangements.

Fully-informed, rational agents "see through" the government budget constraints and thereby recognize the dependence between the levels of government spending, and the implied tax liabilities and seigniorage revenue. The resulting consolidation of the household and government, (2) and (4), together with (5a) implies:

$$W \equiv Y_1 + RY_2 - \left(G_1 + RG_2\right) + M_0/P_1 + \theta B + F_0. \tag{6}$$

Observe that, given the pattern of government spending, domestic public debt affects real private wealth because of the perception that the fraction θ of this debt will be monetized in the second period.[4]

3.2 Optimal Domestic Household Behavior and Equilibrium

The domestic household is assumed to maximize lifetime utility with respect to its consumption and real money balance holdings in periods 1 and 2, subject to the intertemporal budget constraint, (2), and its initial money and asset holdings. Lifetime utility is defined as the following log-linear function[5]:

$$V = \ln C_1 + D\ln C_2 + \ln m_1 + D\ln m_2, \tag{7}$$

where $m_t \equiv M_t/P_t$ denotes real domestic money balances held at the end of period t; $D = 1/(1+d)$, $0 < D < 1$ denotes the subjective discount factor; and d denotes the corresponding subjective rate of time preference. Real money balances are assumed to affect household utility because of the liquidity services that they provide. This specification is functionally equivalent to alternatives such as cash-in-advance constraints or money appearing in the budget constraint through liquidity costs (see Feenstra, 1986). Note that only domestic money provides liquidity services; this rules out currency substitution.

The solution to this optimization problem implies that the domestic household will choose consumption and real money balances which satisfy:

$$C_1 = \frac{W}{2\left(1+D\right)}, \tag{8a}$$

$$C_2 = \frac{DW}{2R\left(1+D\right)}, \tag{8b}$$

$$m_1 = \left[\frac{1}{1 - R\pi_2^e}\right] \frac{W}{2(1+D)} , \tag{8c}$$

$$m_2 = \frac{DW}{2R(1+D)} . \tag{8d}$$

The wealth coefficients represent the marginal (and average) propensities to consume or hold money out of wealth in each period. Observe that these propensities are all less than 1. Note also that these demands depend on household real wealth, the price structure, and the interest rate.

To determine the equilibrium price structure, we utilize the equilibrium money market conditions, (8c), (8d), and (5a), and assume rational expectations, that is $\pi_2 = \pi_2^e$. In particular, we rearrange (5a) and substitute for m_1 with (8c):

$$\theta B/R = m_2 - m_1\pi_2$$
$$= m_2 - \left[\frac{1}{1 - R\pi_2^e}\right] \frac{W\pi_2}{2(1+D)} . \tag{9}$$

Substituting in for m_2 with (8d) and equating π_2 and π_2^e yields:

$$\pi_2 = \pi_2^e = \frac{WD - 2\theta(1+D)B}{R(1+D)(W - 2\theta B)} . \tag{10}$$

By taking partial derivatives of (10), it can be established that π_2 is increasing in W and decreasing in θ, B, and R. Thus greater government debt to be repaid or a higher proportion of debt to be monetized in the second period raises the inflation rate. In addition, a higher interest rate or a rise in private real wealth, by increasing the demand for real balances in period 2, reduces the inflation rate (i.e. raises π_2).

To solve for the equilibrium price level in period 1, P_1, note that the definitions $m_1 \equiv M_1/P_1$ and $\equiv M_1/M_0$, and condition (8c) imply

$$\frac{1}{P_1} = \left[\frac{1}{1 - R\pi_2^e}\right] \frac{W}{2(1+D) M_0} . \tag{11}$$

Substituting for π_2^e with (10) gives

$$\frac{1}{P_1} = \frac{W - 2\theta B}{2 M_0} . \tag{12}$$

Solving (12) for W and equating with (6) implies:

$$W/2 = Y_1 - G_1 + R(Y_2 - G_2) + F_0. \tag{13}$$

Substituting back in (12) gives the inverse of the price level in terms of fiscal and monetary policy variables:

$$\frac{1}{P_1} = \frac{Y_1 - G_1 + R(Y_2 - G_2) + F_0 - \theta B}{M_0}. \tag{14}$$

Observe that P_1 is increasing in , θ, B, G_1, and G_2; it is decreasing in Y_1, Y_2, and F_0. Thus a more expansionary monetary policy in the first period increases the first-period price level. Issuing more debt in the first period or monetizing a greater proportion in the second period also are inflationary in the first period since the private sector realizes that this will lead to future inflation, thereby inducing lower real money demand in the current period. Given output levels, greater government spending in either period has the same effect. Increases in output or initial asset holdings raise private real wealth, increase money demand, and lead to lower current prices.

The government intertemporal budget constraint may be expressed solely in terms of policy variables by substituting (14) along with (5a) and the definition $M_1/M_0 = $ into (4):

$$G_1 + RG_2 = T_1 + RT_2 - B_0 + \frac{-1}{2-1}\left[Y_1 - T_1 + R(Y_2 - T_2) + (B_0 + F_0)\right] + \frac{\theta B}{2-1}. \tag{15}$$

The righthand side of (15) may be interpreted as the present value of government resources. These resources come from three sources: (i) tax receipts, (ii) seigniorage in the first period (if $\mu > 1$), and (iii) monetization of debt in the second period (if $\theta > 0$).

A rise in first-period money supply growth, μ, or in monetization of debt, θ, both allow greater government expenditures by generating more seigniorage revenue.[6] Moreover, present-value neutral budget changes, i.e. $\Delta (G_1 + RG_2) = \Delta (T_1 + RT_2)$, will generally violate the budget constraint if $\mu \neq 1$. The reason is that households know the rate of nominal supply growth and anticipate the effects of government expenditure and tax changes on the changes on the price level and hence on seigniorage revenue. Thus, for example, in the case of a current balanced budget change, i.e. $\Delta G_1 = \Delta T_1$, the increase in government spending raises the first-period price level and reduces the real seigniorage revenue associated with the existing nominal money supply growth rate. This implies that the government will need to increase taxes further or raise more seigniorage revenue in the future by increasing borrowing or monetizing a greater proportion of the existing debt.

3.3 World Equilibrium and Interest Rate Linkages with Flexible Exchange Rates

Analogous results for private consumption and money demand as well as the price structure can be obtained for households of the foreign country. Since the good produced and consumed by the two economies is assumed identical, purchasing power parity holds i.e., nominal price level differences are offset by nominal exchange rate flexibility. In equilibrium the world supply of the single good, defined to include current output and the initial endowment of foreign real assets, must equal demand in each period. Thus, in period 1

$$Y_1 + F_0 + Y_1^* + F_0^* = \left[\frac{1}{2(1+D)}\right]W + \left[\frac{1}{2(1+D^*)}\right]W^* + G_1 + G_1^*, \tag{16}$$

where (8a) has been used to substitute for C_1, and the foreign variables, denoted by asterisks, are defined analogously to those for the domestic country.[7]

Upon substituting the definition for domestic wealth W, (13), and the analogous one for W^* into (16) and assuming real interest equality, we obtain an equation that relates the equilibrium interest rate factor, R, to government spending levels, G_t and G_t^*; output levels, Y_t and Y_t^*; and subjective time preference factors, D and D^*:

$$R = \frac{\left(Y_1 - G_1 + F_0\right)D(1+D^*) + \left(Y_1^* - G_1^* + F_0^*\right)D^*(1+D)}{\left(Y_2 - G_2\right)(1+D^*) + \left(Y_2^* - G_2^*\right)(1+D)}. \tag{17}$$

We will discuss the determinants of the equilibrium interest rate below. Before doing so, we note that the home country's trade balance surplus in period 1, TB_1, is given by the difference between its income and absorption, $TB_1 = Y_1 + F_0 - G_1 - C_1$.[8] Substituting with (8a), (13), and (17) yields the following expression:

$$TB_1 = \frac{D\left(Y_2^* - G_2^*\right)\left(Y_1 - G_1 + F_0\right) - D^*\left(Y_2 - G_2\right)\left(Y_1^* - G_1^* + F_0^*\right)}{\left(Y_2 - G_2\right)(1+D^*) + \left(Y_2^* - G_2^*\right)(1+D)}. \tag{18}$$

Observe that in the special case of balanced growth, fiscal spending, and initial foreign asset positions across countries and time (i.e. $Y_1 - G_1 = Y_2 - G_2 = Y_1^* - G_1^* = Y_2^* - G_2^*$ and $F_0 = F_0^*$), equation (18) reduces to $TB_1 = (D - D^*)(Y - G + F_0)/(2 + D + D^*)$ which is negative if $D < D^*$, that is, if $d > d^*$. Thus the home country runs a trade deficit in the first period if it has a higher rate of time preference and is more "impatient" than the foreign country.

Equation (17) indicates that fiscal policy shifts will be transmitted across countries through changes in the interest rate. The multiplier effects of fiscal policy changes on the equilibrium foreign interest rate $1 + r = 1/R$ may be determined from (17). For example, an increase in first-period domestic government expenditures leads to a rise in the real interest rate r (fall in R).[9] Intuitively, the fiscal spending increase leads to an excess demand for goods in the first period. To eliminate this excess demand, the relative price of present goods in terms of future goods, i.e. the interest rate, must rise.[10]

Observe from (8a) and (8b) that the resulting increase in r and corresponding decline in R imply the substitution away from current consumption and towards future consumption in *both* countries. Thus an increase in first-period domestic government spending crowds out not only current domestic consumption, but also current foreign consumption. Part of the rise in domestic government spending is "financed" through the crowding out of foreign consumption. Thus in an interdependent world, fiscal spending in one country is financed by higher interest rates and the crowding out of private spending in both countries. From (18), it may be discerned that even though home consumption is crowded out, on balance the home country's trade balance worsens in response to the fiscal stimulus.

Fiscal policy shifts also affect the price structure. The particular effects depend on the manner in which the increased spending is financed. Equation (14) implies that an increase in either current or future fiscal spending has an inflationary effect on current prices.[11]

3.4 World Equilibrium and Price Level Linkages

The assumption that domestic and foreign goods are perfect substitutes implies that their nominal price levels are linked by the purchasing power condition $P_t = E_t P_t^*$, where E_t is the domestic currency price of foreign exchange. Solving for E_1 and substituting for P_1 with (14) and analogously for P_1^* implies[12]

$$E_1 = \frac{\mu M_0 \left[Y_1^* - G_1^* + R\left(Y_2^* - G_2^*\right) - \theta^* B^* + F_0^* \right]}{\mu^* M_0^* \left[Y_1 - G_1 + R\left(Y_2 - G_2\right) - \theta B + F_0 \right]} \qquad (19)$$

As long as the nominal exchange rate is flexible, there is considerable scope for the independent conduct of monetary and fiscal policies in the two countries. In fact, as long as price level divergences are allowed through exchange rate flexibility, the transmission of fiscal policy between the two countries occurs only through the real interest rate. Observe that the domestic price level rises and domestic currency depreciates (E_1 rises) in response to domestic money supply expansion (higher μ or M_0), fiscal policy stimulus (higher G_1 or G_2), decline in domestic supply (lower Y_1 or Y_2), or a rise in debt monetization (higher θ or B). The effects of foreign shifts are symmetric.

These effects abstract from any impact on R. To the extent that changes in output or government spending in one country affect the equilibrium interest rate there will be additional effects on the nominal exchange rate. Thus, for example, an increase in G_1 raises the equilibrium interest rate (see equation (17)) as well as raises the domestic price level (see equation (14)).[13] The rise in r, i.e. fall in R, implies that the domestic fiscal spending increase will be transmitted to the foreign economy in the form of higher foreign prices as well. Thus, this model displays the well-known property that flexible exchange rates do not insulate an economy from foreign real disturbances.

In contrast, as long as R is unaffected, nominal disturbances will not be transmitted. An increase in μ or M_0, for example, that does not require any fiscal spending adjustments by the domestic government to satisfy its budget constraint, implies that only the domestic price level will rise. The nominal value of the domestic currency falls; the foreign price is unaffected.

4. IMPLICATIONS OF FIXED EXCHANGE RATES AND MONETARY INTEGRATION

We now turn to analyzing the implications of increased monetary integration for the feasible configurations of fiscal policy. We focus first on the case where monetary integration involves a perfectly fixed nominal exchange rate. Subsequently we address the implications of convergence in the money supply growth through policy coordination in the two countries.

4.1 Fixed Exchange Rates

Assume that a fixed exchange rate regime requires E_1 is constant, and, for simplicity, equal to unity. This implies nominal price levels are tightly linked, and in our framework must be equalized across the two countries. According to (19), such a regime then implies an additional constraint on the configuration of monetary and fiscal policies in the two countries:

$$\frac{Y_1 - G_1 + R(Y_2 - G_2) - \theta B + F_0}{\mu M_0} = \frac{Y_1^* - G_1^* + R(Y_2^* - G_2^*) - \theta^* B^* + F_0^*}{\mu^* M_0^*}. \tag{20}$$

If, for example, current monetary policy in the domestic country is more expansionary than the foreign country, i.e. $\mu M_0 > \mu^* M_0^*$, the following constraint is implied on the possible divergence of fiscal policies (in present value terms):

$$G_1 + RG_2 - (G_1^* + RG_2^*) < (Y_1 + RY_2) - (Y_1^* + RY_2^*) + (\theta^* B^* - \theta B) + (F_0 - F_0^*). \tag{21}$$

Condition (21) implies that if both countries are endowed with similar output levels $(Y_1 + RY_2 = Y_1^* + RY_2^*)$, monetize to an equal extent $(\theta B = \theta^* B^*)$, and have equal initial foreign asset positions $(F_0 = F_0^*)$, then the domestic country must follow a *less* stimulative fiscal policy than the foreign country. To the extent that domestic and foreign monetary policy parameters, as well as foreign fiscal variables, are set exogenously, the domestic fiscal authority is faced with a more binding constraint when fixed exchange rates are introduced. This constraint is mitigated the relatively greater is the domestic country's present value of output, the greater the extent to which the foreign country engages in debt financing, or the greater the initial foreign asset position of the domestic country relative to the foreign country.[14]

Analogously, if current fiscal policy is more expansionary in the domestic country than in the foreign country, i.e., $G_1 > G_1^*$, a corresponding constraint is implied for the divergence of monetary policies between the two countries. In this case, in order to generate a matching increase in its price level and sustain the fixed exchange rate, the foreign country will need to adopt relatively higher money supply growth. The extent to which this is necessary is dampened the greater its willingness to engage in more debt finance.[15] This example illustrates that fixing exchange rates in this context necessitates the targeting of a common price level in both countries, thereby forcing the coordination of monetary and fiscal policies. If foreign policies and the foreign price level are taken as given, domestic monetary and fiscal instruments together must be coordinated to achieve the price level target. Further, if domestic fiscal policy is also set independently, domestic monetary policy is the only instrument available to achieve the price level target and must therefore be set accordingly if a fixed exchange rate is to be maintained.

To put this analysis in an EC context, assume that money supply growth in Italy, the domestic country, exceeds that in Germany, the foreign country, i.e. $\mu M_0 > \mu^* M_0^*$. Given that Italy also has a smaller output level than Germany $(Y_1 + RY_2 < Y_1^* + RY_2^*)$, tends to monetize more debt $(\theta B > \theta^* B^*)$, and has a smaller net initial foreign asset position $(F_0 < F_0^*)$, a more expansionary Italian monetary policy suggests greater upward pressure on its price level. Condition (21) correspondingly implies that a commitment to exchange rate fixity on the part of the Italian fiscal authorities under these circumstances with unchanged German policies (i.e., both a "dominant" domestic monetary policy with foreign monetary and fiscal policies given exogenously), will necessitate relatively greater restraint on Italian government expenditures.

Analogously, consider the case with a "dominant" domestic fiscal policy, monetary policy in Italy adjusts to maintain exchange rate stability, and the present value of Italian government spending (relative to output) is large compared to Germany. This divergence in fiscal position would place relatively greater pressure on the Italian price level and, with unchanged German policies, necessitates a correspondingly tighter domestic monetary position ($\mu M_0 < \mu^* M_1^*$) to maintain exchange rate stability.

These examples illustrate that the commitment to maintain fixed exchange rates places an additional constraint on the configuration of feasible monetary and fiscal policy in each country beyond that imposed through the intertemporal budget constraint. In addition to real interest rate linkages associated with capital and goods mobility, in a fixed exchange regime nominal price levels are also linked across countries. A fiscal policy shift in one country is now transmitted to the other through both real interest rates and pressure on the nominal exchange rate. In the former case, the intertemporal budget constraint is directly affected; in the latter, adjustment in the price level is needed as well. Both effects necessitate fiscal and/or monetary policy adjustment. The addition of the exchange rate constraint reduces the degree of freedom countries face in setting independent monetary and fiscal policies, and magnifies the international impact effects of fiscal policy shifts.

4.2 Money Supply Coordination

We now investigate the implications arising from coordination of money supply policies. In particular, assume that the initial money supply levels and growth rates are equated across countries each period, i.e. $M_0 = M_0^*$, $M_1/M_0 = M_1^*/M_0^*$ and $M_2/M_1 = M_2^*/M_1^*$. The first condition requires $\mu = \mu^*$. Note that the second condition together with (5a) requires $\theta B P_2 = \theta^* B^* P_2^*$. The assumption that fixed exchange rates prevail in both periods implies that, if $E_2 = 1$, then $P_2 = P_2^*$ and hence $\theta B = \theta^* B^*$. Thus seigniorage revenue in the second period must be equalized between the countries. Note that the latter condition does not necessitate that either the degree of debt monetization or government debt levels in the two countries be the same, i.e. θ need not equal θ^* and B need not equal B^*.

Upon imposing these conditions, (20) implies

$$\left(G_1 + RG_2\right) - \left(G_1^* + RG_2^*\right) = Y_1 + RY_2 - \left(Y_1^* + RY_2^*\right) + \left(F_0 - F_0^*\right) \qquad (22)$$

Thus exogenously determined and coordinated money supplies limit the scope for fiscal divergence beyond what is necessary to maintain a fixed exchange rate. The present value of fiscal expenditures can differ only to the extent that output levels and initial foreign asset positions differ.

In the European context, three implications of the above analysis stand out. First, monetary coordination together with a commitment to fixed exchange rates considerably narrows the ability for countries to monetize deficits, and will necessitate much greater convergence in this area. If those countries with relatively high inflation rates and high debt monetization attempt to attain the norms set by Germany, for example, considerable adjustment will be necessary in these countries. This is consistent with the empirical analysis of Gros (1989), the concerns expressed in the Delors report (1989), and analysis by the Commission of the European Community (CEC, 1990).

Second, convergence in monetary positions combined with a commitment to fixed exchange rates will necessitate a significant narrowing of the existing budgetary divergences among the EC countries. To the extent that the norms of the largest countries are established for the EC as a whole (small deficit or surplus positions of Germany, France, and the United Kingdom), this implies large fiscal contractions for a number of the smaller countries if the credibility of their commitment to exchange rate stability and monetary integration is to be established.

Third, a contraction in fiscal policy need not imply an immediate decline in expenditures (G_1), but rather a fall in the present discounted value of these expenditures. Hence, there remains considerable scope for differences in the time pattern of policies, although in discounted terms the overall stance of policy is considerably constrained.

5. OPTIMAL FISCAL POLICY AND MONETARY INTEGRATION

It is clear from the analysis of feasible fiscal policy configurations above that a significant convergence in budgetary policies will be required to establish monetary integration and exchange rate fixity. This is consistent with the view expressed by Thygesen (1989), the Delors committee (1989), and others. However, it stands in contrast with one part of the statement by Germany's Board of Academic Advisors to the Federal Ministry of Economics (quoted in Section 1) that in itself monetary union does not require any formal restrictions on national autonomy in fiscal policy beyond a ban of monetization of deficits. The analysis above suggests that convergence in budget policy will be necessary, in effect limiting national autonomy in fiscal policy. The Board of Advisors goes on to note, however, that informal pressures towards smaller deficit positions, and hence towards convergence at a lower level, would face countries as they commit themselves to monetary integration.

To address this issue, we now turn to the analysis of optimal fiscal policy within our framework. This will shed light on how monetary integration, viewed as a shift in the institutional monetary environment faced by fiscal authorities, affects the incentives of policy makers to spend and finance, and how changes in incentives may induce fiscal policy shifts.[16] Before proceeding, we point out that the assumption of real interest rate parity implicitly presumes that domestic and foreign assets are perfect substitutes. This precludes the existence of any risk premium mechanism through which excessive spending and borrowing in any given country generates differentially greater borrowing costs for that country in the world capital market. Nevertheless, we show below that greater monetary policy coordination affects the equilibrium world interest rate in a manner that enhances the incentive for fiscal policy convergence.

Following Tabellini (1988) and Masciandaro and Tabellini (1988), we assume that the money supply parameters, μ and θ, as well as the tax levels, T_1 and T_2, are given institutionally. This leaves the domestic government with three choice variables: G_1, G_2, and B. To model the government's decision problem in the simplest possible way it is assumed that it cares only about public expenditures and maximizes

$$V_g = \ln G_1 + D\ln G_2, \tag{23}$$

where it is assumed that it has the same rate of time preference as local households. This problem is subject to the two constraints (5b) and (15). Assuming for simplicity that the government treats the interest rate as given in its optimization problem, the associated first-order conditions imply

$$\frac{1}{G_1} = \frac{\phi D}{G_2 R}, \tag{24}$$

where $\phi[\theta, \mu] \equiv \dfrac{(2\mu - 1)(1 - \theta)}{2\mu(1 - \theta) + 2\theta - 1}$, $\phi_\mu > 0$, $\phi_\theta < 0$, $1 > \phi > 0$, if $\mu > 1$.

Condition (24) represents an equilibrium intertemporal government spending relation that takes account of financing considerations.

The lefthand side of (24) is the marginal utility of current government spending. The righthand side discounts the marginal utility of future government spending (since $\phi < 1$) by the extent to which spending is financed by issuing public debt. Lower levels of seigniorage revenue or a higher degree of debt monetization, as parameterized by μ and θ, induce more borrowing and hence lower future relative to current government spending. If $D = R$ and $\theta = 0$ then (24) implies $G_1 = G_2$; i.e., it is optimal to balance expenditures across time.

We may solve for the optimal value of G_1 in terms of exogenous tax and financing variables as well as R by substituting out for G_2 and B in (15) with (24) and (5b), and by using the definition of ϕ:

$$G_1(1+D) = T_1 + RT_2 - B_0 + \frac{(\mu - 1)}{2\mu - 1}\left[Y_1 + RY_2 - (T_1 + RT_2) + (B_0 + F_0)\right] + \frac{\theta RT_2}{(1-\theta)(2\mu - 1)}. \tag{25}$$

It can be established that the optimal level of current fiscal spending increases with greater tax receipts (higher T_1 or T_2), output (higher Y_1 or Y_2), and initial foreign assets (higher F_0). Most importantly for our purposes, it can also be shown that G_1 rises with θ or μ.[17] Intuitively, greater monetization of debt repayment in the second period reduces the cost of borrowing and spending by the government in the first period. Similarly, greater current money supply growth generates greater seigniorage revenue and permits more fiscal spending. Lastly, we note that it can be shown that G_1 rises with R (assuming $Y_2 > T_2$ and $\mu > 1$), implying that a fall in the interest rate induces greater current spending.

The results above imply that, given R, lower levels of θ and/or μ associated with monetary policy coordination will tend to reduce the desired level of current fiscal spending. We now turn to take into account the endogenous response of R in the determination of optimal fiscal policy.[18] To obtain an expression for R in terms of G_1 and G_1^* substitute out in (17) for G_2 using (24) and for G_2^* with the foreign analogue, and solve for R:

$$R = \frac{\left[Y_1 - G_1(1-\phi) + F_0\right](1+D^*)D + \left[Y_1^* - G_1^*(1-\phi^*) + F_0^*\right](1+D)D^*}{Y_2(1+D^*) + Y_2^*(1+D)},$$ (26)

where it should be recalled $\phi < 1$, $\phi^* < 1$. Equations (25), its foreign analogue, and (26) constitute a system of three expressions in the three endogenous variables, G_1, G_1^*, and R. The solution of this system and comparative statics are presented in an appendix. It can be shown, under reasonable conditions, that the comparative statics results obtained for G_1 when R was held constant also hold when R is treated endogenously. That is, G_1 rises with θ or μ.

Allowing R to vary endogenously, however, implies that the optimal level of G_1 will depend on foreign factors transmitted through changes in the equilibrium interest rate. In particular, an increase in μ^* or θ^* reduces the optimal level of current domestic fiscal spending. Intuitively, greater seigniorage revenue or monetization of debt abroad enables the foreign government to increase its current spending. This increased spending, however, pushes up the equilibrium interest rate (lowers R). The higher interest rate reduces the present value of resources available to the domestic country. Consequently, the domestic government must reduce its spending.

The configuration of optimal fiscal spending policies in the two countries depends on their financing parameters as well as on their respective output, tax, and initial asset levels. Treating the latter variables as constant across countries, it can be established that sufficient conditions for $G_1 > G_1^*$ are $D^* > D$ (i.e. $d^* < d$), $\theta > \theta^*$, and $\mu > \mu^*$. The last two conditions imply that the domestic country government generates relatively more resources for spending than the foreign government. The condition $d > d^*$ precludes the possibility that this relationship is reversed by an extreme preference for current spending by the foreign government.

Expression (21) implies that with fixed exchange rates and coordinated monetary policies ($E_1 = 1$, $\mu = \mu^*$, $\theta B = \theta^* B^*$) feasible divergences in fiscal policies will be correspondingly constrained. We next ascertain the implications of fixed exchange rates and coordinated monetary policies on the configuration of optimal fiscal policies in the two countries.[19] Note from (14) that P_1 depends on the present value of government expenditures, $G_1 + RG_2$ (as well as on debt monetization, θB, and initial foreign asset positions). It can be shown that under the conditions above a narrowing of the money supply growth differential between countries reduces any differential in the present value of their expenditures. Thus money supply coordination creates an incentive for optimizing governments to reduce the disruptive impact on the exchange rate of differences in spending policies.

These results support the argument by Germany's Board of Academic Advisers noted above that the institutional changes associated with monetary integration may create the appropriate incentives for fiscal adjustment. For example, assume that the relatively high inflation EC countries bring down their money growth rates, μ, and the degree of debt monetization, θ, to the levels set by Germany (μ^*, θ^*). In this instance, with monetary coordination around lower money growth rates, our results indicate that the optimal response in the high inflation countries would be to lower government expenditures and reduce budget deficits. This suggests the institutional change itself, i.e. a monetary regime shift created through the EMU, would create incentives for fiscal convergence. Because the real cost of financing expenditures has increased, pressure automatically would be placed on the fiscal authorities to respond. To the extent that countries with higher than average money growth make the adjustment and decelerate monetary expansion, the present value of their optimal government expenditure stream will unambiguously decline, and create an incentive toward convergence in EC budget positions. It should be reemphasized, however, that these incentives are for fiscal convergence (at a lower average level of budget deficits) on a present value basis. This still leaves considerable scope for spending level differences between countries at any given point in time.

6. CONCLUSION

This paper explores the implications of EC exchange rate and monetary union for the conduct and transmission of fiscal policy. In particular, we investigate how the feasible mix of government expenditure and financing arrangements may change in the new institutional setting of a monetary union, and also how the incentives facing policy makers in their spending and financing decisions may be affected by institutional monetary arrangements. The objective is to provide some insight into the extent to which fiscal policy actions are constrained in a monetary union, and whether the associated constraints on monetary policies provide an incentive for countries to follow more or less divergent fiscal stances.

In this context, we employ a two-country, two-period framework which highlights the role of intertemporal budget constraints and maximizing private and public sector behavior. We preclude the possibility of default and focus on the implications for public sector behavior of commitments to fixed exchange rates and common money growth policies.

We first assume government authorities take as binding the nominal exchange rate and that their feasible mix of policies must be consistent with this commitment by maintaining stability in the price level. We show that a range of feasible monetary and fiscal mixes, and financing patterns, are consistent with this constraint, although it is significantly more binding than with a flexible exchange rate regime.

Second, we impose conditions consistent with tight coordination of monetary growth policies. In this case, the options facing the government are severely reduced: fiscal policy must now be set to fulfill the budget constraint with limited monetary finance as well as to maintain stability in the price level. We show that, although there may be variation across countries in the feasible time pattern of fiscal spending between the present and future periods, differences in the present discounted value of fiscal spending are more tightly constrained.

Third, we look at how the constraints associated with different institutional changes affect the incentives of fiscal policy makers in an optimizing framework. We find that an incentive exists to reduce large budget deficit positions if money growth and debt monetization is reduced to a lower common level. This increases the real cost of borrowing and hence reduces the optimal expenditure level of the government, both in the present and future periods. Hence the convergence of monetary policies provides a corresponding incentive for convergence in fiscal positions.

Our analysis should shed some light on the debate in the past year over the fiscal implications of the process of monetary integration in the European Community. The concern is that large existing divergences in government budget positions and levels of outstanding debt in the EC, as well as marked differences in the extent to which seigniorage and debt monetization have been employed in financing expenditures, may conflict with the objective of coordinated monetary policy and the commitment to fixed nominal exchange rates. Our analysis suggests that governments that are sensitive to intertemporal budget constraints will naturally find the scope for independent fiscal policy reduced as monetary integration proceeds. Moreover, monetary integration should provide incentives for optimizing governments to further converge their fiscal positions.

FOOTNOTES

The views presented in this paper are those of the authors alone and do not necessarily reflect those of the Federal Reserve Bank of San Francisco, the Board of Governors of the Federal Reserve System, or the Bank for International Settlements. We would like to thank William Branson, Michele Fratianni, Linda Goldberg, Daniel Gros, Aris Protopapadakis, Niels Thygesen, Jürgen von Hagen, and Clas Wihlborg for helpful comments.

1. The Delors Committee report, released in April 1989, outlines the specific steps required to achieve the "final stage" of economic and monetary union in Europe. With respect to macroeconomic policy coordination, the final stage of economic and monetary union envisioned involves permanently fixed exchange rates and possibly, though not necessarily, a single EC currency. It also recommends the setting of a Community-wide fiscal policy position and close coordination of national budgetary policies. Specifically, the report recommends "binding rules" be adopted (i) to impose effective upper limits on budget deficits of individual member countries, (ii) to strictly limit monetary finance of budget deficits, and (iii) to limit external borrowing in non-EC member country currencies.

2. The costs associated with the unification of the eastern and western parts of Germany, of course, will modify this picture over the next several years. The rise in the German debt /GNP ratio in 1990, despite very strong output growth and following the debt ratio decline in 1989, reflects the rise in budgetary transfer to the eastern part of Germany.

3. It is also relevant to note that the intertemporal budget constraint implies $TB_1 + RTB_2 + F_0 = 0$, i.e., the discounted sum of trade balance surpluses plus initial foreign assets must equal zero. Thus a trade deficit in the first period must be followed by a surplus in the second.

4. A number of papers have modelled the circumstances under which the Ricardian non-equivalence between taxation and domestic bonds breaks down in an international setting. For example, Frenkel and Razin (1987, Ch. 11) develop a two-country version of Blanchard's (1985) uncertain-lifetime setup in which the relevant household discount rate is below that of the infinitely-lived government. Obstfeld (1989) analyzes the long-term dynamics of fiscal policy in a model with economic growth. In his paper, non-equivalence between domestic debt and taxation arises because new households are assumed to be unconnected with existing households. Since current debt holders do not value the consumption of unborn taxpayers, a fraction of public debt is perceived as net wealth by existing households. In our model, however, domestic debt has real wealth effects not because of Ricardian non-equivalence, but because the assumption that part of debt is monetized implies money is non-neutral. See Leiderman and Blejer (1988) for a survey of the modelling and testing of Ricardian equivalence.

5. The log-linear specification of lifetime utility is employed for tractibility. It implies a constant unit elasticity of substitution between consumption and money at any two points in time. The results would not be affected

by including government spending levels in the utility function as long as preferences for the privately and publicly provided goods were separable.

6. A sufficient condition for the partical derivative of the righthand side of (15) with respect to μ to be positive is $Y_1 + RY_2 - B_0 > T_1 + RT_2 + 2\theta B$.

7. A corresponding condition pertains to equilibrium in period 2. It can be shown, however, that this conditon is redundant.

8. This relation is consistent with the summing of equations (1a) and (3a) which implies $Y_1 - C_1 - G_1 + F_0 = F = TB_1$, i.e. national savings (inclusive of initial foreign asset earnings) equal the capital account deficit, which, in turn, equals the trade balance surplus.

9. An increase in current foreign fiscal expenditures has the same effect on r. An increase in second-period fiscal spending in either country has the opposite effect. Inspection of (17) indicates that the effects of exogenous supply shocks are symmetrical.

10. In our benchmark model, output levels in the two periods are assumed fixed and given by endowments. Extending the model to allow real investment provides a richer "supply side" to the model by causing output growth to become endogenous. This would focus attention on production opportunities of each economy, as government policies influence private investment decisions and hence the future capital stock and output potential. This supply mechanism generally dampens the effects of exogenous changes, such as stimulatory fiscal policy, on interest rates. In addition, it implies that the net impact of fiscal stimulus on aggregate income and consumption could be positive, as suggested by typical Keynesian models. Another possible extension to the model involves introducing non-tradable goods anf focusing attention on the intratemporal terms of trade, i.e., the real exchange rate, defined as the inverse of the relative price of non-tradable goods to tradable goods. In this case the effects of government depend on the commodity composition and time pattern of the spending. See Ch. 9 of frenkel and Razin (1987) for a detailed exposition of the effects of fiscal policy in a two-country, two-period model with tradable and non-tradable goods.

11. It can be shown that a bond-financed increase in spending is more inflationary than one that is tax financed.

12. An analogous expression is obtainable for $E_2 = P_2/P_2^*$ through use of (10), (13), and (14).

13. Note that the "indirect" effect of a lower R in response to a higher level of G_1 reinforces the "direct" effect of G_1 on P_1.

14. Strictly speaking, the assumption that second period money supply growth is fixed as a proportion of government debt implies monetary and fiscal policies are not fully independent within each country.

15. This discussion implicitly assumes that the domestic country is "dominant" in a game theory sense.

16. Throughout this section we abstract from issues of time consistency in government policies. Since by assumption all lending and borrowing is in real terms, time consistency is not generally a problem that should affect the interaction of the household sector and government sector in each country.

17. These results are equivalent to those in Proposition 2 of Tabellini (1988) and Masciandaro and Tabellini (1988). The effect of θ on G_1 presumes μ on G_1 is $Y_2 > T_2 (1+\theta)/(1-\theta)$.

18. The assumption that each government takes R as given in its optimization problem implicitly implies that it takes the actions of the other country's government to be given as well. Thus the equilibrium derived below may be interpreted as a Nash-Cournot equilibrium.

19. In our analysis we have not formally made the constraint associated with monetary coordination part of the government optimization problem. In addition, we continue to abstract from game theory interactions among the two governments.

APPENDIX

To solve for the equilibrium G_1, G_1^*, and R we arrange (25), its foreign analogue, and (26) into the following matrix expression:

$$
\begin{bmatrix}
1+D & 0 & -a_2 \\
0 & 1+D^* & -a_2^* \\
(1-\phi)(1+D^*)D & (1-\phi^*)(1+D)D^* & y_2
\end{bmatrix}
\begin{bmatrix}
G_1 \\
G_1^* \\
R
\end{bmatrix}
=
\begin{bmatrix}
a_1 \\
a_1^* \\
y_1
\end{bmatrix}
\tag{A.1}
$$

where

$$
a_1 = T_1 - B_0 + \frac{\mu-1}{2\mu-1}\left[Y_1 - T_1 + \left(B_0 + F_0\right)\right]
$$

$$
a_1^* = T_1^* - B_0^* + \frac{\mu^*-1}{2\mu^*-1}\left[Y_1^* - T_1^* + \left(B_0^* + F_0^*\right)\right]
$$

$$
a_2 = T_2 + \frac{\mu-1}{2\mu-1}\left(Y_2 - T_2\right) + \frac{\theta T_2}{(1-\theta)(2\mu-1)}
$$

$$
a_2^* = T_2^* + \frac{\mu^*-1}{2\mu^*-1}\left(Y_2^* - T_2^*\right) + \frac{\theta^* T_2^*}{(1-\theta^*)(2\mu^*-1)}
$$

$$
y_1 = \left(Y_1 + F_0\right)(1+D^*)D + \left(Y_1^* + F_0^*\right)(1+D)D^*
$$

$$
y_2 = Y_2(1+D^*) + Y_2^*(1+D)
$$

Solving

$$
\begin{bmatrix}
G_1 \\
G_1^* \\
R
\end{bmatrix}
= \frac{1}{\Delta}
\begin{bmatrix}
y_2(1+D^*)+a_2^*(1-\phi^*)(1+D)D^* & -a_2(1-\phi^*)(1+D)D^* & a_2(1+D^*) \\
-a_2^*(1-\phi)(1+D^*)D & y_2(1+D)+a_2(1-\phi)(1+D^*)D & a_2^*(1+D) \\
-(1-\phi)(1+D^*)^2D & -(1-\phi^*)(1+D)^2D^* & (1+D)(1+D^*)
\end{bmatrix}
\begin{bmatrix}
a_1 \\
a_1^* \\
y_1
\end{bmatrix}
\tag{A.2}
$$

where $\Delta = y_2(1+D)(1+D^*) + a_2(1-\phi)(1+D^*)^2D + a_2^*(1-\phi^*)(1+D)^2D^*$.

To establish specific results, we make the simplifying assumptions $a_1 = a_2 > 0$ and $a_1^* = a_2^* > 0$. These assumptions imply that in each country the profile of government resources from taxes, seigniorage, and monetization is "balanced" across time (see equation (25)). It follows from (A.2) that

$$G_1 = (y_1 + y_2)(1 + D^*)a_2/\Delta$$
$$G_1^* = (y_1 + y_2)(1 + D)a_2^*/\Delta \tag{A.3}$$
$$R = [y_1(1 + D)(1 + D^*) - a_2(1 - \phi)(1 + D^*)^2 D - a_2^*(1 - \phi^*)(1 + D)^2 D^*]/\Delta$$

To determine comparative statics results it is further assumed that a_2 and $a_2(1 - \phi)$ are positive functions of u and ϕ. Sufficient conditions are $\mu > 1$ and $Y_2 > T_2(1 + \theta)/(1 - \theta)$. Analogous assumptions are made for a_2^* and $a_2^*(1 - \phi^*)$. It is straightforward to show that G_1 is a positive function of μ and θ and a negative function of μ^* and θ^*. In addition, it can be shown that R is a negative function of μ, θ, μ^*, and θ^*.

Observe next that (A.3) implies

$$G_1 - G_1^* = (y_1 + y_2)[a_2(1 + D^*) - a_2^*(1 + D)] /\Delta \tag{A.4}$$

Expression (A.4) implies that $G_1 > G_1^*$ if and only if $a_2/a_2^* > (1 + D)/(1 + D^*)$. If $Y_2 = Y_2^*$ and $T_2 = T_2^*$ sufficient conditions for this to be true are (i) $\theta > \theta^*$, (ii) $u > u^*$ and (iii) $D^* > D$, i.e. $d^* < d$.

An expression for $G_1 + RG_2$ solely in terms of R can be obtained by substituting appropriately with (24) and (25), using the matrix notation of (A.1) above:

$$G_1 + RG_2 = a_2(1 + R)(1 + \phi D)/(1 + D) \tag{A.5}$$

where, as above, it is assumed that $a_1 = a_2$. Define $Z = G_1 + RG_2 - (G_1^* + RG_2^*)$. It can be shown that under the same conditions ensuring $G_1 > G_1^*$, $Z > 0$ as well. It can also be shown that Z falls with μ. This supports the assertion in Section V that a narrowing of money supply growth rate differences also induces the convergence of fiscal policy positions that is requisite for maintaining a fixed exchange rate.

REFERENCES

Barone, E., G. Majnoni, G. and G. Marchese (1989), "International Interest Rate Linkages and Monetary Implications in Italy," in International Interest Rate Linkages and Monetary Policy, Basle, Bank for International Settlements, March.

Blanchard, O.(1985), "Debt, Deficits, and Finite Horizons," Journal of Political Economy, April, 93, 223-247.

Commission of the European Communities (CEC) (1989), European Economy, No. 8/9, August/September, Supplement A.

Committee for the Study of Economic and Monetary Union (Delors Committee) (1989), "Report on Economic and Monetary Union in the European Community," April 12, Chairman Jacques Delors.

de Larosière, M. (1990), Speech delivered to the Belgian Royal Society for Political Economy in Brussels on December 4, 1990. Reproduced in BIS Review, No. 251 (December 1990), Basle.

Djajic, (1987), "Effects of Budgetary Policies in Open Economies: The Role of Intertemporal Consumption Substitution," Journal of International Money and Finance, 6, No. 3, 373-383.

Dornbusch, R. (1989), "Europe 1992: Macroeconomic Implications," Brookings Papers on Economic Activity, No. 2, 341-362.

Eichengreen, B. (1990), "One Money for Europe? Lessons from the U.S. Currency Union," Economic Policy, No. 10, April, 118-187.

Feenstra, R. (1986), "Functional Equivalence between Liquidity Costs and the Utility of Money," Journal of Monetary Economics, 17, 271-291.

Frankel, J., and A. MacArthur, A. (1988), "Political vs. Currency Premia in International Real Interest Differentials: A Study of Forward Rates for 24 Countries," European Economic Review, 32, No. 5, 1083-1121.

Fratianni, M., and J. von Hagen (1990), "Public Choice Aspects of European Monetary Unification," paper presented at London Monetary Conference on "Global Monetary 1992 and Beyond," London, U.K., February 22-23.

Frenkel J. A. and A. Razin (1985), "Fiscal Expenditures and International Economic Interdependence," in Willem Buiter and Richard Marston, eds., International Economic Policy Coordination, Cambridge: Cambridge University Press, 37-73.

_____ (1987), Fiscal Policies and The World Economy, Cambridge, MIT Press.

Giavazzi, F. and A. Giovannini, A. (1986), "The EMS and the Dollar," Economic Policy, No. 2, April.

Giavazzi, F. and M. Pagano (1985), "Capital Controls and the European Monetary System," in F. Giavazzi ed. Capital Controls and Exchange Legislation, Milan, Euromobiliare Occasional Papers, No. 1, June.

Glick, R. and M. Hutchison (1990), "Economic Integration and Fiscal Policy Transmission: Implications for Europe in 1992 and Beyond," Federal Reserve Bank of San Francisco Economic Review, Spring.

Greenwood, J., and K. P. Kimbrough (1985), "Capital Controls and Fiscal Policy in the World Economy," Canadian Journal of Economics, November, 18, No. 4, 743-765.

Gros, D. (1989), "Seigniorage in the EC: The Implications of the EMS and Financial Market Integration," International Monetary Fund Working Paper No. 89-7, January.

Key, S. J. (1989), "Financial Integration in the European Community," Board of Governors of the Federal Reserve System, International Finance Discussion Paper No. 349, April.

Lane, T. and L. Rojas-Suarez (1989), "Credibility, Capital Controls, and the EMS," International Monetary Fund Working Paper No, 89-9, January 26.

Leiderman, L., and M. Blejer (1988), "Modeling and Testing Ricardian Equivalence: A Survey," International Monetary Fund Staff Papers, March, 1-35.

Masciandaro, D. and G. Tabellini (1988), "Monetary Regimes and Fiscal Deficits: A Comparative Analysis," in H. Cheng, ed., Monetary Policy in Pacific Basin Countries, Kluwer,.

Obstfeld, M. (1989) "Fiscal Deficits and Relative Prices in a Growing World Economy," Journal of Monetary Economics, 23, 461-484.

Padoa-Schioppa, T. (1990), "Fiscal Prerequisites of a European Monetary Union," Paper presented at Bank of Israel Conference on "Aspects of Central Bank Policymaking," Tel Aviv, Israel, January.

Tabellini, G. (1988), "Monetary and Fiscal Policy Coordination with a High Public Debt," in F. Giavazzi and L. Sparenta, eds., High Public Debt: The Italian Experience, Cambridge University Press.

Tanzi, V., and T. Ter-Minassian (1987), T., "The European Monetary System and Fiscal Policies," in S. Cnossus, ed., <u>Tax Coordination in the European Community</u>, Kluwer.

Thygesen, N. (1989), "Fiscal Constraints and EMU," <u>The AMEX Bank Review</u>, September 12, 16, No. 7, 5-7.

von Hagen, J. (1990), "A Note on the Empirical Effectiveness of Formal Fiscal Restraints," Indiana University School of Business, mimeo, January.

Watrin, C. (1989) (Chairman of the Board of Academic Advisers to the German Federal Ministry of Economies) "A Monetary Order for the Single European Market," Bonn, 1989, English translation of quotations given in G. Baer, "The Need for Formal Fiscal Constraints in an Economic and Monetary Union," mimeo, October 19.

Financial Regulation and Monetary Arrangements after 1992
C. Wihlborg, M. Fratianni and T.D. Willett (Editors)
© 1991 Elsevier Science Publishers B.V. All rights reserved

Comment

Linda S. Goldberg

Department of Economics, New York University, 269 Mercer Street, 7th Floor, New York, N.Y. 10003, USA

This provocative paper by Reuven Glick and Michael Hutchinson contributes to the heated policy debate over what constraints on policy formation are necessitated by progress toward economic and monetary union within the European Community. As Glick and Hutchinson clearly elucidate, some policy makers argue that rules which define acceptable divergences in budgetary positions must be imposed on countries participating in the monetary union. On the other side of the debate are proponents of the view that rules on fiscal activities are unnecessary and redundant, since market pressures for fiscal convergence will be induced by the institutional shift to a monetary union.

The intent of this interesting paper by Glick and Hutchinson is to determine whether, in fact, fiscal policies will tend to converge across the European countries engaged in the monetary union. Of course, it can be argued that this is not the most pressing or relevant issue for policy-makers. However, it is not the goal of the authors to judge the relative importance of this question: since it has been posed as a policy issue, Glick and Hutchinson set up a stylized model from which some insights can be drawn.

The paper proceeds first by setting up a general framework in which governments choose monetary and fiscal positions in the absence of behavioral constraints. The resulting positions are compared with solutions generated in the presence of institutional constraints intended to roughly correspond to the increasing degree of monetary integration within the European Community.

The framework of analysis is a two period model in which two countries interact. There are households in each country assumed to behave as price takers in international goods markets and in capital markets. The output of each household in each country is assumed to be exogenously given, and households in each country consume and produce the same single good. This good is perfectly substitutable, and the price of the good equalizes across markets. In the consumption and investment choice of households, first period savings can take the form of investments in home bonds and foreign bonds, and by placing part of their unspent earnings into domestic currency. This decision is made when the household maximizes it's lifetime utility: the economic agents choose consumption and investment so as to maximize the discounted present value of consumption in each of the two periods and from real money balances retained at the end of each period.

The governments of these two countries seek to use fiscal policy to attain the goal of maximum possible spending. The resulting optimal fiscal policy is compared under different policy regimes: Glick and Hutchinson compare the constraints on monetary and fiscal policy setting under fixed nominal rates and when monetary rules are imposed.

Based on this model, the authors conclude that when exchange rates are fixed and money growth rates are constrained across countries, fiscal policies tend to converge. However, this is quite a strong policy conclusion and should be received cautiously. Below, I discuss the shortcomings of the model applied for generating these results. In order to extend the results to provide greater generality, directions for modification and further development of their framework are provided. Such extensions could widen the appeal of resulting policy conclusions.

First, the policy conclusions drawn by Glick and Hutchinson are generated in a model which incorporates a particular ideal of consumer behavior, through the utility function specification, and an unusual treatment of money balances. For example, the channel by which money enters the welfare maximizing problem faced by consumers is not realistic. The authors can justify some form of this artifice by arguing that money balances provide some liquidity services and invoking a cash in advance argument. Despite my objection to this specification, it is probably the case that this problem would not change greatly the qualitative conclusions of the paper.

Second, the authors assume that domestic households receive positive utility is they have excess money balances at the time of their death. In the European Community, at least, this is not a valid and universally accepted behavioral description. It should be eliminated from the model.

Third, Glick and Hutchinson treat domestic and foreign goods as perfect substitutes and allow goods trade across countries. In this context, a strong currency substitution argument should hold. This implies that the domestic agent should realize utility gains from holding both domestic and foreign currency, not just from holding domestic currency as specified in the model. This latter point is especially important for the question of determining optimal monetary and fiscal policies.

Without an undisputed motive for holding money balances, it is difficult to reach a clear understanding of the linkages between the monetary and budgetary policies of countries in the European Community. For instance, it is often argued that inflation tax or seignorage revenues are important sources of finance for some countries. [For example, see Dornbusch (1988) and Canzoneri and Rogers (1990).] When consumers in each country hold some of their own currency as well as the currency of their trading partner, there is an incentive for the domestic government to print excess money since it can therefore export some of the inflation tax. It is now a well-known result that equilibria are possible in which gaming countries can generate excessive inflation as they try to exploit this externality.

Another set of criticisms of the Glick and Hutchinson model concerns the specification of the government and the assumed substitutability between domestic and foreign debt. Instead of treating the government as achieving bliss purely through spending, the government might be more richly modelled: perhaps they are concerned with maximizing some combination of consumer welfare and inflation. Indeed, such a formulation can introduce a role for a policy by considering the a weighted combination of the welfare of residents in each of the two countries. Policy can be set so as to correct or counter negative externalities.

Generality of the results could also be broadened by: i) eliminating the assumption that domestic and foreign bonds are perfect substitutes, thereby providing the markets with some additional methods for disciplining habitual spenders; and ii) allowing for endogenous output in each of the countries with specific and shared shocks.

Despite these criticisms, I believe that the authors have taken a strong positive step toward addressing the question of fiscal convergence under the European Community. With some straight-forward modifications of their existing paper, they will be able to provide quite rich and extremely useful policy conclusions of general applicability.

REFERENCES

Canzoneri, M.B. and C.A. Rogers (1990), "Is the European Community an Optimal Currency Area? Optimal Taxation Versus the Cost of Multiple Currencies", American Economic Review, 10, 419.

Dornbusch, R. (1988), "The European Monetary System, the Dollar and the Yen", in F. Giavazzi, et.al. (eds.), The European Monetary System, Cambridge University Press, Cambridge.

Financial Regulation and Monetary Arrangements after 1992
C. Wihlborg, M. Fratianni and T.D. Willett (Editors)
251

Comment

Richard J. Sweeney

School of Business Administration, Georgetown University, Washington, DC 20057, USA

The theme of "Europe after 1992" looks to the future, for the rest of this century and well into the twenty-first century, but the issues the theme raises are in many ways a review of some of the key economic discussions of the past four decades.

Start with the Mundell-Fleming model of the late 1950s and early 1960s. Of course there are many problems with this model, but I want to review two of its features that are relevant today. One is that international disturbances affect domestic real output and employment and domestic disturbances spillover to affect real variables in other countries. Disturbances have real effects in the model because of price level stickiness, an assumption that is not so fashionable since the new classical revolution of the 1970s and 1980s, where total price flexibility and continuous market clearing are the base-case assumption. The new classical view has not eliminated other views, but the older fixed-price models have now been recast to have only temporary sluggishness of prices due to contracts, asymmetric information, non-neutralities and other frictions. The excellent paper by Glick and Hutchison relies on the new classical flex-price, market-clearing view for their results. I think their key results, that fixed exchange rates require more harmonization of monetary policy and fiscal policy than flexible rates, are intuitively plausible and hold in a much wider class of models. They have done a lot in the paper, but it would be good to see some indication of the robustness of their results across models, including sticky-price models. Similarly, the new classicals use either monetary surprises (in the models of the 1970s) or real business cycle supply-side shocks (in the models of the 1980s) to generate the ups and downs that characterise the real world; it would be good to have an indication that the results are robust across these modifications (in their paper for this conference, Fratianni and von Hagen consider asymmetric shocks in a monetary rational expectations model).

The second feature of the Mundell-Fleming model is its "degrees of freedom" problem, often raised by Harry Johnson. If there are two countries with only monetary policy available, and one sets its policy, fixed rates dictate the other's policy. But who gets to use up the degree of freedom, to choose the base monetary policy to which the other country must adapt? Over the longer run, we may be willing to believe that even if fiscal policy is available, the follower has to adapt its monetary policy to the leader's; this gives the leader choice of both monetary and fiscal policy. The Glick and Hutchison paper takes the base policy as given, but its choice is of great importance. Put simplistically, it appears that the Bundesbank has been the monetary policy leader under the EMS. A major issue is who will be the leader under a strengthened EMU.

There is some debate about the form of the EMU. Some argue for a common currency, others for permanently fixed exchange rates. It is not at all clear that the Bundesbank would have the same influence under a common currency as in the past; a common currency EMU may have an inflationary bias as compared to the past. Those of us who went to graduate school in the 1960s can see startling resemblances between the issues of making a permanently fixed-rate EMU work and the issues of preserving the Bretton Woods system. One of the main lessons of the collapse of Breton Woods may be that a "permanently fixed-rate system" is a contradiction in terms; fixed rates last only as long as the costs of maintaining them are not too high, and with probability one, the costs eventually become too high. Thus, adopting a common currency may give an inflationary bias, but a fixed rate system may well be only temporary.

There are good reasons for doubting the permanency of an EMU based on fixed rates. Under the criteria laid out in the optimum currency area literature of the the 1950s-1970s[1], the EC does not appear to be an optimum currency area, and this is so even when the discussion is updated to take account of theoretical developments since the mid-1970s[2]. A non-optimal currency area is innately fragile in the face of disturbances. To take one example, Sweeney (1990) argues that stock market reactions to various events in the collapse of the Soviet eastern European empire show that the EC members are differentially affected by real disturbances from that area, with Germany much more sensitive than many other EC members. No one knows what shocks will come from eastern Europe or the Soviet Union in the future. It is clear that many of these shocks will most easily be met by exchange rate changes; these pressures will work to undermine any system of fixed rates.

In the 1970s and 1980s a major theoretical, empirical and policy issue has been the Ricardian Equivalence Proposition (REP). By now it is clear that theoretical arguments can be constructed to make tax cuts either expansionary or contractionary[3]; the scientific issue is the empirical effect. To overstate, but only by a bit, there is really no scientific evidence that tax-financed deficits have a positive effect on interest rates, and there is a great deal that either there is no effect or that any effect is contractionary. The Glick and Hutchison paper argues its model in non-Ricardian, but it is wholly Ricardian. In part this disagreement is semantic. The REP says that given the level of government spending and that the spending is tax financed, the timing of the taxes is irrelevant. Glick and Hutchison make spending and monetary policy depend on debt; this violates the assumptions of the REP. Their model is not wrong and their assumptions may be very appropriate, but if one performs the REP experiment in the model (that is, without their structural assumptions about government behavior), one gets Ricardian results.

I want to discuss one issue raised by Branson (1991) and Montgomery's paper in this conference. They argue that monetary authorities in an integrated world of fixed rates can retain some real handle on the economy by operating on banks that deal at the local or regional level, rather than competing at the global level. The smaller banks attract funds from depositors that are too small to be of interest to the really big banks and lend to firms that are also too small to attract the attention of the giant banks. Certainly there are many such banks, both in the EC and the US.

Governments can try to affect regions by working on the regional banks. One way to do this is by funnelling funds to them. This is unlikely by itself to work, for these smaller banks may simply lend these funds to larger banks if the world market pays a better return than local areas. The government could try tying the funds, but we know from the example of tied foreign aid that this may not result in many more loans. The government might try lowering the regional banks' costs from the regulatory burden; this assumes that there is scope for making these costs lower. If competition across countries' governments reduces these costs to a minimum for the large global banks, there is no scope for making them lower for regional banks. I am skeptical of the cost effectiveness of pursuing such regional monetary policy.

The model that lies behind the discussion is similar to Duesenberry's discussion in the 1950s of investment. In his view, firms faced an upward sloping marginal cost of funds schedule, with debt financing more expensive than using retained earnings. Firms that could not finance all of their growth internally then faced a cost of capital equal to the rate at which they could borrow from banks. As I read his paper, this is the view in the model Montgomery uses; certainly it views banks as the marginal source of funds, and presumably the regional firms borrowing from banks have positive retained earnings. This view of banks as the marginal cost of funds is directly contrary to the pervasive view in modern finance. Financial economists view equity funds as in general more expensive than funds from debt, and retained earnings are just one form of equity. To be sure, transactions costs can make equity funds from retained earnings more attractive than equity funds raised by issuing stock; this is part of the frequent argument about dividend policy, that a firm requiring equity funds perhaps ought to be paying no dividends in order to avoid the underwriting costs of issuing shares and the brokerage costs of current stockholders buying the new shares to prevent dilution of their ownership positions. Miller and Modigliani (1958) formalized the relationship that the cost of equity capital exceeds the overall cost of capital for the debt-using firm, which exceeds the cost of debt funds. A firm that gets this relationship backwards and assumes that it can give its stockholders a lower rate of return than its bank makes a major conceptual mistake and uses too low a cost of capital; it will pay heavily for this mistake in the future. This is not to say that the firm might not prefer a bank loan to raise marginal funding. It is to say that the marginal cost of funds is not the explicit cost of the marginal loan.

FOOTNOTES

1. For the definitive survey of the older literature, see Tower and Willett (1976)

2. See Wihlborg and Willett's paper in this volume for an excellent update on this literature

3. For example, see Sweeney (1988, Ch. 9)

REFERENCES

Branson, W.H. (1991), "Financial Market Integration, Macroeconomic Policy and the EMS" in Bliss, C. and J.B. de Macedo (eds) <u>Unity with Diversity in the European Community</u>, Cambridge University Press

Duesenberry, J. (1958), <u>Business Cycles and Economic Growth</u>, New York: McGraw-Hill Book Co.

Modigliani, F. and M. H. Miller (1958), "The Cost of Capital, Corporation Finance and the Theory of Investment", <u>American Economic Review</u>, 48, June, 261-297.

Sweeney, R. J. (1988), Wealth Effects and Monetary Theory, Oxford and New York, Basil Blackwell.

_____(1990), "Outlook for European Monetary Union: The Message from Eastern Europe." Contemporary Policy Issues (forthcoming).

Tower, E. and T. D. Willett (1976), The Theory of Optimum Currency Areas and Exchange Rate Flexibility, Special Paper in International Economics, Princeton, NJ, Princeton University, Department of Economics,

Financial Regulation and Monetary Arrangements after 1992
C. Wihlborg, M. Fratianni and T.D. Willett (Editors)
© 1991 Elsevier Science Publishers B.V. All rights reserved   255

11 Policy Coordination in the EMS with Stochastic Asymmetries

Jürgen von Hagen and Michele Fratianni

Department of Business Economics and Public Policy, Graduate School of Business, Indiana University, Bloomington, IN 47405, USA

1. INTRODUCTION

When the European Monetary System (EMS) was created in 1978, it was generally met with great skepticism by economists on both sides of the Atlantic. In view of the wide inflation differentials among the member states the exchange rate mechanism of the EMS seemed to be destined to break down soon.[1] More than ten years later, the EMS has surprised its many critics by the sheer fact of having survived so long. In fact, the EMS has remained the only practicable multilateral exchange rate arrangement among industrialized countries since the breakdown of the Bretton Woods system. Today, many economists and economic policy-makers view the EMS as a successful arrangement for exchange rate management and policy coordination in Europe. This favorable assessment is clearly reflected in the recent Report of the Delors Committee, which takes the EMS as the launching pad for a future European Monetary Union.

Despite this generally positive judgement, however, there is little agreement as to what exactly the successes and achievements of the EMS are. Two views have been offered in the literature. The earlier view of the EMS interpreted the system mainly as a cooperative arrangement, in which exchange rate management serves as a surrogate for more complete monetary policy coordination. Exchange rate management helps the members to improve their policy responses to exogenous shocks. Fixing exchange rates need not be the best form of policy coordination, but has the advantage of providing easily observable policy standards and thereby mitigates the adverse incentive problems associated with international coordination. Viewed this way, the EMS is primarily a shock-absorbing device (see Melitz 1985, Laskar 1986, Canzoneri and Gray 1985, Fratianni and von Hagen 1990a).

A recent interpretation of the EMS stresses instead the disinflationary character of the system. The exchange rate mechanism allows high-inflation countries to delegate their monetary policies to low-inflation Germany and to achieve a greater degree of credibility of their own commitment to price stability. Since enhanced credibility lowers the cost of disinflation, the high-inflation countries find it in their interest to join the system and accept the discipline of the Bundesbank's monetary policy rather than pursue disinflation based on their own, autonomous monetary policies. According to this view, the EMS is primarily a disciplinary device facilitating a lower inflation trend (see Giavazzi and Giovannini 1989, Giavazzi and Pagano 1988, Fratianni and von Hagen 1989, 1990a, b, von

Hagen 1990). The two interpretations are not mutually exclusive: The credibility argument emphasizes the role of the EMS in determining trend inflation in the region, while the cooperative view stresses the importance of the system in determining the variance of money growth, output and inflation around a given trend.

Elsewhere, we have discussed the theoretical and empirical weaknesses of the credibility argument and have shown empirical evidence supporting the cooperative interpretation (Fratianni and von Hagen 1990a, b, von Hagen and Fratianni 1989). Fratianni and von Hagen (1990a) also provide statistical evidence showing that the EMS has resulted in a significant reduction of nominal and real exchange rate risk among the member economies, and has changed the covariance structure of inflation surprises between the EMS and a group of non-EMS economies, evidence which is consistent with the shock-absorber interpretation of the system. This paper goes further into this direction. We explore the shock-absorbing properties of the EMS for a group of 'representative' countries under different assumptions regarding the stochastic characteristics of their economies.

Recent literature on exchange rate management has taken three different roads. The game-theoretic literature generally derives and compares optimal central bank strategies on the basis of highly simplified open-economy models which assume that the economies participating in a coordination arrangement are perfectly symmetric (e.g. Canzoneri and Gray 1985, Canzoneri and Henderson 1988a, Laskar 1986, Melitz 1985). Policy coordination in those models is welfare-increasing because it internalizes the spill-overs of economic policies between countries. In this framework, exchange rate management is a special case of policy coordination. As noted by Fratianni and von Hagen (1990a), the justification for a fixed exchange rate arrangement such as the EMS in those models depends critically on the relative size of common and idiosyncratic shocks to the participating countries. More traditional open-economy models (e.g. Marston 1984, 1985) highlight the role of structural diversity among the members for the performance of an exchange rate arrangement, without considering, however, the formulation of optimal central bank strategies. Finally, recent empirical studies of the welfare gains from international coordination have used large-scale, multi-country econometric models to compare coordinated and non-coordinated policy regimes. The results of such exercises have disappointed many of the optimistic proponents of coordination, because the welfare gains from coordination seem to be of relatively small magnitude.[2] Yet, the complexity of these models makes it hard to see why this is so.

In this paper, we follow an alternative approach which is similar in spirit to the analysis of Basevi et al (1988). We take a small, relatively simple model of policy-making in the EMS and use numerical simulations to evaluate the consequences of stochastic asymmetries among the members for the performance of optimal central bank strategies. By focusing on a relatively simple model, we can assess more precisely the importance of different kinds of stochastic asymmetries. The simulations are helpful because the closed-form solutions of the model are too complex to provide any straightforward insights.

Our paper raises two main questions. First, how robust are the results generated by game-theoretic models when the symmetry assumption is relaxed? Second, how will the shock-absorbing qualities of the EMS change as a result of completing economic integration as envisioned by the Single Market program? The latter will cause major structural changes in these economies, as capital and labor are reallocated and competition becomes more effective in the integrated market. By designing a set of simulation exercises which mimic the expected structural changes, we intend to gain some insights into the future stability and desirability of the EMS.

The organization of the paper proceeds as follows. Section 2 formulates our model of policy-making in the EMS and characterizes the policy regimes considered within its framework. Sections 3, 4, and 5 present the simulation exercises. The main results and conclusions are summarized in Section 6.

2. A THREE-COUNTRY MODEL OF POLICY-MAKING IN THE EMS

2.1 Set-up of the Model

We base our analysis on an extended version of the open - economy rational - expectations model developed in Canzoneri and Henderson (1988a) and Fratianni and von Hagen (1990a). The model is linear in logarithms. There are three countries called Germany, Italy, and the US, indexed by i = 1, 2, and 3, respectively. Subsequently, time subscripts are suppressed wherever possible to simplify notation.

Each country produces a homogeneous output good y_i assumed to be an imperfect substitute for output produced by other countries. Production takes place according to Cobb-Douglas production functions with labor n_i as variable factors:

$$y_i = \alpha_i n_i + a_{i1}\xi_1 + a_{i2}\xi_2, \tag{1}$$

where (ξ_1, ξ_2) are serially uncorrelated, mutually independent supply shocks with zero expectation. With profit maximizing firms, these production functions imply the labor demand functions

$$w_i - P_i = \ln\alpha_i - (1 - \alpha_i)n_i + a_{i1}\xi_i + a_{i2}\xi_2, \tag{2}$$

where w_i and P_i are country i's nominal wage rate and output price, respectively. We assume that labor is immobile across countries. Current output prices, output, employment and money supplies are inobservable to all agents in the labor market, while financial asset prices, nominal interest rates and exchange rates are observable. The labor supply schedule is described by the wage-setting equations

$$w = P^e_i + \lambda_i(R_i - R^e_i), \tag{3}$$

where R_i is the nominal interest rate and the superscript 'e' denotes an expectation based on all information available at the end of the previous period. Equation (3) thus stipulates that price level expectations are updated in the current period on the basis of the unexpected innovation in the nominal interest rate. Labor supply is perfectly elastic at the contracted wage rate determined by (3).

Next, we introduce some notation necessary to derive the aggregate demand functions. Let M_i and Q_i denote country i's money supply and consumer price index, respectively. We define the real interest rate as $r_i = R_i - (P_{i,+1}^e - P_i)$. Let S_{ij} be the nominal exchange rate between the currencies of countries i and j, defined as units of currency i per unit of currency j. We define the real exchange rates in terms of CPIs, namely $q_{ij} = S_{ij} + Q_j - Q_i$, and the vector $q = (q_{12}\ q_{13}\ q_{23})'$. Let β_{ij} be the share of a country's expenditures allocated to the purchase of country j's output, such that

$$\beta_{ii} = 1 - \sum_{j \neq i} \beta_{ij}. \text{ The CPIs are defined as } Q_i = P_i + \sum_{j \neq i} \beta_{ij} q_{ij}.$$

We now have the following demand functions for country i's output

$$y_i^d = \phi_i'q - \gamma_i\, r_i + \sum_{j=1}^{3} \beta_{ji}\rho_j y_j + \sum_{j=1}^{3} c_{ij}\eta_j .$$

(4)

Here, $\rho_i < 1$ is the marginal propensity to spend out of income; ϕ_i is the vector of real exchange rate elasticities of output demand, γ_i is the interest rate elasticity of output demand and $\eta = (\eta_1\ \eta_2\ \eta_3)'$ is a vector of serially and mutually uncorrelated demand disturbances with expectation zero.

Domestic money of each country is held only by domestic residents. The money market equilibria are described by the conditions

$$M_i - P_i = y_i - y_i^e - \theta_i(R_i - R_i^e).$$

(5)

Equation (5) implies that the expected output price is proportional to the expected price level, $P_i^e = M_i^e$. Furthermore, the innovation in the nominal interest rate carries information about the unobserved price level. This justifies the specification of the wage-setting equations (3). Yet, it is only a noisy signal, because of the direct effect of the money supply and the innovation in current domestic output. In a conventional rational-expectations framework, the adjustment parameter λ_i in equation (3) would be chosen in light of this as the regression coefficient of the interest rate innovation on the current price level innovation, a choice which minimizes the variance of the expectation error. For the analysis intended in this paper, such a choice is not practical. Being a non-linear function of the remaining parameters, the regression coefficient would be different for each simulation. Its numerical calculation would therefore greatly increase the computational requirements. To avoid these additional complications, we choose a plausible value for λ_i but do not require variance minimization. Specifically, the choice $\lambda_i = \theta_i$ yields the convenient simplification for the reduced form of the employment level

$$n_i = n_{i0} + (M_i - M_i^e),$$

(6)

where n_{i0} is the normal level of employment.

Nominal interest rates in the three countries are linked through open interest parity

$$R_1 - (S_{13,+1}^e - S_{13}) = R_2 - (S_{23,+1}^e - S_{23}) = R_3.$$

(7)

The nominal exchange rates obey the triangular arbitrage conditions

$$S_{23} = S_{13} - S_{12}.$$

(8)

2.2 Stochastic Environments

The model has five aggregate shocks affecting the three economies, two on the supply side and three on the demand side. By an appropriate choice of the parameters a_{ij} and c_{ij}, we generate the stochastic asymmetries of interest for our simulations. Let $A = [a]_{ij}$ be the (3x2) matrix specifying the impact of the two supply shocks ξ_1 and ξ_2 on the production functions of the three economies (cf. equ. (1)), and let $C = [c]_{ij}$ be the (3x3) matrix specifying the impact of the three demand shocks on the output demand functions (cf. equ. (4)). For our simulations below, we design these matrices as follows:

$$A = \begin{bmatrix} 1 & 1 \\ a_{21} & 1 \\ 0 & 1 \end{bmatrix} \qquad C = \begin{bmatrix} 1 & 0 & 0 \\ c_{21} & 1 & 0 \\ c_{31} & 0 & 1 \end{bmatrix} \qquad (9)$$

The second column of matrix A specifies that ξ_2 affects all three countries in the same way. Thus, ξ_2 is a 'global supply shock' common to the three countries, the kind of shock analyzed in Canzoneri and Henderson (1988a) and Fratianni and von Hagen (1990a). A first type of stochastic asymmetry is created by the first column of this matrix. It specifies ξ_1 as a 'European' supply shock, which affects only Germany and Italy directly. The impact of this shock may be different between Germany and Italy, depending on the value of the parameter a_{21}. This set-up is useful in analyzing the effects of a European policy coordination in the presence of asymmetric supply shocks, which are likely to arise in the process of market integration.

On the demand side, we consider two types of stochastic asymmetries. The first is a 'European demand shock', which affects only Germany and Italy directly. In this scenario, $c_{31} = 0$, and the choice of c_{21} specifies how differently the shock affects Italy compared to Germany. This permits us to study the importance of relative demand shocks among the members of the exchange rate system, an aspect highlighted in Fratianni and von Hagen (1990a). The second is a 'US-German demand shock', for which we set $c_{21} = 0$, so that it has no direct effect on Italy, while the parameter c_{31} determines the how differently the shock affects the US compared to Germany.

A special case of the US-German demand shock is given by $c_{31} = -1$, that is a perfect negative correlation of its impact in Germany and the US. With such an assumption, the reduced form of the model is equivalent to the reduced form obtained with a shock to the relative demand for US and German money.3 Giavazzi and Giovannini (1987), among others, argue that a major goal for the Bundesbank in the EMS is to spread out more evenly the effects of such shifts among the participating economies. The US-German demand shock therefore permits us to study the importance such shifts for the coordination of policies in the EMS.

2.3 Model Calibration

To simulate policy scenarios we need to specify the numerical values for some of the model's basic parameters. To obtain an empirically plausible set of parameters, we take long-run elasticity estimates for Germany, Italy and the US of Taylor's (1988) multicountry model. Where necessary, first derivatives in Taylor's model are transformed into elasticities for the period 1974 - 1984 which underlies Taylor's estimation. Following common practice in the literature, we choose parameter values that make the two European economies symmetric. For our purpose, the most important aspect of these estimates is that differences in parameter values across the three countries determine the extent to which individual shocks affect differently the economies and generate different responses in prices, interest rates and exchange rates. With the emphasis on structural differences, the use of long-run elasticities is justified although our model has no dynamics and is more short-run oriented than the use of long-run elasticities would suggest.

Taylor (1988) provides estimates of the income and interest elasticities of aggregate consumption and investment. To translate these parameters into the income and interest elasticities of aggregate output demand required by our model, we multiply Taylor's elasticity estimates by the average 1974 - 1984 shares of consumption and investment in national income.[4]

To derive the expenditure shares $ß_{ij}$, we first approximate $ß_{ii}$ as one minus the share of total imports in national income. Next, the share of total imports of each country is allocated between the remaining two countries of the model, using their actual average import shares over 1981 - 1987. The resulting estimates obviously overstate the importance of, say, Italy's market share in German imports. However, our procedure provides a convenient way to reconcile empirical estimates with the natural limitations of a three-country model. Finally, the real exchange rate elasticities ϕ_{ij} of output demand are approximated by the weighted sum of Taylor's estimates of the terms of trade elasticities of export and import demand, the weights being the shares of exports and imports in national income. Here, we do not obtain different estimates for intra-European and US-European exports and imports in the basic model.

Table 1
Parameter Values for the Symmetric Baseline Model

Para-meter	Germany	Italy	US	Parameter	Germany	Italy	US
α	.634	.634	.682	θ	-.0213	-.0213	.0473
ρ	.486	.486	.645	γ	-.144	-.144	-.079
$ß_{ij}$	Germany	Italy	US	δ_{ij}	Germany	Italy	US
Germany	.720	.223	.057	Germany	-	.223	.00
Italy	.223	.720	.057	Italy	-.223	-	.10
US	.057	.057	.890	US	.00	.00	-

Table 1 summarizes the parameter estimates. There are marked differences in the elasticities among the US and the two European countries. The European income elasticity of aggregate demand is lower than the US elasticity. The demand for money is considerably less interest elastic in Germany and Italy than in the US, while the opposite holds for the interest elasticity of output demand. The European economies are more open with larger import shares in total expenditure than the US. The European aggregate demand elasticity with respect to the real exchange rate is about twice as large as the US elasticity.

2.4 Monetary Policy Strategies and Regimes

The monetary authorities in each country aim at stabilizing fluctuations of employment around the natural employment level and at price stability. Their policy objectives are summarized by the preference functions

$$U_i = -\sigma(n_i - n_{i0})^2 - (Q_i - Q^e_i)^2, \tag{10}$$

which, after substituting equation (7), becomes

$$U_i = -\sigma(M_i - M^e_i)^2 - (Q_i - Q^e_i)^2. \tag{10'}$$

Central bank strategies to maximize the objective functions are defined by the choice of a policy instrument. We consider two types of strategies: a monetary control strategy, where the central bank uses its domestic money supply as policy instrument, and an exchange rate strategy, where the central bank pegs an exchange rate. With flexible exchange rates, the three central banks adhere to monetary control strategies. To model the EMS we assume that the Banca d'Italia pegs the DM/Lira exchange rate, while the Bundesbank and the Fed adopt monetary control strategies. The full solution of the model is obtained by optimizing the utility functions with respect to the relevant policy instruments and subject to the constraints of equations (1) - (9). These solutions are derived in the Appendix.

Policy regimes are defined by the rules of international policy coordination. We distinguish four different regimes. The first is the 'Nash'-regime, in which the three central banks pursue independent monetary control strategies, taking as given the policies in other countries. Our Nash regime is therefore a flexible exchange rate regime.

Trade and capital flows among the three countries create international economic interdependencies which imply that monetary policy in one country has spill-over effects on output and inflation in the other two countries. For example, an unexpected monetary expansion in Germany, while raising German employment and inflation, causes a depreciation of the Mark and reduces inflation in the other two countries. Policy-makers under the Nash regime do not take into account these spill-overs. The Nash regime therefore yields an inefficient equilibrium. Policy coordination can improve on the Nash outcome by internalizing the spill-overs. Our analysis limits policy coordination to coordination between the two European countries. Since each European country can always attain at least the utility level associated with the Nash regime, the Nash equilibrium becomes the reference point to evaluate policy coordination between the two European countries.

We consider three forms of policy coordination. Under the 'cooperative regime', the Bundesbank and the Banca d'Italia jointly maximize the aggregate preference function $U_E = U_1 + U_2$. Under this regime, the spill-over between the two European countries is fully recognized. With the money supplies used as policy instruments, exchange rates are flexible in the cooperative regime.

The main problem with the cooperative regime is that simple agreements to cooperate are often not incentive compatible. As discussed in more detail in Canzoneri and Gray (1985), Canzoneri and Henderson (1988a) and Fratianni and von Hagen (1990a), once a coordinated policy has been agreed upon, each country has an incentive to 'cheat', i.e. to deviate tacitly from it, given that the other country sticks to the agreement. Given the complexity of national policy processes and the definition of policy variables such as 'money', efficient international monitoring of monetary policies is impossible, and cheating is therefore relatively easy (Canzoneri and Gray 1985). In the absence of enforceable international policy rules, the cooperative regime therefore is not likely to be sustainable.

In contrast, a fixed exchange rate arrangement provides a policy standard which is easy to monitor, so that tacit cheating is impossible. The essence of the cooperative interpretation of the EMS is that pegging the exchange rate specifies a simple but sustainable coordination rule, which may allow the members to reap some of the benefits from cooperation. We consider two EMS regimes, an 'asymmetric' and a 'symmetric' EMS. In the former, the Banca d'Italia fixes the DM/Lira rate, while the Bundesbank unilaterally maximizes her preference function without regard to the effects of her policy on the EMS partner. The asymmetric EMS thus imbeds the popular notion of a hegemonic Bundesbank in the EMS. In the 'symmetric EMS', Italy again pegs the DM/Lira rate, but the German money growth rate is set taking into account its spill-over effects on the Italian policy targets.

3. POLICY SIMULATIONS FOR THE EMS

3.1 The Baseline Case
Our first set of simulations takes the most simplified version of the model to evaluate the performance of the policy regimes in the presence of various exogenous shocks. We recall that the two European countries are structurally perfectly symmetric. The degree of monetary policy spill-over can be described by the ratio of country i's CPI multipliers of country j's and country i's money supplies, $(dQ_i/dM_j)/(dQ_i/dM_i)$. We call this the monetary spill-over index between country j and i. The index is -0.62 between the two European countries, -0.26 between the US and Europe, and -0.18 between Europe and the US. The baseline parameterization has the plausible characteristic that cross-country effects are more important in Europe than between Europe and the US.

3.2 Policy Responses to Supply and Demand Shocks
Table 2 reports the differences between Germany's and Italy's best policy responses under the Nash regime and the other three regimes together with the relative welfare improvements over the Nash outcomes for four different types of shocks. The upper panel has the responses to a negative world supply shock affecting all three countries simultaneously and equally. As in the two-country model of Canzoneri and Henderson (1988a), the Nash policies are 'too restrictive'. Coordination leads to less contractionary policies in the three alternative regimes. The cooperative regime and the asymmetric EMS regimes yield the same policy responses and relative improvements for both countries. The symmetry of the model implies that the two regimes are identical for this type of shock (see Fratianni and von Hagen 1990a). In contrast, the symmetric EMS yields an improvement over the Nash outcome, but is a smaller one than the other two

coordination schemes. This result carries an important message for the design of the rules of decision-making in the EMS. By choosing the German money growth rate so as to incorporate the spill-over effects on Italy's CPI may worsen the outcome for the system compared to the asymmetric case. That is, the assumed hegemony of the Bundesbank may benefit all participants.

The second panel of Table 2 adds a 'European' supply shock $\xi_1 = -1$ to the previous situation and compares the outcomes for three different values of the impact parameter a_{21}. If the shock affects both European countries symmetrically ($a_{21} = 1$), the differences in the money supply changes between the Nash regime and its alternatives become larger, but the relative welfare improvements are the same as before. Things change as a_{21} begins to decline. The cooperative regime becomes more contractionary, but remains less so than the Nash regime. In contrast, the EMS regimes become even more contractionary than the Nash policies with $a_{21} = -1$. At the same time, the stochastic asymmetry results in remarkable changes of the distribution of the welfare gains from coordination.

With $a_{21} = -1$, the cooperative regime is worse than Nash for Germany, and hence unacceptable. Furthermore, the fixed exchange rate regimes become unfavorable for Germany and Italy, when $a_{21} = -1$.

Similar findings emerge from the third panel. Here we add a 'European' demand shock, $\eta_1 = 1$, to the world supply shock and compare the outcomes for three different values of c_{21}. Again, the relative welfare improvements are the same as in the upper panel if the shock affects the two European countries equally ($c_{21} = 1$), although the difference between the coordinated and the Nash policy responses is smaller. As the impact of the shock on Italy declines, the cooperative policies become more uneven and the EMS policies more restrictive than the Nash policies. Coordination in all three regimes is unfavorable for Germany, while Italy continues to gain from full cooperation, but looses under the symmetric EMS; the asymmetric EMS is favorable for Italy if $c_{21} = .5$ and unfavorable if $c_{21} = -1$.

The final panel considers a US-German demand shock, $\eta_1 = 1$ combined with a non-zero value of c_{31}. Again, the distribution of the gains from full cooperation shifts in favor of Italy. However, the fixed exchange rate arrangements perform differently than before. With a positive effect of the shock on the US the symmetric and the asymmetric EMS yield worse outcomes than the Nash solutions for Germany and Italy. But if the shock affects the US in the opposite direction, Germany gains in both fixed exchange rate systems. This is consistent with the conjecture that Germany has a preference for the EMS when there are significant shifts in the relative demand for German and US assets. However, the German interest in the EMS in this case contradicts the Italian preference for flexible exchange rates.

The baseline simulations indicate that the performance of policy coordination arrangements depends crucially on the degree of stochastic asymmetries between the participating economies, a result which confirms and generalizes a characteristic of our earlier two-country model (Fratianni and von Hagen 1990a). An arrangement like the EMS, or even the cooperative regime, which promises welfare gains in a perfectly symmetric world, may leave one or all members worse off in the presence of asymmetries.

Table 2
Baseline Simulations

	Cooperative Regime	Asymmetric EMS	Symmetric EMS

World Supply Shock
Difference in Money Growth between Coordinated and Nash Policy

	Cooperative Regime	Asymmetric EMS	Symmetric EMS
Germany	.50	.50	.17
Italy	.50	.50	.17

Relative Welfare Improvements over Nash

	Cooperative Regime	Asymmetric EMS	Symmetric EMS
Germany	.21	.21	.11
Italy	.21	.21	.11

European Supply Shock

	$a_{21}=1$			$a_{21}=.5$			$a_{21}=-1$		
	C	A	S	C	A	S	C	A	S

Difference in Money Growth between Coordinated and Nash Policy

	C	A	S	C	A	S	C	A	S
Germany	.85	.85	.28	.78	.60	.19	.57	-.15	-.07
Italy	.85	.85	.28	.75	.32	-.09	.43	-1.30	-1.65

Relative Welfare Improvements over Nash

	C	A	S	C	A	S	C	A	S
Germany	.21	.21	.11	.18	-.02	-.10	-.89	-5.20	-5.21
Italy	.21	.21	.11	.23	.26	.07	.24	-1.06	-.95

European Demand Shock

	$c_{21}=1$			$c_{21}=.5$			$c_{21}=-1$		

Difference in Money Growth Between Coordinated and Nash Policy

	C	A	S	C	A	S	C	A	S
Germany	.43	.43	.14	.49	.19	-.02	.55	-.52	-.50
Italy	.43	.43	.14	.41	-.13	-.34	.35	-1.82	-1.80

Relative Welfare Improvements over Nash

	C	A	S	C	A	S	C	A	S
Germany	.21	.21	.11	-.02	-.46	-.58	-8.74	-3.80	-3.80
Italy	.21	.21	.11	.24	.07	-.14	.21	-1.04	-1.02

Table 2 - cont.

US - German Demand Shock

	$c_{31}=1$			$c_{31}=.5$			$c_{31}=.1$		
	C	A	S	C	A	S	C	A	S
Difference in Money Growth between Coordinated and Nash Policy									
Germany	.80	.22	-.09	.67	.09	.14	.28	.31	.27
Italy	.65	-.43	-.74	.52	-.57	-.79	.13	-.96	-.92
Relative Welfare Improvements over Nash									
Germany	-.17	.79	-.91	-.48	1.38	1.52	-2.30	.31	.29
Italy	.24	-.02	-.23	.24	-.14	-.33	.21	-1.33	-1.23

Note: C = Cooperative Regime, A = Asymmetric EMS, S = Symmetric EMS

The simulations thus corroborate an important implication of more simplified models: Policy coordination can result in worse outcomes than the Nash regime (Rogoff 1985, Canzoneri and Henderson 1988a, b, Fratianni and von Hagen 1990a). There are two reasons for this. The first was raised by Rogoff and Canzoneri and Henderson. A coalition of a subgroup of players may have a worse set of equilibrium outcomes than independent players have individually, because the agreement to coordinate policies changes incentives and constraints. The other is that the distribution of the gains from coordination becomes uneven in the presence of asymmetries, so that one country may loose from coordination where the other gains.

3.3 The Robustness of the Welfare Gains from Coordination

These results underline the critical role of asymmetries among the participants in determining the welfare benefits from policy coordination. They imply that the robustness of welfare benefits to asymmetries is an important aspect of the shock-absorbing properties of an arrangement for coordination. The less robust its benefits are, the more likely an arrangement would be welfare-reducing for at least one participant, if asymmetries are empirically significant. But if countries can withdraw freely and unilaterally from coordination arrangements, it is obvious that no arrangement can prevail that leaves one or both partners with lower welfare levels than those achievable in the Nash equilibrium. Realizing that it could fare better by pursuing an independent policy, the losing member would revert to the Nash strategy, and the best response of the other member would be to do the same. Coordination therefore breaks down if at least one of the partners suffers a welfare loss relative to the Nash equilibrium. Consequently, the robustness to asymmetries plays a critical role in determining the stability of the arrangement. We now intend to evaluate the robustness of the gains in the cooperative and the two EMS regimes.

Let the realization of the world supply shock be $\xi_2 = -1$, which guarantees benefits in the symmetric case. To measure the robustness of the welfare benefits from coordination in the presence of, say, a European supply shock given a value of the parameter a_{21}, we compute the range of values of the shock for which coordination yields a benefit to both Germany and Italy. This range can be found by simulating the model with different realizations of the shock and identifying those simulations where the German and Italian utility levels increase relative to their Nash levels. We call this range the maximum acceptable range, MAR, for the European supply shock. By definition, a realization of the shock outside its MAR means that at least one country is worse off from coordination. Coordination would therefore break down when such a realization occurs. Thus, the smaller the MAR, the less robust are the benefits from coordination, and the less stable is the international arrangement for coordination under consideration.

MARs for the European demand shock and the US-German demand shock are defined in a similar way. Given the world supply shock, the MAR for each type of shock is a function of the relevant impact parameter a_{21}, c_{21}, or c_{31}, which determines the degree of stochastic asymmetries among the European countries. Therefore, by varying the parameters a_{21}, c_{21}, and c_{31}, we can show how a changing degree of asymmetry affects the robustness of the benefits from coordination. Note that the size of the MARs and their location depend on the realization of the world supply shock. While the location seems of little interest, the MARs should therefore be interpreted as indicating the relative size of the three shocks, compared to a global shock, supported by the EMS or the cooperative regime.

To calculate the MARs in the simulations, values of a_{21}, c_{21}, and c_{31} are taken over the interval -1.0 to 1.0, proceeding in increments of 0.1. The European supply shock, the European demand shock, and the US-German demand shock each are given values between -1.5 to 1.5, also in increments of 0.1. The '(0)' columns of Tables 3A-C show the MARs from the simulations using the parameters of baseline model (Table 1). Both fixed exchange rate regimes support only very small MARs for all three types of shocks. The smallest ranges occur for the European demand and supply shocks when they affect Italy negatively. Thus, the benefits from coordination in the fixed rate arrangements disappear even in the presence of relatively small shocks if they affect the partner economies differently. The cooperative regime is more robust than the two EMS regimes, but still has quite small MARs particularly for a negative correlation of the European demand shock.

The simulations demonstrate that the case for coordination becomes increasingly weaker as the degree of stochastic asymmetries increases. Furthermore, they indicate that the potential benefits from using fixed exchange rates as a surrogate for full cooperation are sharply limited by the size of asymmetric stochastic shocks to the participating economies. The lower robustness of the benefits from coordination in the EMS is a significant price of not achieving the cooperative regime.

4. POLICY COORDINATION AND THE PROCESS OF EUROPEAN INTEGRATION

The European Community's Internal Market program aims at completing greater integration of the markets for goods and services by eliminating the remaining non-tariff barriers to trade and financial market integration through the elimination of regulations prohibiting cross-border business in financial services. In the context of our analysis, we hypothesize that the program will bring about two major structural changes in the

European economies. First, the elimination of barriers to trade will increase intra-European trade. With more trade a larger share of total expenditures will be spent on European imports by the member countries. Second, financial markets deregulation is bound to increase the interest elasticity of the demand for money as it did in the US when financial deregulation was implemented in the 1980s. We take up these issues in two steps, first considering the consequences of increasing expenditure shares on imports, demand and then the consequences of increasing interest elasticities of money demand.

Our first set of simulations proceeds as follows. Starting from the parameter values of Table 1, we let the intra-European imports expenditure shares β_{12} and β_{21} increase in three steps from .223 over .323, .423, to .523. Their increase comes at the expense of the domestic expenditure shares β_{11} and β_{22}, which decline from .72 over .62, .52, to .42. As a result of these changes, the monetary spill-over index between the European countries goes from -.62 over -.79, -.91, to -.96, while the spill-over of US monetary policy on Europe goes from -.18 over -.09, -.04, to -.02. Trade integration increases the importance of the intra-European spill-over and diminishes the importance of the US-European spill-over.

In the second set of simulations we start again from the parameter values of Table 1, and let the interest elasticities of money demand change from -.0223 over -.0323, -.0623, to -.1123. Again, the monetary spill-over index between the two European countries increases numerically, going from -.62 over -.63, -.71, to -1.16. However, the coefficient between the US and Europe moves in the same direction, from -.18 over -.19, -.21, to -.31. Financial integration, unlike trade integration, increases the importance of spill-over among the European countries and among Europe and the US.

Tables 3A-C and 4A-C report the MARs with increasing European import expenditure shares and increasing interest elasticities, respectively. The central message of the tables is that the structural changes increase the MARs for all shocks and thus increase the scope for beneficial policy coordination. There are, however, some marked differences between the two sets of simulations. Increasing the import expenditure shares raises the MARs considerably for all three regimes and all three types of shocks. As a result, the large differences between the cooperative and the fixed exchange rate regimes vanish for large import expenditure shares, particularly so if the shocks are positively correlated across countries. In contrast, the higher interest elasticity of money demand raises the MARs significantly only for the cooperative regime. The MARs for the fixed exchange rate regimes remain small even with a large interest elasticity. Consequently, this type of parameter change preserves the large difference in the robustness of the benefits from full cooperation as compared to the benefits from a fixed exchange rate regime.

Table 3A
Maximum Acceptable Ranges for European Supply Shock
Increasing Import Expenditure Shares

a_{21}	Cooperative Regime (0) (1) (2) (3)				Asymmetric EMS (0) (1) (2) (3)				Symmetric EMS (0) (1) (2) (3)			
- 1	1.0	1.0	1.0	1.4	0.2	0.3	0.6	1.4	0.1	0.4	0.7	1.3
-.9	1.1	1.0	1.0	1.5	0.2	0.4	0.7	1.4	0.1	0.4	0.7	1.3
-.8	1.2	1.1	1.1	1.7	0.2	0.5	0.8	1.5	0.2	0.4	0.9	1.4
-.7	1.3	1.1	1.1	1.7	0.2	0.5	0.9	1.6	0.2	0.5	0.9	1.5
-.6	1.3	1.3	1.3	1.9	0.2	0.5	0.9	1.6	0.2	0.6	0.9	1.5
-.5	1.4	1.3	1.4	2.0	0.3	0.6	1.0	1.9	0.2	0.6	1.0	1.7
-.4	1.5	1.4	1.5	2.1	0.3	0.6	1.1	2.1	0.3	0.6	1.1	1.9
-.3	1.8	1.6	1.6	2.3	0.3	0.6	1.2	2.3	0.3	0.7	1.3	2.0
-.2	1.9	1.8	1.9	2.3	0.3	0.7	1.4	2.4	0.3	0.7	1.4	2.3
-.1	2.2	2.0	2.1	2.5	0.4	0.9	1.6	2.4	0.3	0.9	1.5	2.4
0.0	2.3	2.2	2.4	2.5	0.5	1.0	1.9	2.4	0.4	0.9	1.8	2.4
0.1	2.3	2.3	2.3	2.4	0.5	1.1	1.9	2.5	0.4	1.0	2.1	2.4
0.2	2.3	2.3	2.3	2.5	0.6	1.3	2.0	2.5	0.5	1.2	2.1	2.5
0.3	2.4	2.3	2.4	2.5	0.6	1.7	2.0	2.5	0.6	1.4	2.2	2.5
0.4	2.4	2.4	2.4	2.6	0.9	1.9	2.1	2.6	0.7	1.9	2.2	2.6
0.5	2.5	2.4	2.5	2.6	1.2	2.0	2.1	2.6	0.8	2.1	2.3	2.6
0.6	2.6	2.5	2.5	2.6	1.7	2.1	2.2	2.7	1.1	2.2	2.4	2.6
0.7	2.6	2.6	2.6	2.7	2.0	2.2	2.3	2.7	1.6	2.3	2.5	2.7
0.8	2.7	2.7	2.7	2.8	2.1	2.3	2.5	2.8	2.2	2.4	2.6	2.8
0.9	2.8	2.8	2.8	2.8	2.4	2.5	2.6	2.8	2.5	2.6	2.7	2.8
1.0	3.0	3.0	3.0	3.0	3.0	3.0	3.0	3.0	3.0	3.0	3.0	3.0

Note: Simulation (0) is based on the baseline parameterization of Table 2. Simulations (1) through (4) increase the expenditure shares of European imports to .329 (1), .429 (2), .529 (3), and decrease the expenditure shares of domestic output correspondingly.

Table 3B
Maximum Acceptable Ranges for European Demand Shock
Increasing Import Expenditure Shares

c_{21}	Cooperative Regime (0) (1) (2) (3)				Asymmetric EMS (0) (1) (2) (3)				Symmetric EMS (0) (1) (2) (3)			
-1.0	.4	.8	1.6	2.8	.1	.6	1.0	1.7	.1	.6	2.1	2.9
-0.9	.4	.8	1.6	3.0	.1	.6	1.0	1.8	.1	.6	2.3	3.0
-0.8	.5	.8	1.8	3.0	.1	.6	1.1	1.9	.1	.7	2.3	3.0
-0.7	.6	1.0	1.9	3.0	.2	.6	1.2	2.0	.1	.7	2.4	3.0

Table 3 B cont.

c_{21}	Cooperative Regime (0) (1) (2) (3)				Asymmetric EMS (0) (1) (2) (3)				Symmetric EMS (0) (1) (2) (3)			
-0.6	.6	1.0	2.0	3.0	.2	.7	1.2	2.0	.1	.8	2.4	3.0
-0.5	.6	1.0	2.1	3.0	.2	.8	1.3	2.0	.1	.8	2.5	3.0
-0.4	.6	1.2	2.3	3.0	.2	.9	1.4	2.1	.2	.9	2.6	3.0
-0.3	.8	1.2	2.5	3.0	.2	.9	1.6	2.1	.2	1.0	2.7	3.0
-0.2	.8	1.3	2.7	3.0	.3	.9	1.7	2.1	.3	1.1	2.8	3.0
-0.1	.9	1.5	2.8	3.0	.3	1.1	1.9	2.2	.3	1.2	3.0	3.0
0.0	1.0	1.7	2.9	3.0	.3	1.2	2.1	2.3	.3	1.3	3.0	3.0
0.1	1.1	1.8	3.0	3.0	.4	1.3	2.3	2.3	.3	1.4	3.0	3.0
0.2	1.3	2.0	3.0	3.0	.5	1.5	.4	2.4	.4	1.6	3.0	3.0
0.3	1.5	2.5	3.0	3.0	.5	1.8	2.6	2.6	.5	1.9	3.0	3.0
0.4	1.7	2.7	3.0	3.0	.7	2.0	2.7	2.7	.6	2.3	3.0	3.0
0.5	2.1	2.9	3.0	3.0	.7	2.4	3.0	3.0	.7	2.8	3.0	3.0
0.6	2.6	3.0	3.0	3.0	.9	2.8	3.0	3.0	.9	3.0	3.0	3.0
0.7	2.9	3.0	3.0	3.0	1.3	3.0	3.0	3.0	1.3	3.0	3.0	3.0
0.8	3.0	3.0	3.0	3.0	2.0	3.0	3.0	3.0	2.1	3.0	3.0	3.0
0.9	3.0	3.0	3.0	3.0	3.0	3.0	3.0	3.0	2.6	3.0	3.0	3.0
1.0	3.0	3.0	3.0	3.0	3.0	3.0	3.0	3.0	3.0	3.0	3.0	3.0

Note: See Table 3A

Table 3C
Maximum Acceptable Ranges for US-German Demand Shock
Increasing Import Expenditure Shares

c_{31}	Cooperative Regime (0) (1) (2) (3)				Asymmetric EMS (0) (1) (2) (3)				Symmetric EMS (0) (1) (2) (3)			
-1	1.2	2.0	2.3	2.5	.3	1.2	2.0	2.7	.3	1.5	2.5	2.6
-.9	1.1	2.0	2.3	2.6	.3	1.2	2.6	2.7	.3	1.5	2.6	2.7
-.8	1.1	2.1	2.4	2.6	.3	1.3	2.7	2.8	.3	1.4	2.6	2.8
-.7	1.0	2.1	2.4	2.7	.3	1.2	2.8	2.9	.3	1.4	2.7	2.9
-.6	1.0	1.9	2.5	2.8	.3	1.2	2.9	3.0	.3	1.3	2.8	3.0
-.5	1.0	1.9	2.5	2.9	.3	1.2	3.0	3.0	.3	1.4	2.9	3.0
-.4	1.0	1.8	2.6	3.0	.3	1.2	3.0	3.0	.3	1.3	3.0	3.0
-.3	.9	1.8	2.7	3.0	.3	1.2	3.0	3.0	.3	1.3	3.0	3.0
-.2	1.0	1.7	2.7	3.0	.3	1.2	3.0	3.0	.3	1.3	3.0	3.0
-.1	1.0	1.7	2.8	3.0	.3	1.1	2.9	3.0	.3	1.3	3.0	3.0
0	1.0	1.7	2.9	3.0	.3	1.2	2.8	3.0	.3	1.3	3.0	3.0
.1	1.0	1.6	3.0	3.0	.3	1.2	2.7	3.0	.3	1.3	3.0	3.0
.2	1.0	1.6	3.0	3.0	.3	1.2	2.6	3.0	.3	1.3	2.9	3.0
.3	1.1	1.7	2.9	3.0	.3	1.3	2.6	3.0	.3	1.4	2.8	3.0

Table 3C cont.

c_{31}	Cooperative Regime				Asymmetric EMS				Symmetric EMS			
	(0)	(1)	(2)	(3)	(0)	(1)	(2)	(3)	(0)	(1)	(2)	(3)
.4	1.0	1.6	2.8	3.0	.3	1.3	2.5	3.0	.3	1.3	2.7	3.0
.5	1.0	1.7	2.7	3.0	.3	1.4	2.5	3.0	.3	1.3	2.6	3.0
.6	1.0	1.7	2.6	3.0	.3	1.5	2.5	3.0	.3	1.4	2.6	3.0
.7	1.0	1.7	2.6	3.0	.3	1.5	2.4	3.0	.3	1.4	2.5	3.0
.8	1.0	1.8	2.5	2.9	.3	1.6	2.3	3.0	.3	1.5	2.5	2.9
.9	1.0	1.9	2.5	2.8	.3	1.6	2.3	3.0	.3	1.5	2.4	2.8
1	1.0	2.0	2.4	2.7	.3	1.7	2.2	3.0	.3	1.5	2.4	2.7

Note: See Table 3A

Table 4A
Maximum Acceptable Ranges for European Supply Shock
Increasing Interest Elasticity of Money Demand

a_{21}	Cooperative Regime			Asymmetric EMS			Symmetric EMS		
	(1)	(2)	(3)	(1)	(2)	(3)	(1)	(2)	(3)
-1.0	1.0	1.4	2.6	.2	.3	.5	.2	.3	.5
-.9	1.2	1.6	2.7	.2	.3	.5	.2	.3	.5
-.8	1.2	1.7	2.8	.2	.3	.5	.2	.4	.5
-.7	1.3	1.8	2.8	.2	.3	.5	.2	.4	.5
-.6	1.4	1.9	2.8	.3	.4	.7	.2	.4	.6
-.5	1.5	2.1	2.8	.3	.5	.7	.3	.4	.6
-.4	1.7	2.2	2.8	.3	.5	.8	.3	.4	.8
-.3	1.8	2.4	2.7	.3	.6	.8	.3	.5	.8
-.2	2.0	2.4	2.7	.3	.6	.9	.3	.6	.9
-.1	2.3	2.4	2.7	.5	.7	1.1	.4	.6	1.0
0	2.3	2.4	2.7	.5	.7	1.2	.4	.7	1.2
.1	2.3	2.5	2.7	.6	.8	1.4	.5	.7	1.4
.2	2.4	2.5	2.7	.6	1.0	1.7	.5	.9	1.6
.3	2.4	2.5	2.7	.7	1.1	2.0	.6	1.1	2.0
.4	2.5	2.6	2.7	1.0	1.5	2.0	.8	1.3	2.0
.5	2.5	2.6	2.7	1.2	1.9	2.1	.9	1.7	2.1
.6	2.6	2.6	2.7	1.8	2.0	2.2	1.2	2.1	2.1
.7	2.6	2.7	3.0	2.0	2.1	2.2	1.8	2.2	2.2
.8	2.7	3.0	3.0	2.1	2.2	2.3	2.2	2.3	2.3
.9	3.0	3.0	3.0	2.6	2.4	3.0	2.5	2.5	3.0
1.0	3.0	3.0	3.0	3.0	3.0	3.0	3.0	3.0	3.0

Note: Interest elasticities of money demand are increased for Germany and Italy in these simulations. The elasticities are -0.0223 in the baseline simulation (see Tables 4 column 0), -.0323 in simulation (1), -0.0623 in simulation (2), and -0.1123 in simulation (3).

Table 4B
Maximum Acceptable Ranges for European Demand Shock
Increasing Interest Elasticity of Money Demand

c_{21}	Cooperative Regime			Asymmetric EMS			Symmetric EMS		
	(1)	(2)	(3)	(1)	(2)	(3)	(1)	(2)	(3)
-1.0	.4	.6	.8	.2	.2	.3	.1	.2	.3
-.9	.4	.6	1.0	.2	.2	.3	.1	.2	.3
-.8	.6	.6	1.0	.2	.2	.3	.1	.2	.3
-.7	.6	.8	1.1	.2	.2	.3	.1	.2	.3
-.6	.6	.8	1.1	.2	.3	.4	.1	.2	.3
-.5	.6	.8	1.2	.2	.3	.5	.2	.3	.5
-.4	.7	.9	1.4	.3	.3	.5	.3	.3	.5
-.3	.8	1.0	1.5	.3	.3	.5	.3	.4	.5
-.2	.8	1.1	1.6	.3	.3	.6	.3	.4	.6
-.1	1.0	1.2	1.9	.3	.5	.6	.3	.4	.6
0	1.0	1.3	2.2	.3	.5	.8	.3	.5	.7
.1	1.2	1.5	2.2	.4	.5	.9	.4	.6	.9
.2	1.3	1.7	2.3	.5	.6	1.0	.4	.6	1.0
.3	1.5	1.9	2.3	.5	.8	1.3	.5	.8	1.2
.4	1.7	2.3	2.4	.7	.9	1.6	.6	.8	1.5
.5	2.2	2.6	2.4	.8	1.1	2.0	.8	1.1	1.9
.6	2.7	2.8	2.5	1.0	1.4	2.0	.9	1.3	2.0
.7	3.0	3.0	2.5	1.4	2.0	2.1	1.4	1.9	2.1
.8	3.0	3.0	2.6	2.1	2.4	2.3	2.1	2.6	2.2
.9	3.0	3.0	3.0	3.0	3.0	2.5	2.9	3.0	2.4
1.0	3.0	3.0	3.0	3.0	3.0	3.0	3.0	3.0	3.0

Note: See Table 4A.

Table 4C
Maximum Acceptable Ranges for US-German Demand Shock
Increasing Interest Elasticities of Money Demand

c_{31}	Cooperative Regime			Asymmetric EMS			Symmetric EMS		
	(1)	(2)	(3)	(1)	(2)	(3)	(1)	(2)	(3)
-1	1.2	1.4	1.9	.4	.4	.7	.4	.5	.7
-.9	1.1	1.3	1.9	.4	.5	.7	.4	.5	.7
-.8	1.1	1.3	1.9	.4	.5	.7	.3	.5	.7
-.7	1.1	1.4	2.0	.4	.5	.7	.3	.5	.7
-.6	1.1	1.3	1.9	.3	.5	.7	.3	.5	.7
-.5	1.0	1.3	2.0	.3	.5	.7	.3	.5	.6
-.4	1.0	1.3	2.0	.3	.5	.7	.3	.5	.6
-.3	1.1	1.3	2.1	.3	.5	.8	.3	.5	.6
-.2	1.1	1.3	2.0	.3	.5	.8	.3	.5	.7
-.1	1.0	1.3	2.1	.3	.5	.8	.3	.5	.7
0	1.0	1.3	2.2	.3	.5	.8	.3	.4	.7
.1	1.0	1.3	2.2	.3	.5	.8	.3	.4	.7

Table 4C cont.

c_{31}	Cooperative Regime			Asymmetric EMS			Symmetric EMS		
	(1)	(2)	(3)	(1)	(2)	(3)	(1)	(2)	(3)
.2	1.0	1.4	2.1	.3	.5	.8	.3	.4	.7
.3	1.0	1.3	2.1	.3	.5	.7	.3	.5	.7
.4	1.1	1.3	2.1	.3	.5	.7	.3	.5	.7
.5	1.1	1.4	2.1	.3	.5	.7	.3	.5	.7
.6	1.0	1.4	2.1	.3	.5	.7	.3	.5	.7
.7	1.0	1.5	2.1	.3	.5	.8	.3	.5	.8
.8	1.1	1.5	3.0	.3	.5	.8	.3	.5	.8
.9	1.1	1.6	3.0	.3	.5	.8	.3	.5	.8
1.0	1.1	1.6	3.0	.3	.5	.8	.3	.5	.8

Note: See Table 4A

5. CONCLUSION

Our simulations underline the critical role of stochastic asymmetries in determining the benefits from international monetary policy coordination. While the exact numerical results naturally suffer from the limitations of model simulations, they suggest several generalizing conclusions.

Stochastic asymmetries among the participating countries strongly reduce the scope for international policy coordination, both in the form of full cooperation and in the form of fixed exchange rate arrangements. Welfare benefits from policy coordination derived in models exhibiting a high degree of symmetry are highly sensitive to asymmetries. This lack of robustness stems from two sources, the problem of adequately distributing the gains to make coordination acceptable for all participants, and the problem that coordination, by changing incentives and constraints for third parties, changes the attainable outcomes.

Economic integration contributes strongly and positively to the robustness of the gains from coordination. Our results indicate that trade integration contributes more to robustness than financial integration. Yet, this particular finding may be due to the rather narrow aspects of financial integration we have considered. Our results suggest that economic and financial deregulation in the course of the 'Europe 1992' program promise to strengthen monetary policy coordination in Europe, within the limits of the EMS or not.

It seems plausible to assume that asymmetric demand and supply shocks in Europe predominantly arise from independent monetary and fiscal policies in the individual countries, including government interventions in individual markets to regulate market forces or to redistribute income. If this is true, the Single Market process will have two consequences for the importance of stochastic asymmetries. In the short run, stochastic asymmetries will become more important, as idiosyncratic market interventions are removed. In the long run, stochastic asymmetries will lose importance as greater mobility of goods, services and productive factors will reduce the scope and incentives for independent market intervention. The results in this paper indicate that the robustness of monetary policy coordination in the EC will first deteriorate and then improve as a consequence. This suggests that any attempt for more complete coordination or for making the EMS a tighter constraint should be postponed until the Single Market has been achieved.

Appendix A: Model Solution

Define the parameter matrices $A = [a]_{ij}$, $B = [\beta]_{ij}$, $\Delta = [\delta]_{ij}$, $C = [c]_{ij}$, $\Lambda_\alpha = \text{diag}(\alpha_i)$, $\Lambda_\rho = \text{diag}(\rho_i)$, $\Lambda_\gamma = \text{diag}(\gamma_i)$, and $\Lambda_\theta = \text{diag}(\theta_i)$. The three aggregate demand functions can be written in matrix form as

$$Y^d = \Delta q - \Lambda_\gamma r + B'\Lambda_\rho Y + C\eta, \tag{A1}$$

where Y^d, Y, q, and r are the vectors of aggregate demand, aggregate income, and real interest rates in the three countries. Using the permutation matrices

$$F = \begin{bmatrix} 1 & 0 & 0 \\ 0 & 1 & 0 \\ -1 & 1 & 0 \end{bmatrix} \quad G = \begin{bmatrix} 1 & -1 & 0 \\ 1 & 0 & -1 \\ 0 & 1 & -1 \end{bmatrix} \quad H_0 = \begin{bmatrix} 1 & 0 & -1 \\ 0 & 1 & -1 \\ 0 & 0 & 0 \end{bmatrix} \quad H_1 = \begin{bmatrix} 0 & 1 & 0 \\ -1 & 1 & 0 \\ 0 & 0 & 0 \end{bmatrix}$$

the triangular arbitrage condition and open interest parity are $S = SF$, $H_0 R = H_1(S^e_{+1} - S)$, and the real exchange rates are $q = S - GP$. With these definitions, the three output market equilibria are

$$[I - B'\Lambda_\rho]Y = \Delta F S - (\Delta FG + \Lambda_\gamma(I + \Lambda_\theta^{-1}))P + \Lambda_\gamma\Lambda_\theta^{-1}M + C\eta$$
$$= [I - B'\Lambda_\rho][Y_0 + \Lambda_\alpha(M - M^e) + A\xi], \tag{A2}$$

where M is the vector of money supplies and P the vector of output prices. The matrix I is the (3x3) identity matrix. The triangular arbitrage condition and open interest parity imply that, of the three interest rates and three exchange rates, only two each are independent. We choose the two Deutsche Mark exchange rates as the independent ones and the German and US nominal interest rates as the independent interest rates. The output and money market equilibria are sufficient to determine five dependent variables, namely the three output prices P_i, and the two independent exchange rates.

Augmenting the system by the definitional equations for the CPIs, we obtain the following eight equation system:

$$\begin{bmatrix} T & 0 & -\Delta F \\ -B' & I & -B'F \\ 0 & 0 & H_1 \end{bmatrix} \begin{bmatrix} P \\ Q \\ S \end{bmatrix} = \begin{bmatrix} -(I-B'\Lambda_\rho) & (I-B'\Lambda_\rho + \Lambda_\gamma\Lambda_\theta^{-1})\Lambda_\alpha & 0 & \Lambda_\gamma \\ 0 & 0 & 0 & 0 \\ 0 & 0 & H_1 & 0 \end{bmatrix} U$$

$$+ \begin{bmatrix} \Lambda_\gamma\Lambda_\theta^{-1} - \Lambda_\alpha(I-B'\Lambda_\rho + \Lambda_\gamma\Lambda_\theta^{-1}) \\ 0 \\ H_0\Lambda_\theta^{-1}(I-\Lambda_\alpha) \end{bmatrix} M + \begin{bmatrix} -(I-B'\Lambda_\rho + \Lambda_\gamma\Lambda_\theta^{-1})A & C \\ 0 & 0 \\ 0 & 0 \end{bmatrix} \begin{bmatrix} \xi \\ \eta \end{bmatrix} \tag{A3}$$

or

$$K_0 X = K_1 U + K_2 M + K_3 \Xi \tag{A3'}$$

where $\tau = \Delta FG + \Lambda_\gamma (I + K_\theta^{-1})$, $U = (Y_0 \, M^e \, S^e_{+1} \, P^e_{+1})'$, and $\Xi = (\xi \, \eta \,)'$. The rational expectations solution for this model is

$$K_0 (X - X^e) = K_1 (M - M^e) + K_2 \, \Xi. \tag{A4}$$

This yields the reduced forms of the system

$$X = X^e + K_0^{-1}[K_1(M - M^e) + K_2\Xi]. \tag{A5}$$

Note that X^e is a vector of constants. The full solution can be found by maximizing the central bank preference functions subject to (A5).

FOOTNOTES

1. In 1978, the largest inflation differential among the EMS nations was 9.4 percent between the Italian and the German CPI inflation rate.

2. For a recent overview of the literature, see Portes (1989) and Currie, Holtham and Hughes-Hallett (1989).

3. In the present model, the reduced-form effect of stochastic shocks to the individual money demand functions is similar to the effect of aggregate demand shocks.

4. The use of national income instead of GNP as a measure of aggregate demand is justified by the fact that our model neglects capital consumption.

REFERENCES

Basevi, G., P. Kind and G. Poli (1988), "Economic Cooperation and Confrontation between Europe and the USA: A Game-Theoretic Approach to the Analysis of International Monetary and Trade Policies'" in: R.E. Baldwin, C.B. Hamilton and A. Sapir (eds.), Issues in US-EC Trade Relations. Chicago: University of Chicago Press.

Canzoneri, M.B. and J.A. Gray (1985), "Monetary Policy Games and the Consequences of Noncooperative Behavior", International Economic Review 26, 547-64

Canzoneri, M.B., J.A. Gray, and Dale W. Henderson (1988a), "Is Sovereign Policymaking Bad?" in K. Brunner and A.H. Meltzer (eds.), Stabilization Policies and Labor Markets, Carnegie Rochester Conference Series on Public Policy 28, Amsterdam: North Holland.

_____._____ (1988b), Noncooperative Monetary Policies in Interdependent Economies: Three Countries and Coalitions, mimeo.

Currie, D.S., G. Holtham and A.H. Hallett (1989), "The Theory and Practice of International Policy Coordination: Does Coordination Pay?" in R.C. Bryant, D.A. Currie, J.A. Frenkel, P.R. Masson and R. Portes (eds.), Macroeconomic Policies in an Interdependent World, Washington DC: International Monetary Fund .

Fratianni, M. and J. von Hagen (1989), "Credibility and Asymmetries in the EMS", forthcoming in P. DeGrauwe and V. Argy (eds.), Exchange Rate Policies in Industrial Countries, IMF, Washington DC.

_____._____ (1990a), "The European Monetary System Ten Years After", in A.H. Meltzer and C. Plosser (eds.), Carnegie Rochester Conference Series on Public Policies 32.

_____._____ (1990b), "German Dominance in the EMS: The Empirical Evidence", Open Economies Review 1, 67-87

Giavazzi, F. and A. Giovannini (1987), "Models of the EMS: Is Europe a Greater Deutschmark Area?" in R.C. Bryant and R. Portes (eds.) Global Macroeconomics, New York: St. Martin's Press.

_____._____ (1989), Limiting Exchange Rate Variability: The European Monetary System,

Giavazzi, F. and M. Pagano (1988), "The Advantage of Tying One's Hands", European Economic Review 32, 1055-82.

Laskar, D., (1986), "International Cooperation and Exchange Rate Stabilization", Journal of International Economics 21, 151-64

Marston, R.C., (1984), "Exchange Rate Unions as an Alternative to Flexible Rates: The Effects of Real and Monetary Disturbances", in J. F. O. Bilson and R. C. Marston (eds.), Exchange Rate Theory and Practice, Chicago: University of Chicago Press.

_____ (1985), "Financial Disturbances and the Effects of an Exchange Rate Union", in J.S. Bhandari (ed.), Exchange Rate Management under Uncertainty, Cambridge, MIT Press

Melitz, J., (1985), "The Welfare Case for the European Monetary System", Journal of International Money and Finance 4, 485-506.

Portes, R. (1989), Macroeconomic Policy Coordination and the European Monetary System. Working Paper, CEPR

Rogoff, K. (1985), "Can International Monetary Policy Cooperation be Counterproductive?" Journal of International Economics 8, 199-217.

Taylor, J.B. (1988), "The Current Account and Macroeconomic Policy: An Econometric Analysis", in A.E. Burger (ed.), The U.S. Trade Deficit: Causes, Consequences and Cures, Boston: Kluwer Academic Publishers.

von Hagen, J. (1990), Policy-delegation and Fixed Exchange Rates, Working Paper, School of Business, Indiana University.

Financial Regulation and Monetary Arrangements after 1992
C. Wihlborg, M. Fratianni and T.D. Willett (Editors)

Comment

Thorvaldur Gylfason

Department of Economics, University of Iceland, IS 101 Reykjavik, Island, and
Institute for International Economic Studies, S-106 91, Stockholm, Sweden

The intensification of monetary and financial integration in Europe as the year 1992 approaches bears unambiguous witness to the powerful appeal of international policy coordination as a potentially effective means of promoting economic efficiency and social welfare. Originating with the important contributions of Hamada (1974, 1976), the idea behind harmonizing international economic policy decisions in a cooperative game-theoretic sense is essentially to reduce friction in the policy making process and to internalize externalities through cooperation rather than competition. But just as increased cooperation in the microeconomic sphere through oligopolistic behavior and mergers tends to benefit some at the expense of others, so increased harmonization of macroeconomic policies can entail significant costs for some as well as benefits.

The European Monetary System (EMS) is a case in point. It was designed to produce two major benefits for participants. First, the EMS was initially intended as an exchange and trade stabilizing device. However, increased exchange and trade stability per se does not guarantee greater output stability. The effect depends on the source of the shock. On the one hand, increased exchange and trade stability tends to reduce fluctuations in domestic output when, for example, a Mundell-Fleming type of economy is hit by a domestic monetary shock. In this case, domestic credit fluctuations are automatically offset by foreign reserve flows, regardless of capital mobility. This, essentially, is why the EMS is sometimes described as a shock-absorbing device. On the other hand, increased exchange and trade stability may destabilize domestic output when, for example, a Mundell-Fleming type of economy is hit by a foreign demand shock. In this case, the effects of fluctuations in export earnings on domestic output tend to be amplified by induced foreign reserve flows, implying that increased stability of exchange rates and trade is achieved at the cost of greater fluctuations in domestic output.

In the second place, the EMS gradually came to be intended as a disinflationary device, stabilizing prices at the cost of greater unemployment. Since the inception of the EMS in 1979, consumer price inflation has decreased from an average annual rate of 11 percent in 1980 to 3 percent in 1989 in the EMS countries, while unemployment has increased from 5 percent to 10 percent on average. It is tempting to attribute this development at least partly to the exchange rate policy discipline imposed by the EMS (as well as to fiscal restraint in Europe), even though careful econometric studies have been inconclusive on this point to date (see De Grauwe 1989). The argument is simple and straightforward: within the EMS, exchange rate policies are jointly geared toward stable exchange rates and trade and low inflation, whereas without EMS membership, individual countries might have felt free to depreciate their currencies to strengthen their current account position at the expense of others. Sweden, for example, is not a participant in the EMS precisely because the Swedish government has wanted to reserve the right to devalue the Swedish krona unilaterally when need arose. This is undoubtedly one reason why the Swedish inflation rate has been two to three times as high as the EMS average in recent years. And this may also be one of the reasons why the registered open unemployment rate in Sweden has remained far below the EMS average (Gylfason 1990).

The paper by von Hagen and Fratianni emphasizes the shock-absorbing potential of the EMS by developing a simple three-country rational expectations open economy model, and by simulating the model in an attempt to quantify the effects of different external shocks under different forms of policy coordination, and also to quantify the sensitivity of these effects to stochastic asymmetries, with shocks having different effects on different countries.

The numerical calibration strategy adopted by the authors is well suited to the task at hand considering that their model does not easily lend itself to a full-fledged econometric investigation and that analytical solutions to the model are too complicated to lead to simple or straightforward conclusions. The numerical simulation results reported by the authors are interesting: within their rational expectations market clearing model, von Hagen and Fratianni find that stochastic and structural asymmetries generally tend to reduce the welfare gains from policy coordination. Specifically, they find that (a) stochastic asymmetries weaken the case for coordination; (b) by reducing structural asymmetries, Europe's single market after 1992 is likely to strengthen the case for coordination; and (c) side payments (representing the theoretical counterpart of international fiscal income redistribution or regional policies) can increase the robustness of the welfare benefits of policy coordination in some cases, but not always.

These results are suggestive. However, they leave open the question how the welfare effects of international policy coordination would be affected by stochastic asymmetries, and by side payments, in a more general--and, to my mind, more realistic--macroeconomic model in which employment does not depend solely on unanticipated monetary policy changes as it does in the market clearing model of von Hagen and Fratianni, but in which employment could be systematically influenced by monetary, fiscal, and structural adjustment policies in the short to medium term. By this I mean primarily a non-market clearing model of an open economy, with or without rational expectations--that is, a model which would contain the rational expectations market clearing solution as a special case, in the form of a vertical aggregate supply schedule. Viewed this way, the model presented by von Hagen and Fratianni is an interesting special case of a more general model that remains to be developed and simulated numerically by the same techniques. When that has been accomplished, I think we can expect to know much more about the potential benefits and costs of policy coordination. But von Hagen and Fratianni have shown us the way and taken an important step in that direction.

It is important, in my view, to take the next step and analyze European policy coordination within a non-market clearing framework for comparison with the rational expectations market clearing approach of von Hagen and Fratianni. The main reason for this is that labor market institutions, incentive structures, and wage formation are quite different in Europe and the United States. Partly because of the nationwide importance of labor unions in Europe (including Germany and Italy where, for instance, about one half of the labor force is unionized, compared with about one sixth in the United States), wages in Europe do not adjust solely to price expectations as assumed by von Hagen and Fratianni. On the contrary, in practice wages are to a considerable extent determined through complicated negotiations among nationwide unions and employer associations. Unsurprisingly, therefore, empirical evidence indicates that the adjustment of wages to price expectations varies considerably across countries. For example, real wages are generally more rigid in Europe than in the United States (see Branson and Rotemberg 1980 and Alogoskoufis and Manning 1988). In view of this potentially important structural asymmetry, any attempt to analyze the benefits and costs of policy coordination in Europe risks being partial and perhaps misleading if it does not take wage bargaining and its consequences into account. Even if national governments could achieve full coordination, the potential welfare gains from their cooperation might be offset by the refusal of powerful labor unions to go along. Therefore, to be wholly successful, international policy coordination perhaps should not be confined to the fiscal, monetary, and structural adjustment policies of national governments, but should be extended to incorporate the wage policies of labor unions and employer associations.

Nevertheless, by highlighting the uncertainty surrounding the benefits of international policy coordination and their distribution across countries in the presence of the stochastic asymmetries considered, the paper by von Hagen and Fratianni makes a valuable contribution to our understanding of the benefits and costs of international economic integration.

REFERENCES

Alogoskoufis, G. S., and A. Manning (1988), "On the persistence of unemployment", Economic Policy 7, October, 427-469.

Branson, W. H., and J. J. Rotemberg (1980), "International adjustment with wage rigidity", European Economic Review, vol. 13, no. 3, May, 309-332.

De Grauwe, P. (1989), The cost of disinflation and the European Monetary System, Discussion Paper No. 326, Centre for Economic Policy Research, London.

Gylfason, T. (1990), "Exchange rate policy, inflation, and unemployment: The Nordic EFTA countries", in V. Argy and P. De Grauwe (ed.), Choosing an Exchange Rate Regime: The Challenge for Smaller Industrial Countries (International Monetary Fund, Washington, D.C.), 163-192.

Hamada, K. (1974), "Alternative exchange rate systems and the interdependence of monetary policies", in R. Z. Aliber (ed.), National Monetary Policies and the International Monetary System (University of Chicago Press, Chicago and London), 13-33.

Hamada, K. (1976), "A strategic analysis of monetary interdependence", Journal of Political Economy, vol. 84, no. 4, August, 677-700.

Financial Regulation and Monetary Arrangements after 1992
C. Wihlborg, M. Fratianni and T.D. Willett (Editors)

12 Optimum Currency Areas Revisited on the Transition Path to a Currency Union

Clas Wihlborg
Department of Economics, Gothenburg School of Economics and Commercial Law,
Gothenburg University, Viktoriagatan 30, 411 25 Gothenburg, Sweden

Thomas D. Willett
Department of Economics, Claremont Graduate School and Claremont McKenna
College, Claremont, CA 91711, USA

1. INTRODUCTION

Jürg Niehans has commented to us that the label "optimum" currency area is misleading, since the literature on this subject has developed too many criteria for an optimum configuration to be determined. While misleadingly labeled we believe the approach is important in shifting the debate over fixed versus flexible exchange rates from an abstract level to systematic analysis of the conditions favoring one system over the other.

The optimum currency area approach to exchange rate analysis considers factors which may make fixed exchange rates more efficient for one country and flexible rates more efficient for another. Given the frequency with which optimum currency area theory is discussed in relation to the European Monetary System (EMS) it should be stressed that, as originally conceptualized in the literature, the adjustable peg of Bretton Woods or the Exchange Rate Mechanism (ERM) of the EMS would be classified as a category of flexible rather than fixed rates. In other words, the theory was developed to deal with the choice of permanently fixing exchange rates or moving to a single currency, not temporarily pegging rates. Though a permanently fixed rate would have to become a currency area (as we argue below), it is of relevance in the European context to consider fixed rates among countries with independent central banks as well, since during a transition period the EMS may be intended to take this form.

In the following sections we shall briefly discuss major criteria for optimum currency areas. We apply the criteria impressionistically to the EC.[1] Original contributions to the literature are reviewed in Section 2. Initially, criteria were based on explicit or implicit assumptions about the pattern of shocks and the nature of imperfections in factor and goods markets. In Section 3 the pattern of shocks is considered in more detail. Discipline and political economy arguments are reviewed in Section 4. Public finance aspects are discussed in Section 5. In Section 6 we reconsider the choice of exchange rate regime within the framework of rational expectations models with flexible prices. The informational role of the exchange rate regime is emphasized. Specifically, we argue that although flexible rates tend to be superior to pegged rates from the informational points of view, a currency unon may be superior to flexible rates. Finally, in Section 7, issues of transition to a common currency are discussed. Political economy considerations are especially important here as is the degree of financial capital mobility.

2. THE ORIGINAL OPTIMUM CURRENCY AREA CRITERIA

2.1 Factor Mobility

While it had been previously understood that there were limits to how small an economic unit could have a viable independent currency (see, for example, Friedman, 1953) the optimum currency area concept was not labelled and formalized until Robert Mundell's classic contribution in 1960. Mundell's contribution pioneered analysis of the degree of economic integration among areas as a criterion for the desirability of monetary integration, focusing primarily on the role of factor mobility.[2] In the absence of a high degree of wage and price flexibility, factor mobility in response to shifts in regional or product demand and supply is essential to avoid prolonged unemployment. Exchange rate flexibility may serve as a substitute, shifting the composition of international trade and production by influencing relative real wages and product prices. With nominal wage stickiness, factor mobility becomes a key criterion for the delineation of optimal currency areas.

In these terms, it can be strongly questioned whether the EMS meets the criterion of an optimum currency area (see Thygesen, 1987), although factor mobility may increase with moves towards the internal market of the EC. On the other hand, national impediments to factor market adjustments caused by social policy and other factors have increased over the past decade as reflected in the much higher average rates of unemployment in the 1980s as compared with the 1970s and 1960s.[3] It is by no means certain, however, that individual countries qualify as optimum currency areas on this criterion. Most countries have regional unemployment problems and substantial unemployment has persisted in spite of realignments of exchange rates on several occasions.

At the EC level, the less is the progress made in increasing wage-price flexibility and factor mobility, the greater will be the demands for financial transfers to depressed areas. As Eichengreen (1990) has recently documented, even increasing the funding for such short run fiscal redistribution among countries within the EC by several hundred percent would still leave interregional fiscal cushioning in the EC far below the levels in the United States. Major intercountry redistribution via a central EC fiscal unit is not required, however, to the extent that imbalances occur among regions and industries within each country as opposed to a situation of imbalances among countries.

2.2 Size and Economic Integration

Ronald McKinnon (1963) extended Mundell's analysis to focus in more detail on the role of openness and the usefulness of money.[4] For a small open economy where the ratio of traded to non-traded goods is high, a change in the exchange rate in response to a balance of payments shock may be expected to have a subantial impact on the domestic price level, reducing the effectiveness of devaluation as an expenditure switching device. In the extreme of an economy with all traded goods there would be no special allocation effects of exchange rate adjustments, and the price level effect of exchange rate changes would be large.

A high degree of openness would furthermore make expenditure adjustment policies under fixed rates more "effective" in the sense that with a high marginal propensity to import a smaller expenditure adjustment is required to restore external balance.

These arguments indicate that large economies with low marginal propensities to import and a large share of non-traded goods in production and consumption are well suited for flexible exchange rates. Empirical studies indicate that size and openness are correlated with exchange rate regime in the way suggested here.[5] There are counter-arguments, however. Presley and Dennis (1985) note that if one associates greater openness with higher elasticities of demand and supply for exports and imports, then increased openness increases the effectiveness of exchange rate adjustment, disregarding feedback effects on domestic wages and prices.

Kenen (1969) also suggests that large rather than small economies may be better candidates for fixed rates. He emphasizes product diversity as a criterion for fixed exchange rates. Smaller, relatively specialized economies would be subject to larger and more frequent terms of trade shocks and thus have greater need for exchange rate adjustment. If specialized regions join in a currency area they would become diversified, however, and thus be better candidates for a fixed exchange rate.[6]

3. PATTERNS OF SHOCKS AND POLICY PREFERENCES

Over time the literature on optimum currency area theory began to include analysis of stabilization policies in open economies based on Keynesian sticky price models. Jerome Stein's treatment of "The Optimum Foreign Exchange Market" (1963) was an important example. This literature focused on the role of the exchange rate regime as an automatic stabilizer in the face of different shocks. One conclusion from this literature was that neither fixed nor flexible exchange rates would be optimal. Different patterns of shocks would call for different optimal policy responses. It was easy to show that assuming a country was large enough to have a viable independent currency, then an ideally managed float would be superior to either fixed or flexible exchange rates.

The literature has grown quite complicated over time as richer patterns of shocks and assumptions about the behavior of economies were introduced and policy objectives were broadened to include concern with inflation as well as the stabilization of output and expenditure. There remains a general presumption, that despite counter examples, typically pegged rates are more attractive, ceteris paribus, for countries for whom most disturbances are internal and flexible exchange rates are more desirable for countries where disturbances more often originate abroad.[7] If all countries based their regime choice on these criteria, then choices of regime would often be incompatible.[8]

The insulation properties of flexible exchange rates tend to weaken with capital mobility. Henderson (1979) and Boyer (1982) emphasize instead the distinction between real and monetary disturbances in the balance of payments and show that if monetary disturbances are the major source of variability, then fixed exchange rates are superior in terms of output variability, while flexible rates are superior when (aggregate) real disturbances dominate as a source of variability. If shifts in the demand for money or asset preferences among currency denominations are frequent, then a monetary area based on fixed exchange rates and unsterilized intervention would reduce economic instability caused by real exchange rate changes (see, for example, Henderson, 1979, and McKinnon, 1982). Currency substitution would strengthen this argument further and in the extreme make a flexible exchange rate indeterminate.[9] In Section 5 we present counterarguments to these conclusions based on broader welfare criteria.

It must be remembered that this analysis typically assumes that disturbances are independent or reversed so that they do not give rise to cumulative balance of payments problems. The standard conclusion that fixed rates are to be preferred in the face of a domestic money shock would not hold if the shock were, for example, an increase in the rate of monetary expansion. For this case the continuation of fixed exchange rates would not normally be feasible over the longer run.

A weakness of this literature is that it rarely considers the possibility that most real shocks require relative price adjustment among industries rather than among countries or regions, and that the relative price changes vary across industries. An exchange rate adjustment between countries is in this case, at best, a second best solution, when the industry composition differs significantly among countries. We consider it an important area for further research to analyze more exactly first best, second best, etc. adjustment to different kinds of shocks.

4. THE DISCIPLINE ARGUMENT AND POLITICAL ECONOMY ANALYSIS

While the literature referred to above focuses on the distinction between a currency area and flexible rates, most political economy arguments for different exchange rate arrangements apply to the choice between fixed and flexible rates among currencies managed by different national central banks. Many articles analyze the incentive structure within the EMS (see, for example, Giavazzi, Micossi, and Miller, 1988). We return to these in more detail under the discussion of transition issues.

The traditional political economy argument applying to the choice of currency area versus flexible rates concerns coordination of monetary policy.[10] Although coordination is possible under any regime, a currency union is by definition a coordinated policy area. Benefits of coordination from lack of opportunities to devalue competitively will be obtained. However, recognizing, as Frankel (1989) does, that monetary policy is conducted by imperfect central bankers with imperfect information, lack of coordination implies also a "diversification" of policy risk for the private sector. Under flexible exchange rates we are likely to see different and imperfectly correlated inflation rates and policy induced output fluctuations. Thus, a richer menu of denominations of contracts exists under flexible rates, providing opportunities for diversification of risk, as well as competition among currencies.

An important question is whether the exchange rate system among the central banks provides incentives for cooperative behavior to lower inflation rates or whether it instead inparts an inflationary bias. One line of reasoning argues that exchange rate regimes should be designed to maximize domestic policy autonomy. Thus countries with preferences for different rates of inflation would not be good candidates to join in a currency area (see, for example, Corden, 1972).

The other view is that governments cannot be trusted to act in the public interest with respect to macroeconomic policies, perhaps in part because of political pressures from a short-sighted public, so that exchange rate systems should be chosen so as to impose discipline on domestic policy choices. This discipline view has received more careful analysis in recent years through the application of public choice analysis (see, for example, Willett, 1988a). Such analysis has emphasized the need to carefully specify concepts of policy bias and to distinguish the influence of alternative exchange rate regimes on policy makers' incentives from the constraints they face.

The discipline argument for fixed exchange rates requires an affirmative answer to all the following questions. First, are there biases in the operation of domestic policy inducing an excessive rate of inflation and/or policy instability that cannot be corrected directly?[11] If yes, will the monetary and international reserve financing and adjustment policies associated with the fixed exchange rate regime be effective in constraining such policy biases? If yes, then, third, are fixed exchange rates (as apposed to, say, a domestic money growth rule and flexible exchange rates) the best way to constrain such biased policy processes?[12] For example, in the absence of direct monetary constraints pegged exchange rates by themselves could increase the incentive to engage in anti-social macroeconomic policies (see Rogoff, 1985, and Willett and Mullen, 1982) and Section 7 below).

The main counter argument in favor of pegging within the EMS is essentially that Germany imposes a deflationary discipline on other more inflation prone countries.[13] We return to this issue in Section 7 in connection with transition issues.

5. PUBLIC FINANCE ASPECTS AND CURRENCY COMPETITION

The traditional literature on currency areas gave a good deal of attention to whether monetary union requires fiscal harmonization. Many of the implications of these interrelationships will be discussed in detail in the paper by Glick and Hutchison (see also Fratianni and von Hagen, 1990). We shall comment here only on a few aspects. We have already indicated how factor immobility may contribute to political demands for fiscal redistribution to ease adjustment burdens.

Another public finance aspect of monetary union which has received recent attention concerns the inflation tax. As noted above, a good while ago national differences in desired rates of inflation were added to the list of criteria for optimum (or reasonable) currency areas. Originally this addition was based on the idea that countries might wish to select different points on their long run inflation - unemployment trade-offs. Today, however, few believe that such trade-offs exist past the short or, at most, medium run. Thus, the traditionally formulated argument has lost its weight. It has been replaced, however, with the possibility that desires for seigniorage to help finance public expenditures may lead to different desired secular rates of inflation. Dornbusch (1988), Drazen (1989), Canzoneri and Rogers (1990) and Grilli (1989) have all focused on the loss of seigniorage as an important cost for some countries of joining a European monetary union. While for a number of the European countries such as Belgium, Germany, and the U.K. seigniorage has tended to account for less than one per cent of tax revenues, for Italy this percentage is over six, and for Greece and Portugal it is around ten per cent (see Drazen, 1989, p. 14).

Again we may look at this from different perspectives. Drawing upon the traditional optimal policy literature perspective, we could calculate the costs of the deviations from the national optimal inflation tax rates that would be required by joining a currency union. Recent analysis that includes the uncertainty costs of inflation variability in optimal tax calculations shows, however, that for most of the industrial countries the optimal inflation tax is zero, or close to it (see Banaian, McClure, and Willett, 1990). Thus, from an optimal policy perspective, lost seigniorage would typically present little if any cost to joining a European currency area. From a broader political economy perspective, however, the governments of a number of countries appear to find non trivial inflation rates to be politically, if not economically, efficient. To these governments the consequent loss of seigniorage could be quite important.

A more severe problem arises in a completely or nearly irrevocably fixed rate system with independent central banks issuing different currencies. Currency substitution may become strong in such a system, since monies issued by different central banks would be nearly perfect substitutes. As a consequence "Gresham's law" could take effect. The principle of a "bad money driving out good money" can here be interpreted to mean that an individual central bank might print money excessively, behaving as a "free rider" since the inflationary costs would be borne to a large extent by residents in other jurisdictions. A large public debt would increase a government's incentive to act as a "free rider". Aizenman (1990) discusses potential competition for seigniorage in detail. Within this volume Giovannini discusses the issue, arriving at somewhat different conclusions.

This argument speaks in favor of flexible rates when currency substitution is high unless central banks are able to coordinate fiscal and monetary policy perfectly. The traditional currency substitution literature arrives at the opposite conclusion. As noted in Section 3, a flexible exchange rate might become unstable. On the other hand, currency substitution under flexible rates implies that individuals are able to substitute for a high expected inflation currency at a relatively low cost. Essentially a currency area could be formed spontaneously from a flexible regime with the low inflation central bank becoming dominant, as emphasized by proposals for increased currency competition.[14]

6. RATIONAL EXPECTATIONS AND IMPERFECT INFORMATION

While developed in a closed economy context, rational expectations models were quickly seen by international monetary economists as having important implications for exchange rate policy. At first view the monetary policy ineffectiveness conclusions of the intitial generation of rational expectations models were seen as strengthening the case for monetary integration, because the freedom to pursue discretionary monetary policy was eliminated and with that the major objection to joining a monetary union.

However, in richer rational expectations models that pay more attention to the problem of information processing and wage and price adjustments, it is no longer true that any money growth rule is as good as another. As will be discussed below some types of monetary policy cum exchange rate arrangements may provide better information than others. Furthermore, even where continuous market clearing from wage and price flexibility eliminates unemployment, the costs of changing wages and prices may be relevant. In this section we focus on the information aspects of alternative exchange rate regimes and abstract from costs of changing wages and prices.

Within the rational expectations (RE) framework with flexible prices and wages and imperfect information, the criteria for evaluation of alternative monetary regimes shifts from the variability of output or the rate of inflation to the variability of output caused by confusion about the source of disturbances. Disturbances of different kinds are not generally directly observed but inferred from observable prices and/or quantity variables. We consider a regime more "informative" if variability caused by confusion is smaller. In the RE-literature it is generally assumed that the structure of the economy is known by agents and that expectations are formed based on this knowledge.[15] This assumption turns out to be relevant for the comparison of different exchange rate regimes. After reviewing the literature on informativeness of alternative exchange rate regimes under standard RE-assumptions, we argue that a case for a currency union can be made by relaxing the strong RE-assumptions under imperfect information while retaining the criterion that output fluctuations caused by confusion should be minimized.

Kimbrough (1983a, 1983b, and 1984) argues that a flexible exchange rate regime is more "informative" for a small country than a fixed regime because the exchange rate conveys information about real shocks. Glick and Wihlborg (1990) extend these results to large countries with independent monetary authorities. Assuming that foreign exchange reserves or the aggregate money supply are not directly observed without a considerable time lag, the information potentially conveyed by the exchange rate is lost if monetary authorities peg the exchange rate using an intervention rule incorporating unobservable variables. By releasing speedy and accurate information about monetary aggregates the informativeness of the fixed regime can be enhanced, however.[16]

It is interesting to compare the criteria for absolute and relative superiority of fixed and flexible exchange rates in the RE framework with flexible prices, and with criteria in the traditional fixed price, optimal regime models. For example, in Henderson (1979) and Boyer (1982) it is shown that when the relative variability of monetary shocks dominates the variability of real shocks, fixed exchange rates are advantageous. Furthermore, the degree of foreign exchange market intervention should increase as relative montetary variability increases.

In the RE-framework, on the other hand, the exchange rate intervention rule is irrelevant as long as it is based on observable variables (Flood and Hodrick, 1982). Intervention in response to unobserved shocks influence information available to agents, however. Kimbrough shows that when there is monetary variability along with at least one more source of variability, flexible exchange rates are always superior, thus reversing the conclusion from the Keynesian model. However, the *relative* superiority of the flexible regime decreases as the relative variability of money shocks rises (Glick and Wihlborg, 1990). Thus Henderson's and Boyer's criterion for fixed versus flexible rates holds in relative terms in the RE-model. Intuitively, if there are *only* monetary shocks, then they would not cause confusion under any regime. In this case, regime choice is irrelevant. As the relative importance of monetary variability decreases, the superiority of flexible rates increases.

The RE-models of fixed and flexible exchange rates presented in, for example, Kimbrough (1983 and 1984), Flood and Hodrick (1985) and Glick and Wihlborg (1990) rest on a number of strong assumptions. A more realistic evaluation of regimes requires analysis of the effects of relaxing these assumptions.

We focus here on two assumptions.[17] First, we discuss the possibility that monetary variability is not exogenous as the above RE-models assume. Second, we relax the assumption that expectations formation can be based on known structural parameters, including those describing policy authorities' behavior over time.

6.1 Endogenous monetary variability

We have discussed the choice of regime as a function of the variance of disturbances but, if the regime is chosen on other grounds, then the variance of monetary disturbances can be influenced by authorities' desire to achieve specific objectives. If monetary policy effectiveness is considered important, there might be an optimal degree of monetary variability. In the RE-framework of Glick and Wihlborg(1990), unanticipated monetary shocks have a larger short-term real effect as well as a greater inflationary effect under flexible rates than under fixed at given variances of shocks. Thus, a central bank's incentive to use unanticipated monetary policy depends on its preferences for inflation and output changes. If the "costs" of inflation are relatively low we expect more frequent use of monetary policy increasing monetary variability under flexible rates. In this case the correlation between exchange rate flexibility and monetary variability may be positive. Wihlborg and Willett (1990) argue, on the other hand, that the short-term inflation-output trade-off after a monetary shock on the other hand is steeper under flexible rates than under fixed. In this case monetary variability may be more "costly" under flexible rates, providing an incentive to lower the variance of monetary shocks under flexible rates.

Glick, Kretzmer, and Wihlborg (1990b) show that the correlation across countries between a measure of exchange rate flexibility and the variance of monetary shocks is negative, -.34. The rank-correlation is -.45 for 31 countries. Both figures are marginally significant. The negative correlation supports the contention that the costs in terms of increased inflation of monetary surprises are higher under flexible rates. It is also consistent with governments' choice of exchange rate flexibility based on the argument that the relative superiority of flexibility increases as (relative) monetary variability decreases.

6.2 Knowledge about structure and the formation of a currency area

Most analyses of exchange rate regimes within the RE-framework compare the effects of intervention on informativeness under the assumption that the sources of shocks remain unchanged and that agents know the structural characteristics of the economy including the time-series properties of shocks. These simplifications need not be serious for most comparisons of regimes. However, in the current discussions about forming an irrevocally fixed regime in the form of a currency area within Europe, the analysis must be modified.

The formation of a currency area with one central bank implies automatically that the number of independent sources of noise to the money supply is reduced. Similarly, the integration of money and financial markets in several countries associated with the formation of a currency union would reduce the independence of disturbances to money demand as well. The general conclusion of reduced informativeness relative to a flexible regime would still hold within the framework of the RE-models as described as long as exchange rates contain some information about real shocks.

Additional modifications of the above analysis may be necessary to describe appropriately the consequences of the formation of an expanded currency area. First, it is possible that within one currency area not only monetary disturbances but also real disturbances become less independent. Second, we did not consider the possibility that the structure of the economies and the time-series properties of disturbances are not known, and that such knowledge could be influenced by the formation of a currency union.[18]

While we do not have evidence concerning the first issue it is logical that if the formation of a currency area reduces the costs of real transactions among member states, it should serve to reduce the independence of real disturbances as well. The reduction in transactions costs may be seen as a reduction in non-tariff trade barriers among member states thereby increasing the correlation among disturbances in goods markets of member states.

The second modification of the analysis is likely to be more significant. The conclusions of the RE-models hold if rules for expectations formation have converged to equilibrium in a setting with stable economic structures and stable monetary policy rules. However, each time a monetary authority shifts from one money growth rule to another with different time-series characteristics, it would take time for agents to adjust their expectation formation and for firms to adjust their rules for price and output response to exchange rate changes. In general, it takes time to establish a new RE-equilibrium under the new set of circumstances. During a period of learning, expectations will be systematically biased and deviations from RE-output will occur (see e.g. Lewis, 1988). Under such circumstances the criteria for evaluating alternative exchange rate regimes should include welfare losses incurred during learning processes.

The point we want to make here is that with the reduction of the number of independent central banks associated with the formation of a true currency area, there are possibly fewer independent disturbances which agents must learn about in terms of time pattern and impact. If, as it seems, each independent monetary authority changes its policy rule frequently, then a currency union substantially reduces the need for learning, and for adjustment of rules for expectation formation and firms' rules for output adjustment to exchange rate changes. The number of sources of systematic forecast errors about real disturbances and errors of output adjustment that exist with independent central banks is reduced in a currency union.

To illustrate the point assume that in two countries with a flexible exchange rate the exchange rate, s, is a money market signal reflecting domestic (m), and foreign (m') unanticipated money supply changes, as well as one real disturbance, r. There is also a price level signal (x) originating in the money market of the other country. Assume that the signals take the following form:

$$s = a_1 m + a_2 m' + a_3 r \qquad (1)$$

$$x = a_4 m' + a_5 r \qquad (2)$$

Under fixed rates with independent monetary authorities there is no exchange rate signal but only one price level signal in the one money market with two money shocks:

$$x = b_1 m + b_2 m' + b_3 r \qquad (3)$$

Within a currency area with integrated financial markets there is only one money market disturbance M. Thus, the one money market signal can be written as

$$x = B_1 M + B_2 r \qquad (4)$$

Within a conventional RE-model with all parameters known the currency area and the fixed exchange rate is inferior to the flexible system in terms of informativeness, since the information obtained from (1) and (2) would in general be superior to information obtained from (4) and (3).

If structural uncertainty is considered, then agents' information extraction is conditional on an evaluation of structural parameters, a_1-a_5, b_1-b_3, and B_1-B_2. A structural shift caused, for example, by a change in monetary policy rule induces a period of learning of the parameter a_1. During this period, there is additional uncertainty about the inference of r. Thus, the variance of the forecast error of r increases relative to the situation when structural parameters are known.[19] It seems reasonable to assume that this additional forecast error is proportional to the number of uncertain structural parameters on which agents base their inference. As long as there are two independent central banks there are two potentially uncertain independent monetary policy rules reflected in uncertainty about a_1, a_2 and a_4 under flexible rates, and b_1 and b_2 under fixed rates. Within a currency union there is only one monetary policy rule causing uncertainty about B_1.

In summary, conventional RE models favor flexible exchange rates. However, applying the criterion for evaluating regimes from RE models there are potential gains from forming a currency area. The sources of these potential gains occur at the microlevel in reduced confusion about real disturbances when the number of independent monetary authorities applying uncertain policy rules decreases. This gain is additional to and potentially more important than other microeconomic benefits described in Gros and Thygesen (1990), such as the reduction in exchange rate risk and transactions costs.

7. CAPITAL MOBILITY AND THE TRANSITION TO A CURRENCY UNION

Economists have typically argued that high capital mobility may render middle-ground regimes between a common currency area and perfectly flexible exchange rates non-sustainable.[20] Goodhart (1989) argues on these grounds that the transition to a common currency area should be characterized by a rapid shift to credibly and irrevocably fixed rates. The main problem we see with such an intermediate regime is, as noted, that unless a currency area with one central bank has been created currency substitution could become substantial with associated incentives for individual countries to inflate and to finance fiscal deficits by money creation. Goodhart's proposal includes fiscal policy coordination that would help alleviate this problem. The mechanism by which coordination can be enforced is yet to be created, however.[21]

We think there is an inherent contradiction in the concept of fully credible fixed exchange rates. Some incentive to change rates in the long run will always remain, even if fixed rates may be credible in the short and the medium run. If one favors the "big-bang" approach to fixing exchange rates irrevocably then it would be necessary to go directly to currency unification.

Political constraints and caution may make such an approach infeasible. We see considerable danger, however, to the strategy of progressive hardening of the stickiness of exchange rates which appears to be advocated in the Delors report.

If a gradual approach to the transition is to be pursued, then we suggest that, contrary to the approach outlined in the Delors report, exchange rates should be allowed to float freely while mechanisms and institutions for a strictly enforced joint monetary policy are created.[22] Once the coordination mechanism is working exchange rates can be fixed. If no strictly enforceable mechanism can be found among individual central banks, then the intermediate step would be to create the rules for a common central bank, which would exchange a new currency for the members' currencies on a specific date but not at a prearranged price.

To elaborate on this suggestion it is useful to consider the role of financial capital mobility for the choice of exchange rate regime in general as well as for the transition problem in particular. Much of the early literature on currency areas and regional payments adjustment assumed that higher financial capital mobility strengthened the case for fixed exchange rates.[23] This was based on the proposition that higher capital mobility would make transitory balance of payments deficits easier to finance.

On the other hand, at least up to a point, increased international capital mobility can help flexible exchange rates work better. While some have pointed to high capital mobility as a cause of exchange rate instability, there is no unique relationship between increased capital mobility and the size of exchange rate fluctuations. The relationships will vary depending upon the nature of underlying shocks, the degree of wage and price stickiness, the initial level of capital mobility, and the behavior of speculation (see Willett and Wihlborg, 1990). While the assumption of perfect international capital mobility has become quite popular in theoretical models, most of the available empirical evidence suggests that capital mobility, while certainly important and higher than in the immediately preceding decades, is still far from perfect. Indeed, it is quite possible that insufficiencies of stabilizing speculative capital flows have made as much or more of a contribution to exchange rate instability as have an excess of overtly destabilizing speculative capital flows.[24]

While the effects of increases in international capital mobility on the relative merits of fixed versus flexible exchange rates remain unclear, increased capital mobility does have some unambiguous implications for monetary arrangements among the European countries. One is that the cost imposed on its trading partners by monetary and fiscal policy instability in a particular country are clearly increased. Thus, the case for limits on monetary and fiscal policy variability is increased, whatever the exchange rate regime. Another implication is that higher capital mobility will generally reduce the short term pressure that increased budget deficits will place on domestic interest rates (at least in non-Ricardian models) although under flexible rates the potential appreciation increases the costs imposed on the traded sector.

Does the exchange rate mechanism (ERM) within the EMS lend sufficient credibility to fixed rates for the system to serve as a suitable transition arrangement? How is credibility influenced by increased capital mobility, goods market integration, and political commitments?

One common interpretation of EMS is that Germany serves as the anti-inflation anchor and pegging to the German mark by other countries enables the latter to lower inflation expectations by acquiring some of Germany's reputation. The sustainability of EMS as a credibly fixed rate system with infrequent exchange rate changes hinges both on the willingness of Germany to serve as an anchor and the credibility of other less inflation averse countries' adherence to coordinated monetary targets.

Inflation rates in member countries of the EMS have converged to a relatively low level in the 80s and the frequency of realignments seems to have declined. There is still considerable controversy about the proposition that the ERM helped high inflation economies to lower inflation rates at less costs in terms of unemployment by fixing exchange rates to the German mark (see, for example, Collins, 1988, and Fratianni and von Hagen, 1989). Two reasons for the skepticism, summarized by Thygesen in an introductory chapter in Giavazzi, Micossi and Miller (1988) is that EMS has had periods of both diverging and converging inflation rates and that inflation rates were converging outside as well as inside the EMS during the 80s. An alternative hypothesis is that the ideological thrust in most countries during the '80s has been inflation averse, partly as a reaction to the inflationary period of the late '60s and the 70s. If this interpretation is correct, then the convergence to a low inflation rate is vulnerable, indeed, and any substanstial shock, such as an increase in oil prices, could induce a divergence among ERM-members with respect to the desirability of restrictive monetary policies.

Kenen (1989) argues that political agreements are in themselves strong enforcement mechanisms. However, de Cecco and Giovannini (1989) point out that the disciplinary effects are weakened in times of crises. Then the near term temptation may be dominant in a central bank's objective function. Carraro presents evidence in de Cecco and Giovannini (1989) that EMS-government's objectives are short term while the weights of different objectives seem similar across countries (see also Willett, 1988).

Wihlborg and Willett (1990) conclude that as long as exchange rates are not irrevocably fixed, and central bank's objectives are dominated by short-term considerations, then there is a strong temptation to "cheat" on coordination partners by expanding the money supply in a situation when, for example, unemployment is relatively high or the political incentives for lowering a particular level of unemployment are unusually high as before elections. Only when the future costs of such actions would be quite high would pegged rates be expected to have a high degree of credibility. We note that the evidence from interest differentials suggests that the credibility of the current EMS exchange rates is far from complete (see Giovannini, 1991).

According to the analysis based on the model in Wihlborg and Willett (1990) outlined in the Appendix, credibility of a fixed rate would be enhanced by higher capital mobility and, in the extreme with perfect capital mobility, there is no incentive to "cheat" under pegged rates. However, as long as exchange rates are not made irrevocably fixed, capital mobility is going to be imperfect even in the absence of exchange controls. Under these conditions, a country's joining the ERM has the effect of increasing the short term credibility of a pegged rate while realignments remain possible. In this case, Wihlborg and Willett argue that the increased short term credibility increases the incentive to "cheat" on coordinated monetary targets with the paradoxical result that the credibility of a monetary target as well as the pegged rate in the longer term may actually be reduced.

The alternative transition route considered is to allow exchange rates to float while mechanisms for coordination of monetary policy and procedures for a common central bank are worked out. The advantage of a float while coordination of monetary targets is practiced is that the output-unemployment trade-off in the short run is less favorable, because monetary shocks have an immediate impact on the price level, as well as on output.

These arguments contrast with those of, for example, Giavazzi and Pagano (1988) who argue that a central bank's adherence to a monetary rule gains credibility under a pegged regime as opposed to a float. The Wihlborg-Willett model in the Appendix differs from theirs, as well as those of Melitz (1988) and other contributions in Giavazzi, Micossi and Miller (1988), in that a richer menu of transmission mechanisms for monetary shocks on output are allowed for. Furthermore, the very short run price effect under pegged rates is zero while output increases due to higher credit availability. This mechanism contributes to making the short run inflation-unemployment trade-off flatter under pegged rates. This is consistent with Rogoff (1985) and Willett and Mullen (1982).[25] In contrast, in most of the recent economic policy models for EMS there is a fixed relation between unexpected inflation and output effects.

Another feature of Giavazzi and Pagano's model is that exchange rate realignments can occur only with a fixed interval. If this interval is long enough, negative output effects in later periods tend to discourage "cheating". Thus, as Obstfeld (1988a) points out in his comments on Giavazzi and Pagano, if realignment-periods were to be predetermined with full credibility, then the optimal regime choice in their framework would be to have an irrevocably fixed rate. As long as a currency union has not been created, there must be a positive probability of realignment and some potential gain to policymakers of making use of this probability must be considered. The time horizon of policy makers, the flexibility of timing of realignments, and expectations about realignments should all be considered when investigating central banks' benefits of the EMS and the policy incentives under the EMS.

8. CONCLUDING REMARKS

Europe as a whole does not display the degree of factor mobility and wage-price flexibility necessary for a currency union to be an optimal institutional arrangement on traditional criteria. A serious adjustment problem may arise for countries like Spain, Portugal and Greece if exchange rate adjustment is ruled out. On the other hand, it is not obvious that exchange rate adjustment is an effective mechanism for adjustment to many shocks requiring relative price changes among industries. Several major EMS-members are similar in industrial structure and, therefore, little factor mobility among these countries may be required in response to external shocks and relative cost and demand shocks among European industries. Much of the required adjustment can and needs to occur among industries within each of these countries. Nevertheless, the argument advanced in the Delors report that monetary union is an essential complement to economic union must be viewed as mainly political rhetoric although there are microeconomic benefits to be gained from the elimination of exchange risk and a reduction in the number of sources of confusion as we argued in Section 6.

A political argument in favor of a currency union can be made if the Delors report's emphasis on the creation of a truly politically independent European Central Bank could be effectively implemented.

The basis for this argument is the belief that there is a strong need for a monetary constitution to constrain the inflationary tendencies of discretionary macroeconomic policy makers. Financial innovation has undercut the appeal of simple monetary rules (Mayer and Willett, 1988) and complicated constraint systems have displayed little political appeal. Thus, central banks without strong dependence on fiscal authorities may at the current time be the best hope of those who see a need for a new monetary constitution (See Burdekin and Willett, 1990). The creation of a European Central Bank to achieve this objective is not a riskless strategy, however, since there is a danger that in the process of negotiation the independence of the new monetary authority would be substantially weakened.[26]

In order to enjoy the benefits of a currency union it must be complete in the sense that a common monetary policy is conducted. The need for coordination of fiscal policies within a genuine monetary union with one central bank is less than with fixed rates and multiple central banks. While some types of temporarily pegged exchange rates could increase the political incentives for excessive national fiscal expansion, the existence of common monetary authority, especially if it has a good deal independence, such as say the Bundesbank, would help promote fiscal discipline.[27] A remaining source of a free riding by independent fiscal authorities would be an implicit guarantee by member governments' of each others' public debt as Goodhart has pointed out.

The transition path towards a currency union is an important policy issue. The country that attempts to join a union by pegging to Germany while still having a higher inflation rate will accumulate real exchange rate appreciation until the inflation rate is down to Germany's level. At this time, the country's inflation rate must become lower than Germany's for a period in order to restore real exchange rates to a long run equilibrium. Furthermore, private or central bank net foreign asset position may have to be restored.

Thus, the transition path for high inflation countries with pegged rates is likely to be very costly, unless the peg is credible. But credibility is hard to achieve as long as the option to realign remains, and adjustment costs in terms of an overvalued currency are perceived.

At the time this paper is written increasing resistance to a fast transition has appeared in Germany and other countries although Jacques Delors has proposed to shorten stage two in the transition. At the end of this stage the European Central Bank would take over responsibility for monetary policy after a period of increasingly close coordination of policies. According to our line of argument there is considerable danger to this proposal. It provides a specific time at which a final realignment can occur. This time is sufficiently close for individual central banks to be able to defend pegged rates in the meantime and far enough away that an expansionary monetary policy may have considerable success. In our analysis, there is a considerable incentive to "cheat" on coordinated targets.

To avoid starting off the currency union with a number of countries having created monetary expansions before submitting to a common monetary authority, the final transition should either be far enough away and its specific timing sufficiently uncertain that individual central banks would have to consider the inflationary consequences of expansion or close enough that the expansion cannot have a substantial impact.

Giovannini (1990b) has suggested that the gradualism of the original Delors plan can be rescued by central banks pledging not to change parities, combined with a "threat" that if countries expand "excessively" and disruptions occur in foreign exchange markets, then the transition to a common currency would be speeded up. It is hard for us to see how this threat could be credible if the institutional framework for the common central bank has not been agreed upon. On the other hand, if it has been, then there is little reason to delay the transition in any case. Furthermore, if a final realignment may occur under an accelerated schedule there is no reason for the speculators to fear the acceleration.

Since a commitment to an irrevocably fixed rate cannot become credible unless a common monetary authority or a binding set of coordination rules exist, any transition path with pegged rates runs the risk of breaking down in recurring realignments, or, as noted, becoming costly.

While it seems unlikely to be politically acceptable our analysis suggests the seemingly paradoxical possibility that the most economically efficient transition strategy for monetary union involves the use of exchange rate flexibility while the institutional framework is worked out and monetary policy coordination is practiced.[28] A couple of core countries with similar low inflation preferences may naturally follow the Delors plan but for many countries with less tolerance for unemployment, the temptation to conduct expansionary policy at a low short run cost in terms of inflation within the EMS may be irresistable.

Appendix: A Model for Analysis of the Output Inflation Trade-Off after Monetary shocks over Different Time Horizons

The model describes formally a small country but all variables can be interpreted as values relative to those which have been targeted in coordination with other central banks.

The price level (p in log) is defined by prices of traded (s) and non-traded (p^{NT}) goods;

$$p_t = \alpha s_t + (1-\alpha)p_t^N \tag{A1}$$

where s_t is the log of the exchange rate in domestic currency units per unit of foreign currency and α is the share of traded goods for which the "law of one price" holds.

The price of non-traded goods adjusts slowly once the relative price deviates from equilibrium but it adjusts perfectly to expected changes in the equilibrium price ($\overline{p}^{NT}$ in log).

$$p_t^{NT} - p_{t-1}^{NT} = E_{(t-1}[\overline{p}_t^{NT}] - \overline{p}_{t-1}^{NT}) + \theta(\overline{p}_{t-1}^{NT} - p_{t-1}^{NT}) \tag{A2}$$

In the absence of real disturbances purchasing power parity (PPP) holds in equilibrium, where $p_t^{NT} = s_t$. Eq. 2 can then be rewritten as

$$p_t^{NT} = E_{t-1}[s_t] - (1-\theta)(s_{t-1} - p_{t-1}^{NT}) \tag{A2a}$$

The parameter θ describes the speed of adjustment of the relative price. This parameter in combination with α, the share of traded goods, captures the speed of exchange rate pass-through on prices and openness of the economy. E_{t-1} refers to expectations in period t-1.

The money market is in equilibrium in every period:

$$m_t = p_t + by_t - \beta i_t \tag{A3}$$

where m_t is the log of the money supply, y_t the log of real output and i_t the nominal interest rate.

If all variables are interpreted as deviations from long run equilibrium values, then real output in excess of long run full employment output can be written in the following way:

$$y_t = \delta_1(m_t - p_t) + \delta_2(p_t - E_{t-1}[p_t]) + \delta_3(p_t - p_{t-1}) + \delta_4(s_t - p_t^{NT}) \tag{A4}$$

The δ_1-term is a real-balance effect capturing the effect on output of increased real credit availability in a banking system practicing credit rationing to some degree.

The α_2-term is the output effect caused by confusion about monetary and real disturbances as in a Lucas supply function, while the δ_3-term captures output effects due to contractual rigidities in the labor market. A one period lag for wage adjustment is assumed. The δ_4-term finally shows the output effect of a real depreciation.

Finally, the (short-term) interest rate is specified as

$$i_t = -a(m_t - p_t) + (E_t[s_{t+1}] - s_t) \tag{A5}$$

A higher real supply of domestic money reduces the interest rate. With perfect capital mobility a = 0, and the interest rate exceeds the one in the rest of the world only if there is an expected depreciation as described by the second term in (5).

Exchange rate expectations under pegged as well as floating exchange rates are characterized by a term γ_t describing the probability that the exchange rate will be allowed to reach its non-intervention equilibrium (s_t^*)

$$(E_{t-1}\lfloor s_t\rfloor - s_{t-1}) = \gamma_t(E_{t-1}\lfloor s_t\rfloor - s_{t-1})$$

(A6)

Note that γ_t is dated and may vary over time.

We can now to solve for output and price level effects of unanticipated monetary shocks relative to a coordinated target, and the output-inflation trade-off over different time horizons and exchange rate policies. Under pegged rates, real balances are endogenous. Thus, (m_t-p_t) from (3) is inserted into the output equation (4). The price level is determined by the exogenous exchange rate, and (2a) for the price of non-traded goods. Under flexible rates, the price level p_t at an exogenous m is inserted into (4) while the exchange rate is determined by the price level from (3) and the price of non-traded goods from (2a).

Wihlborg and Willett (1990) develop expressions for output and price effects under pegged and flexible rates and discuss the role of capital mobility, goods market integration, and expectations formation regarding realignment.

REFERENCES

Aizenman, J. (1984), Competitive Externalities and the Optimal Seigniorage, Working Paper, IMF

Banaian, K., H. McClure, and T.D. Willett (1990), "Uncertainty and the Inflation Tax". Claremont Working Papers

Basevi, G. et al (1976), "Towards Economic Equilibrium and Monetary Unification in Europe" (OPTICA Report 1976). Brussels, Commission of the European Committees

Bertola, G. (1989), "Factor Mobility, Uncertainty and Exchange Rate Regimes" in De Cecco and Giovannini, (eds), 95-130

Boyer, R.S. (1978), "Optimal Foreign Exchange Market Intervention", Journal of Political Economy, Dec, 1045-55

Canzoneri, M. and C. Rogers (1990), "Is the European Community an Optimal Currency Area? Optimal Taxation Versus the Cost of Multiple Currencies", American Economic Review, 419-433

Collins, S. (1988), "Inflation and the European Monetary System" in Giavazzi, F, S. Micossi and M. Miller (eds), The European Monetary System, Cambridge University Press, 112-139

De Cecco, M. and A. Giovannini (1989), A European Central Bank? Perspectives on Monetary Unification After Ten Years of the EMS, Cambridge University Press

Dornbusch, R. (1988), "The European Monetary Systems, the Dollar and the Yen" in Giavazzi et al, 23-47
Dowd, Kl (1989), "The Case Against a European Central Bank", World Economy, Sept, 361-372

Drazen, A. (1989), "Monetary Policy, Capital Controls and Seigniorage in an Open Economy" in De Cecco and Giovannini (eds), 13-52

Edison, H. and M. Melvin (1990), "The Determinants and Implications of the Choice of An Exchange Rate System" in Haraf and Willett (eds), Monetary Policy for a Volatile Global Economy, AEI Press, Washington DC

Eichengreen, B. (1989), "Is Europe an Optimum Currency Area?", Working Paper, University of California, Berkely.

_____ (1990) "One Money for Europe? Lessons from the US Currency Union", Economic Policy, 10, 117-187

Emerson, M. (1988), What Model for Europe? Cambridge, MIT Press

_____ (1990), "The Economics of EMU" in Pöhl, K.O. et al, <u>Britain and EMU</u>, London School of Economics, 15-45

Frankel, J. (1988), "Obstacles to International Macroeconomic Policy Coordination", Princeton Studies in International Finance, 64

Fratianni, M. and J. von Hagen (1990), "Public Choice Aspects of European Monetary Unification". Presented February 1990 at the London Monetary Conference on "Global Monetary Order 1992 and Beyond"

Friedman, M. (1953), "The Case for Flexible Exchange Rates" in <u>Essays in Positive Economics</u>, Chicago, University of Chicago Press

Giavazzi, F. and A. Giovannini (1988), "The Role of the Exchange-Rate Regime in a Disinflation: Empirical Evidence on the European Monetary System" in Giavazzi, F., S. Micossi and M. Miller (eds) <u>The European Monetary System</u>, Cambridge University Press, 85-111

_____ (1989), <u>Limiting Exchange Rate Flexibility</u>, Cambridge, Mass, MIT Press

Giavazzi, F. and M. Pagano (1988), "The Advantage of Tying One's Hands: EMS Discipline and Central Bank Credibility", <u>European Economic Review</u>, June

Giavazzi, F., S. Micossi and M. Miller (1988), <u>The European Monetary System</u>, Cambridge University Press

Giovannini, A. (1990), "European Monetary Reform: Progress and Prospects", <u>Brooking Papers on Economic Activity</u>, 2, 217-291

Glick, R. and C. Wihlborg (1990), "Real Exchange Rate Effects of Monetary Shocks under Fixed and Flexible Exchange Rates", <u>Journal of International Economics</u>, May, 267-290

Glick, R., P. Kretzmer and C. Wihlborg (1990a), "Real Exchange Rate Effects of Monetary Disturbance under Different Degrees of Exchange Rate Flexibility; An Empirical Analysis", Gothenburg Studies in Financial Economics No 1990:5

_____ (1990b), "Measuring Degree of Exchange Rate Flexibility and Informativeness of Exchange Rate Regimes", Gothenburg Studies in Financial Economics, No. 1990:12

Goodhart, C. (1988), "The Foreign Exchange Market: A Random Walk with a Dragging Anchor", <u>Economica</u>, Nov.

_____ (1990), "The Delors Report: Was Lawson's Reaction Justifiable?", Special Papers No 15, Financial Markets Group, London School of Economics

Grilli, V. (1989), "Seigniorage in Europe" in De Cecco and Giovannini (eds) 53-94

Gros, D. (1989), "Paradigms for the Monetary Union of Europe", <u>Journal of Common Market Studies</u>, vol 27, no 3, March, pp 219-230

Gros, D. and N. Thygesen (1990), "The Institutional Approach to Monetary Union in Europe", <u>Economic Journal</u>, Vol. 100, Sept. 925-935

Henderson, D. W. (1979), "Financial Policies in Open Economies", <u>American Economic Review</u>, May

Kenen, P. B. (1969), "The Theory of Optimum Currency Areas: An Eclectic View" in Mundell, R.A. and A.K. Swoboda (eds) <u>Monetary Problems of the International Economy</u>, Chicago, University of Chicago Press, 41-60

_____ (1989), <u>Exchange Rates and Policy Coordination</u>, Ann Arbor, University of Michigan Press

Kimbrough, P. (1983a), "The Information Content of the Exchange Rate and the Stability of Real Output under Alternative Exchange Rate-Regimes", Journal of International Money and Finance, 27-38

_____ (1983b), "Exchange Rate Policy and Monetary Information", Journal of International Money and Finance, 333-346

_____ (1984), "Aggregate Information and the Role of Monetary Policy in an Open Economy", Journal of PoliticalEconomy, 268-285

Lawrence, R. Z. and C. L. Schultze (1987), Barriers to European Growth, A Transatlantic View, Washington, DC, The Brookings Institution

Lewis, K. (1989), "Changing Beliefs and Systematic Rational Forecast Errors with Evidence from Foreign Exchange", American Economic Review, September, 621-636

Marston, R. (1984), "Exchange Rate Unions as an Alternative to Flexible Rates" in Bilson, J.F.O and R.C. Marston (eds) Exchange Rate Theory and Practice, Chicago, University of Chicago Press

Mayer, T. and T. Willett (1988), "Evaluating Proposals for Fundamental Monetary Reform" in Willett (1988a)

McKinnon, R. I. (1963), "Optimum Currency Areas", American Economic Review, 53, September 1963a, 717-725

_____ (1982), "Currency Substitution and Instability in the World Dollar Standard", American Economic Review, June, 320-333

Melitz, J. (1988), "Monetary Discipline and Cooperation in the European Monetary System: A Synthesis" in Giavazzi, F., S. Micossi and M. Miller (eds) The European Monetary System, Cambridge University Press, 51-84

Mundell, R. A. (1961), "A Theory of Optimum Currency Areas", American Economic Review, 51, September, 657-665

Presley, J. R. and G.E.D. Dennis (1985), Currency Areas: Theory and Practice, Toronto, Macmillan of Canada

Rogoff, K. (1985), "Can International Monetary Policy Cooperation be Counterproductive?", Journal of International Economics, 18, 199-217

Stein, J. L (1963), "The Optimum Foreign Exchange Market", American Economic Review, 53, 384-402

Thygesen, N. (1987), "Is the European Economic Community an Optimum Currency Area?" in Levich, R. and A. Somariva (eds) The ECU Market, Lexington, Lexington Books, 163-185

Tower, E. and T.D. Willett (1975), "The Theory of Optimum Currency Areas and Exchange Rate Flexibility", Special Papers in International Economics, no 11. Princeton, Princeton University Press

Vaubel, R. (1990), "Currency Competition and European Monetary Integration", Economic Journal, Vol. 100, Sept., 936-945

Wihlborg, C. (1990), "Costly Information and Financial Market Efficiency", Journal of Economic Behavior and Organization, June, 347-366

Wihlborg, C. and T.D. Willett (1990), "The Instability of Half-Way Measures in the Transition to a Common Currency" in Grubel, H (ed.) EC 1992 - Perspectives from the Outside, MacMillan, London

Willett, T.D. (1984), "Macroeconomic Policy Coordination Issues under Flexible Exchange Rates", <u>ORDO</u>, Band 35, 137-149.

_____ (1988a), <u>Political Business Cycles; The Political Economy of Money, Inflation and Unemployment</u>, Durham, N C, Duke University Press.

Willett, T.D. (1988b), "National Macroeconomic Policy Preferences and International Coordination Issues" <u>Journal of Public Policy</u>, Vol. 8, July-Dec, 235-263

Willett, T.D. (1989), "A Public Choice Analysis of Strategies for Restoring International Economic Stability" in Vosgerau, ? (ed.) <u>Studies in International Economics and Institutions</u>, New Institutional Arrangements for the World Economy, Springer-Verlag Berlin Heidelberg.

Willett, T.D. et al (1987), "Currency Substitution, US Money Demand, and International Interdependence", <u>Contemporary Policy Issues</u>, V, July, 76-82

Willett, T.D. and J.E. Mullen (1982), "The Effects of Alternative International Monetary Systems on Macroeconomic Discipline and the Political Business Cycle" in Lombra, R. and W. Witte (eds) <u>Political Economy of International and Domestic Monetary Relations</u>, Ames, IA, Iowa State University Press, 143-159

Willett, T.D. and E. Tower (1970), "The Concept of Optimum Currency Areas and the Choice Between Fixed and Flexible Exchange Rates" in Bergsten, F. et al Approaches to Greater Flexibility of Exchange Rates: The Burgenstock Papers, Princeton, Princeton University Press, 507-515

_____ (1970), "Currency Areas and Exchange-Rate Flexibility", <u>Weltwirtschaftliches Archiv</u>, September, 48-65

Willett, T.D. and C. Wihlborg (1990), "International Capital Flow, the Dollar, and US Financial Policies" in W.S. Haraf and T.D. Willett (eds) <u>Monetary Policy for a Volatile Global Economy</u>, Washington DC, AEI Press

Financial Regulation and Monetary Arrangements after 1992
C. Wihlborg, M. Fratianni and T.D. Willett (Editors)

298

Comment

John Driffill

Queen Mary and Westfield College, Economics Department, University of London, Mile End Road, London E1 4NS, United Kingdom

The article by Wihlborg and Willett gives a very wide-ranging tour of the arguments surrounding the issue of whether a group of economies does or does not constitute an optimum currency area. It starts from the arguments put forward by Mundell based on the degree of factor mobility and the degree of integration, progresses through consideration of the pattern of shocks hitting these countries, and goes on to a discussion of the anti-inflationary discipline imposed by alternative currency arrangements. It takes in public finance issues, informational issues, and issues raised by the transition to a currency union. I would like first to make some remarks addressed to some of these individual aspects of the paper, and then turn to one or two overall comments.

The need for factor mobility, especially labour mobility, in a currency union, stressed by Mundell, arose out of the assumption that labour markets do not respond quickly enough, with flexible wages and prices, to maintain equilibrium employment continuously. With wage and price flexibility in the labour markets of individual countries, the need for labour mobility between countries disappears. In addition, the degree of symmetry or asymmetry of shocks hitting members of the putative currency union becomes unimportant, at least in the sense that it causes no departure from efficient resource allocations within individual countries.

A crucial element in the assessment of the effects of currency union is therefore the degree of wage and price flexibility in constituent countries. I find myself disagreeing with the authors on the interpretation of higher unemployment in the 1980's and the direction in which "national impediments to factor market adjustment" have been moving. Arguably unemployment developments in the 1980's represent supply factors rather than shortage of aggregate demand, i.e., the increase in unemployment is an increase in the equilibrium unemployment rate. The thrust of economic policy in a number of European countries, not only the United Kingdom, has been to make factor markets more flexible, by limiting the availability of unemployment and other benefits, and by weakening the position of insiders relative to outsiders in the labour market. On this view, the persistence of unemployment despite realignments reflects the persistence of differences in equilibrium unemployment rates in various parts of the EC which monetary policies are powerless to affect more than temporarily.

An additional point that may be worth making in relation to wage and price flexibility, is that it is usually treated as being independent of the degree of economic and monetary integration, whereas it may be argued that it will be affected by, inter alia, exchange rate arrangements and the integration of goods and labour markets. Fixed exchange rates and the completion of the single European market may increase competition in goods and labour markets in each member state, changing the constraints on firms and labour unions (where these exist) in a way which alters wage formation. An example is the demand of East German workers for West German wages after the economic integration of the two countries. Whether integration in Europe increases the demands from workers in low-productivity parts of the EC for the same wages as in the highest-productivity parts and thereby worsens the regional problem, or whether increased competition in labour markets induces wage moderation and greater flexibility of wages, is an open question. But it should perhaps not be presumed that wage and price formation are independent factors.

Pursuing further the question of what factors are regarded as being exogenous to the analysis, it may be worth remarking that the macroeconomic analysis generally assumes that the level and growth rate of productivity are independent of the monetary and exchange rate arrangements. From this viewpoint, removing a policy instrument (the exchange rate) by going to a monetary union cannot improve the ability of governments to achieve their policy targets, problems of time-inconsistency and credibility aside. When there are more independent sources of disturbances than policy instruments, the loss of an instrument usually causes a loss in the ability to achieve policy targets. A move to monetary union cannot look attractive.

However, there are arguments that a move to EMU will increase productivity by increasing product market competition and causing changes in the location of production in the EC (see, for example, Venables and Smith, 1986). If monetary union is a necessary part of the process which increases competition in national markets, then there are benefits to it which are not captured in the typical macroeconomic analyses. A further benefit of monetary union is suggested by recent models of endogenous growth (see, for example, Romer, 1989). These are based on the hypothesis that there are externalities associated with the aggregate capital stock, human capital stock, or the number of varieties of products available in an economy. At some point in the process of integration, externalities which extended only to the individual member countries become available to the whole community, so that firms in each country benefit from the externality generated by the whole community's capital stock rather than just that generated by the national capital stock. Again, if monetary integration is necessary to get these spillovers, the gains are greater than the macroeconomic analysis indicates.

The effect of monetary union on the anti-inflationary discipline exerted by the monetary and exchange rate regime, is unclear, as the authors note. Assuming Germany has disciplined other more inflationary countries so far, the question seems to be whether Germany provides a firmer anchor in the current EMS, controlling its money supply to meet domestic inflation targets, or in a monetary union, as one voter among twelve on the board of the European Central Bank, voting for low-inflation monetary policies.

It may well be begging the question to suppose that other European countries have different objectives than Germany, and need discipline. The discipline argument for the EMS has predominated, but is not universal (see, e. g., Melitz, 1988). It has been argued that disinflation would have occurred anyway, and that the EMS is a symptom of this, not a cause.

The public finance argument for differential inflation rates is based on differential efficiency of tax collection and different marginal distortions caused by taxes in various European countries. Optimal taxes equalize the marginal efficiency losses from alternative means of collecting revenue, and lead to higher optimal inflation tax rates in some countries than others. On this issue, it has been remarked that the single European market will reduce some of the high bank reserve ratios current in some of the higher inflation countries, and make seigniorage a less attractive and less potentially significant source of revenue. This may weaken the case for differential inflation rates on public finance grounds, and consequently strengthen the case for monetary union.

The authors look at issues raised by the transition to monetary union, particularly concerning the possibility that under an interim regime of fixed exchange rates countries may have incentives to create monetary expansion the effects of which will spill over into other EC countries. This possibility has been analyzed by Aizenmann (1989), as they note. It involves having many suppliers of one currency, effectively. While this is a theoretical possibility, one wonders how practically significant it might become. The dangers of such a situation seem so apparent that Central Bankers would surely fight hard to avoid its emergence.

The issue of the need for central limits on fiscal deficits in a monetary union is discussed. The assertion in the Delors report that upper limits on the deficits of individual countries should be centrally set has provoked much debate. It appears to have been motivated by fears of Central Banks that the European Central Bank might otherwise have been obliged to bail out by monetizing the debt of a country with high deficits. This seems to be an important practical problem which underlines the importance of independence of the European Central Bank. This argument apart, the need for fiscal coordination in a monetary union is not clear (Buiter and Kletzer, 1990) in any case, and there is no reason to suppose that the form of coordination should take a centrally imposed upper limit (Goodhart, 1990).

A discussion which is absent from the present paper, perhaps because it would take an already broad discussion too far afield, is that concerning the need for greater interregional transfers in a monetary union. The arguments are rehearsed, for example, by Eichengreen (1990). Transfers of income between regions, it is argued, may provide insurance against local disturbances which reduces their impact, and reduces unemployment fluctuations in the EC. They might partly offset the loss of exchange adjustment as a policy tool for local disturbances. The scale of transfers which operates in the US via Federal tax, transfer, and expenditure programmes is on a much larger scale than occurs in the EC, suggesting the need for much bigger central budgets in Europe. To the extent that fiscal federalism can replace exchange rates as a response to local shocks, the arguments against monetary union based on wage/price stickiness and factor immobility may lose some of their force.

These comments have taken up some of the very many points made in Clas Wihlborg and Tom Willett's paper, where it seemed appropriate to suggest a different view or emphasis, or to mention another argument touching on the issue. Notwithstanding such small differences, I found that their paper brings together a very useful and comprehensive perspective on the issues surrounding European monetary union, and the question of whether Europe could be an optimal currency area.

REFERENCES

Buiter, W. H., and K. M. Kletzer (1990), "The Welfare Economics of Cooperative and Non-Cooperative Fiscal Policy," CEPR Discussion Paper 420, June.

Eichengreen, B. (1990), "Is Europe an Optimal Currency Area?" CEPR Discussion Paper, 478, November.

Goodhart, C. A. E. (1990), "Fiscal Policy and EMU," in M. Beber and J. Driffill (eds.), <u>A Currency for Europe</u>, Lothian Foundation Press, London.

Melitz, J. (1988), "Monetary Discipline and Cooperation in the European Monetary System: A Synthesis," in F. Giavazzi, S. Micossi and M. Miller (eds.), <u>The European Monetary System</u>, Cambridge University Press, Cambridge.

Romer, P. M. (1989), "Capital Accumulation in the Theory of Long-Run Growth," in R. J. Barro (ed.), <u>Modern Business Cycle Theory</u>, Blackwell: Oxford.

Venables, A. J., and A. Smith (1986), "Trade and Industrial Policy under Imperfect Competition," <u>Economic Policy</u>, 3, October, 621-672.

Part Five

**Economic Policy Perspectives on Financial Market Regulation
and Supervision**

Financial Regulation and Monetary Arrangements after 1992
C. Wihlborg, M. Fratianni and T.D. Willett (Editors)
© 1991 Elsevier Science Publishers B.V. All rights reserved

13   Financial Markets, Regulation and Supervision: The Major Issues

Tad Rybczynski

City University, Northampton Square, London EC1V 0HB, United Kingdom

1. INTRODUCTION

The regulation and supervision of financial markets raise a number of important issues for policy makers, practitioners as well as members of the economics profession. The latter should be able to throw useful light on the design of the new system in view of recent developments. The new issues deal with the impact of reduction and elimination of barriers to capital mobility, as well as the impact of this new freedom on the actual and optimal architecture of the regulatory framework.

To help arrive at some answers I will first comment briefly on the broad effects of reducing obstacles to international capital mobility. Then I present a view of the financial system, its functions and its development. Thereafter, I discuss how approaches to control of the financial system have developed and are being adapted in the EC countries. I conclude with a challenge for economists.

2. GENERAL CONSEQUENCES OF INCREASED CAPITAL MOBILITY

The first point I want to make is that the removal of or reduction in barriers to capital mobility in relation to the structure and process of financial intermediation will depend on what type of barriers are being reduced or eliminated, and on what type of exchange rate regime is to prevail. There are three major types of barriers to capital mobility. They are exchange controls, different taxation, and different regulatory systems. While exchange controls, like tariffs, are highly visible, different taxation and regulatory systems, which can be likened to non-tariff barriers, are equally important.

On the micro-economic level, we are now witnessing the policy of creating a single market in financial services in the E.C. The relevant issues - already being examined - include first, what is the optimum nature of the regulatory structure reducing systemic risk while encouraging efficiency, stability, flexibility and the balanced nature of financial system as evaluated by conventional criteria? These include allocative, operating and dynamic efficiency, ability to adjust, and to create and use a sufficiently wide mix of financial practices facilitating the absorption of exogenous and endogenous shocks. Second, how reconcile in the international context the different regulatory approaches based on universal banking principles or specialised financing arrangements, respectively? Third, what is the optimum type of deposit and investment insurance policy and lender of the last resort policy to help financial institutions to operate efficiently? Fourth, what are the implications of a common regulatory policy for the structure of industry, especially the extent of conglomeration, the control of financial firms and the competition policy? Finally, what are the implications for the cost of capital and the convergence of the term structure of interest rates in the context of globalisation of finance?

Both macro-economic and micro-economic problems arising from reduction in barriers to capital mobility must also take into account that the removal of such obstacles is merely one of the factors facilitating cross-border financial flows influencing real and nominal exchange rates and domestic and world money supply. It should be stressed that international capital movements are also propelled by advances in technology, above all those in the area of information, communication and calculation which are changing the character of financial industry and would have been doing so in a closed economy.

Liberalisation of capital movements is thus one of the factors which accelerates the transformation of the financial system and speeds up the pace of advance towards "securitisation" with important implications for the behaviour of an economy.

3. THE FINANCIAL SYSTEM

The financial system includes, first, depository institutions accepting deposits transferable at call or notice; second, other savings collecting institutions, such as life assurance companies, pension funds and mutual funds; and finally, the complex of capital markets and capital market intermediaries bringing together ultimate savers and savings collecting and depository institutions with ultimate or proximate fund users. The basic financial services can be performed by one institution or they can be made available separately by different organisations.

The financial system performs three basic functions. The first one is the running and administration of the payment system, i.e. the transfer of funds among individuals and institutions relating to current and capital transactions as well as transfer payments. The second function is to collect such new savings from those who generate but cannot directly employ them and allocate them where they earn the highest rate of return consistent with the savers' proclivity to assume risk. The third function is to provide facilities for transfer of ownership, i.e. the market for corporate control, thus helping to ensure that past savings embodied in real and financial assets are also used in the manner yielding optimum returns.

In discharging these basic functions the financial system is dealing with risk. There is a credit risk, exchange rate risk and interest rate risk involved in running the payments system, allocating newly generated savings, and re-allocating past savings embodied in real and financial assets. In dealing with risk the financial system assumes risks, pools risks, prices risks and trades risks. What type of functions are discharged by various institutions and the amount or risk they assume and carry is determined to a considerable degree by the regulatory framework.

Needless to say, financial systems are not static. Like the real economy which in the process of development moves from an agricultural one into an industrial one and then a de-industrialised one, the financial system also evolves as described in Rybczynski (1988). In brief, in the first stage, there is a bank-oriented system, when banks collect and allocate the bulk of new savings and when other savings collecting institutions and capital markets play a relatively modest role. The re-allocation of old savings is of negligible importance. The second stage is a market-oriented system when other savings collecting institutions collect and allocate a much larger proportion of new savings, and the capital market plays a more important role as regards the channelling of new savings and helping re-allocate old savings. In the final stage we have a securitised system when savings collecting institutions play a very important role as regards the collection and allocation of new savings and capital markets play a very significant part in assisting to direct new savings and a dominant role in reallocating old savings. The relative importance of the last function increases in the securitised stage.

There is nothing deterministic about this pattern of development of the financial system. It corresponds to facts; it does not conflict with the views of various theorists, and it includes the developments now underway. I present it here, even though it is not a part of the conventional wisdom, because European and world financial integration involves linking together financial systems in various stages of development. In turn, financial systems in different countries have different regulatory regimes which reflect not only political preferences but even more so the stage of the development of the financial system. This approach also emphasises that institutional development, as is now increasingly recognised, is an integral part of economic growth. This was accepted and formed a part of economics in the past, was abandoned for the fifty years or so until recently, but being reintroduced again at present.

Taking a bird's eye view, one can say that developing countries and also some industrial countries have a bank-oriented system, more developed industrial countries either have or are now moving into a market-oriented financial system, and finally those experiencing de-industrialisation or where industrialisation has passed its peak, have or are now moving into a securitised system.

4. APPROACHES TO CONTROL OF THE FINANCIAL SYSTEM

It has always been accepted that there is a need to have a regulatory framework for finance to protect savers and investors from fraud, to decrease informational asymmetry diminishing the allocative, operational and dynamic efficiency of the financial system, to prevent individual institutions from assuming risks they cannot absorb, and to eliminate the systemic risk. However, there is at present no established, accepted and comprehensive body of theory giving guidance to what is the optimal structure of regulation during different stages of economic and financial evolution.

It should therefore not be surprising that policy makers in all countries, when imposing regulatory requirements and erecting safety nets, have always responded and still respond to external pressures, be they economic or political. This was true when the Bank of England assumed the role of the lender of the last resort and gradually introduced liquidity ratios. It was true at the time of the creation of the Federal Reserve System in 1913 in the US, and the introduction of the US Glass-Steagall Legislation of 1933. Other important regulatory events include the creation of the Specialised Financial System in France in the last quarter of the last century and its restructuring in the 30's, the restructuring of the Italian financial system in the 30's, the Swiss legislation of the 1920's, and the recent changes in the British, US, Japanese, French, and other continental countries' regulatory framework.

The EC 1992 Single Financial Market Programme aims to remove European regulatory barriers for the performance of the three basic functions undertaken by various financial

institutions among member countries with financial systems in different stages of
evolution. The Programme has tried to introduce a 'level playing field' in the area of
finance within the Community in an ad hoc, pragmatic manner with limited and rather
modest input and help from academia, most of it produced to meet certain specifications.
An outstanding example of this approach is the famous, or notorious, Reciprocity Clause
in the EC legislation. This was originally transplanted lock, stock and barrel from the UK
Financial Services Act, 1986, where it was inserted to provide U.K. authorities with
safeguards and bargaining counters vis-à-vis foreign institutions. The Commission inserted
it without considering its consequences and changed it only after head-on clashes with
non-EC countries.

The EC Single Financial Programme raises two different sets of issues. The first issue
concerns relations with non-EC countries while the second issue has to do with intra-EC
relations. In each case the Programme covers depository-, savings-, collecting-, and capital
market functions be they undertaken by one or more institution. It also covers the macro
and micro aspects of the financial system. The former has to do with the mix and thrust
of economic policy with special reference to monetary controls, while the latter has to do
with measures concerned with safety and stability of the system and competition.

With respect to the intra-EC relations, the basic principle adopted by the EC is that of
a single passport based on or linked to the principle of a universal banking form of
organisation. These principles have been embodied in the Second Banking Directive
which allows banks authorised in the home country to offer services specified in the
directive, covering depository, savings collecting and capital market participation services,
in other member countries subject to observation of marketing rules in force in the host
country. Complementing this directive are the capital requirement and the solvency
directives as well as those dealing with listing requirements and insider dealing. The
capital adequacy directive requires the acceptance of the unified risk-adjusted capital
ratios. These ratios apply to all banks regardless of whether or not they also undertake -
as they are free to do under Second Banking Directive - investment banking business, i.e.
underwriting, market making, acting as dealers/brokers and offering fund management
services. Also, the Second Banking Directive sets a relatively high minimum level of
capital for institutions wishing to operate as a bank. As a result, depository institutions
with small deposit business but large investment activity, as is the case of many firms in
the UK and the US, let alone investment banks doing no deposit business find themselves
at a disadvantage.

The difficulties so arising will be resolved in the final draft of the Investment Services
Directive and, accompanying it, the Capital Adequacy Directive for non-banks and
securities firms. The new draft, still to be approved by the European Parliament, allows
universal banks to opt for separate capitalisation of securities business and allied activities
on a net basis using capital ratios applicable to banks and allowing companies not
undertaking banking business to use lower capital ratios.

This is merely one example of attempts to create a new comprehensive regulatory
framework with the preventive safeguards covering different types of activity, but as yet
leaving aside a number of questions as regards the nature of protective measures such as
deposit insurance, and rules to be relied upon as regards the lender of a last resort role
of Central Banks. The example illustrates the formidable issue raised by the conflict
between the so-called functional and institutional approaches, and the significance of the
institutional framework within which different financial functions are discharged.

Regulatory arbitrage and tax havens are other important issues. It remains to be seen to what extent these will be affected by the race of different countries to attract financial business to become major world financial centres.

So far, within the EC there is no common approach towards ownership links between bank, non-bank, savings collecting institutions and capital market intermediaries on the one hand, and non-financial business on the other. Similarly, there is no common approach to ownership links for deposit insurance. These issues bear on the provision of liquidity and control of exchange and interest rate risk, controlled directly as far as depository institutions are concerned but not through prudential capital requirement.

Many of the regulatory problems arising within the EC are common to the EC framework vis-à-vis that in the rest of the world. The institutional vs. the functional approach, and the prudential capital ratios established under the auspices of the BIS are among them. Towering above them is the question of the meaning of national treatment to be accepted as a basis for international trade in financial services, and forming a part of the Uruguay round of GATT negotiation.

National treatment involves according foreign financial institutions and above all banks, the same privileges as to the domestic banks. However, differences in institutional structures and regulatory frameworks make implementation of the principle difficult, especially in relation to branches of parent banks registered outside the host country.

While within the EC the principle of mutual recognition is ultimately based on agreement to harmonise essential *rules* and also implicit agreement on common goals for regulatory convergence, such agreement does not extend internationally except for capital adequacy requirement. These requirements apply to traditional banking business only.

There are some difficult problems in the international area, both as regards the major groupings, such as the EC, North America, Japan, and other developed countries (EFTA members and other OECD countries) and as regards developing countries. These problems arise mainly because of differences in the institutional framework. In some cases it is based on universal banking with traditional banking activity determining the capital ratios, or on separate capitalisation of various activities, i.e. traditional banking and different types of investment banking activities. Institutional differences in turn influence the shape of the path leading towards regulatory convergence. Ultimately, it involves the acceptance of common principles and the assumption of common obligations resulting in the acceptance of a common approach to supra-national regulatory structure.

The securitisation of the financial system in the EC, as reflected in the Investment Services Directive yet to be agreed upon, is already causing the EC to move towards the adoption of the main features of regulatory architecture now evolving in the US, the country with the most developed financial (securitised) system. This architecture includes the acceptance of a financial holding company structure, "firewalls" between subsidiaries undertaking different activities and separate capitalisation. A number of issues such as the separation of deposit banking and investment banking, the competence of various regulatory bodies in the US (the FED, SEC, the Controller of Currency, state authorities) and the design of various futures and option regulatory bodies remain unresolved.

5. CONCLUSION

The broad problem of what is the optimum balance between self-regulation and public regulation, not only nationally and regionally but also internationally, still remains. The

1992 EC Single Financial Market Programme has brought these issues to the top of the agenda. But important though the 1992 Programme is, the ultimate factor forcing the pace of advance is technology (informational, computational etc), financial innovations and deregulation. This development is opening a rich area for economists, for analysts of institutional elements in the new evolving structure of regional and international integration, where first class understanding and clear guideposts are desperately and urgently needed. The challenge is there and is being responded to as shown in this volume. Let us hope that new analyses and policy recommendations will come in time not only to prevent another collapse but also help contain the risk while helping efficient allocation of new savings and the use of and re-allocation of old savings with the consequent increase in welfare.

REFERENCE

Rybczynski, T. (1988), "Financial System and Industrial Restructuring", The National Westminster Review, Aug.

Financial Regulation and Monetary Arrangements after 1992
C. Wihlborg, M. Fratianni and T.D. Willett (Editors)
1991 Elsevier Science Publishers B.V.

14   A U.K. View of Financial Market Regulation and Supervision

Nigel Carter

Bank of England, Threadneedle street, London EC 2R 8AH, United Kingdom

1. INTRODUCTION

I have been invited to comment on economic and political factors shaping the regulation and supervision of "international"[1] financial institutions after 1992 from the point of view of a large EC member state. However, it is worth noting at the outset that the U.K. perspective may differ significantly from that of most other EC countries for two reasons in particular. First, the activities of almost all major U.K. financial institutions, and hence the interests of U.K. regulators, have long been strongly oriented towards global financial markets. Second, London has long been host to a uniquely wide range of financial firms from around the world which contribute enormously to the large volume of international financial business conducted from the U.K. as well as playing an active role in our domestic markets. These factors have fundamentally affected our approach to regulation both domestically and internationally. The European Community dimension is only one - albeit increasingly important - aspect of that picture. The U.K. approach to regulation has been, and after 1992 will continue to be, firmly based on a wider concern for world markets as a whole. A key priority for the U.K. will continue to be the development of the European Community as a centre for global rather than regional financial business.

My remarks will focus on a number of important factors affecting the response of regulatory authorities to the competitive pressures and changes in risk which will be reinforced by creation of the single European market. I shall begin by noting briefly those aspects of worldwide economic and financial developments which, in my view, have greatest significance for regulation. Turning to the U.K. I shall outline the U.K. government's basic economic policy stance and describe how this relates to the principles which underlie our approach to financial market regulation in the U.K. and internationally. My purpose in so doing will be to cast some light on the factors which may influence other regulatory authorities too. I shall conclude by considering in a little more detail the regulatory response to prospective changes in competition and risk.

2. GLOBAL ECONOMIC AND POLITICAL BACKGROUND

Let me begin with the global economic and political background. I would identify four major influences on the development of financial markets which are of particular concern to regulators. First - the increasing pace of technological change which has greatly enhanced the links between different aspects of financial markets and which has accelerated and magnified the transmission of effects between them. Second - the intensification of competition between regions and between different types of financial institution (which has greatly increased the pressure towards innovation). Third - persistent significant external payments imbalances associated with large and volatile international capital flows in which the financial services industry is the principle intermediary. Fourth - a global political climate which continues to encourage liberalisation of financial markets.

Worldwide developments have intensified the need to refine regulatory techniques to meet the new types and magnitudes of risk. It is partly with these developments in mind that the U.K. authorities have in recent years engaged in a major overhaul of the regulatory framework for a large part of the financial sector spanning banks, building societies and other financial services.

3. THE U.K. PHILOSOPHY OF ECONOMIC MANAGEMENT

The approach adopted by the U.K. both in revising the domestic regulatory framework, and in international negotiations on financial regulation, is in keeping with the prevailing U.K. philosophy of economic management. Our approach - as seen particularly clearly over the past decade - has been based on the belief that promoting the efficient operation of markets offers the best means of maximising economic welfare. Under the Thatcher government this policy stance has been manifested in positive efforts to reduce the role of government in the economy coupled with a preference for market, rather than legal or regulatory, solutions wherever possible. This is seen in our open-door policy towards inward investment including investment in the financial services industry. The U.K. Government's role in industry and commerce is largely restricted to attempts to promote the functioning of markets for example by improving private business incentives through tax reduction or by enhancing transparency of information for market participants.

4. THE U.K. REGULATORY SYSTEM: TRADITIONS AND PRINCIPLES

Regulation in the U.K., therefore, has generally been designed to allow the free play of market forces so far as is consistent with a reasonable degree of protection for individual users of financial services and consistent with maintenance of the soundness and smooth functioning of the markets as a whole. Thus traditionally there has been an emphasis on lightness of regulation in the sense that detailed rules and burdensome supervisory procedures have generally been avoided in the U.K.. There has also been an emphasis on flexibility in recognition of the fact that many financial institutions (particularly banks) differ greatly in their nature and size and that they need to be able to adapt to changing market conditions. It would therefore be wrong in our view to impose too many rigid supervisory requirements. Although more of U.K. financial regulation is now enshrined in statute than in the past, the new laws have on the whole been limited to a general statement of principles and establishment of a broad framework for authorisation and control. The statutes are intended to be flexible enough to allow for changes over time in financial techniques and for institutional developments.

The principles which apply to financial regulation in the U.K. are rather simple. They are basically the same as those commonly applied elsewhere in G10 countries. The twin objectives, namely the protection of individual investors and depositors and avoidance of systemic risk, are to be ensured by achieving first - the fitness and properness of the owners and managers of a financial institution; second - the adequacy of capital for the types of business undertaken; third - adequacy of continuing control systems; and fourth - high standards of conduct of business (usually backed by some form of insurance or compensation arrangements).

5. THE EC DIMENSION

At the European level the U.K. government's basic economic policy stance translates into a desire to see liberalisation extended throughout the Community (and in due course more widely to EFTA countries and the rest of Europe). By liberalisation I mean the removal of artificial restrictions on competition whether they result from official controls or from features of market structure or practice. It is worth stressing that liberalisation is not the same thing as deregulation. Indeed some, even new, regulation may be necessary in order to ensure basic standards in the more competitive market conditions which may result from liberalisation. This has been well illustrated recently in the U.K.. The so-called "Big Bang" of 1986 was prompted by competitive considerations namely the wish to break up traditional restrictions in the operation of the securities markets in the U.K.. The Financial Services Act, which was implemented subsequently, is sometimes seen as inconsistent with the general policy of liberalisation. This view, however, arises from confusion between the notions of "restriction" and "regulation". In the case of the U.K. the removal of artificial and anti-competitive restrictions in the securities markets necessitated strengthened regulation to ensure standards in the freer market conditions which ensued. One may argue, as many do, that the Financial Services Act is unnecessarily complex and burdensome, but this does not invalidate the reasons for its introduction.

In the European Community our aim in the field of financial services is to lighten and where possible lift national restrictions on the design as well as the marketing of financial products while ensuring that regulatory and fiscal variations do not sustain other kinds of competitive inequality. Solid progress in these areas is being achieved through negotiations in Brussels. It can usefully be reinforced through the operation of market forces. Competition can impel market participants to put pressure on governments to reduce or remove regulatory and fiscal variations in Europe where these distort markets unacceptably. This suggests that detailed harmonisation through negotiation is unnecessary since market pressures may be relied on gradually to smooth out most significant remaining unevenness in the playing field. The U.K. is a strong advocate of this basic approach to completing the single European market. However, this does not imply endorsement of a general levelling-down of standards. Care is needed to ensure this does not occur. For, while it is no doubt true that competition can lead to the erosion of regulatory discrepancies between countries, it is hard to predict where such a process might end. Hence the wisdom of the European Community's approach involving agreement on a basic regulatory framework and key prudential standards.

The U.K. authorities' emphasis on a liberal approach in the EC is in line with global trends. However, we accept that this approach must in practice be qualified in some degree. Complete liberalisation in the financial services industry (in the sense of allowing all appropriately qualified firms to operate in markets of their choice) is clearly a long-term goal. But this must be based on the assurance of adequate regulation throughout the EC. The aim is to achieve this on the basis of sufficient harmonisation of key standards to enable mutual recognition of supervisory regimes within the Community.

U.K. domestic efforts to reduce the role of government are also reflected in our approach to the role of the European Community, and our support for the principle of "subsidiarity"[2] in regulatory and other matters. In pursuing this goal we would also hope to minimise the Community administrative burden on individual businesses and on regulatory procedures. Of course we readily acknowledge that the Commission has a significant role to play, one which is likely to increase over time. Our main concern is that the Community should not become unnecessarily involved in functions best handled on a national or local basis, and that any increased involvement at the Community level should not be premature or unplanned.

I have briefly considered the global financial market trends of particular concern to regulators and have outlined the U.K.'s broad approach to economic management and financial regulation both domestically and at the European and wider international level. I hope this has given some indication of the main themes we would expect to see reflected in EC financial market regulation after 1992. Let me now discuss the regulatory implications of two specific topics - competitive developments and changes in risk.

6. CHANGES IN COMPETITION IN FINANCIAL MARKETS

Competition may be seen as the driving force behind the single market process. Within the European Community the impact of competition on financial services (particularly through a reduction in the cost of capital to industry and the cost of services to individual consumers) should make an important contribution to the welfare gains from market integration. Externally, by reducing or removing certain distortions in the market, by encouraging some rationalisation and concentration of investment, and by promoting efficiency, increased competition in the EC should help strengthen the capacity of EC financial institutions to compete in global markets with non-EC firms (particularly the large US and Japanese groups).

However, the benefits of competition could not be achieved if the EC sought isolation. For the Community to realise its full potential it must create an open relationship with the rest of the world and readily accept the contribution that institutions from other countries can offer. This is the basis on which the U.K. financial services industry has flourished.

The latest formulation of reciprocity provisions in EC financial market legislation therefore represents a welcome advance on earlier more narrowly defensive (and bureaucratic) proposals for reciprocal treatment of institutions from third countries. The new version, based on the principle of national treatment, should encourage an open competitive relationship between the European Community and the rest of the world.

7. COMPETITIVE PRESSURES ON REGULATORY STANDARDS

However, increased competition, while generally beneficial, also entails difficulties. It will intensify certain kinds of pressure both on regulators themselves and on the firms they regulate. The principal potential manifestation of competitive pressure on regulators is sometimes described as "competition in laxity". The EC approach to legislation sets basic regulatory standards leaving scope for variation in the application of regulation by a firm's "home" state. It is argued that this could encourage home supervisory authorities to attempt to outbid each other in the lightness of their supervisory requirements in order to give competitive advantage to institutions already based in their own market and to attract financial institutions from third countries to make that their "home" base inside the Community.

Clearly there are risks of this kind although it is in the interest of every Member State to ensure that the key prudential requirements are harmonised at a minimum standard which is prudentially sound. Moreover, market participants are coming increasingly to recognise the importance of operating in markets, and dealing with counterparties, of established integrity. Even if it chose to adopt a somewhat stricter regime than the agreed minimum, a Member State might therefore not be putting its national market place and its own financial institutions at a competitive disadvantage. In the U.K. we are firmly convinced that London's attraction as a financial centre is derived in part from the reputation for sound markets based on firm but flexible and balanced regulation which does not necessarily imply a minimalist approach.

8. CHANGES IN RISKS: ISSUES FOR REGULATORS

The combination of expanding financial services activity and intensified competition in the single market will tend to increase the level of risk in the financial markets. This could arise from several sources. The pressure on financial institutions to try to restructure and reposition themselves in Europe ahead of their competitors could lead some firms to invest in expansion or diversification based less on a realistic assessment of opportunities than on concern "not to miss the boat", or for reasons of public profile, or simply out of fear. In other words intensified competition might make firms more inclined to take risks. This inherent danger could be exacerbated by the arrival of other relatively inexperienced (or unscrupulous) firms in newly liberalised sectors. Some of these negative effects of increased competition could appear before the potential benefits begin to be felt. If not accompanied by adequate regulatory safeguards, such developments could increase unacceptably the risks of loss to individual users of financial services and of wider loss to the economy at large.

9. INFORMATION ASYMMETRIES

The risks faced by individual users of financial services derive in large measure from problems associated with imperfect information ("information asymmetries" between producers and consumers). Users of financial services, particularly at the retail end of the market, do not generally have the will or capacity to evaluate financial institutions properly. Consequently they often fail to distinguish clearly between sound and unsound firms. Imperfect information about firms exposes users of financial services to several kinds of risk. In particular a client may be at risk because the firm deals fraudulently, unfairly (in the sense of taking excess profits) or incompetently. A client also faces the risk that the firm itself may fail. However, it is difficult on the whole for an individual client to make a judgment on such matters ex ante. Information asymmetries, therefore, are widely held to justify regulatory control in order to provide at least some measure of protection for investors and depositors.   Information problems may well intensify in the fast changing and unsettled conditions which will be associated with the initial phases of creating the single market in financial services.

10. SYSTEMIC RISK

I have so far only discussed the risks which can arise at the micro level from individual clients' dealings with firms. However, at the macro level there is also the aggregate effect of the accumulation of such risks in the financial system which can have a wider impact on the economy - so-called systemic risk. In the past systemic risk was most commonly discussed in the context of the banking system where it arises, on the one hand, from the close inter-linkages between banks (eg through the inter-bank market), and, on the other, from the central role played by banks in the economy. Over recent years, with the rapid development of securities businesses and their widespread, multiple links with banks and individual clients, the range of institutions and markets involved in systemic risk has expanded. The additional losses to the economy, which can arise from failures in certain financial markets, are the main justification for provision of support through lender-of-last-resort functions and/or deposit insurance. Such support may, however, lead firms to pursue more risky business than otherwise. Financial supervision is justified in part by the need to limit such excessive risk-taking.

11. REGULATORY IMPLICATIONS

I have already indicated possible sources of increased risk arising from greater European and global competition. The question arises: Will the potential increase in risks require an intensification of financial market regulation? Some economists argue that most regulation is distortionary, restrictive and anti-competitive and therefore only in the interest of those who benefit from constraints on competition. This begs the question whether regulation serves a purpose in reducing other even more distortionary, restrictive or anti-competitive features of the market. In practice, there is always a balance to be struck between the marginal costs and benefits of regulation.

I would make two points in particular about the changes in competition and risk after 1992. The first concerns a distinction which can be drawn between market professionals and private users of financial services. While both face risks arising from information assymetries, such problems are generally significantly less for competent market professionals than for private individuals. In the case of professionals, responsibility for dealing with these difficulties can reasonably be placed squarely on the market operators' own shoulders. But some regulatory systems may not differentiate adequately in this context between business involving private individuals on the one hand and purely inter-professional operations on the other. In such circumstances market professionals may be subjected to tougher regulation than necessary and thus impeded in normal business activities or even disadvantaged vis-a-vis foreign competitors. Increased competition will add to the pressure on regulatory authorities in Europe and elsewhere to remove such unnecessary obstacles to business by relaxing regulation of inter-professional operations and concentrating it where there may be greatest need namely in the protection of individual investors and depositors.

The second point relates to overall trends in regulatory standards. It is to be hoped that efforts to coordinate the approach to financial market regulation in Europe will lead to some levelling-up rather than a levelling-down in average prudential standards. This is the aim of wider international coordination efforts - e g through the Basle Committee of Banking Supervisors, or through IOSCO in the case of securities market supervisors. These efforts towards further convergence in regulatory standards on the basis of internationally accepted good practice will be reinforced by other types of cooperation between supervisors particularly the exchange of information. Thus regulatory authorities are already responding positively, through coordinated efforts, to the potential increases in risk in the financial markets in Europe and worldwide.

12. CONCLUSION

In conclusion, I would stress that progress in European and wider international regulatory cooperation in recent years has been encouraging but that efforts must be intensified and sustained long after 1992. The processes of liberalisation, innovation and technological advance are accelerating in financial markets and constantly changing (in some ways extending) the risks to be dealt with in the system. It will therefore be necessary to reinforce efforts to achieve greater regulatory convergence worldwide and to strengthen arrangements to contain systemic risk in particular. This is the challenge to which regulators in Europe, the USA, Japan and elsewhere will have to rise now and after 1992.

FOOTNOTES

These remarks are not an official statement of Bank of England opinion and they do not carry the Bank's formal endorsement. I believe, nevertheless, that my colleagues would generally agree with the main substance of this paper.

1. "International" financial institutions defined here as a foreign-owned institution operating domestically or a domestically owned institution operating abroad.

2. "Subsidiarity" here means the principle that you should not do something at the central, community level if it can be done at least as well at a national or local level.

Financial Regulation and Monetary Arrangements after 1992
C. Wihlborg, M. Fratianni and T.D. Willett (Editors)
© 1991 Elsevier Science Publishers B.V. All rights reserved

15 An EFTA View of Financial Market Regulation and Supervision

Emil Ems

EFTA Secretariat, 9-11 Rue de Varembe, CH 1211 Geneva 20, Switzerland

1. INTRODUCTION

This paper provides an overview of the process of liberalization of capital movements and financial services in the EFTA countries. It describes the status of financial liberalization in the EFTA countries and assesses, against this background, the consequences of West European financial integration in terms of the structure of financial markets, policy issues and economic welfare in the EFTA countries.

The analysis concentrates on capital movements, banking and investment services. Insurance, which is normally considered to be part of financial services, is not being treated here.

Financial liberalization involves liberalizing capital movements as well as liberalizing financial services.

Concerning capital movements, the EFTA countries, except Switzerland, have until fairly recently had rather restrictive regimes. These are now being loosened, with the exception of restrictions on inward direct investments and real estate. Capital movements in Austria, Norway and Sweden are largely free. Finland is following this example. Iceland is also considering liberalization.

In financial services the EFTA countries, again except Switzerland, have traditionally had rather restrictive regimes concerning the establishment of financial institutions. Reciprocity is applied by all countries except Iceland and Sweden. There are still severe limitations on foreign ownership of shares in financial institutions in the Scandinavian EFTA countries. In some countries, like Austria, Norway and Sweden, the establishment of branches by foreign banks has also been limited until recently. Restrictions on cross-border trade in financial services are now being eased.

2. STRUCTURAL CONSEQUENCES OF FINANCIAL INTEGRATION

The rapid developments of the international financial markets during the past fifteen years have had their impact on the EFTA countries. International markets have become more sophisticated and interlinked due to the challenge posed by, among other factors, the two oil crises and the accompanying redistribution of international liquidity on a global scale. New financial instruments have been invented and new techniques for planning and carrying out financial operations have been introduced, especially in the field of information processing. In many countries, not least the Scandinavian EFTA countries and Austria, there has also been a trend; away from the intensive regulation of domestic financial markets; building up momentum in the mid-1980s.

In Europe, the EC has become a fore-runner for financial integration within the framework of its internal market to be established by 1993. Capital movements were already liberalized in most EC countries by 1989. Liberalization of banking and investment services is imminent and will be virtually complete with the adoption of a few remaining strategic legal instruments.

Market reaction in EFTA countries to these changed conditions is both offensive and defensive, although somewhat different due to differences in the structure of the markets and public policy directed towards financial markets. In all countries, most markedly in Switzerland, banks and investment brokers have sought to establish themselves in foreign countries.

All EFTA countries, with the possible exception of Switzerland (which consistently applies reciprocity to open up foreign markets) have had a defensive stance when it comes to allowing foreign financial institutions to enter their markets. Most EFTA countries have, or have recently had, cartel-like arrangements with predictable effects on profits, on prices of the services offered and on non-price competition. In Scandinavia these arrangements were underpinned by public regulation of the credit market which is now abolished.

Thus, the future effects of increased competition due to internationalization of financial markets and to easing restrictions on capital movements and on entry of foreign institutions would mostly be felt in the EFTA countries' home markets. Abolishing public restrictions on foreign establishment will probably lead to some regrouping of domestic institutions through mergers and alliances. This process is already pronounced, in the banking sector, in Sweden and in Norway.

The threat of new entrants from abroad will lead to falling prices and rents in the financial sectors, which are considerable in some countries. In countries with an oligopolistic banking structure, in particular Sweden and Switzerland, financial institutions can be expected to lower prices in order to discourage entry. Substantial restructuring will probably occur in countries like Austria and Finland with a relatively large number of small enterprises. After restructuring, defensive pricing behaviour might also emerge in these countries.

Increasing foreign competition may also lead to the emergence of regional solutions in Scandinavia. In corporate banking a joint venture already exists in the form of the Scandinavian Banking Partners, a co-operation between banks from all the Scandinavian countries. Similar co-operation can be foreseen in investment services and in the Nordic stock exchanges, in particular since foreign customers tend to perceive the Nordic financial market as a single entity (The Nordic Perspective Group, 1990). In Switzerland, the cantonal stock markets will eventually be merged into a national market.

Additional adjustments in the EFTA countries would result, if they decided to join the EC financial area. In a single West European financial area all the EC and EFTA financial institutions would be subject to a single licence and to home-country control, wherever they did their business. Participating in such a scheme would sharpen the competition at home in the EFTA countries and hasten the structural adjustment of domestic financial institutions. It would also necessitate an overview and a revision of public regulation of financial markets, in order not to give domestic institutions a disadvantage (or advantage) due to "competition in rules".

Greater freedom of cross-border trade in financial services would also follow if the EFTA countries joined the EC financial area. The principle of "free movement of financial services" would have to be adopted. This would mean, among other things, that some EFTA countries might have to abolish some "modalities" on international capital transfer (see below), which would lead to still more competition at home.

Finally, adopting the EC scheme would mean that the EFTA countries would adhere to the EC's reciprocity policy towards third countries concerning establishment of foreign financial institutions. This scheme is analogous to and has the same advantages and disadvantages as the common trade policy inherent in a customs union. However, seen from the side of the EFTA countries, the structural effects on financial markets of introducing such a scheme might not be large, compared to applying an "erga omnes" solution. The EFTA countries would in any case open their borders to all West European financial institutions, which, considering the rather restrictive stance towards foreign ownership in most EFTA countries at the outset, would already provide a substantial increase in foreign competition. The additional effects on competition from opening the borders towards the rest of the world would probably be marginal.

All in all, the winners in joining a common West European integrated financial area would be consumers, and not primarily owners and workers in the financial sector.

At the start of the negotiations with the EC in July 1990 concerning the establishment of a common European Economic Area (EEA), all EFTA Member States made it clear that they are prepared to liberalize capital movements, to shape, together with the Community, an integrated market for financial services in Western Europe and to accept the "acquis communautaire" as the basis for such a market. Thus the first steps towards West European financial integration have already been taken.

3. POLICY ISSUES

Policy concerns in EFTA countries arise mainly in four respects. First, and above all in the Scandinavian countries, the taxation issue will have to be tackled by political decision-makers. Second, again in the Scandinavian countries, the free flow of short-term and long-term capital inhibits the traditional way of carrying out economic policy. Third, competition between rules induces a revision of public regulation. Fourth, an EFTA position will have to be reached concerning establishment of financial institutions from third countries.

Concerning the issue of taxation, Sweden, and to a limited extent Austria, Finland and Norway, intend to keep so-called "modalities" on international capital transfer for reasons of tax control. In Sweden, payments must be made through authorized domestic banks, deposit accounts in foreign currency may only be held in authorized domestic banks and foreign securities must be held in depot at authorized domestic institutions. These and similar solutions to the tax evasion problem would also in the future restrict cross-border trade in financial services, although this trade might otherwise be free.

However, these "modalities" would have to be abolished or modified if the EFTA countries joined the EC financial area. Thus, the last effective barrier in the Scandinavian countries enabling relatively high capital tax rates would disappear. An adjustment of capital tax rates would then have to be considered by the authorities in order to avoid distorting tax evasion.

Taxes, such as turnover and stamp taxes, also have a direct impact on the functioning of domestic capital and money markets. For example, a high turnover tax in Sweden had the effect of wiping out the options market and putting a "sourdine" on the rest of the capital markets when capital movements were being liberalized. The only solution to such problems would be to abolish, or at least drastically diminish, such taxes.

In economic policy, public decision-makers in the Scandinavian countries have now accepted fully the macro-economic restrictions to which the Austrian and Swiss authorities adapted, albeit in different ways, already a decade ago: there is no such thing as an independent economic policy in a small country in an integrated financial world. The main remaining challenge for the authorities in Scandinavia is to get acceptance by the general public of that fact.

Public regulation of financial services is primarily carried out to protect the consumer and should reasonably be employed only if found to be more effective than private measures on the market.

In financial services, abiding by this rule is complicated by the fact that prudential supervision nowadays mostly consists of measures by the public to compensate for other efforts to protect consumers. Nearly all countries provide a safety net of deposit insurance, together with "lender of last resort" guarantees from the side of the central banks. This creates a moral hazard problem (Krugman, 1987) which has to be kept at bay by prudential supervision designed to discourage excessive risk-taking by the financial institutions.

Against this background, the system of control of banking and investment services to be applied in a West European financial area could lead to an improvement in the overall package of supervision, deposit insurances and guarantees in all participating countries. The EC has chosen only to set common minimum standards of essential supervisory rules and prudential requirements, and to allow each country to apply additional supervision if deemed desirable. The EC's essential rules are similar to those agreed upon internationally, e.g. in the Cook Committee, although being somewhat wider in scope. "Competition between rules" will eventually restrain public ambitions to regulate financial markets above that minimum.

As for relations with third countries, EFTA countries considered, at an early stage of the EEA negotiations, alternatives to taking over the EC's common reciprocity policy concerning the establishment of financial institutions, as prescribed, for example, in the Second Banking Coordination Directive. Switzerland desired to keep its seemingly efficient reciprocity policy and other countries expressed concern that the adhering to the EC policy might lead to conflicts with other international obligations, e.g. the OECD Codes of Liberalisation (OECD, 1990).

One of these alternative options borrows some elements from traditional trade policy. In trade in goods, the EFTA countries are equally adverse to accepting a common trade policy towards third countries. The implication of this refusal is the need to accept rules of origin. In a similar way, rules of origin would have to be introduced in the field of establishment of financial institutions as the price of avoiding a common policy against non-EEA countries.

Such rules would allow limiting to financial institutions originating from an EC or EFTA country the right of free establishment with a single licence and with home-country control throughout Western Europe. This right would, thus, not be automatically extended to subsidiaries of third-country institutions which were established in an EFTA country or in the EC. Such a subsidiary, first established in an EFTA country, would be treated as a third-country institution by the other EFTA countries and the EC, and vice versa. By proposing such a scheme to the Commission, EFTA countries hoped to become part of the EC's level financial playing field without building a common wall around it.

At the present stage of the negotiations (February 1991), a compromise between this autonomy scheme and the EC's scheme of common reciprocity policy seems likely to emerge. This compromise has the character of concertation of policies.

Whenever the EC would be negotiating, with a third country, for national treatment or effective market access it would have to make an eventual agreement conditional on extending all attainments to the EFTA credit institutions. On the other hand, the EC, if deciding to place an embargo on a third country, would be allowed to extend the embargo to subsidiaries from the third country in the EFTA area, which were established after the EC decision. EFTA countries would maintain their autonomy but would, in general, not be allowed to apply a comparable "rules of origin" principle vis-à-vis subsidiaries of third country institutions established in the EC.

4. WELFARE EFFECTS OF FINANCIAL INTEGRATION

Welfare effects in EFTA countries from liberalizing capital movements and financial services in Western Europe would mainly arise in three respects: through a net transfer of capital among countries; through enhanced possibilities for diversifying investment portfolios; and through more effective and competitive markets for financial services.

The net transfer of capital effect would appear if EFTA countries, prior to liberalization of capital movements, still applied effective restrictions on capital transfer. Abolishing these would imply that capital flows would be redirected towards countries with relatively scarce capital and away from countries where capital was relatively abundant.

Recent studies show, however, that capital restrictions had lost, at least during the second half of the decade, most of their ability to restrict these flows (EFTA, 1989). Assuming reasonable arbitrage between the money and the capital markets, the effectiveness of restrictions on long-term capital flows would then also be largely eroded. Thus, no substantial gains from capital liberalization by itself, via a net capital transfer effect, are to be expected in the EFTA countries.

Although the capital controls remaining until fairly recently did not strongly hinder the net transfer of capital between countries, they did represent serious obstacles to investment in securities for residents in EFTA countries as well as for foreigners and thus for diversification of investment portfolios. For instance, private residents in several EFTA countries (though not in Switzerland) were not allowed to freely buy and sell bonds and shares abroad as recently as 1988. Such transactions were either forbidden outright, limited in scope, or had to be channelled through authorized domestic institutions.

Abolishing these and similar capital restrictions will lead to direct welfare gains for residents in the EFTA countries. EFTA residents will. get general access to the international market for financial assets for investment and borrowing purposes, and will thus be able to improve their investment portfolios by choosing freely from the vast and diversified international supply of bonds, shares and other securities. Remaining "modalities" in the EFTA countries would not restrain these opportunities. Their negative effect exercises itself more in encumbering transactions and making them more costly, rather then in restricting them outright.

As for welfare gains through more effective and competitive markets for financial services, these gains are broadly believed to be dominating the first two, although the assessments made of their impact are far from uncontroversial.

Generally speaking, these gains would stem from largely two developments (EC, 1988b). On the one hand analysts expect that financial integration will enable banks and investment brokers to better utilize economies of scale and scope by expanding on the large integrated West European market. By this increase of efficiency, costs for producing financial services would decrease at least for the large enterprises which would be able to realize these potentials, with secondary effects on prices of financial services. To assess directly the magnitude of such effects would demand extensive methodological and empirical studies, which are beyond the scope of this article.

On the other hand it surely can be expected that financial integration will be accompanied by increased competition on domestic markets. This might also have some effect on the efficiency and, thus, the costs of providing financial services, since inefficient enterprises would tend to be crowded out by increased competition. But above all, increased competition will put downward pressure on prices and profits, especially in the EFTA countries where prices are determined by cartels or by cartel-like agreements.

The empirical assessments of welfare effects in Western Europe that have been carried out centre largely on these two types of development. The main study, done by Price Waterhouse (EC, 1988a), deals with the price effects of financial integration in the EC countries. It tries to assess by how much prices for financial services would fall in the different EC countries if the law of one price prevailed. Obviously, this type of study cannot encompass the full impact on welfare of the two developments mentioned above. The approach used concentrates on consumer effects. EFTA has commissioned a similar analysis (Gardener & Teppett, 1990), which uses the same methodology as the Price Waterhouse study, so as to obtain comparable results.

In the EC study, consumer gains due to financial integration (wherein insurance services are included) would amount to about 0.7 per cent of GDP in the European Community as a whole. The EFTA study shows that, if prices would adjust towards the common hypothetical EC prices estimated by the EC study, the Alpine EFTA countries would exhibit consumer gains far above the EC average, whereas the Scandinavian countries would cluster more or less around this average.

A direct comparison of prices for financial services, sector by sector, paints a more disparate picture. With the exception of Switzerland, EFTA countries exhibit prices in investment services far above those in comparable EC countries like the FGR, France, Luxembourg and the UK. This illustrates the sheltering effect that earlier regulations of the capital market and restrictions on capital movements had and still have on these types of services. Thus a substantial restructuring can be expected in these countries. In Switzerland, in contrast, capital movements have been virtually free for over a decade and the country has developed a relatively competitive market for investment services.

On the other hand, in banking, Switzerland exhibits, together with Austria, prices substantially above those in other EFTA countries and comparable EC countries. Third in line is Sweden. Thus the two countries broadly believed to be the most efficient in banking among EFTA countries, also distinguish themselves with high prices. From this, the tentative conclusion may be drawn that financial integration will, in banking, mainly affect competition in Sweden and Switzerland, whereas the other countries to a larger degree will experience increased efficiency by restructuring in their banking sectors in addition to increased competition.

5. CONCLUSION

Financial integration in Western Europe will lead to considerable welfare effects in EFTA countries. Substantial benefits will accrue to these countries, since consumers of financial services will get better access to investment instruments and enjoy lower prices of financial services.

These benefits will, to some extent, be gained at the cost of producers of financial services. In most EFTA countries some restructuring of the banking and investment services sectors will occur and profits will decrease in hitherto sheltered parts of the industry.

The public sector will experience some loss in tax revenues due to the need to adjust capital taxes and taxes on financial transactions to West European standards.

There is a risk that public decision makers will try to renege on their pledges to liberalize capital movements and financial services in the light of problems encountered along the way. They might succumb to the pleas of ailing companies in the financial sector and try to soften their plight by accommodating policies, be it by introducing subsidies or new barriers to entry. Misdirected concerns for consumers might also entice decision makers to reregulate the financial industry. They might try to keep or introduce some barriers to cross-border trade for tax reasons.

Joining a West European financial area would diminish this risk. The international discipline imposed by signing a treaty on free capital movements and free movements of financial services would make it costly, if not impossible, to renege on the liberalization and on agreed upon measures to deregulate the financial markets. Such an agreement, with its inherent principles of freedom of establishment, of cross-border trade in financial services and of "competition in rules" would discourage public decision makers in the EFTA countries from taking political measures too far off the European mainstream.

FOOTNOTE

The author is solely responsible for the views expressed, which do not necessarily represent the views of the EFTA council or of the member governments.

REFERENCES

EC (1988a), "The Economics of 1992", European Economy No. 35.

EC (1988b), "Creation of a European financial Area", European Economy No. 36.

EFTA (1989), "Consequences and Problems of Liberalizing Capital Movements in the EFTA Countries", EFTA/EC 7.

Ems, E. (1989a), "European Banking Reform - The EFTA Perspective", in Stauder (ed.) Liberalization and Regulatory Reform in the Field of Banking Services in Europe: The Swiss Consumer's Point of View, Schulthess Polygraphischer Verlag Zürich.

_____ (1989b), "Liberalizing Capital Movements in EFTA - A First Step towards financial Integration", EFTA Bulletin No. 3/89.

Gardener, E. & D. Teppett (1990), "The Impact of 1992 on the Financial Services Sector of EFTA Countries", EFTA Occasional Paper No. 32.

Krugman, P.R. (1987), "Economic Integration in Europe: Some Conceptual Issues", in Padoa-Schioppa (ed.) Efficiency, Stability and Equity, Oxford University Press..

The Nordic Perspective Group (1990), Growth and Integration in a Nordic Perspective, ETLA, IFF, IUI and NÖI.

OECD (1989), Competition in Banking, Paris.

OECD (1990), Liberalisation of Capital Movements and Financial Services in the OECD Area, Paris.

Wijkman, P. (1988), "Implications of 1992 for Regulation, Competition, and the Structure of the Financial Services Industry: Research Issues", Gothenburg Studies in Financial Economics No. 1989:1.

Financial Regulation and Monetary Arrangements after 1992
C. Wihlborg, M. Fratianni and T.D. Willett (Editors)

16   Economic Reforms in the USSR and 1992

Igor G. Doronin

Institute of World Economy and International Relations, 117859 Moscow, USSR

1.   MARKET-ORIENTED REFORMS IN EASTERN AND WESTERN EUROPE

Whatever the differences between the economic reforms in the USSR and the construction of a single market within the European Community may be, they are of the same nature since they aim at a more active use of market forces that will lead to structural changes and a more effective use of the productive, scientific, financial and intellectual potential. There are, however, some obvious differences.

One difference has to do with the position from which these reforms start. If the EC follows the path of deepening market relations and removes the obstacles to free movements of goods, services, capital and manpower, then the USSR is at an initial stage of movement toward a market economy. The state sector is being transformed, and a market structure parallel to the state sector has originated.

Another difference concerns the nature of the problems and the dynamics of the ongoing transformations. For the EC the formation of a common market can be seen already, while the formation of a market economy and the concrete ways to achieve it in the USSR are less certain. Moreover, it is obvious that the consequences of the transformation, especially at the initial stages, will be different.

According to the predictions, the construction of a single market within the EC will lead to higher rates of economic growth, lower rates of inflation, increased employment, as well as improvements in the balance of payments. However, problems will emerge even under such favorable conditions due to structural adjustment and the formation of a unified financial market. The shift toward a market economy in the USSR requires a reduction of public expenditure, and above all a curtailment of centralized investments. This entails a reduction of the growth of the public sector which must be made up for by increased activity in the non-public sector, first and foremost in the processing industry, the production of consumer goods, and in the building sector.

A gradual liberalization of the price formation under the existing inflation potential is likely to increase the rate of inflation. This will stimulate the production of goods, and for this purpose it is necessary to remove administrative restrictions on enterprise activity. Furthermore, the change to an economically substantiated exchange rate calls for a depreciation. The effects of this depreciation is far from unambiguous. It can serve as an important stimulus for expanding exports and reducing imports. This is important in order to improve the unbalanced international payments position of the USSR. Hence, it is only logical to conclude that, compared to the EC, the future of the Soviet economy looks less certain in a short-term perspective. It is difficult to say how the process of decentralization will proceed. But there is no doubt that local markets of sovereign republics, territories and regions will emerge.

In the nearest future, the most difficult task will be to keep control over the economic situation, while introducing new principles and instruments of a market economy. In the meanwhile, we have to lay the foundation for a sustained economic growth on the basis of the development in other countries and in the EC in particular.

The importance of the financial integration in the EC reaches far beyond the framework of the Community itself. Practically all third countries will have to adapt their domestic and external financial policies to the process that takes place within the EC. In its relations to third countries the Commission proceeds from a desire to fulfill the obligations of international agreements and not to give unilateral advantages to third countries in spheres where international obligations are absent. This principle applies first of all to the markets for financial services, which are not yet covered by GATT rules. In such cases the principle of reciprocity is applied. Though it does not normally run counter to the process of liberalization, it may serve as an instrument of a protectionist policy.

Under the influence of the financial integration within the EC, third countries can rationalize and deregulate the banking system, simplify their control systems, liberalize the order of admittance for foreign banks and encourage activities in rendering financial services. These processes can be observed in the East European countries as well. In line with these developments, radical changes are expected in Soviet financial, taxation, banking and currency systems. It is the USSR and the East European countries that are in a less favorable position compared to other European countries. Owing to the existing structure and the management of their economies, which demonstrate a considerable force of inertia, the adaptation proceeds much slower and lags constantly behind the rapid international development. Hence, the vulnerability of restrictions in these countries under the principle of reciprocity is enhanced rather than slackened. The EC is aware of this and has made it clear that an all-out liberalization of the relations with the USSR and the East European countries calls for fundamental economic reforms in, for instance, price formation, credit policy, taxation, demonopolization, recognition of private property, and convertibility of currencies. The Commission believes that the principle of mutual economic benefit will be violated without these reforms.

At present, the EC has liberalized trade and economic relations considerably relative to some European countries, while others are in a less favorable situation. To our minds, there is a contradiction between the demands declared by the EC concerning the economic reforms in the USSR and the East European countries, on the one hand, and the economic processes in these countries, on the other. The obstacles to free trade, motivated by the absence of market structures, hinders the development of such structures, because these countries have to overcome both the resistance of a state-bureaucratic system, as well as the barriers on external markets.

Take the banking sector in the USSR, as an example. It has to protect its interest within the country, as well as surmount obstacles in foreign markets. At present, the number of cooperative and commercial banks engaged in commercial operations in the USSR is about 300. They are distinguished by high initiative and enterprise. At some time or another they will search for a way out to conduct operations on external markets. One of the problems likely to arise is whether, and under what conditions, they will have the possibility to carry out operations within the EC.

2. EC REFORMS AND CAPITAL REQUIREMENTS OF THE USSR

Today it is more or less clear that the transformation which take place in the EC will act as a serious pressure in favour of efficiency and speed of economic reforms. This pressure has already made itself felt directly and indirectly. The direct consequences will affect the movement of capital between the USSR and EC. Since the USSR is a net importer of capital, it is important to answer the question how the creation of a single financial market will affect the possibilities and the conditions for importing capital from EC. Furthermore, it is important to assess the changes in the volumes of financial flows.

Regarding the evaluation of future flows of capital, it is necessary to bear in mind that one of the major tasks of a common financial market is to create the most favourable conditions for mobilizing savings and financing of investments within the EC. One can expect that the trend towards a narrowing of opportunities for the USSR to obtain credit and investment resources is likely to become more pronounced due to an invigorated investment strategy, structural changes and an accelerated scientific and technical progress within the EC. Also, one has to consider the fact that the coordinated credit policy of the member states will play an ever greater role with respect to the USSR.

It is reasonable to presume that the opportunities to attract foreign capital on commercial terms will become more and more limited. These limitations are caused not only by developments within the Community, but also by considerations of the USSR's balance of payments situation. The necessity to limit the growth of external debt will be one of the major reasons for a more prudent policy on foreign capital markets.

The Soviet Union needs and will need foreign capital, however. It is becoming more evident that it is impossible to overcome the present crisis and restructure the economy by internal efforts only. A much greater role must be played by foreign investment capital in the Soviet economy. When considering the prospects of attracting foreign capital, it is necessary to consider different aspects; legal regulation, structural policy, as well as forms and methods of foreign capital participation. The fact that all these aspects are not sufficiently elaborated is one of the obstacles to foreign investments in the Soviet economy on a wide scale.

It is becoming evident that foreign partners in the USSR should enjoy the same rights and possibilities as Soviet enterprises and organizations. It is clear that the practice of special privileges does not pay off. Therefore, considerable reforms in the legal framework are necessary. While defining our structural economic policy it is necessary to determine the priorities and the ways of linking up the interests of domestic and foreign investors. As for the forms and methods of attracting foreign capital they should be flexible, and include, among other things joint ventures, special economic zones and concessions.

3. THE EC AS A MODEL

The creation of a common financial market in the EC shows the directions for carrying out reforms in money, tax and currency systems in ways that are in line with the requirements of the rest of the world. These aspects are of considerable importance to the USSR, since steps are taken to make the transition to market structures more efficient.

The common market within the EC is a realization of supply side economics. The experiences from a number of states give a positive answer to the question whether deregulation and encouragement of competition promote reduction in costs and stimulates economic activity. It seems reasonable to take account of the fact that supply side economics has been elaborated on and verified in practice in developed market economies with relatively balanced economies.

The implementation of the economic reforms in the USSR has revealed two aspects in the transition toward a market economy. The first aspect concerns measures aiming at increasing the economic independence of enterprises and organizations. During 1987 and 1988, this was reflected in the laws on state enterprises and cooperatives, reforms in the banking system, and in a number of decrees concerning foreign economic activities. However, these reforms took place in a system of widespread state owned properties that displays strong monopolistic structures. As a consequence, the monopolistic tendencies in the economy have increased and the possibilities of the state to manage the economic process have been reduced.

The second aspect is that a lot of proposals are being reduced to basic stabilization policy measures, like the withdrawal of excess money by any means, strict control of wages and prices, etc. This situation has arisen as a reaction to the weakening of the state control over the economic process and the growing negative tendencies in the economy.

4. REFORMS IN THE FINANCIAL SECTOR IN THE USSR

Economic reforms call for deep transformations of state property. Specifically privatization, the creation of market structures as well as alterations in the the management of state bodies are necessary. The bank sphere will play an important role in forming the market structures of the economy. In the near future, substantial alterations will take place in this sector, as reflected in the preparation of laws on the State bank of USSR, and on bank and banking activity. These legal acts contain a number of fundamentally new propositions which affect both the structure of the banking system and the functioning of the credit markets;

1. The State bank of the USSR will be under the jurisdiction of the Supreme Soviet of the USSR, implying that the conduct of monetary policy will be under direct control of the highest body of legislative power.

2. The banking system will consist of two levels. The first level is the State bank of USSR, and the second level consisting of the rest of the banks having the status of commercial banks.

3. Free movement of credit should be allowed between banks, creating the basis for a regular money market.

4. The rates of interest on credits will be set by the commercial banks on the basis of contracts with the borrowers. The State bank will regulate the levels through changes in the rates of interest on credits granted to the commercial banks.

5. Regulation has been established for opening, implementing and terminating the activities of foreign banks, their affiliates as well as representatives thereof. Their affairs will be covered by the Law on economic activity on the Soviet territory by foreign legal persons and citizens, the Law of the State bank of the USSR, and the Law of banks and banking.

6. Rules have been determined for setting up commercial banks owned by Soviet and foreign legal persons. These may be registered upon submission of required documents; an application for granting permission, feasibility studies (economic substantiation), and data on the qualifications of the administrative staff. Also, foreign owners should present a charter or other documents in support of their legal status and a balance sheet for the three preceding years, a decision of the relevant authorities on participation in the joint bank, a written application from the controlling authorities of the residence country of a foreign founder showing that they have no objections to the participation in a joint bank on the territory of the USSR, or a document of an authoritative legal representative showing that such a permission is not required by the laws of the residence country of the foreign founder.

The importance of foreign banks and joint banking activities is that they undermine the existing monopoly of the Vnesheconombank, which is the administrative organ for currency distribution within the country. The first joint bank was "The International Moscow Bank" established late in 1989. Its founders were several Soviet banks and banks from Italy, Germany, France, Finland and Austria. The latter group holds 60 percent of the capital. It intends to offer traditional banking services, as well as to cooperate in the search for counterparts, participate in feasibility studies of projects, conduct "leasing" and "factoring" operations, and to manage portfolios of clients. The bank is expected to function by the end of 1990 and is therefore timed to operate under the new laws on banking.

5. REQUIREMENTS FOR REFORMS

The problem of harmonization in the financial sphere is not so much a problem of benefits as an objective necessity, and should first and foremost be associated with a global trend of internationalization of economic activities. For the USSR the problems identified above should first of all be tackled with the purpose of bringing the adjustment mechanisms in line with the the requirements imposed by a market economy. First, the work should start with bookkeeping and cost accounting as it is known in the West. Secondly, adequate statistics on the supply of money, credit, and the balance of payments including the foreign debt, must be collected and processed according to standards in the Western countries.

A policy of harmonization is impossible without making international comparisons. The rouble exchange rate, whose unreality should be evident by now, has an important role to play in this context. The introduction of a new exchange rate would have a significant effect on foreign economic activities, and would call forth activities that deal with the reliability of economic and commercial information. It seems that harmonization must first of all begin with a cooperation between statistical services and an exchange of information about methods for the coordination of statistics.

Part Six

Economic Policy Perspectives on Monetary Arrangements

Financial Regulation and Monetary Arrangements after 1992
C. Wihlborg, M. Fratianni and T.D. Willett (Editors)
© 1991 Elsevier Science Publishers B.V. All rights reserved

17   A Japanese Central Banker's View of the EMS

Yoshiharu Oritani

The Bank of Japan, CPO Box 203, Tokyo 100-91, Japan

1. INTRODUCTION

It is a great pleasure for me to discuss or even just observe the development of monetary union, especially a plan for establishing a supernational central bank in Europe.

I have been working for the Central Bank of Japan for almost twenty years. During this time I have experienced various aspects of central banking including bank examination, business condition analysis, and designing of payment systems. I have been considering what money is, what the essence of central banking is. The establishment of the European Central Bank seems to be the birth of a new central bank. As the birth of a new star provides a lot of information about the universe, the observation and discussion of the new central bank give us a very precious information about central banking and money.

Developments towards a European Monetary Union has been attracting a lot of attention not only in the Bank of Japan, but also in the financial community in Japan as a whole. Since the Bank of Japan's roles in the economy like other central banks are to conduct monetary policy, supervise private financial institutions, and provide payment services together with the function of the lender of last resort (LLR), I focus on these aspects.

As for the development towards an EMU, two major reactions in the Japanese financial community can be pointed out. Firstly, it is basically received favorably by our financial community. Secondly, it has stimulated reform of the Japanese financial system.

2. REASONS FOR THE FAVORABLE REACTION TO A EUROPEAN MONETARY UNION

Among the various reasons why the Japanese financial community welcomes the development towards the EMU, the following two reasons seem to be the most important.

2.1 Deregulation of Financial Markets in the European Community

When the 1992 program for the EC market was unveiled, there was a controversy about its characteristics in Japan. Some argued that the plan implies further deregulation of the financial market in the EC, while others asserted that it potentially implies the building of higher walls between markets of the EC and third countries, such as the United States and Japan. The former opinion, the deregulation hypothesis, has been proven right by the declaration that the reciprocity principle would not be strictly adopted. Many Japanese financial institutions have been establishing subsidiaries in European countries to take advantage of the single European market.

2.2 The EC Economy and a European Central Bank

The second reason for a favorable reaction is due to expectations that the EMU will have positive effects on the real economy of EC. If this happens, it would be favorable for Japan since the economies of EC and Japan are interdependent nowadays.

Whether or not the EMU can bring positive effects on the EC economy depends in my opinion mainly on the structure and policy of the European Central Bank, a "European System of Central Banks". The first and the most important point for establishing the ESCB is that it should conduct stable monetary policy to control inflation. In other words, no economy can prosper without price stability. To achieve this goal, the ESCB should be independent from any political power in EC.

The second point is that the ESCB should develop a network which links existing central bank's payment systems in EC member countries. Without the linked payment network, it would be impossible to transfer funds smoothly from country to country and, consequently, capital movements among EC countries would be costly. Then, the difference among interest rates in member countries would not be diminished, which could cause volatility of foreign exchange rates. From this standpoint, it may be helpful to study the outcome of the funds transfer network among District Reserve Banks in the United States.

The third point is that it is necessary to shift the supervisory and rule-making power from government agencies, (national banking commission or ministries of finance) to the ESCB or national central banks. Since the central bank is also a kind of a bank, it is much more familiar with financial markets than government agencies. Therefore, supervision and rule-making are conducted better by the central bank than by individual government agencies. From this angle, it may be beneficial to compare central banks with or without their own supervisory power.

A fourth and related point is that in order to solve systematic risk problems in EC's financial markets, the lender of last resort function should be provided by the agency supervising the banking system, i.e. the ESCB or national banks.

3. REFORM OF THE JAPANESE FINANCIAL SYSTEM

Responding to the developments towards the EMU, there is in Japan a lively discussion about reforming the Japanese financial system. In Japan, banks are prohibited from engaging in securities activities according to Article 65 of the Securities and Exchange Law which was established after the World War II imitating the Glass-Steagall Act. The Financial System Research Council, an advisory body to the Minister of Finance, has recommended abolishment of the separation between banking and securities business by allowing a bank to establish a subsidiary engaging in securities business. In the discussion by the Council, the universal banking system in EC has been one of the most influential factors to consider for reform of the Japanese financial system even after the declaration that the reciprocity principle would not be strictly adopted. The reason is a concern about the possibility that the EC may effectively require Japan to adopt the universal banking system.

Although the separation principle will be abolished, banks will still not be allowed to engage in securities business within the same entity. Since it is not permitted in Japan to establish a bank holding company, a "fire-wall" betwen a parent bank and affiliates would be an instrument to avoid risk transmission from a securities subsidiary to a parent bank.

4. JAPANESE PERSPECTIVES ON A EUROPEAN MONETARY UNION

Let me discuss aspects of the EMU based on impressions from this volume. Since I am a member of the BIS payment system group, I would like to comment from this position.

My first comment is that the discussion of the EMU and the ESCB is unreasonably limited to monetary policy. As mentioned, the central bank is responsible not only for monetary policy, but also for payment services, the function of lender of last resort and for supervision.

It is therefore necessary to discuss those aspects of central banking when we think about integration of central banks. In this respect, the paper by Folkerts-Landau, Garber and Weisbrod is very interesting, since their argument stimulated me to think about the effect of linked payment systems on reserve requirement set by national central banks.

Furthermore, the presentation by Alberto Giovannini is also very interesting, because his instability hypothesis is strongly related to the lender of last resort-function of central banks.

My second comment is that the discussion on Monetary Union is unreasonably limited to the discussion of a single currency approach versus a competing currency approach. I think there is another type of distinction between, say, "top down approach" versus "bottom up approach". "Top down approach" means that the Monetary Union starts with the establishment of the ESCB which is responsible only for monetary policy. Then, the ESCB expands its scope to payment service, lender of last resort-function and supervision.

Conversely, "bottom up approach" means that the Monetary Union starts with the linking of payment systems of national central banks, and cooperation of national central banks in the function of lender of last resort. Then, the Monetary Union expands its scope to monetary policy. Since the central bank is also a kind of bank, it is very important to discuss the banking aspect of central banks when we discuss the supernational central bank. It is impossible to imagine a Federal Reserve System without linkage of payment systems of district reserve banks.

Thirdly, and finally, when we talk about money or currency, I think it is necessary to define the concept of money. Whether money means deposit money or cash money is very important, when we discuss different aspects of the Monetary Union.

In conclusion, I hope the European countries will succeed in establishing the ESCB through the bottom up approach, and then we would like to establish a global central bank by linking the ESCB, the Bank of Japan and the US Federal Reserve System.

FOOTNOTE

This paper represents the views of the author and are not those of the Bank of Japan.

Financial Regulation and Monetary Arrangements after 1992
C. Wihlborg, M. Fratianni and T.D. Willett (Editors)
© 1991 Elsevier Science Publishers B.V. All rights reserved

18   A Large Outsider's View of the EMS

Sven W. Arndt

Lowe Institute, Claremont McKenna College, Bauer Center, 500 E9th Str., Claremont, CA 91711-6400, USA

1. INTRODUCTION

The analysis of trade and monetary integration has traditionally focused on the implications for member countries, while paying relatively scant attention to its effects on outsiders. In developing its plans for completion of the internal market and for further monetary integration, the European Community has largely observed that tradition. Of the many studies carried out or commissioned by the Community, the majority has focused on the internal effects. Much of the independent research since then has preserved that perspective.

It is, of course, well-known that outsiders cannot insulate themselves entirely against the consequences of regional integration. Although some of the typical spillovers may be welfare-enhancing, many are welfare-reducing from the outsider's perspective. The negative consequences can be particularly severe for outsiders who are the low-cost producers in a given industry. They feel the full weight of trade diversion associated with regional tariff liberalization and at least some of the burden of other forms of regional goods market integration.

Among the spillovers likely to be significant after completion of the internal market in Europe, will be those associated with the enhanced competitiveness of European firms whose industries will have benefited from cost reductions precipitated by the region-wide rationalization of production. These developments do not generate the trade diversion of static tariff liberalization, but they nevertheless impose adjustment costs on outside producers.

The extent of the adjustment problem, and hence the potential need for policy intervention, depends at least in part on the flexibility of relative prices and on the inter-industrial and inter-sectoral mobility of resources in the EC's trading partners. The need to adjust to changes in relative prices may very well turn out to be a key consequence if completion of the internal market generates significant improvements in the efficiency of resource utilization within the Community. If the number of outsider industries affected by this competitive challenge is significant, the shock may have a depressing effect on overall economic activity and thereby provoke calls for activist monetary and fiscal policies.

The overall effect on outsiders need not be negative even where significant elements of trade diversion are present. To the extent, for example, that integration abroad produces faster economic growth, it may generate positive prospects for the exports of outsiders which may more than offset the negative effects of the initial act of liberalization itself.

Similarly, monetary integration in Europe may have positive as well as negative implications for the outsider - positive if, for example, it contributes to lower world inflation and reduced exchange rate volatility; negative if it contributes to lower growth rates. From the perspective of the large outsider, who is likely to bear greater responsibility for the maintenance of global monetary stability, the completion of a large integrated monetary entity in Europe may be positive or negative in its implications depending upon its effect on global stability and on burden-sharing.

2. THE NATURE OF SHOCKS

The range of likely shocks and possible outcomes is large indeed, and so is the range of possible policy responses. Disturbances that would be of immediate interest or concern in large outsider countries would be those that significantly change the level and/or variability of demand or supply in domestic markets for goods, services and assets. For a large outsider like the United States with perceived global leadership responsibilities, shocks to world markets may be of concern as well even where they exert no immediate effect on the domestic economy.

Disturbances can be beneficial or harmful. Beneficial shocks would include those that increase growth rates or reduce exchange rate volatility, while harmful shocks are those that deliver opposite results. Since large regime shifts of the kind currently underway in Europe typically generate both positive and negative spillovers, it is their net effect that is of interest. If the repercussions of shocks on residents and interest groups in outsider countries are skewed, policy makers may be faced with complex problems in managing the political economy of adjustment.

Not all the shocks likely to emanate from Europe will be of interest to policy makers at the aggregate level and not all those that are of interest will require changes in monetary arrangements. Shocks that are industry or sector specific often do not affect overall economic conditions or are not amenable to treatment by broad monetary policies. Changes in industrial structure and competition in Europe may generate significant spillovers from the perspective of U.S. producers, without changing the rules and conditions pertaining to macro policy and monetary arrangements.

This is not to say, however, that sector-specific shocks cannot have repercussions at the aggregate level. As already noted, significant new competition from restructured European industries may, at least temporarily, exert a depressing effect on employment and output in outsider countries, thereby exposing governments to political pressure aimed at greater macro policy activism. Pressures toward that end may also mount if the Community attempts to address adjustment difficulties during the transition to Europe 1992 by means of protectionist policies aimed at exporting the burden of structural change (one of the feared aspects of the so-called "fortress Europe" scenario). It is easy to see that developments of this sort have the potential of destabilizing the policy environment in outsider countries.

On the monetary side, the regime that is eventually installed in the Community may contribute to or detract from global monetary stability. Its effect on the rest of the world will depend in part on its intrinsic structure and in part on the rules and conditions that will govern monetary policy processes. It is useful to recall in this context that the United

States has over the years been criticised by other countries for the destabilizing global consequences of its macroeconomic policies. Only very large monetary entities have broad and consequential external effects, and the EC of the future may become a member of that exclusive club.

A European Community with a centralized monetary system is likely to have a larger effect on world monetary, exchange rate and macro conditions than one composed of many decentralized monetary policy regimes. Increased global monetary influence is, moreover, compatible with a considerable range of specific monetary regimes - including greater policy harmonization in a modified EMS, various types of permanently fixed exchange rate systems, and currency union.

An integrated monetary regime which achieves Europe's internal objectives and at the same time contributes to enhanced global monetary stability would clearly serve the interests of both the Community and the large outsider. A monetary regime, on the other hand, which achieved greater internal exchange rate stability at the expense of increased external instability would create new monetary management problems for the outsider. There is some evidence that such a trade-off may have been in effect during the first ten years of the present EMS system.

Another potentially troublesome trade-off may arise between internal exchange rate stability and average economic growth in the Community. In EMS-type exchange rate regimes, convergence of inflation is a key collective policy objective. If convergence must take place at relatively low inflation rates, high-inflation countries may be able to achieve such outcomes only at the expense of lower growth rates. This, in turn, may bring down average growth rates. Even if adverse growth effects last only as long as it takes the private sector to adjust to the new policy regime, they can create major problems of transition. We return to this issue in the next section.

Any future monetary arrangements subject to such anti-growth biases would clearly be less attractive to outsiders than systems capable of achieving exchange rate and monetary stability without impairing economic growth.

As the United States has clearly demonstrated during the past decade, fiscal policy in a large economy has non-trivial consequences for global macroeconomic stability, real exchange rates and competitiveness. In the Europe of many uncoordinated fiscal policy regimes, the policies of individual countries tend often to be offsetting, at least in part. This reduces the size and intensity of the fiscal shocks that spill over into world markets.

Policy regimes that harmonize and hence synchronize fiscal policies among separate national entities within Europe and those that replace fiscal federalism with more centralized fiscal processes promise to enhance the impact of EC fiscal developments on the world economy. Whether this increased EC profile works to raise or reduce global macro stability depends on the nature of the new regime and on the details of the policy process. Very little is known about the effects on global macroeconomic stability of the interaction between two large, integrated economic blocs.

3. THE TRANSITION PERIOD

As noted in the previous section, trade-offs among policy targets within the Community may generate undesirable spillovers. Although some of these may persist over the long run, others may be more short-term in nature and may be particularly troublesome during the transition to 1992. This may be so for a number of reasons.

If industrial restructuring and the consequent reallocation of resources leads to large transitional unemployment problems among members of the Community, greater macro policy activism on the part of some governments may be difficult to escape. This may make maintenance of convergent monetary policies more difficult and hence introduce greater variability of internal and external exchange rates.

Greater policy divergence and a higher incidence of policy variability, as governments attempt to cope with the changing conditions of the transition to 1992, are bound to occur if the transition runs into trouble. In that event, the EC is likely to be the source of destabilizing disturbances, not only at the level of various industries and sectors, but in aggregate terms as well. Such an outcome would place great pressure on large outsiders like the United States and Japan, as policy makers are pressed to devise offsetting policies.

4. CONCLUDING OBSERVATIONS

That the transition to Europe 1992 will generate spillovers is not in dispute. Nor is the likelihood that there will be negative effects among the spillovers. What is subject to debate is the net effect and the duration of disturbances likely to emanate from Europe, as well as their implications for global monetary arrangements and for monetary policies on the part of large outsiders.

Both the completion of the internal European market and further integration in the monetary sphere have the potential of enhancing or diminishing world-wide monetary and macroeconomic stability. Transformation of the European Community from a collection of largely independent and weakly coordinated policy regimes into a more fully integrated economic and monetary entity is bound to increase the external weight and influence of the Community. The net effect on global stability will depend upon the nature of the new arrangements and is likely to be different in the transition from the steady state.

Financial Regulation and Monetary Arrangements after 1992
C. Wihlborg, M. Fratianni and T.D. Willett (Editors)
© 1991 Elsevier Science Publishers B.V. All rights reserved

19   Current Account and Fiscal Policy Adjustment in the EMS

Karen K. Lewis

Department of Economics, University of Pennsylvania, 3718 Locust Walk, Philadelphia
PA 19104-6297, USA

The upcoming unification of financial markets in Europe has led economists to consider its economic implications. In particular, financial integration raises a number of different issues dealing with the likely effects upon the union as a whole. Below, I raise some of these issues and, in some cases, question the validity of the arguement economists have put forth.

The first issue addresses the balance of payments of a unified Europe. Conjectures about the future balance of payments of the unified European community have recently been made given current trends in payments balances of the individual European countries. During the 1980's, the surplus countries such as Germany have compensated for the deficits from countries such as Italy. It is therefore argued that the future integrated economic system of Europe would have a current account surplus vis a vis the rest of the world.

However, this type of argument raises at least two questions: First, since these trends have occured without integration, how would economic integration affect future current account imbalances? The removal of goods and financial restrictions should increase the volume of trade. In particular, the capital account depends upon financial variables that affect intertemporal decisions. Therefore, if integration affects the interest rate faced by investors and consumers, the rate at which they discount the future relative to the present will also change. A different discount rate can clearly alter savings decisions, and therefore the aggregate current account surplus of the European community. For example, if the increased competition for funds from greater integration leads to lower interest rates, then standard current account models would say spending should increase relative to income. In this case, the current account would worsen, not improve. Thus, the overall impact upon the payments balance of a unified Europe relative to the rest of the world cannot be directly determined from current trends in the individual countries.

The argument that the surplus countries can finance the deficit countries after integration leads to a second, more important, question. Namely, do individual countries become less concerned about their imbalances just because they have become economically integrated with other European countries? As long as countries remain culturally and socially distinct, current account imbalances across European countries can remain politically sensitive even within an economically unified Europe. For instance, although the individual states in the United States are financially integrated, trade imbalances across states can be a source of political discord. During the run-up in oil prices following the embargos of the 1970s, bumper stickers frequently seen on the highways of oil exporting states such as Texas and Oklahoma read: "Let the Yankees freeze in the dark." This type of anecdotal evidence suggests that trade imbalances among European countries will remain politically sensitive even after integration.

A second issue of financial integration concerns its potential effects upon fiscal discipline. It has been argued that financially unified markets enforce fiscal discipline because governments that wish to borrow must face international markets. Since governments must compete for funds in these competitive markets, they must pay a risk premium in order to make creditors willing to lend their funds.

This argument raises a deeper question, however. That is, since countries already borrow internationally, will this risk premium rise or fall? Table 1 reports the ratio of foreign to domestic debt outstanding and the ratio of new foreign to total net borrowing for four European countries (as well as the United States for comparison.) As these numbers show, the countries were already borrowing in world markets for the years 1984 to 1988. Furthermore, the domestic Treasury bill rate exceeded the Libor rate for each currency. These numbers should be interpreted with some caution. For example, the Libor rates are rates on three-month deposits, while the Treasury bill rates are rates on differing short term maturities. Therefore, these interest differentials may include term premia due to differences in maturity. Given this caveat, these numbers suggest that the countries were already paying a premium on their debt.

Since many of the countries were already borrowing at rates potentially including a risk premium, it seems quite plausible that economic integration could actually reduce the risk premium. For example, greater integration could increase economic trade and, hence, productivity. This increased productivity would lead investors to develop more faith in the country's creditworthiness. In such a scenario, the risk premium may actually fall with no obvious impact upon fiscal discipline.

A third issue involves the collection of seigniorage revenues. If countries are integrated monetarily, the center country in the monetary arrangement will collect these revenues. In a system of monetary union but fiscal autonomy, distribution of these seigniorage revenues becomes politically contentious. Thus, in order to avoid political conflicts arising from the revenue redistribution, the issue of how to allocate seigniorage must be addressed before a centralized monetary system is established.

A fourth and related issue is how non-member countries of the ERM will adjust to lower inflation and, therefore, to lower seigniorage revenues. That is, as these countries join the ERM, they will be forced to reduce inflation in order to maintain fixed parities vis a vis other European countries. Since seigniorage revenues must fall during the transition period to lower inflation, this process will force the countries to combine fiscal austerity with monetary contraction. Such a combination may induce a costly adjustment process for the economies in question.

Given this costly adjustment, it has been argued that countries should first reduce inflation on their own at a slower rate. This gradual adjustment could ease the budgetary adjustments required in the transition. Then, only after inflation is brought into line with the rest of Europe should these countries join.

However, this argument raises an important question. If these countries can conduct policy to reduce inflation outside of the ERM, why have they not done so already? The answer may be that they cannot stick with an anti-inflation policy on their own. The fixed exchange rate system becomes attractive to these countries precisely because joining the system provides a way to precommit to reducing and, then, stabilizing inflation. If so, reducing inflation gradually first, and then joining later may not be a feasible alternative.

Table 1
Measures of Foreign Government Debt

	1984	1985	1986	1987	1988
Germany					
Foreign to total debt	.24	.27	.32	.33	--
Foreign to total net borrow.	.34	.70	1.25	.56	--
Libor rate	5.8	5.4	4.6	4.1	4.3
T-bill rate	5.7	5.0	3.9	3.3	3.6
France					
Foreign to total debt	.04	.04	.03	.03	.03
Foreign to total net borrow.	-.01	.01	-.00	.01	--
Libor rate	12.8	10.8	9.5	8.6	8.1
T-bill rate	12.5	10.9	8.4	8.2	7.8
United Kingdom					
Foreign to total debt	.08	.09	.10	--	--
Foreign to total net borrow.	.06	.26	.30	--	--
Libor rate	10.0	12.3	10.9	9.8	10.3
T-bill rate	9.3	11.6	10.4	9.3	9.8
Spain					
Foreign to total debt	.09	.08	.05	--	--
Foreign to total net borrow.	.05	.02	-.14	--	--
Libor rate	14.4	11.4	12.3	11.7	--
T-bill rate	13.4	10.9	8.6	11.3	10.8
United States					
Foreign to total debt	.14	.14	.15	.15	.17
Foreign to total net borrow.	.09	.16	.18	.11	--
Libor rate	10.9	8.4	6.9	7.2	8.0
T-bill rate	9.6	7.5	6.0	5.8	6.7

Data from International Monetary Fund, <u>International Financial Statistics</u>, 1990

The fifth and final issue concerns the effects of unification upon financial market segmentation. Through capital controls across countries, the financial market of local savers in Europe is segmented from the market of large savers. Furthermore, financial regulators have been found to alter the differentials between interest rates earned by different savers using data in the United States. Differentials due to market segmentation affect the rate of return investors must pay to obtain funds for investment purposes. In particular, when small local savers are segmented from large savers, investors may obtain funds at a lower cost and thus expand economic activity.

Hence, the question is: how does integration affect this segmentation and,thereby, investment? Of course, the answer to this question will remain unknown until after the unification is complete. However, some casual observations on people's expectations about financial integration may help shed some light on the issue. To this point, Grilli (1989) cites a recent Eurobarometer survey that asked people: "The coming into being of the single European market by 1992 will mean the free circulation of persons, goods and property within the European Community Countries ... Can you tell me, ... whether you personally think it will be an advantage or disadvantage?" In particular, this question was asked concerning different aspects of integration. Interestingly, about 70% of those questioned responded that the ability to open a bank account in any country within the Community was an advantage.

If people's expectations are correct, unification will lead to substantially greater competition for the funds of savers. If so, then the increased competition should erode the ability of banks to segment the markets. As a result, this erosion should reduce the ability of financial regulators to affect investment.

Overall, the future unification of financial markets in Europe raises a number of issues ranging from the financing of current account balances to the implications for fiscal austerity. Of course, the questions raised by these issues elude definitive answers since the exact form of unification envisaged does not have a precedent. In most cases, however, the answers depend systematically upon how the financial markets affect the aggregate economic system.

FOOTNOTES

1. For example, see Branson (1991)

2. See Giavazzi and Giovannini, Ch. 5

REFERENCES

Branson, W.H. (1991), "Financial Market Integration, Macroeconomic Policy and the EMS" in Bliss, C. and J.B. de Macedo (eds) Unity with Diversity in the European Community, Cambridge University Press

Giavazzi, F. and A. Giovannini (1989), Limiting Exchange Rate Flexibility: The European Monetary System, MIT Press, Cambridge

Grilli, V. (1989), "Europe 1992: Issues and Prospects for the Financial Markets," Economic Policy, October, 388 - 411.

Financial Regulation and Monetary Arrangements after 1992
C. Wihlborg, M. Fratianni and T.D. Willett (Editors)
347

20 A Swedish Central Banker's View of the EMS

Thomas Franzén

Sveriges Riksbank, P O Box 16283, S-103 25 Stockholm, Sweden

1. INTRODUCTION

Europe enters the 1990s with a new-found confidence that would have seemed fanciful only a few years ago. Gone is the pessimism and talk of "Eurosclerosis". Instead, confidence has returned, employment expansion has resumed, and business investment has surged. Western Europe's real GDP grew 3.7 percent in 1988 and nearly as much in 1989. In 1990, the major economies in Western Europe should again manage a real GDP growth of 3 percent or more.

The strong growth of business investments and GDP is partly the product of structural improvements. Some of the credit must of course go to the EC's 1992 "single market" project. Another important factor is that the business community has gained confidence in the policy environment. For much of Europe, the EMS offers policy stability.

2. THE EMS - CONVERGING ON STABILITY

I would like to discuss some aspects of the European Monetary System. The results of the cooperation are - in many respects - admirable.

The EMS is now widely regarded as having functioned satisfactorily for nearly a decade. In retrospect, skeptics underestimated the ability of the EMS to meet the different circumstances of its members. The critics also underestimated the potential for combining rules with discretion in the operation of the ERM and, above all, they underestimated the cohesion and commitment attributable to larger cooperation and integration objectives within the EC.

Evaluation of the effects of the EMS can be focused on three areas: (1) exchange rate movements; (2) policy coordination; (3) and convergence of economic performance.

Let us look at the first area - exchange rate movements. The parities of EMS currencies participating in the exchange rate mechanism (ERM) have not been realigned since January 1987, apart from the fairly recent adjustment bringing the Italian lira into the narrow 2.25 percent band. Furthermore, empirical assessment of the impact of the ERM on exchange rate variability shows a reduction in the volatility of intra-ERM nominal and real exchange rates.

Sometimes it has been argued that the reduction in exchange rate variability has been bought at the cost of increased variability in interest rates. This does not seem to be the case. On the contrary, the exchange rate cooperation has helped reduce speculative movements, thereby making sharp changes in short-term interest rates less necessary. The reduced interest rate variability has been facilitated by an increased symmetry in the economic policy goals among the EMS-countries and by an increased convergence of the economic performance.

There has been significant progress in the coordination of monetary policies. Such coordination has been part and parcel of the trend - also visible outside the EMS - towards tighter monetary policy to bring down inflation. However, coordination of fiscal policies has shown notably less progress. Specifically, large fiscal imbalances have continued to persist in some EMS countries. I think that the divergencies in the fiscal policies among the EMS-countries can prove to be one of the largest problems in the implementation of a workable EMU. I will return to this topic later on.

The third area - convergence of economic performance - has been most marked in the area of inflationary developments. The inflation rate has been reduced and the inflation differentials have tended to narrow significantly during the 80s. In addition the interest rate differentials between the member countries have also been reduced.

I do not think that the success in reducing inflation in the member countries can be ascribed to the EMS cooperation alone. One very important explanation is the focus on anti-inflationary policies in each member country. Each country has invested a lot of effort in achieving credibility in the anti-inflationary policy.

One should not underestimate the importance of the EMS in the anti-inflationary policy, however. The EMS has facilitated the reduction of the inflation rates by providing a form for cooperation in which anti-inflationary policies could be pursued more effectively. By participating in a fixed exchange rate system that includes the Federal Republic of Germany, with its specific adherence to price stability, the other member countries have been able to increase the credibility of their efforts to combat inflation.

An area where there has not been any convergence is the development of the current account balances. The spread of surpluses and deficits has not narrowed between the participating countries. However, one should not automatically view current account imbalances as a large problem. With internationalised economies and free capital movements, current account imbalances are harder to interpret. For example, a widening of the current account imbalances may be judged analytically to be a harmless and even positive by-product of Europe's economic integration. Having said this, I still want to stress that policy makers should keep an eye on the current account development. A current account imbalance is often a sign of instability. Furthermore, a current account deficit is often an indication of too strong domestic demand and strong inflationary pressure. That is, for instance, the case in Sweden.

During the first years of EMS' existence if was often emphasised that EMS-partcipation gives a disciplinary effect on the economic policy. However, the disciplinary effect was not sufficient to create stability. There were frequent realignments during the first years of the EMS. But gradually the member countries have achieved something that is of vital importance for stability - symmetry in their policy goals. This symmetry has changed the character of the EMS from being disciplinary to being mainly cooperative. Consequently, realignments have become very rare.

I have read summaries of the papers written for this conference. Some of the papers discuss the lack of symmetry in the economic structure of the member states and that the EMS-area, in fact, is not an optimal currency area - at least not according to the traditional definition of an optimal currency area. The discussion of the symmetry problem is interesting but, in my view, it does not highlight the most important aspect of symmetry - that being policy goals among the member countries. These countries have gradually adopted the common goals of low inflation, high factor mobility and price and wage flexibility. The increased symmetry in the policy goals and the resulting increased cooperation are the reasons for EMS' success and the driving forces behind the further development of the EMS into an Economic and Monetary Union.

3. THE EMU

Intensive work is being put into the preparation of the EC intergovernmental conference in 1991. It is going to map the remaining stages of the proposed EMU.

The first stage in the three-stage progression towards European monetary union envisaged in the Delors Report, commits EC members to closer policy coordination and performance convergence. It also includes the participation of all members - most notably Britain - in the EMS exchange rate mechansim, (ERM), albeit with no target date agreed. Even though the first step does not imply a transfer of the monetary policy decisions away from the individual countries to a common decision-making body, it is important, I think, not to underestimate the impact of this step.

The second step is a transitory step where the conduct of monetary policy gradually will be transferred from the member countries to the gradually strengthened common central bank. However there is, from what I understand, a discussion among the EMS-countries about the implications of this step. Step 2 could cause uncertainty and instability and consequently hamper the progress towards the ultimate goal of a monetary and economic union.

The third step of the Delors plan outlines fundamental changes in the structure of economic policy coordination and in the conduct of monetary policy among the EC-countries. The ultimate goals are irrevocably fixed exchange rates, a single common currency and a common monetary policy conducted by a common central bank.

Given the risks implied in the second step it seems to be more desirable to move directly from step 1 to step 3 or at least that step 2 should be very short-lived.

A workable EMU must resolve major issues of institutional structure and control - issues inescapably dominated by political and national sovereignty concerns as well as economic objectives. One important issue is the mandate and the position of the common central bank.

In a common central bank the monetary policy will be formulated collectively by all member states. Consequently, there is a risk of getting a monetary policy which is less anti-inflationary. But hopefully, the emphasis on anti-inflationary developments is by now so deeply rooted in all the member states, that a single monetary policy conducted by a common central bank would be as anti-inflationary as the policies we see today.

In my view, it is crucial that the common central bank is given a mandate that will create the necessary conditions for pursuing an anti-inflationary policy. An important condition, I believe, is that the common central bank is given an independent position. It is thus of utmost importance to find suitable forms for achieving central bank independence.

Presently, there is a discussion about central bank independence in Sweden. In the Swedish discussion I think that a very important distinction has been forgotten - the distinction between central bank independence and central bank accountability. This distinction is highlighted in the discussion about the EMU, however.

It is obvious that there must be central bank accountability in order to guarantee democratic control. However, central bank independence is also necessary to guarantee that the monetary policy is guided by long run considerations and focused on preserving a low-inflationary environment. It is important to make absolutely clear that central bank independece is not in conflict with the goal of democratic control.

Another area of importance, but also somewhat controversial, is the coordination of fiscal policies. As I mentioned before I think that a large problem - perhaps the largest problem - is to find suitable and acceptable forms for fiscal policy coordination.

Today the way EMS countries mix fiscal and monetary policy varies. If a country pursues an expansionary fiscal policy this is reflected in a higher interest rate in that country. The fact that an expansionary fiscal policy leads to a higher interest rate hopefully increases the discipline in the formulation of the fiscal policy.

This disciplinary effect disappears in a monetary union because the interest rate is equal throughout the entire union. However, another type of disciplinary effect arises in a monetary union. The European governments will have to finance their budget deficits in the open market at a risk premium that reflects the market's assessment of the difficulty the country will experience in servicing its debt. The risk of getting a larger and larger risk premium will help in creating discipline in the formulation of the fiscal policy.

A very important question is whether this disciplinary effect will be strong enough to guarantee a sound development of the fiscal policies of the member states. I personally doubt that.

This problem was recognized in the Delors Report. The report stated that the monetary structure should be complemented by binding rules on national fiscal policies to assure an appropriate overall fiscal stance for the Community. At present, however, such strict fiscal policy rules do not seem to have strong support among the member countries. Instead pragmatic solutions seem to be favoured.

I think that such an approach would be the correct one. It would be hard to formulate binding rules for the fiscal policy. Instead the fiscal policy issues have to be solved by intensive economic policy discussions.

Even with all parties constructively engaged, the formulation of a mandate for the common central bank and the implementation of the necessary institutions will likely take some time. Each member country has to adjust its domestic legislation. Thus, the completion of EMU may lie some time in the future. I am convinced, however, that not only the ultimate goals are valuable, but also the process towards EMU. On the way there will be a gradual strengthening of economic policy coordination.

4. SWEDEN AND THE EMS

There have been voices raised in Sweden advocating a Swedish association to the EMS. The proponents of a Swedish EMS association underline that such a step would have a disciplinary effect on our economic policy and thereby put an end to the high inflation rate.

Participation in the European exchange rate system would increase the credibility in our fixed exchange rate the proponents say, since it would imply that we no longer autonomously could change the exchange rate. Increased credibility would in turn facilitate a reduction of the inflation rate, the proponents argue.

As I mentioned before the EMS-countries have succeeded in reducing their inflation rates. Again I want to stress that the decrease in their inflation rate can not only be explained by their participation in the EMS. The main reason is, in my opinion, the domestic priority of an anti-inflationary policy in the participating countries. Sweden still has some way to go in this respect.

There does not exist a shortcut - in the form of EMS-participation - in attaining a lower inflation rate. We have to undertake clear economic policy measures domestically, in order to achieve an inflation rate that is in line with our competitors in the world market.

Sweden must actively participate in the process of internationalisation, cooperation and integration - particularly in Europe. The Swedish objectives have been set out by a broad majority in Parliament. Parliament has decided that we should aim at achieving close cooperation with the EC in all economic and social fields on a non-discriminative basis with the exception of foreign policy and defence issues. We are of course aware of that in order to move closer to the EC and benefit from the European integration, we also have to fulfill the obligations that are necessary.

Today we are taking many unilateral steps to adjust our rules and legislation to the ones prevailing in the EC. We have also undertaken a number of structural measures aimed at greater integration with the rest of Europe, for example the abolition of our foreign exchange controls last summer. Furthermore, Sweden is actively working for the implementation of a European Economic Space between the EC and the EFTA countries.

A necessary condition for seriously raising the issue of a Swedish association to the EMS has been that there are clear indications showing that the overall domestic policy forcefully strives to reduce inflation. When convincing measures are taken to reduce inflation then participation in the exchange rate mechanism could decrease inflationary expectations and strengthen credibility. Furthermore a Swedish association is in line with our ambition to achieve closer cooperation and integration with the EC. An association of a larger number of countries to the EMS would further expand the area of exchange rate stability and contribute to intra-European trade and growth. (Editors' note: Sweden pegged unilaterally to the ECU in May 1991 without formally joining the ERM and the EMS.)

A Swedish EMS-association should - from my point of view - strive to get the closest possible association to the EMS. We should aim at participating in the discussions and the cooperation - not only concerning technical issues related to the ERM but also concerning general economic matters. An EMS-association is only an interesting alternative for Sweden if it goes beyond a technical exchange rate cooperation. The objective of a very close cooperation is also well in line with the goal of greater integration between Sweden and the EC declared by Parliament.

I fully understand that it is hard for the EC to discuss an association to the EMS of non EC-countries at present. A lot of energy has to be put into the completion of the internal market. This is probably the reason why the EC has not yet answered the questions concerning third-country association, put forward by Norway and Austria. However, when the EC has resolved the most acute internal issues I do hope and believe that the EC will strive for finding arrangements for close asscociation with non EC-countries. An association of a third country must be characterized by pragmatic solutions and guarantee that the cooperation will include substantial involvement and cooperation over a large range of economic policy issues. It is in the interest of us all to work for increasing exchange rate stability and the enhancement of economic cooperation.

Financial Regulation and Monetary Arrangements after 1992
C. Wihlborg, M. Fratianni and T.D. Willett (Editors)
© 1991 Elsevier Science Publishers B.V. All rights reserved

21 A U.K. View of the EMS

Sir Alan A. Walters

Putnam, Hayes & Bartlett Inc., 1776 Eye Street N.W., Washington DC 20006, USA

1. THE COST OF EMS

I shall start by repeating one criticism of the EMS which I think is of some importance and I am pleased to see that Gros and Thygesen seem to consider it of some importance too. My problem is one which is fundamental to pegged or EMS type of arrangements. This is not at present a free exchange rate system, nor is it an absolutely fixed system; a pegged system it is.

I am talking about capital movements. We have seen an example of the problem caused by such movements in Britain since early 1987. The pound was pegged at DEM3 at this time. It was not an official peg, but pegged it was. Britain has no exchange controls and only prudential control on domestic capital markets. What happened was that as a result of exchange rate pegging, the real rate of return on assets in Britain was very high, higher than in any other OECD country. The nominal rate of interest was obviously very high too at about 12 percent. In Germany the interest rate was 5.5 or 6 percent. At a pegged rate, all you have to do is to get into sterling, collect the 12 percent and get out again after a year, six months or whatever period. Britain was thus deluged with capital inflows. What to do? Of course, the normal procedure for Bank of England is to sterilize it.

In order to keep the sterling from appreciating the chancellor was selling sterling. At the same time he was controlling the interest rate. There was consequently automatic sterilization. Much was sterilized because sterilized intervention does not stop movements in exchange rates. Some people think it has a few days effect. The pressure for the sterling to appreciate went on.

To relieve the pressure on sterling the chancellor brought the interest rates down and down and down. By June or July 1988 they were down from 12 percent to 7.5 percent.

At this time the inflation pressure in the United Kingdom became clear for all to see. It was clear in asset markets. Monetary growth ballooned. The great inflation was back and interest rates went up in stages. By October 1989 they were up at 15 percent.

We note that the same thing happened to the Spanish peseta when it joined the EMS. The interest rates came down and went up again.

The pegged exchange rate system as the EMS is a half-baked system. It is a mishmash of fixed and floating systems. The members of EMS have had exchange and capital controls. Some still shelter behind these controls.

It seems to me that the entry of Britain into the EMS, was quite a critical decision made for political reasons. It would be politically disastrous if Britain leaves the EMS after 6 months or 12 months. Britain has to stick to it. With the interest rates Britain would first be at the bottom but people would expect the pound to go to the top. Britain will agree with this part of it. There would be a massive short term capital inflow, more massive than in 1987-88 with a monetary expansion and inflation as a consequence. Ultimately the exchange rate will be free. The pound cannot be tied up for long, and it will come down and quite a long way.

Britain's joining may do no good to the EMS. On the contrary, it will open up the weak seams of the EMS to enormous capital movements.

My view on this issue has been critizised by Mr Giovannini and others. The argument is that this sort of thing does not happen although it has been going on since capital movements brought down the sterling in 1967. The critics are right that it does not happen when, as a close approximation, inflation rates are equal.

France and Italy have had real problems with inflation rates. One would like to think there exists a mechanism which restores appropriate movements of interest rates and adjustment of monetary policy. But since most countries' monetary policies are conducted with interest rate targets the movements are exactly the *opposite* of the way you want them. This is the nature of the pegged system. I am glad to see that this point has been presented by Gros and Thygesen (1990) though they argue that my description is a caricature. It is a caricature because countries have been protected by exchange controls.

On this subject I am also stunned to see the cost of Britain de facto entering the exchange rate mechanism 1987-88. Britain increased foreign exchange reserves from 10 to 50 billion dollars in today's prices. The real return on those reserves was not more than three percent. What would have happened if we as in 1979 had privatized the reserves? We know that over the 1980's pension funds on the average have made 13.5 percent real return. Most of the private sector did better during the last decade. So the cost of the reserves is 10 maybe 12 percent of 50 billions annually. Take the present value of this figure by multiplying by 20 as most of us in the World Bank tend to do. The present value is about 100 billions or 15 percent of GNP. That is the cost of entering the EMS assuming the reserve target is 50 billions.

This cost of the EMS is also the value of entering the EMU assuming the country is in the EMS. There is a lot more to be said about this but I want to focus more on the EMU.

2. THE EMU

The first thing to notice is that we can, of course, have an economic union without a monetary union. There is an economic union between Canada and the USA and it might be complete in 7-8 years time. You may say that the Canadians should have adopted the U.S. currency but that is not their judgement. The point is that you can have completely free movement of goods and factors without a monetary union. This is worth bearing in mind because certainly the argument in Europe has been that we must have a monetary union.

Secondly, we come to the nature of a monetary union. Let me first make clear that although I obviously see a lot wrong with the EMS mechanism, this does not mean that I see a lot wrong with a monetary union. On the contrary, I think it is probably as good as floating exchange rates. There are limitations to the positive sides of a monetary union. The limitations relate to the question of what sort of monetary union will it be. There must be only one central bank of Europe creating money. The Bank of France, the Bank of England and the Bundesbank will give up the right to create money. The real difficulties, the political difficulties occur when you ask who is going to run this central bank of Europe? Is it going to be run by Brussels bureaucrats or by a gang of politicians? Suggestions have been made and suggestions have been counted. It would make a certain degree of sense if the Bundesbank became the central bank of Europe. After all the reason for joining the EMS is to borrow credibility from the Bundesbank.

Incidentally, those with enough gray hairs remember us saying the same thing about the Federal Reserve Board in the late 50s and the early 60s. We all wandered over to America from Europe and found that inflation had been defeated. All one had to do was to link the currency to the dollar and there would be no inflation. We all know what happened. Very sad indeed.

If you believe in the credibility argument, then, of course, the Bundesbank should rule. Do the Germans and the Bundesbank want this? In any case, the French, the British, the Italians, even the smaller countries with the possible exception of Holland will never be willing to completely hand over control over money to the Germans. The French would want to control the Bundesbank and so would the others. It is hard to see a possible solution since the Bundesbank would not want to surrender control.

The question is what sort of central bank can be set up in Europe and avoid all these political problems. There are a number of varieties that could avoid these problems. Remember that the critical condition is that we must avoid subsuming the monetary policy to any other countries or, even worse, to the Brussels bureaucrats. There is a way of doing this.

3. A PARALLEL COMMODITY CURRENCY

We could set up a parallel currency in addition to those existing in Europe. The old-fashioned commodity currency could be issued as paper claims to a bundle of commodities. It could be set up so that private arbitrage induces an expansion or contraction automatically as deflation or inflation pressures build up. Reserve assets would be entitlements to commodities.

There would be no need to worry about problems like in East Germany with changes in the velocity of circulation. The demand for the currency would automatically adjust according to the tastes of participants in Europe. The currency, or the reserve asset, could be defined so that the quantity of the currency would adjust according to all tastes involved. One example is the weighted average retail basket of commodities in Europe, so that nobody would have an incentive to fiddle with the retail price index in any individual country.

The new currency, call it the ECOM, would be issued alongside existing currencies and this is a great advantage as long as the values of different currencies are allowed to change and the ECOM is recognized as legal tender in each country. Much has been written about currency competition elsewhere so I will not go into the advantages of this proposal here.

REFERENCE

Gros, D. and N. Thygesen (1990), "The Institutional Approach to Monetary Union in Europe", Economic Journal, Sept., 925-935.

Financial Regulation and Monetary Arrangements after 1992
C. Wihlborg, M. Fratianni and T.D. Willett (Editors)
© 1991 Elsevier Science Publishers B.V. All rights reserved

22   ERM: A Way Station to One Currency?

Aris Protopapadakis

Department of Economics, Claremont Graduate School, Claremont, CA 91711, USA

One of the most interesting goals of 1992 is to have completely free movement of capital and labor. Even if this goal is achieved in 1992, the system ultimately will fail if monetary and foreign exchange arrangements are not compatible with such extreme factor mobility. Monetary and foreign exchange arrangements that are prone to producing divergent real interest rates or rapid changes and uncertainty in market expectations are likely to create instability in the financial markets. Such instabilities will result in large short-term capital movements and accompanying pressures on the central banks. These large capital movements may or may not be very damaging to the national economies. In either case, there will be pressures to regulate and control the "undesirable" movements, because they generally imply changes in asset prices and therefore sizeable transfers among financial actors. These pressures eventually will erode capital mobility by encouraging government to increasingly invoke the emergency procedures that are already part of the agreement, and they would also encourage the invention of methods to control capital movements without explicitly violating the letter of the EC agreements.

The foreign exchange solution, or perhaps the stop-gap measure, that has been adopted by most of the EC members is the Exchange Rate Mechanism - ERM - within the European Monetary System - EMS. The ERM sometimes is portrayed as an intermediate step to a one-currency regime, and sometimes as an attractive arrangement in its own right, a mini Breton Woods agreement.

The hope seems to have been that national monetary policies would become sufficiently harmonized to Bundesbank policies, and that the laggard central banks will gain enough credibility in the financial markets by some future date, so that it will become possible to establish "permanently" fixed exchange rates. Indeed this seems to be the view espoused by the Delors report.

The theoretical considerations associated with the desirability of permanently fixed exchange rates are discussed in the various contributions to the "optimal currency" literature, and they are reviewed by Wihlborg and Willett in this volume. This literature emphasizes that the potential reduction in transactions costs associated with a currency union must be weighed against the costs of giving up monetary policy independence. These costs are related to the potential ability of monetary policy to offset domestic and foreign shocks to the national economy, to the ability to choose "optimal" national inflation rates, and various other more esoteric benefits associated with a sovereign monetary policy.

1. COSTS OF THE REALIGNMENT OPTION

The events of the last couple of decades must give pause to those who believe that national monetary independence is highly valuable. Consider the nature of the shocks that are to be offset by monetary policy: If these shocks are real supply shocks, then experience indicates clearly that expansionary monetary policy is not a satisfactory response. In fact, the downfall of demand management policies was hastened by government attempts in many countries to offset the first "oil shock" with monetary policy.

In general, non-monetary shocks require adjustments in relative prices within and across countries. The standard argument is that adjustments in the nominal exchange rate can substitute for the absence of wage and price inflexibility. This may be true in a one-good world, i.e., when all the domestic prices need to be adjusted by the same amount. In general, however, even if exchange rate adjustment can attenuate the external imbalance by changing the overall terms of trade, it cannot bring into balance all the relative prices. Monetary policy then is an inadequate tool, because mainly it redistributes rather than redresses imbalances across the various sectors, and it can lead to perverse economic consequences!

This is not to argue that monetary policy is useless. Rather, the argument is that monetary policy operates primarily on credit markets, and the existence of national currencies arbitrarily subdivides credit markets into national units. Thus it appears that there are benefits to having an independent monetary policy for every credit market. But in a single-currency EC with integrated credit markets there will be no clear benefit, in addition to no possibility, of more than one monetary policy.

Monetary union will create a single credit market within the EC, as long as governments do not erect barriers to goods, capital, and labor movements.According to the current agreement, regulation does not need to be harmonized across countries, but financial firms will be able to offer their services everywhere in the EC, under the regulations of their home country,subject to some marketing controls of the host countries. These conditions will invite competition in regulation among governments. Differential regulation will exist only if it has very small economic consequences or if it allows the financial firms operating under the more restrictive regulation to create profitable imperfect substitutes for services provided by competitors licensed under less restrictive regulation. Otherwise, the countries with the more onerous regulation will see financial firms migrating to the most hospitable regulation or going out of business. If the EC can withstand the political strains of competition in regulation and the concurrent movement of financial business, it will emerge as a single financial market, much the same way as the United States is now.

A crucial point that is discussed by Wihlborg and Willett in this volume and that was raised by a number of conference participants is that a "permanently" or "irrevocably" fixed exchange rate is a contradiction in terms and is not a long-run credible policy, unless it is accompanied by the creation of one central bank - a monetary union. This is because a credible regime of permanently fixed exchange rates is stochastically dominated by a single-currency regime. Separate national currencies entail substantial transactions and information costs to consumers, investors, and businesses alike. Government is willing to impose these costs on its voters because it wants to retain the option to conduct independent monetary policy under certain circumstances. However, conducting such independent monetary policy implies that under some future unspecified emergency conditions, government will renege on its promise to keep exchange rates fixed, and it will allow the currency to float or devalue, de-facto or de-juro. This possibility guarantees that national currencies cannot be perfect substitutes, because they retain this risk and also because their use gives rise to transactions and information costs across national boundaries. The inescapable conclusion then is that fixed exchange rate regimes are inherently not credible.

The evidence favors this point. It is very hard to imagine that the current interest rate differentials would exist across EC government securities if the EC was a one-currency area. The markets perceive the various currencies as different, despite the current success of the ERM and the ongoing planning towards "irrevocably" fixed exchange rates!

2. GOVERNMENTS AND MARKETS

An additional cost to government of moving from fixed exchange rates to one currency is that it loses much of its ability to impose national regulation to financial markets and institutions, because differential regulation is made possible by the imperfect substitutability of national currencies.

Even if one believes that monetary policy independence can be beneficial to the national economy, it is unreasonable to assume that government will conduct monetary policies only with the public welfare in mind! If government primarily maximizes consumer welfare, monetary policy independence is beneficial to the extent that it has real effects, even if government makes policy errors. But to the extent that agency problems, political cycles, and myopic behavior play an important role in monetary policy, policy independence saddles the economy with welfare-reducing policies, monetary shocks, and unstable expectations, which by themselves can easily outweigh the benefits of policy independence. Thus, it is not enough to assert that "good" monetary policy can be beneficial at the national level. It is also necessary to assess how frequently monetary policy is likely to be incorrect, misguided, perverse, or even malevolent, and how frequently IT is the problem. It was not so long ago that misguided monetary policy was regarded by monetarists and many others as the cause of all post-war business cycles.

Finally, this discussion assumes that financial markets are reasonably efficient, and that advisors and policymakers alike understand what determines exchange rates and capital movements. My reading of the empirical literature is that the evidence for foreign exchange market efficiency is not altogether persuasive, and that in any case we have much to learn about what determines exchange rates. To the extent that exchange rates or capital move in ways incompatible with our open economy models, there is no reason to assume that such unexplained movements would be generally beneficial to the national economies or would aid government policy. Indeed, during the Breton Woods era of "fixed" exchange rates, many economic policy failures were blamed --rightly or wrongly-- on perverse capital movements. The possibility of such perverse capital movements is one more argument in favor of a single currency.

In sum, it seems to me that it is not possible to realize the full scope of the benefits of economic integration in the absence of a currency union. This is partly because of the transactions costs associated with multiple currencies but even more importantly, it is because the existence of multiple currencies arbitrarily divides financial markets and subjects them to different regulations and policy shocks.

Clearly, the benefits of a single EC currency will be the largest if the EC monetary authority is designed carefully and is given an unequivocal charter that makes price "stability" the overriding objective. A poorly conceived EC monetary authority that is assigned multiple objectives, including real economic growth, and one that is vulnerable to temporary political necessities will be inflation prone and a source of monetary instability. Such a monetary authority would cause chronic economic malaise and would dissipate many of the economic benefits of the single market. However, the stumbling block to a single currency is not going to be the constitution of the EC central bank, the business community, or concern over national economic welfare. Rather, it is more likely to be the unwillingness of governments to give up monetary independence, even if this independence is on balance detrimental to their economies.

Part Seven

**The Transition to a Convertible Currency
for a Centrally Planned Economy**

Financial Regulation and Monetary Arrangements after 1992
C. Wihlborg, M. Fratianni and T.D. Willett (Editors)
© 1991 Elsevier Science Publishers B.V. All rights reserved

23   Germany and a Single Deutsche Mark

Stefan Schönberg

Deutsche Bundesbank, Postfach 10 06 02, 6000 Frankfurt 1, Germany

1. THE REFORM

On May 2, 1990 the Governments of the Federal Republic of Germany and of the German Democratic Republic reached agreement about the basic modalities for the introduction of the D-Mark in East Germany. On July 2, 1990 the East German currency was substituted for by the West German Mark - an operation without a precedent in modern economic history. How was it achieved? According to the agreement reached

- East German residents were entitled to convert at a rate of 1 for 1 up to 4,000 East Marks per person, and 2 for 1 thereafter. For GDR residents of less than 14 years of age and those of 60 years of age and older lower (2,000) respectively higher (6,000) amounts could be exchanged at the 1 for 1 ratio;
- wages, pensions, rents and all other recurrent payments were converted at 1 for 1;
- all other claims and liabilities, *inter alea* the corporate debt to the previously state-owned banking sector - some 260 billion East Marks - were converted at 2 for 1.

The agreement between the two governments was an attempt to square the circle between the Bundesbank's anti-inflation preoccupations, the political and social needs of the East Germans and the competitive and financial situation of East German industry.
In view of East German cash and savings of 170-180 billion East Marks, the reform means that a sum of East German savings of around DM 150 billion was added to potential West German liquidity, amounting to roughly 12 per cent of the West German money supply. Under the Bundesbank's earlier suggestion of 1 for 1 up to 2,000 East Marks, the addition to the money supply would have been only DM 125 billion - hardly a significant difference in view of the size of the West German economy of more than DM 2,000 billion. The increase of 12 percent in money supply was, by the way, similar to the expected increase in GNP. East Germany's GNP is estimated to amount to approximately 10 percent of West Germany's GNP.
Wages and pensions were converted, as I mentioned, at 1 for 1 rather than the 2 for 1 suggested by the Bundesbank. The Federal Government made clear, however, that wages had to be held at their East Mark levels before the conversion, rather than being increased by 30 percent to compensate for the expected increase in the price level in the GDR (following the abolition of subsidies), by an additional 7 percent for higher social security contributions, and by another 10 percent to compensate for the wage spread as

suggested by the Bundesbank. By this arithmetic real wages under the Government's proposal were only about 10 percent higher than under the Bundesbank recommendation.

The agreement on the rates for the conversion of East Marks into D-Marks is part of a treaty ("intergovernmental agreement") between the two Germanys. It was ratified by both parliaments, went into force on July 1, and implies the transfer of the basic elements of West Germany's monetary, economic and social system to the GDR.

With respect to the extension of the currency area of the Deutsche Mark to the territory of the GDR the agreement guarantees that solely the Bundesbank Act and the regulations issued by the Bundesbank apply in the field of monetary policy in the GDR after July 2, 1990. In order to safeguard that the monetary policy decisions taken by the Bundesbank's Central Bank Council are implemented in the GDR the Bundesbank has established an administrative center in Berlin and has opened 15 branches in the territory of the GDR.

2. EFFECTS OF CONVERSION RATES AND MARKET REFORM

Let me stress at this point that in my view the importance of the conversion rates has been generally overestimated. The notion that West Germany money supply will rise by about twelve percent does not tell very much as long as nobody really knows how much of the newly acquired D-Marks will actually be spent by GDR residents, i.e. what the velocity of money circulation will actually be, and how the real economy will develop after introduction of the D-Mark. Much more important than conversion rates is, therefore, the issue to which extent and how fast market-related economic structures are set up in East Germany and how soon East German industry can be made competitive.

Accordingly, the agreement provides that all basic principles of a social market economy must be taken over by East Germany. Fundamental economic reforms, like price and wage reform, freedom of business acitivities, private property and privatization of conglomerates, and competition are made the *conditio sine qua* non for monetary union. They are also the prerequisite that the country will adequately benefit from the introduction of a convertible currency. There cannot be and there is no "middle-way" between the previously centrally-planned East German economy and the model of a social market economy as established in the Federal Republic.

Of course, this historic task raises formidable problems. Let me just mention four of them:

(1) Foreign trade
East Germany has to remove all foreign trade monopolies and to adjust its foreign trade regime towards EC-conformity; however, for a transitional period intra-German trade will continue to be conducted on the basis of the EC-treaties ("protocolle on German internal trade and related issue"). East Germany is concerned, of course, that it will be swamped by imports from West Germany and western countries once the foreign trade regime is abolished and has asked for the authority to ban certain categories of imports until it has adjusted its economic structures. The inter-governmental agreement stipulates that such temporary import restrictions can be established only with the concurrence of the Federal Republic.

(2) Foreign trade obligations of the old GDR vis-a-vis Comecon-Countries

The Federal Republic has agreed that East Germany's previous obligations in terms of scheduled deliveries to other Comecon-countries (which represent some 70 percent of East Germany's foreign trade) will be honored. This could mean a substantial burden for the federal budget. Moreover, in line with recent decisions taken by the Comecon-countries, East German foreign trade with Comecon-countries shall be carried out in convertible currencies (and at world market prices) beginning 1991. This could sever a major proportion of East Germany's traditional trade ties with its eastern neighbors.

(3) Agriculture

East German agricultural production has been characterised by large agricultural areas per producer and by extreme unproductivity. As a consequence agricultural producer prices have been some 50 per cent higher than those in the Federal Republic whereas consumer prices have been heavily subsidized and been substantially lower than in West Germany. The agreement provides that food subsidies must be phased out and that East Germany may apply quotas for imports of agricultural products for a transitional period.

(4) Public Finances

East Germany has undertaken to introduce in due course the West German tax system. Until such time that East Germany will have sufficient financial resources (tax receipts) at its disposal. West Germany will provide the necessary financial resources. The East German government may also raise credits only with the concurrence of the West German minister of finance.

The two Germanys entered on July 2, 1990 not only a monetary and economic union but a social union, too. This implies that the West German social security system and employment legislation have been effectively transferred to East Germany. At the beginning of the negotiations the East German representatives tried to safeguard some elements of their old social system such as the state-run health-service. However, these plans were dropped ultimately. As a result of the introduction of the West German pension scheme in the East, old-age pensions expressed in D-Mark in most cases are higher than previous pensions expressed in East Marks.

3. RISKS AND OPPORTUNITIES

What are the economic implications of monetary, economic and social union between the two Germanys? It does involve, in our view, both considerable economic risks and even greater opportunities.

One should bear in mind, however, that this venture constitutes a historic task for Germany that justifies the acceptance of some risks. One should also bear in mind that transferring a socialist (centrally-planned) economy to a market economy in one big move is without precedent. The specific method for transition used in the intra-German context probably cannot be applied to the other Middle and East European countries. Particularly, the "instant" approch used for institutional and economic integration of East Germany was only feasible in view of the prospect of an early political unification and in view of massive transfers from West to East Germany to cushion the economic and social consequences of the restructuring process. But East Germany could constitute a "checklist" for other reform-oriented countries. Certainly, if East Germany, with its huge advantage of having a strong partner ready to inject big amounts of capital into its economy, cannot prosper, then the outlook for everyone else in eastern Europe would be bleak.

As a result of economic and monetary unification in Germany we expect stronger potential growth, higher interest rates, more balanced foreign accounts, and higher budget deficits over an extended period of time.

Output in the Federal Republic is expected to increase over the medium term with higher business and infrastructure investment and stronger consumer demand for West German consumer goods in the East. Overall economic growth in the Federal Republic which originally was expected to drop from 4 percent in 1989 to some 3 percent in 1990 is now believed to attain at least the 1989 level.

Output in East Germany is likely to decline during the first stages of the transition from a centrally planned to a market economy. There is widespread disagreement so far how many companies in East Germany will be able to survive and to what level unemployment will rise. Obviously, the situation is very different in the various industrial branches and even within branches. We expect, however, an initial economic acceleration from the service sector and from small and medium-sized industrial companies. Economic restructuring is strengthened by the unique advantage of East Germany over all other countries trying to reform their economies: the risk of financial disturbances (inflation, liquidity bottlenecks, excessive budget deficits) is practically nil as financial conditions are effectively controlled by West Germany. Also, consumer demand has been boosted temporarily by the increased purchasing power associated with the conversion of Mark (East) into Deutsche Mark. Over time, improved infrastructure, higher private investment, and the introduction of superior management and technologies will raise labor productivity allowing real wages to catch up with West Germany.

4. INTEREST RATES AND INFLATION

We experienced in early 1990 in the Federal Republic substantial increases in interest rates, both in money and capital markets in Germany. Some observers have related this development somewhat arbitrarily and one-sidedly to the German economic and monetary union, in particular to speculation concerning the size of necessary capital flows and to worries about inflationary consequences arising from the additional demand for capital. However, this occurred at the time of a global trend of rising interest rates due to various factors, among them higher inflation expectations in Japan, the US and Great Britain. In our view, markets tended to underestimate the positive effects of a unified German economic area.

In any case the Bundesbank's monetary policy has continued to be geared toward keeping inflation at low levels while accomodating only the growth of potential output. There is and will be no monetary financing of the financial consequences of German monetary and economic union. The Bundesbank is fully aware that it carries not only the responsibility for the stability of our money but must also justify the confidence of the countries which have tied their currencies to the D-Mark.

Government expenditure in the Federal Republic can be expected to increase over several years with higher infrastructure investment and social transfers to the East in order to soften the social consequences of economic and monetary reform. However, there will be considerable room of manoeuvre both for restructuring the expenditure side of the budget and for running somewhat higher deficits for a certain period of time. The effects of the expenditure increase on the budget can be partly offset, for instance, by a reduction in subsidies to the East, to West Berlin, and to the regions in West Germany bordering to the former GDR. There will also be a substantial increase in tax revenues due to stronger economic growth in the years ahead. It should be possible, therefore, to finance a large proportion of the remaining budgetary gap via capital markets all the more as the federal budget was roughly in balance in 1989.

We hope that a major part of the financial burden of economic and monetary union will be financed by private capital flows. East Germany is likely to become a significant capital importer, primarily from West Germany, but also from other countries. This means that net capital exports from Germany as a whole will decline. Thus, also Germany's current account surplus will be reduced in the short to medium term.

5. IMPLICATIONS FOR THE EC

The likely implications of German monetary and economic union for the European Community are, above all, a higher medium-term GDP growth trend due to increased exports of other member states to Germany and third countries. The European Commission estimates that GDP will increase by an additional 0.5 percent p.a. for the Community as a whole. The mechanism underlying this process would be a rise in the real exchange rate of the Deutsche Mark reflecting the increase in interest rates in Germany. Real interest rates in other member countries would also tend to rise as Germany's supply of net saving to the rest of the world is reduced.

The rise in domestic demand in Germany can be expected to increase exports and output in countries that are presently operating below full capacity. In countries where resources are fully utilized, there may be some upward pressure on prices, and higher real interest rates would be expected to restrain domestic demand. This process would thus require also some adjustment on the part of the Federal Republic's main trading partners.

6. LESSONS FOR AN EMU

Finally, let me touch on an issue which has been raised frequently recently by representatives of our partner countries in the European Community, i.e. the question whether monetary union in the context of the EC could or should be achieved as fast as a German Monetary Union was achieved. In my view these two processes are not comparable for two reasons:

First, the development of the economic situation in the GDR in the first months of 1990. In particular
- there was a mass exodus of more than 2,000 people a day (more than 110,000 GDR-citizens left for the Federal Republic in January and February 1990 alone);
- there were increasing bottlenecks in industrial production, health care, etc. and other signs of economic and political disintegration that provoked the risk of an economic collapse in the GDR in 1990.

These developments made suggestions for a step-by-step approach towards economic and monetary integration in Germany, similar to the process we are engaged with in the EC, unrealistic. Mass emigration from the GDR, in particular, was not only undermining the East German economy but was also putting the West German social stability at stake. Although many in the Federal Republic would have preferred a slower, more controlled process during which the conditions for an eventual monetary union would have been established step by step, actual events forced a different course of action.

Second, the term "monetary union" in the context of German unification process is, of course, misleading. In Western Europe we are engaged in a process of harmonizing national monetary and economic policies with the aim of achieving ultimately a monetary union by transferring national sovereign powers towards European institutions (European central bank system). In contrast, the abolition of the East German Mark was a part of East Germany's complete loss of sovereignty in monetary policy matters.

There is presumably no need for an explanation that this kind of "monetary integration" is considered inappropriate and unacceptable by many in the European Community. We beleive, however, that monetary and economic unification in Germany will not delay but rather accelerate the European integration process. Events have confirmed this. Another historic task is on the agenda: the ambitious objective of creating a European central bank system and ultimately a European currency.

Financial Regulation and Monetary Arrangements after 1992
C. Wihlborg, M. Fratianni and T.D. Willett (Editors)
© 1991 Elsevier Science Publishers B.V. All rights reserved

24 German Monetary Union

Emil-Maria Claassen

Université Paris Dauphine, Place du Maréchal de Lattre de Tassigny, F-750 16 Paris

"Kommt die DM, bleiben wir. Kommt sie nicht, gehen wir zu ihr."
Slogan in Leipzig and East-Berlin in early 1990.

In this note I discuss alternative paths for monetary stabilization in the transition from centrally planned to market economies. The path chosen by East Germany is used to illustrate the alternatives. I distinguish between monetary stabilization and price liberalization associated with restoration of a system of relative prices. These processes are in principle separable although, for reasons discussed, inflationary pressures may arise as a result of price liberalization.

1. MONETARY STABILIZATION AND PRICE LIBERALIZATION

As any former socialist country, East Germany had two alternatives to eliminate the monetary overhang, either to admit open inflation or to eliminate the monetary overhang by reducing the outstanding quantity of money. These two monetary options for East Germany are illustrated in Fig. 1a. The quantity of money of West Germany is measured on the horizontal axis from point O' to the left. It amounts to O'T. The demand for money is M^d_w. In East Germany, the quantity of Eastmarks measured from point O to the right is OT and its demand for money M^d.

Both options have to be accompanied by liberalizing prices, at least those for tradable goods. The price liberalization concerns the restructuring of *relative* prices. The main problem of East Germany, like that of all other post-socialist countries, is that of the relative price structure. "Basic" consumption goods are highly subsidized and industrial goods are extremely "overpriced". The high prices of industrialized goods was not only an outcome of high production costs (or low productivity), but in particular the consequence of the fiscal system. Since most government revenues were provided by the "surpluses" of enterprises, price liberalization and the subsequent reversal of the total relative price structure must imply simultaneously a fiscal reform in order to replace the transfer of surpluses by ordinary taxes.

The monetary stabilization concerns the level of *absolute* prices. Assume that the price level is at A and that the liberalization of relative prices of tradables (i.e. their adjustment to the price structure in Western countries) would not affect the price level since one category of prices will fall and another rise. The East German price level at A should correspond to the West German price level at C. But at the Eastern level A there is still a monetary problem in terms of the monetary overhang BC = UT. In the case of East

Germany, the monetary overhang UT/OT was estimated to be 58.4/181.5 = 32% (see Table 1, last line).

Table 1
Conversion of Eastmarks into Deutschemarks (M_3), July 1990

	Amount in billions of Eastmarks	Conversion rate	Amount in billions of Deutschemarks
Deposits	167.9	1.44:1	116.3
1. Deposits of 4000 Eastmarks per inhabitant from age of 15 years and below 60 years	40.4	1:1	40.4
2. Deposits of 2000 Eastmarks per child below 15 years	6.4	1:1	6.4
3. Deposits of 6000 Eastmarks per inhabitant from age of 60 years	18.0	1:1	18.0
4. Remaining deposits of residents	108.8	2:1	50.4
5. Deposits of non-residents at 31.12.1989	2.1	2:1	1.0
6. Remaining deposits of non-residents at 1.7.1990	0.2	3:1	0.1
Cash	13.6	2:1	6.8
M_3	181.5	1.47:1	123.1

Source: Deutsche Bundesbank, December 1990

If East Germany had opted for open inflation, its price level would have risen to point D by the proportion DT/CT = OT/OU = 1.47/1 which was the actual conversion rate (Table 1, last line). By establishing the external convertibility, the exchange rate of Eastmarks for one deutschemark would have been DT/CT = 1.47/1.

East Germany opted for a particular type of currency reform which consisted of two separate analytical steps: the elimination of the monetary overhang (UT) by reducing the outstanding quantity of money (OT) by UT/OT = 32%, and the conversion of the remaining quantity of Eastmarks (OU) into deutschemarks by the ratio 1:1. Both steps were undertaken simultaneously, but they could have been made separately in time. The first step would have maintained the East German currency. Fig. 1b illustrates the West German and East German money market after the canceling of the monetary overhang. The East German price level remains at A which is also that of West Germany (at point C) and the exchange rate would have been 1:1. The second step which could have been undertaken one year or several years afterwards would have been the conversion of Eastmarks into deutschemarks.

It should be noted that the inflationary danger of the German Monetary Union was rather limited for the Federal Republic. Assume that the Bundesbank had overestimated the demand for money of East Germany and created an excess liquidity of 10% of the Eastern GDP. Since the GDP was estimated to be roughly one-tenth of the GDP of West Germany, the inflationary impact for the whole monetary area would only have been approximately one percent. This conclusion results from our knowledge about the determination of the inflation rate in open economies which are linked with each other by fixed exchange rates. Due to the law of one price for tradable goods, the inflation rates will tend to be equalized, at least for tradable goods. Furthermore, for the size of the common inflation rate, the country of origin of the inflationary pressure is completely irrelevant.

2. LABOR MARKETS, INFLATIONARY PRESSURES AND MIGRATION IN A MONETARY UNION

For East Germany, there remains still another "inflationary" source which may in crease the overall Eastern price level by 50, 100 percent or even more. In early 1991, most prices of subsidized nontradables (rents, prices of public transport, energy etc.) were still not liberalized. Thus, the rent for one square meter was still 0.85 DM in East Berlin while it was 20 times more in West Berlin. The fare of public transport was ten times higher for West Berliners compared to East Berliners. Since these items may constitute one third of expenditures by an average household, the ultimate price adjustment of nontradables will be accompanied by higher wage claims.

German policy makers face a dilemma. If wages are allowed to rise while monetary policy remains restrictive, then substantial subsidization of East German industry might be required to avoid severe unemployment, and an exodus of people looking for work in the West. On the other hand, if wages do not compensate for price increases on nontradables as they probably would not in East Germany in a stable monetary environment, then the wage differential between East and West could induce migration.

It seems as if, in either case, East Germans may have to receive a direct income subsidy if substantial migration is to be avoided. Inflationary pressures caused by such transfers need not arise, of course, as long as the Bundesbank does not monetize fiscal deficits.

It is somewhat ironic that in the monetary union between East and West Germany, the permanent fixing of the exchange rate occurs in a situation when labor mobility exists but is seen as undesirable. The literature on optimum currency area reviewed in this volume by Wihlborg and Willett emphasizes that either labor mobility or wage flexibility is required for the successful creation of a monetary union.

a. With Monetary Overhang

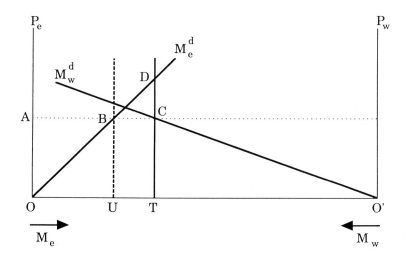

b. Without Monetary Overhang

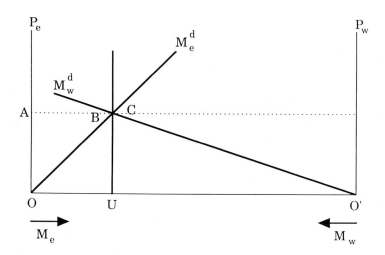

Figure 1 German Monetary Union

Financial Regulation and Monetary Arrangements after 1992
C. Wihlborg, M. Fratianni and T.D. Willett (Editors)
© 1991 Elsevier Science Publishers B.V. All rights reserved

25 Some Reflections on the Convertibility of the Rouble

Stanislav M. Borisov

Institute of World Economy and International Relations, 117859 Moscow, USSR

1. INTRODUCTION

The idea to make the Soviet rouble convertible is of great interest both in our country and abroad at the moment. The volume of the discussion is growing rapidly, even an international competition with a multi-thousand dollar award has been carried out. The quality of the discussion, however, remains quite poor and primitive, which undoubtedly is a matter of serious concern.

The former American ambassador to the USSR, Mr. Averell Harriman, once said that the most dangerous thing in politics is to base it on ignorance and illusions. I think it is our common task to oppose the ignorance and illusions in the case of rouble convertibility to make it more practical and realistic.

2. DEFINING CONVERTIBILITY AND ITS RELEVANCE FOR THE ROUBLE

You may reproach me for oversimplification, but first I have to go back to the definition of convertibility. The reason for this is twofold. First, for a long time, the convertibility of currencies has been considered as a matter of fact and a well established reality in the Western world. A lot of different and complicated issues which were connected with it are almost forgotten. The concept and even the word "convertibility" has disappeared from the Articles of the IMF, and here I quote its legal adviser Mr. Joseph Gold who writes: "It may seem strange that the central legal instrument of the international monetary system no longer refers to convertible currencies and contains no definition of them."

Second, until quite recently, the idea of currency convertibility was unknown to the majority of Soviet economists. Hence, there is a lot of confusion and misunderstanding in oral debates and written publications, especially when many of the contributors are non-professionals or TV- and pressmen.

In the postwar decades, a lot of clever and instructive books were written on the problems of convertibility. In a way this helped the Western countries to rearrange their foreign exchange mechanisms and return to convertibility. After reading these considerations and recommendations, and studying their implementation in real life, we may conclude that convertibility is a pure monetary phenomenon, strictly connected with international payments and transfers when there is a need to exchange one currency (domestic) for another currency (foreign).

Theoretically, currency convertibility belongs to a category of monetary exchange (money-money), which at the same time is accompanied by a shift of the "national uniform" of currencies (money domestic - money foreign). In practical terms, we can define currency convertibility as a certain mechanism, and a state of economic, financial and monetary conditions in a country which allows holders of domestic money, both residents and non-residents, to use it freely at home and abroad, including the unconditional and unrestricted right to exchange it for foreign currency.

Depending on the degree of foreign exchange restrictions there are different types of convertibility. Usually we talk about *full* convertibility when all restrictions are eliminated, and *partial* convertibility if some restrictions still exist. In modern times, the most common type is "the convertibility for current account transactions" in the balance of payments, i.e. for goods and services only, as it is provided by Article VIII of the IMF Articles of Agreement.

Depending on the freedom of action for residents and nonresidents there is a difference between external and internal convertibility. As it is stated in International Monetary Fund (1969, pp. 226-227): " The payments system of a country whose currency is *externally* convertible has two important characteristics. First, all holdings of that currency by nonresidents are freely exchangeable into any foreign (nonresident) currency at exchange rates within the official margins. Second, all payments that residents of the country are authorized to make to nonresidents, may be made in any externally convertible currency that residents can buy in foreign exchange markets. On the other hand, if there are no restrictions on the ability of a country's residents to use their holdings of domestic currency to acquire any foreign currency and hold it, or transfer it to any nonresident for any purpose, the country's currency is said to be *internally* convertible."

I used a lot of space and time for these definitions and quotations on purpose. The aim is to avoid some erroneous and confusing statements which are not unusual in the discussion about rouble convertibility.

Some of our reformers usually argues as follows. First of all, we have to make the rouble convertible "internally" - that is to ensure its free exchange for goods and services *inside* the country. After that the rouble would be ready for "external" convertibility - that is to be freely exchangeable for foreign currencies in *external* transactions. It is not difficult to understand that everything in these suppositions is reversed upside-down.

Certainly, it is extremely important to have a diversified and well-supplied internal market with an unrestricted ability to exchange money for commodities and similar values. But is it correct to designate the common process of buying and selling goods and services on the internal market with the monetary and externally oriented term "convertibility", instead of simply calling it "domestic trade"? The internal convertibility of the rouble is not the freedom of buying and selling in the Soviet domestic market for the Soviet currency - it is something quite different.

In a distant future, I think that the rouble will become internally convertible - that is, when all Soviet citizens and organizations will have the possibility to exchange their rouble funds for the foreign currencies they need. It cannot, however, be at an initial but rather at a more advanced stage in the process of making our currency convertible.

Everybody knows the difficult situation which presently exists in our domestic market as a result of commodity shortages and strong inflationary pressure. It would be a big mistake and a big illusion to put the main responsibility on the "bad" inconvertible rouble, and to try to cure all irregularities in production and trade by introducing the "good" convertible currency - as has been proposed by some of our well-known as well as of some not so well-known economists. Surely, such romantic dreams are only confusing and lead nowhere.

3. IS A NEW ROUBLE REQUIRED?

What can be said about the idea of a new "convertible rouble" also known as "hard rouble", "gold rouble" and other names? Indeed, nobody knows, because we have to deal with more or less general and unprocessed ideas, and not with specific and and well-shaped projects. Some people have put forward the concept of a gold currency, with a gold content and redeemable into gold. Others advocate more progressive devices that are backed by convertible currencies, and are exchangeable into these currencies. As for myself, I am for convertibility of the present Soviet rouble, that is why I oppose any project to substitute it for something else.

Theoretically, it is possible to create a gold rouble taking into account the Soviet Unions's potential gold production and gold reserves. But, in modern times it would be an obsolete construction. Gold has now lost its unique position as a universal means of payments. It plays a much more modest role as a precious and expensive commodity traded for money. Today, no country uses gold as a basis for its monetary system, and it seems inappropriate and short-sighted to recommend such an outmoded device when electronic money systems are successfully introduced in many countries in the West.

Probably similar arguments are valid to reject the idea of making the rouble redeemable into gold. A free exchange for convertible currencies and a global system of international gold trade are amply sufficient to ensure all possible demand for precious metal - for electronics and other industrial purposes, jewellery or investment, without official convertibility into gold which ceased to exist everywhere many years ago.

Some people have proposed a new "convertible rouble" as a replica of the "chervonets" which was introduced in the Soviet Union in the twenties and circulated rather successfully for some time. True, for that specific period, the "chervonets" was "good" money, but the present conditions in our country are utterly different. We know too well that attempts to "repeat history" are more than often doomed to failure. Specifically, during the years of so-called "war communism" the market structure was completely eliminated, together with all market instruments and accessories, like trade, prices, wages, money and credit. Paper notes and bonds, still circulating at that time, were almost nullified, and it was therefore impossible to start the New Economic Policy (NEP) without creating new sound money - so the "chervonets" appeared.

At present, we are also trying to change our centralized administrative economy for a market one. However, I think it would be a great delusion to consider the issue of a new type of currency as a an indispensable or obligatory precondition for performing this. There is absolutely no need to create market instruments anew and again, because in most cases they already exist. True, they are of a poor quality and quite often used improperly. But it is possible to correct and adjust them to the requirements of a genuine and workable market. We can apply the same reasoning to the monetary system. It is also in need of repair and reconstruction, not of demolition and substitution for something new.

The present Soviet currency does not hinder the introduction of a market economy in the USSR. Is it really so necessary to create a new monetary unit in order to demonopolize industry, replace state distribution by genuine trade, reform the price system, put common sense into taxation, etc.?

Also, a new currency would be of little help in eliminating the economic discrepancies which are beyond the scope of monetary matters. On the contrary, it is only a balanced development of all branches in the economy, which we hope to ensure as a result of radical economic reforms, that can stabilize the present rouble and create a climate for its convertibility.

At the moment, there is no money vacuum in the Soviet economy. We have to invent measures and even extraordinary ones, to "tie" surplus money or "pump" it out of circulation. If we issue a new currency instead of, or parallel to, the existing rouble, this move itself does not solve the problem. All other factors being unchanged, the new money will soon inherit all the negative features of its predecessor. In the end, we would have a new name of the currency and perhaps a new price scale while old economic "maladies" remain intact if not sharpened.

By the way, the present (1990) rate of depreciation of the rouble, 10-12 percent a year, is not as catastrophic as some advocates of a new currency claim. At the end of the 1970's many currencies, including the dollar, depreciated by the same percentages. These problems, however, were fought by various anti-inflationary measures, and surely not by currency
reforms.

4. ACHIEVING CONVERTIBILITY

Following the debate about rouble convertibility, one can easily discover that all suggestions and proposals are based upon existing laws and regulations for external economic activities in the USSR. The main principle of these regulations is the state monopoly for foreign trade and exchange transactions. I think it would be another big illusion to try to achieve convertibility while leaving this principle intact.

Under a state monopoly, all external transactions are planned according to the commands of official authorities. There are no problems with convertibility if a certain transaction is included in the plans of foreign trade and exchange allocation. In this case we have only a technical exchange of Soviet roubles for foreign currencies because everything, including the purpose as well as the amount and the type of currency, is decided by central authorities instead of independent holders of currency.

Different principles will be needed if we intend to change from a centralized to a market economy, where economic activity is ruled by an interchange of economic interests and competition through market instruments. The independence of economic units as well as the ability to make their own decisions, and to take risks make up the mainstay of a genuine market mechanism.

When market activities are aiming abroad, a convertible currency is the best way to ensure the independence, and interests of the actors on the market. Of course, a situation like that does not correspond with a state monopoly for international economic relations, which in fact is the antipode to convertibility. Moving toward a convertible rouble, means the elimination of this monopoly and its replacement with more liberal and flexible government regulations.

To reach an advanced stage of rouble convertibility, at least for current account transactions within the meaning of Article VIII of the IMF statute, we must concentrate at three main issues: The first is to steadily follow the path of transition to a market economy by transforming existing mechanisms and instruments, like prices, domestic and foreign trade, banking, taxation, tariffs, foreign exchange rates and many others, into market ones. The second issue is to restructure the national economy in such a way that it becomes more effective and integrated with the world economy. This requires that we stabilize government finances and put the rate of inflation and the balance of payments deficit under control. Finally, we must create the legal and technical mechanisms, including a decentralized foreign exchange market, that are needed for currency convertibility.

The first two points will evidently require a rather long period for implementation. So, it is perfectly clear that rouble convertibility is not a case for the nearest future, and much will depend on the speed of progress towards stable market conditions in the USSR. One can, however, start to work on the third set of problems immediately, by dismantling the state monopoly for international economic transactions.

The Soviet Constitution and other basic laws should be revised to end the monopolistic practice of performing all international transactions through official channels. They should be replaced by a freedom for independent agents to carry out foreign transactions in accordance with government regulations and under government supervision.

The foreign exchange monopoly must be demolished as well. To fulfill this task it will be necessary to stop discriminating against the Soviet rouble as an instrument of financing foreign trade transactions, to deprive the Government of the privilege to be the sole owner and distributor of foreign exchange, and to decentralize the existing system of channeling all foreign exchange services and transactions through the single official banking body, the "Vnesheconombank".

As a first step in this direction, it is essential to alter the existing rules and regulations in such a way that it becomes possible to use, not only foreign currency, but our own currency for external transactions. We have enough of examples where foreign businessmen agree to supply goods and services to the USSR in exchange for roubles. I think it would be expedient to allow these "imports-for-rouble" transactions, while giving non-residents the opportunity to spend rouble earnings according to existing possibilities, and in conformity with Soviet law.

Parallel to this step it is important to stop discriminating non-residents' legal holdings of Soviet currency. Easing the restrictions for using them inside the country would provide good opportunities for non-residents to take more active part in Soviet domestic market activities, deal with cooperative bodies and tenants, participate in local business, as well as scientific and cultural projects. In this way the foreign business community would become more accustomed to Soviet economic conditions, while the participants in the Soviet monetary system would learn what is absolutely indispensable for paving the way to rouble convertibility.

For the future payments relations with the Eastern European countries, the problem of using the rouble for internal transactions is of increasing importance. It may be more rational to carry out these transactions on a basis of world market prices, and to use convertible currencies. But I strongly believe that these movements have to be combined with the development of a certain system for using national currencies, including the Soviet rouble, where special concern is taken for mutual settlements and mutual convertibility. Otherwise, the Soviet currency would again be left behind the present convertible currencies, with eventually negative results for its move to convertibility.

To support currency convertibility it is necessary to have an active well-organized foreign exchange market. It is high time to create such a market in the Soviet Union, with the elimination of the state monopoly for ownership of foreign exchange resources as the main initial move. Instead of the Government, foreign exchange must belong to the holders who earn it, with a guarantee to use their holdings freely at home or abroad, according to established rules. If such a need arises, these rules have to provide freedom of selling foreign currencies for roubles. Regarding the central Government, its demand for foreign exchange can be satisfied by requiring that a part of foreign exchange proceeds must be exchanged with the Government at the official or the market rate for roubles.

These new arrangements of decentralized ownership and disposition of foreign exchange holdings are important preconditions for the establishment of a modern foreign exchange market in the USSR with equal rights and duties for all domestic and foreign participants, including official bodies, public enterprises, cooperative societies, joint ventures and individuals.

It is also of urgent necessity to reconstruct the Soviet banking system, because it would be impossible to serve the huge volume of foreign exchange transactions by thousands of holders in our big country without transferring them from the single center of "Vnesheconombank" to a network of newly created commercial banks given a license to carry out foreign exchange business. We shall have to pay a high price for training personnel and equipping the premises to ensure a modern level of banking that serves foreign exchange transactions effectively. This seems the only way to be ready to implement rouble convertibility after it has been prepared and propped up economically.

5. CONCLUSION

I have to note that some measures recently adopted by the Soviet Government generally follow the lines of a more liberal foreign trade policy which are essential for the idea of convertibility. These first steps, however, are not enough to essentially undermine the present situation of rouble inconvertibility. At the moment, a comprehensive program is prepared for attaining convertibility, stage by stage and alongside the transition to a market economy. I like to believe that this program will put an end to the contest between unnecessary illusions and unattainable hopes, and eventually show the ways and the means of solving this complicated problem in realistic terms.

REFERENCES

Gold, J. (1978), Use, Conversion and Exchange Currency Under the Second Amendment of the Funds's Articles, (Washington).

International Monetary Fund (1969), The International Monetary Fund 1945-1965. Twenty Years of International Monetary Cooperation, Vol. II: Analysis, (Washington).

Subject Index